VITTORIA COULD NOT HAVE SPOKEN JUST THEN, FOR SHE WAS TREMBLING FROM HEAD TO FOOT.
—*Corleone.*

THE COMPLETE WORKS OF
F. MARION CRAWFORD

In Thirty-two Volumes ← *Authorized Edition*

CORLEONE
A Tale of Sicily

BY
F. MARION CRAWFORD

WITH FRONTISPIECE

WILDSIDE PRESS

THE COMPLETE WORKS OF F. MARION CRAWFORD

I.	Mr. Isaacs		XVII.	The Witch of Prague
II.	Doctor Claudius		XVIII.	The Three Fates
III.	To Leeward		XIX.	Taquisara
IV.	A Roman Singer		XX.	The Children of the King
V.	An American Politician		XXI.	Pietro Ghisleri
VI.	Marzio's Crucifix		XXII.	Katharine Lauderdale
	Zoroaster		XXIII.	The Ralstons
VII.	A Tale of a Lonely Parish		XXIV.	Casa Braccio (Part I)
VIII.	Paul Patoff		XXV.	Casa Braccio (Part II)
IX.	Love in Idleness: A Tale of Bar Harbor		XXVI.	Adam Johnstone's Son
	Marion Darche			A Rose of Yesterday
X.	Saracinesca		XXVII.	Via Crucis
XI.	Sant' Ilario		XXVIII.	In the Palace of the King
XII.	Don Orsino		XXIX.	Marietta: A Maid of Venice
XIII.	Corleone: A Sicilian Story		XXX.	Cecilia: A Story of Modern Rome
XIV.	With the Immortals			
XV.	Greifenstein		XXXI.	The Heart of Rome
XVI.	A Cigarette-Maker's Romance		XXXII.	Whosoever Shall Offend
	Khaled			

CORLEONE

CHAPTER I

"If you never mean to marry, you might as well turn priest, too," said Ippolito Saracinesca to his elder brother, Orsino, with a laugh.

"Why?" asked Orsino, without a smile. "It would be as sensible to say that a man who had never seen some particular thing, about which he has heard much, might as well put out his eyes."

The young priest laughed again, took up the cigar he had laid upon the edge of the piano, puffed at it till it burned freely, and then struck two or three chords of a modulation. A sheet of ruled paper on which several staves of music were roughly jotted down in pencil stood on the rack of the instrument.

Orsino stretched out his long legs, leaned back in his low chair, and stared at the old gilded rosettes in the square divisions of the carved ceiling. He was a discontented man, and knew it, which made his discontent a matter for self-reproach, especially as it was quite clear to him that the cause of it lay in himself.

He had made two great mistakes at the beginning of life, when barely of age, and though neither of them had ultimately produced any serious material consequences, they had affected his naturally melancholic temper and had brought out his inherited hardness of disposition. At the time of the great building speculations in Rome, several years earlier, he had foolishly involved himself with his father's old enemy, Ugo del Ferice, and had found himself at last altogether in the latter's power, though not in reality his debtor. At the same time, he had fallen very much in love with a young widow, who, loving him very sincerely in her turn, but believing, for many reasons, that if she married him she would be doing him an irreparable injury, had sacrificed herself by marrying Del Ferice instead, selling herself to the banker for Orsino's release, without the latter's knowledge. When it was all over, Orsino had found himself a disappointed man at an age when most young fellows are little more than inexperienced boys, and the serious disposition which he inherited from his mother made it impossible for him to throw off the impression received, and claim the youth, so to speak, which was still his.

Since that time, he had been attracted by women, but never charmed; and those that attracted him were for the most part not marriageable, any more than the few things which sometimes interested and amused him were in any sense profitable. He spent a good deal of money in a careless way, for his father was generous; but his rather bitter experience when he had attempted to occupy himself with business had made him cool and clearheaded, so that he never did anything at all ruinous. The hot temper which he had inherited from his father and grandfather now rarely, if ever, showed itself, and it seemed as though nothing could break through the quiet indifference which had become a second outward nature to him. He had travelled much, of late years, and when he made an effort his conversation was not uninteresting, though the habit of looking at both sides of every question made it cold and unenthusiastic. Perhaps it was a hopeful sign that he generally had a definite opinion as to which of two views he preferred, though he would not take any trouble to convince others that he was right.

In his own family, he liked the company of Ippolito best. The latter was about two years younger than he, and very different from him in almost every way. Orsino was tall, strongly built, extremely dark; Ippolito was of medium height, delicately made, and almost fair by comparison. Orsino had lean brown hands, well knit at the base, and broad at the knuckles; Ippolito's were slender and white, and rather nervous, with blue veins at the joints, the tips of the fingers pointed, the thumb unusually delicate and long, the nails naturally polished. The elder brother's face, with its large and energetic lines, its gravely indifferent expression and dusky olive hue, contrasted at every point with the features of the young priest, soft in outline, modelled in wax rather than chiselled in bronze, pale and a little transparent, instead of swarthy,— feminine, perhaps, in the best sense of the word, as it can be applied to a man. Ippolito had the clear, soft brown eyes which very gifted people so often have, especially musicians and painters of more talent than power. But about the fine, even, and rather pale lips there was the unmistakable stamp of the ascetic temperament, together with an equally sure indication of a witty humour which could be keen, but would rather be gentle. Ippolito was said to resemble his mother's mother, and was notably different in appearance and manner from the rest of the numerous family to which he belonged.

He was a priest by vocation rather than by choice. Had he chosen deliberately a profession congenial to his gifts, he would certainly have devoted himself altogether to music, though he would probably never have become famous as a composer; for he lacked the rough creative power which hews out great conceptions, though he possessed in a high degree the taste and skill which can lightly and lovingly and wisely impart fine detail to the broad beauty of a well-planned whole. But by vocation he was a priest, and the strength of the conviction of his conscience left the gifts of his artistic intelligence no power to choose. He was a churchman with all his soul, and a musician with all his heart.

Between the two brothers there was that sort of close friendship which sometimes exists between persons who are too wholly different to understand each other, but whose non-understanding is a constant stimulant of interest on both sides. In the midst of the large and peaceable patriarchal establishment in which they lived, and in which each member made for himself or herself an existence which had in it a certain subdued individuality, Orsino and Ippolito were particularly associated, and the priest, when he was at home, was generally to be found in his elder brother's sitting-room, and kept a good many of his possessions there.

It was a big room, with an old carved and gilded ceiling, three tall windows opening to the floor, two doors, a marble fireplace, a thick old carpet, and a great deal of furniture of many old and new designs, arranged with no regard to anything except usefulness, since Orsino was not afflicted with artistic tastes, nor with any undue appreciation of useless objects. Ippolito's short grand piano occupied a prominent position near the middle window, and not far from it was Orsino's deep chair, beside which stood a low table covered with books and reviews. For, like most discontented and disappointed people who have no real object in life, Orsino Saracinesca read a good deal, and hankered after interest in fiction because he found none in reality. Ippolito, on the contrary, read little, and thought much.

After Orsino had answered his remark about marriage, the priest busied himself for some time with his music, while his brother stared at the ceiling in silence, listening to the modulations and the fragments of tentative melody and experimental harmony, without in the least understanding what the younger man was trying to express. He was fond of any musical sound, in an undefined way, as most Italians are, and he knew by experience that if he let Ippolito alone, something pleasant to hear would before long be evolved. But Ippolito stopped suddenly and turned half round on the piano stool, with a quick movement habitual to him. He leaned forward towards Orsino, tapping the ends of his fingers lightly against one another, as his wrists rested on his knees.

"It is absurd to suppose that in all Rome, or in all Europe, for that matter, there is nobody whom you would be willing to marry."

"Quite absurd, I suppose," answered Orsino, not looking at his brother.

"Then you have not really looked about you for a wife. That is clear."

"Perfectly clear. I do not argue the point. Why should I? There is plenty of time, and besides, there is no reason in the world why I should ever marry at all, any more than you. There are our two younger brothers. Let them take wives and continue the name."

"Most people think that marriage may be regarded as a means of happiness," observed Ippolito.

"Most people are imbeciles," answered Orsino, gloomily.

Ippolito laughed, watching his brother's face, but he said nothing in reply.

"As a general rule," Orsino continued presently, "talking is a question of height and not of intelligence. The shorter men and women are, the more they talk; the taller they are, the more silent they are, in nine cases out of ten. Of course there are exceptions, but you can generally tell at a glance whether any particular person is a great talker. Brains are certainly not measurable by inches. Therefore conversation has nothing to do with brains. Therefore most people are fools."

"Do you call that an argument?" asked the priest, still smiling.

"No. It is an observation."

"And what do you deduce from it?"

"From it, and from a great many other things, I deduce and conclude that what we call society is a degrading farce. It encourages talking, when no one has anything to say. It encourages marriage, without love. It sets up fashion against taste, taste against sense, and sense against heart. It is a machinery for promoting emotion among the unfeeling. It is a—"

Orsino stopped, hesitating.

"Is it anything else?" asked Ippolito, mildly.

"It is a hell on earth"

"That is exactly what most of the prophets and saints have said, since David," remarked the priest, moving again in order to find his half-smoked cigar, and then carefully relighting it. "Since that is your opinion, why not take orders? You might become a prophet or a saint, you know. The first step towards sanctity is to despise the pomps and vanities of this wicked world. You seem to have taken the first step at a jump, with both feet. And it is the first step that costs the most, they say. Courage! You may go far."

"I am thinking of going further before long," said Orsino, gravely, as though his brother had spoken in earnest. "At all events, I mean to get away from all this," he added, as though correcting himself.

"Do you mean to travel again?" enquired Ippolito.

"I mean to find something to do. Provided it is respectable, I do not care what it is. If I had talent, like you, I would be a musician, but I would not be an amateur, or I would be an artist, or a literary man. But I have no talent for anything, except building tenement houses, and I shall not try that again. I would even be an actor, if I had the gift. Perhaps I should make a good farmer, but our father will not trust me now, for he is afraid that I should make ruinous experiments if he gave me the management of an estate. This is certainly not the time for experiments. Half the people we know are ruined and the country is almost bankrupt. I do not wish to try experiments. I would work, and they tell me to marry. You cannot understand. You are only an amateur yourself, after all, Ippolito."

"An amateur musician — yes."

"No. You are an amateur priest. You support your sensitive soul on a sort of religious ambrosia, with a good deal of musical nectar. Your ideal is to be Cardinal-Protector of the Arts. You are clever and astonishingly good, by nature, and you deserve no credit for either. That is probably why I like you. I hate people who deserve credit, because I deserve none myself. But you do not take your clerical profession seriously, and you are an amateur, a dilettante of the altar. If you do not have distractions about the vestments you wear when you are saying mass, it is because you have an intimate, unconscious artistic conviction that they are beautiful and becoming to you. But if the choir responded a flat 'Amen' to your 'per omnia sæcula sæculorum,' it would set your teeth on edge and upset your devout intention at the beginning of the Preface. Do you think that a professional musician would be disturbed in conducting a great orchestra, by the fact that his coat collar did not fit?"

Ippolito smiled good humouredly, but did not answer.

"Very well," continued Orsino at once, "you are only an amateur priest. It does not matter, since you are happy. You get through life very well. You do not even pretend that you do any real work. Your vocation, as you call it, was a liking for the state of priesthood, not for the work of a priest. Now I do not care about any state in particular, but I want work of some sort, at any cost. I was never happy but once, during that time when I worked with Contini and got into trouble. I preferred it to this existence, even when we got into Del Ferice's clutches. Anything rather than this."

"I thought you had grown indifferent," said Ippolito.

"Indifferent? Yes, I am indifferent — as a machine is indifferent when the fire is out and there is no steam. But if the thing could think, it would want work, as I do. It would not be satisfied to rust to pieces. You ought to know a little theology. Are we put into the world with a purpose, or not? Is there an intention in our existence, or is there not? Am I to live through another forty or fifty years of total inactivity, because I happen to be born rich, and in a position — well, a position which is really about as enviable as that of a fly in a pot of honey? We are stuck in our traditions, just as the fly is in the honey —"

"I like them," said Ippolito, quietly.

"I know you do. So does our father. They suit you both. Our father is really a very intelligent man, but too much happiness and too much money have paralyzed him. His existence seems to have been a condition of perpetual adoration of our mother."

"He has made her happy. That is worth something."

"She has made him happy. They have made each other happy. They have devoured a lifetime of happiness together in secret, as though it were their lawful prey. As they never wanted anything else, they never found out that the honey of traditions is sticky, and that they could not move if they would."

"They are fond of us —"

"Of course. We have none of us done anything very bad. We are a part of their happiness. We are also a part of their dulness; for they are dull, and their happiness makes us dull, too."

"What an idea!"

"It is true. What have we accomplished, any of us four brothers? What shall we ever accomplish? We are ornaments on the architecture of our father's and mother's happiness. It is rather a negative mission in life, you must admit. I am glad that they are happy, but I should like to be something more than a gargoyle on their temple."

"Then marry, and have a temple of your own!" laughed Ippolito. "And gargoyles of your own, too."

"But I do not want that sort of happiness. Marriage is not a profession. It is not a career."

"No. At least, you might turn out a dilettante husband, as you say that I am an amateur priest." Ippolito laughed again.

Orsino laughed dryly, but did not answer, not being in a humour for jesting. He leaned back in his chair again, and looked at the carved ceiling and thought of what it meant, for it was one of those ceilings which are only to be found in old Roman palaces, and belong intimately to the existence which those old dwellings suggest. Orsino thought of the grim dark walls outside, of the forbidding gateway, of the heavily barred windows on the lower story, of the dark street at the back of the palace, and the mediævalism of it all was as repugnant to him as the atmosphere of a prison. He had never understood his father nor his grandfather, who both seemed born for such an existence, and who certainly thrived in it; for the old Prince was over ninety years of age, and his son, Sant' Ilario, though now between fifty and sixty, was to all intents and purposes still a young man. Orsino was perhaps as strong as either of them. But he did not believe that he could last as long. In the midst of an enforced idleness he felt the movement of the age about him, and he said to himself that he was in the race of which they were only spectators, and that he was born in times when it was impossible to stand still. It is true that, like many young men of to-day, he took movement for progress and change for improvement, and he had no very profound understanding of the condition of his own or of other countries. But the movement and the change are facts from which no one can escape who has had a modern education.

Giovanni Saracinesca, Orsino's father, known as Prince of Sant' Ilario, since the old Prince Saracinesca was still living, had not had a modern education, and his mother had died while he was a mere child. Brought up by men, among men, he had reached manhood early, in close daily association with his father and with a strong natural admiration for him, though with an equally strong sense of personal independence.

Orsino's youth had been different. He was not an only son, as Sant' Ilario had been, but the eldest of four brothers, and he had been brought up by his mother as well as by his father and grandfather. There had been less room for his character to develop freely, since the great old house had been gradually filled by a large family. At the same time there had also been less room for oldfashioned prejudices and traditions than formerly, and a good deal less respect for them, as there had been, too, a much more lively consciousness of the outer world's movements. The taking of Rome in 1870 was the death-blow of mediævalism; and the passing away of King Victor Emmanuel and of Pope Pius the Ninth was the end of Italian romanticism, if one may use the expression to designate all that concatenation of big and little events which make up the thrilling story of the struggle for Italian unity. After the struggle for unity, began the struggle for life, — more desperate, more dangerous, but immeasurably less romantic. There is all the difference which lies between banking and fighting.

And Orsino was aware of qualities and feelings and opinions in his father and mother which he did not possess, but which excited in him a sort of envy of what he regarded as their simplicity. Each seemed to have wanted but one thing in life since he could remember them, and that was the other's love, in possessing which each was satisfied and happy. Times might change as they would, popes might die, kings might be crowned, parties might wrangle in political strife, and the whole country might live through its perilous joys of sudden prosperity and turn sour again in the ferment that follows failure, — it was all the same to Giovanni and Corona. As Orsino had told his brother, they had devoured a lifetime of happiness together in secret. He would have added that they had left none for others, and in a sense it might have been true. But he preferred not to say it, even to Ippolito; for it would have sounded bitter, whereas Orsino believed himself to be only indifferent.

Proud men and women hide their griefs and sufferings, when they have any. But there are some who are so very proud that they will hide their happiness also, as though it might lose some of its strength if anyone else could see it, or as if it could be spoiled by the light like a photograph not yet fixed. People sometimes call that instinct the selfishness of love, but it is more like a sort of respect for love itself, which is certainly not vulgar, as all selfishness is.

It was not probable that either Giovanni or Corona should change in this respect, nor, indeed, in any other, for they had never been changeable or capricious people, and time had made solid their lives. To each other they were as they had always been, but to others Giovanni was a man advanced in middle life, and the beautiful Corona Saracinesca was a rose of yesterday.

She could never be anything but beautiful, even if she should live to extreme old age; but those who had known her in her youth had begun to shake their heads sadly, lamenting the glory departed, and seeing only in recollection a vision of it, while they could not see the value of what remained nor appreciate something which had come with years. Strangers who came to Rome and saw the Princess of Sant' Ilario for the first time, gazed in silent surprise at the woman who for nearly a quarter of a century had been the most beautiful in Europe, and they wondered whether, even now, anyone could be compared with her.

The degeneration of age had not taken hold upon her. The perfect features were as calm and regular as fate, the dark skin had still its clear, warm, olive tint, which very rarely changed at all perceptibly; her splendid eyes were truthful and direct still, beneath the strong black eyebrows. There were silver threads in the magnificent hair, but they were like the lights on a raven's wing. She was straight and strong and graceful still, she who had been compared to velvet and steel — slighter perhaps than in her full perfection, for she had in her some of that good Saracen blood of the south, which seems to nourish only the stronger and the finer tissues, consuming in time all that is useless; wearing away the velvet, but leaving the steel intact almost to the very last.

There could be but one such woman in one race, and it seemed in some way natural that she should have been sisterless, and should have borne only sons. But as though nature would not be altogether defeated and stayed out of balance, the delicate feminine element had come to the surface in one of the Saracinesca men. It was too fine to be womanish, too high to be effeminate, as it showed itself in Ippolito, the priest-musician. But it was unmistakably something which was neither in the old Prince, nor in Giovanni, nor in any of the other three brothers, and it made between him and his mother a bond especially their own, which the rest acknowledged without understanding, and respected without feeling that Ippolito was preferred before them. For it was not a preference, but a stronger mutual attraction, in which there was no implied unfairness to the rest.

It is one of the hardest things in the world to explain, and yet almost everyone understands it, for it has nothing to do with language, and everything to do with feeling. We human beings need language most to explain what is most remote from our humanity, and those who talk the most of feeling are often those that feel the least. For conveying a direct impression, what is the sharpened conciseness of Euclid, or the polished eloquence of Demosthenes, what is the sledge-hammer word blow of Æschylus, or the lightning thrust of Dante's two-edged tongue, compared with a kiss, or a girl's blush, or the touch of a mother's hand — or the silent certainty of twofold thought in one, which needs neither blush, nor touch, nor kiss to say that love is all, and all is love?

And that bond which is sometimes between mother and son is of this kind. It is not strange, either, that the father who looks on should misunderstand it, since it is the most especially human feeling which is often the least comprehensible to those who do not feel it, for the very reason that language cannot convey the impression of it to others. Nothing is less ridiculous than love, except death. Yet a man in love is very frequently ridiculous in the eyes of his friends and of the world, the more so in proportion as he shows the more plainly what he feels. Yet most of those who laugh at him have probably been in love themselves. A cynic would say that the humour of it lies in the grim certainty which others feel that it cannot last. Fear is terribly real to him who feels it, but a man who is frightened without cause is always laughable and generally contemptible. It is true that whereas we are all human and feel humanly, humanity is very hard to understand — because understanding is not feeling, any more than the knowledge of evil is temptation, or than the knowledge of good is virtue. The best description of a sunset cannot convey much to a man born blind, though it may awaken longings in him, and sharpen the edge of his old suffering upon the roughness of a new regret. And yet a description means very much more to most people than an explanation.

Sant' Ilario had long ago accepted the fact that his wife was in some mysterious way drawn to her second son, more than to the others. It would be saying too much, perhaps, to assert that Corona was glad when Ippolito took orders and the vow of celibacy. She was not an imaginative woman, nor nervous, nor in any way not normal. Nor were the Saracinesca by any means an excessively devout family, nor connected with the history of the church, as many Roman families are. On the contrary, they had in former times generally opposed the popes when they had not been strong enough to make one of their own, and the absence of any womanly element in the great house, between the untimely death of the old Prince's wife, and Giovanni Saracinesca's marriage with the Duchessa d'Astrardente nearly thirty years later, had certainly not favoured a tendency to devotional practices. When young Ippolito made up his mind to be a priest, the aged head of the family growled out a few not very edifying remarks in his long white beard. Even ten years earlier, he might have gone into a rage about it, which might have endangered his life, for he had a terrible temper; but he was near the end, now, and it would have taken more than that to rouse him. As for Giovanni, he was not especially pleased either, for he had never been fond of priests, and he assuredly did not care to have any in the family. Yet, in spite of this prejudice, there seemed to him to be a certain fitness in the event, against which it would be useless to argue, and after a little discussion with his wife, he accepted it as more or less inevitable.

But Corona was satisfied, if not glad, and what she felt was very like gladness, for, without reasoning at all, she knew that she should be jealous of any woman who came between her and Ippolito. She had never been able to think of a possible wife for him — as she often thought of wives for her other sons — without a sharp thrust of pain which could not be anything but jealousy. It was not exactly like what she should have felt, or fancied that she should have felt, if Giovanni had been momentarily attracted by some other woman. But it was not at all like anything else in the world.

She did not know how far Ippolito was aware of this, but she knew beyond doubt that he was instinctively drawn to her, as she was to him. She had that intuitive certainty, which women know so well, that in a moment of danger he would think first of her, precisely as her husband would. Such instincts are, perhaps, but shadowy inklings of the grey primeval past, when women and children knew to whom they must look for protection against man and beast; but they are known to us all in connexion with those we love best, though they may never cross our thoughts when we are alone.

There was between her and Ippolito a sort of constant mutual echoing of thought and feeling; that sort of sympathy which, between people of sensitive and unhealthy organization, leads to those things, not easily explained, to which the name of telepathy has lately been attached as a tentative definition. But these two were not unhealthy, nor morbidly sensitive, nor otherwise different from normal human beings. Corona had never been ill in her life, and if Ippolito had been thought delicate in his boyhood, it was by contrast with the rest of a family remarkable for most uncommon health and strength.

All this has seemed necessary in order to explain the events which at this time took place in the Saracinesca household. Nothing unusual had occurred in the family for many years, excepting Orsino's rather foolish and most unlucky attempt to occupy himself in business at the time of the great building speculation, and his first love affair, to which reference was made in the beginning of this somewhat explanatory chapter.

CHAPTER II

WHEN the notorious Prince of Corleone died without much ceremony in a small second-class hotel in Nice, and was buried with no ceremony at all worth mentioning, at the expense of the hotel keeper, his titles and what was left of his lands and other belongings went to his brother's children, since his brother was dead also. The Corleone people were never long-lived, nor had their alliances as a rule conduced to long life in others, who had been their wives and husbands. Superstitious persons said that there was upon the whole family the curse of a priest whom they had caused to be shot as a spy in order to save themselves during the wars of Napoleon in Italy. It was even said that they saw, or thought they saw, this priest when they were about to die. But as priests are plentiful in the south of Italy, it might very well be that their vision was not a vision at all, but simply some quite harmless living ecclesiastic who chanced to be passing at the time. It is true that they were said to notice always a small red hole in his forehead and another in his left cheek, but this also might have been only an effect of imagination. Nevertheless they were unfortunate, as a race, and several of them had come to violent or otherwise untimely ends within the century.

The name, Corleone, was only a title, and the town from which it was taken had long ago passed into other hands. The family name was Pagliuca d'Oriani. As often happens in Italy, they went by whichever one of the three names happened to be most familiar to the speaker who mentioned them.

At the time of the Prince's death there were living his brother's widow and four children, consisting of three sons and one daughter; and there was another branch of the family, calling themselves Pagliuca di Bauso, with whom this history is not at present concerned.

The widowed lady was known in Sicily as Donna Maria Carolina Pagliuca. Her eldest son was Tebaldo, to whom came from his uncle the title, Prince of Corleone; and his two brothers were named Francesco and Ferdinando. Their sister, a girl seventeen years of age, was Vittoria, and was the youngest.

In the ordinary course of events, being of the south, the three sons as well as their father and mother would have each borne a distinctive title. Corleone, however, had begun life by quarrelling with his younger brother; and when the latter had died, and the property had been divided according to the code introduced after the annexation of Naples and Sicily, he had absolutely refused to allow his brother any title whatsoever. He could not prevent the division of the lands, of which, however, he had by far the larger share; but he could keep the titles, with which the law of succession does not concern itself, and he did so out of spite. Moreover, he injured and defrauded his brother by every means in his power, which was at that time considerable; and the result was that the said brother and his family became very poor indeed, and retired to live in a somewhat barbarous region of Sicily, very much in the manner of farmers and very little in the style of gentlefolks. He died of the cholera when his eldest son, Tebaldo, was barely of age, and Vittoria was a little girl at a convent in Palermo.

The three young men lived almost in the surroundings of Sicilian peasants, but with the pride and more than the ordinary vanity of a race of nobles. There might not have been much difference had their uncle been generous to them, instead of at once transferring and continuing to them his hatred of their father. But as they were placed, and with their characters, the result was inevitable. They grew up to be at once idle and vindictive, grasping and improvident, half cunning and half fierce, physically brave and morally mean. The many faults and the few virtues were not evenly distributed among them, it is true, for each had some greater or less share of them all. Tebaldo was the most cunning, Francesco the most licentious, Ferdinando was the boldest and the most rash of them all, — perhaps the best, or, at all events, the least bad.

The house which remained to them, with a little land around it, was known as Camaldoli to the peasants and the people of the neighbourhood, though its original name had been Torre del Druso — the Tower of the Druse, or of the fiend, as one chooses to interpret it. It was a good-sized, rambling, half-fortified old monastery, looking down from a gentle elevation in the high valley on one side, and having a deep gorge at the back, through which a torrent tumbled along over dark stones during three-quarters of the year. There was a sort of rampart above this chasm, and at one end rose a square tower with ruined crenellations, built of almost black tufo. It was evidently this tower which had given the place its more ancient name, before the monks had built their white plastered building against it and the rampart, with the little church in the inner court. The village of Santa Vittoria was about three-quarters of a mile distant, hidden by the spur of the hill, and separated from Camaldoli by a barren stretch of burnt lava and scoriæ, which had descended long ago from some lower crater of the volcano.

Far above all, Etna's enormous cone rose against the dark blue eastern sky like a monstrous, streaked sugar loaf. On each side of the great burnt strip between Santa Vittoria and Camaldoli, the woods and fields stretched north and south towards Messina and Catania, and westwards beyond the valley rose a great range of mountains covered high with forests of chestnut trees. No houses were visible from Camaldoli, nor any shed nor hut which could have served for a human habitation, for it was a wild and lonely country.

The three brothers lived with their mother at Camaldoli, and were served in a rough fashion by three men and four women, almost all of whom were expected to do almost anything, from stable work to cooking and waiting at table. There was a sort of slovenly abundance of coarse food and drink, but there was little else, and many a well-to-do peasant lived better than the sister-in-law and the nephews of Prince Corleone. Donna Maria Carolina scarcely ever left the house in winter or summer. She had been married from a convent, a mere child, had enjoyed a brief taste of luxury and something of happiness at the beginning of life, and had spent the years of subsequent poverty between spasmodic attempts to make gentlemen of her wild sons, bitter outbursts of regret for her marriage, and an apathetic indifference such as only comes upon women of southern races when placed in such hopeless situations as hers. She was a thin, dark woman, with traces of beauty, dressed generally in shabby black, but strangely fond of cheap and tasteless ornaments, which contrasted horribly with her worn-out mourning. As her sons grew up they acquired the habit of contradicting everything she said. Sometimes she argued her point, whatever it might be, and generally in total ignorance of the subject. Her arguments frequently ended in a passionate appeal to the justice of Heaven, and the right feeling of the saints, though the matter under discussion might not be more important than the planting of a cabbage, or the dressing of a dish of greens. Or else, as sometimes happened, she sullenly bent her brows, while her once handsome mouth curled scornfully, and from her scarcely parted lips one word came in an injured and dramatic tone.

"Villani!" she would exclaim.

The word may be translated 'boors,' and the three boys did not like it, for it is an outrageous insult from a man to a man. But it is worth noting that such rudeness to their mother did not go beyond flat contradiction in argument, and when she called her sons boors, they bore it in silence, and generally went away without a retort. There are no Italians without some traces of manners and of that submission to parents which belonged to the old patriarchal system of the Romans. It must be remembered, too, so far as this and the rest of their behaviour may be concerned, that although their father died when they were young, he had lived long enough to give them something, though not much, in the way of education, chiefly by the help of the parish priest of Santa Vittoria, and to teach them the rudimentary outward manners of young gentlemen. And these they were quite able to assume when they pleased. He had succeeded in having them taught at least enough to pass the very easy examination which entitles young men to serve but a year and a few weeks in the army, instead of the regular term; and he had taken first Tebaldo, then Tebaldo and Francesco, and then all three in successive years to Messina and Palermo for a fortnight at a time, so that they were not wholly ignorant of the world beyond Camaldoli, Santa Vittoria, and the one or two larger towns which lay within a day's ride of their remote abode.

It must not be forgotten, either, in order to understand how the brothers were able afterwards to make a tolerably decent appearance in Rome, that Italians have great powers of social adaptation; and, secondly, that the line between the nobility and the people is very clearly drawn in most parts of the country, especially in the matter of manners and speech, so that what little the young men learned from their father and mother belonged distinctively to their own class and to no other. Even had they been outwardly less polished than they really knew how to appear, their name alone would have admitted them to society, though society might have treated them coolly after a nearer acquaintance.

Vittoria, their sister, remained at the convent in Palermo after their father's death. He, poor man, seeing that his house did not promise to be a very fit place for a young girl, and especially not for one delicately organized as his daughter seemed to be, had placed her with the nuns while still a young child; and under the circumstances this was by far the wisest thing he could do. The nuns were ladies, and the convent was relatively rich. Possibly these facts had too much weight with Pagliuca, or perhaps he honestly believed that he should be able to pay regularly for Vittoria's education and living. Indeed, so long as he lived he managed to send small sums of money from time to time, and even after his death Donna Maria Carolina twice remitted a little money to the nuns. But after that nothing more was sent for a long time. Fortunately for herself, Vittoria was extremely unlike her turbulent brothers and her disappointed mother, and by the time she was ten years old she was the idol of the religious household in which she had been placed. Even had she been very different, of low birth, and of bad temper, the nuns would have kept her, and would have treated her as kindly as they could, and would have done their best by her, though they would very justly have required her to do something towards earning her living under their roof when she grew older. But apart from the child's rare charm and lovable disposition, being of an old and noble name, they would have considered her unfit for menial work, though cast adrift and helpless, and they would have thought her quite as worthy of their sympathy as though she had belonged to the family of one among themselves. All this, however, was quite forgotten in their almost exaggerated affection for the child. They showed their love for her as only such women could; for though there were a dozen other daughters of nobles under their care, of ranging ages, the nuns let no one know that Vittoria was brought up by their charity after her father's death. They gave her all she needed of the best, and they even gave her little presents which she might think had been sent from home. They told her that 'her mother desired her to have' a Book of Hours, or a writing-case, or a silk handkerchief, or any such trifles. Her mother, poor lady, doubtless did desire it, though she never said so. It was a pious and a gentle fraud, and it prevented the other girls from looking down upon her as a charity scholar, as one or two of them might have done. In dress there was no difference, of course, for they all dressed alike, and Vittoria supposed that her parents paid for her things.

She was a very lovely girl as she grew up, and exquisite in all ways, and gentle as she was exquisite. She was not dark as her brothers were, nor as her mother. It is commonly said that all the region about Palermo is Saracen, but that the ancient Greek blood survives from Messina to Catania; and the girl certainly seemed to be of a type that differed from that of her family, which had originally come from the other side of the island. Vittoria had soft brown hair and clear brown eyes of precisely the same color as the delicate, arched eyebrows above them, a matching which always helps the harmony of any face. There was a luminous clearness, too, in the skin, which both held and gave back the light like the sheen of fine satin in shadow. There was about all her face the dream-like softness of well-defined outline which one occasionally sees in the best cut gems of the Greeks, when the precious stone itself has a golden tinge. The features were not faultless by any standard of beauty which we call perfect, but one would not have changed the faults that were there to suit rule and canon. Such as they were, they will appear more clearly hereafter. It is enough to say now that Vittoria d'Oriani had grace and charm and gentleness, and, withal, a share of beauty by no means small. And she was well educated and well cared for, as has been seen, and was brought up very differently from her brothers.

The existence of the Pagliuca at Camaldoli was not only tolerably wild and rough, as has been seen; it was, in a measure, equivocal; and it may be doubted whether all the doings of the three brothers, as they grew up, could have borne the scrutiny of the law. Sicily is not like other countries in this respect, and, at the risk of wearying the reader, it is better that something should be said at the outset concerning outlawry and brigandage, in order that what follows may be more clearly understood.

Brigandage in Sicily has a sort of intermittent permanence which foreigners cannot easily explain. The mere question which is so often asked — whether it cannot be stamped out of existence — shows a total ignorance of its nature. You may knock off a lizard's tail in winter with a switch, as most people know, but you cannot prevent the tail from growing again in the spring and summer unless you kill the lizard outright.

Brigandage is not a profession, as most people suppose. A man does not choose it as a career. It is the occasional but inevitable result of the national character under certain conditions which are sure to renew themselves from time to time. No one can change national character. The success of brigandage, whenever it manifests itself, depends primarily upon the almost inaccessible nature of some parts of the island, and, secondly, upon the helplessness of the peasants to defend themselves in remote places. It is manifestly impossible to arm a whole population, especially with weapons fit to cope with the first-rate repeating rifles and army revolvers which brigands almost invariably carry. It is equally impossible to picket troops all over the country, at distances not exceeding half a mile from station to station, in every direction, like cabbages in a field. No army would suffice. Therefore when a band is known to have formed, a large force is sent temporarily to the neighbourhood to hunt it down; and this is all that any government could do. The 'band,' as it is always called, may be very small. One man has terrorized a large district before now, and the famous Leone, when at last surrounded, slew nearly a score of men before he himself was killed, though he was quite alone.

Almost every band begins with a single individual, and he, as a rule, has turned outlaw to escape the consequences of a murder done in hot blood, and is, in all probability, a man of respectable birth and some property. It is part of the national character to proceed instantly to bloodshed in case of a quarrel, and quarrels are, unfortunately, common enough. The peasants break one another's heads and bones with their hoes and spades, and occasionally stab each other with inefficient knives, but rarely kill, because the carabineers are constantly making search for weapons, even in the labourers' pockets, and confiscate them without question when found. But the man of some property rarely goes abroad without a shot-gun, or a revolver, or both, and generally knows how to use them. He may go through life without a serious quarrel, but should he find himself involved in one, he usually kills his man at once, or is killed. If there are witnesses present to prove beyond doubt that he has killed in self-defence, he may give himself up at the nearest station of carabineers, and he is sure of acquittal. Otherwise, if he can get away, his only course is to escape to the woods without delay. This seems to be the simple explanation of the fact that such a large proportion of brigands are by no means of the lowest class, but have often been farmers and men of property, who can not only afford good weapons, but are able to get licenses to carry them. Brigands are certainly not, as a rule, from the so-called criminal classes, as foreigners suppose, though when a band becomes very large, a few common criminals may be found in the whole number; but the brigands despise and distrust them.

These things also account for the still more notable fact that the important bands have always had friends among the well-to-do landed proprietors. Indeed, they have not only friends, but often near relations, who will make great sacrifices and run considerable risks to save them from the law. And when any considerable number of brigands are caught, they have generally been betrayed into an ambush by these friends or relations. Sometimes they are massacred by them for the sake of a large reward. But to the honour of the Sicilian character, it must be said that such cases are rare, though a very notable one occurred in the year 1894, when a rich man and his two sons deliberately drugged six brigands at a sort of feast of friendship, and shot them all in their sleep, a massacre which, however, has by no means ended the existence of that particular band.

As for the practices of the bandits, they have three main objects in view: namely, personal safety, provisions wherewith to support life, and then, if possible, money in large sums, which, when obtained, may afford them the means of leaving the country secretly and for ever. With regard to the first of these ends, they are mostly young men, or men still in the prime of strength, good walkers, good riders, good shots, and not rendered conspicuous marks at a distance by a uniform. As for their provisions, when their friends do not supply them, they take what they need wherever they find it, chiefly by intimidating the peasants. In the third matter they have large views. An ordinary person is usually quite safe from them, especially if armed, for they will not risk their lives for anything so mean as highway robbery. It is their object to get possession of the persons of the richest nobles and gentlemen, from whom they can extort a really large ransom. And if they once catch such a personage they generally get the money, for the practice of sending an ear or a piece of nose as a reminder to relations is not extinct. Few Sicilian gentlemen who have lands in the interior dare visit their estates without a military escort when a 'band' is known to be in existence, as happens to be the case at the present time of writing.

It chanced that such a band was gathered together, though not a large one, within a few years of Pagliuca's death, and was leading a precarious and nomadic life for a time not far from Santa Vittoria. It was said that the Pagliuca men were on good terms with these brigands, though of course their mother knew nothing about it. In the neighbourhood, no one thought much the worse of the brothers for this. When brigands were about, every man had to do the best he could for himself. The Corleone, as many of the peasants called them, were well armed, it is true, but they were few and could not have resisted any depredations of the brigands by force. On the other hand, they had the reputation of being brave and very reckless young men, and even against odds might send a bullet through anyone who tried to carry off a couple of their sheep, or one of their mules. They knew the country well, too, and might be valuable allies to the carabineers, which meant that they could be useful friends to the outlaws, if they chose. Everyone knew that they were poor and that it would not be worth while to take one of them in the hope of a ransom, and no one was surprised when it was hinted that they sold provisions to the brigands for cash when they could get it, and for credit when the brigands had no money, a credit which was perfectly good until the outlaws should be taken.

There was very little direct proof of this alliance, and the Pagliuca denied it in terms which did not invite further questioning. To make a brilliant show of their perfect innocence, they led a dozen carabineers about for two days through a labyrinth of forest paths and hill passes, and brought them three times in forty-eight hours to places where a fire was still smouldering, and remains of half-cooked meat were scattered about, as though the brigands had fled suddenly at an alarm. It was very well done, and they received the officer's thanks for their efforts, with sincere expressions of regret that they should have been unsuccessful. In one of the camps they even found the skin of a sheep which they identified as one of their own, with many loud-spoken curses, by the brand on the back. It was all very well done, and the result of it was that the carabineers often applied for news of the brigands at Camaldoli, a proceeding which of course kept the d'Oriani well informed as to the whereabouts of the carabineers themselves.

It was certainly as well in the end that Vittoria should have stayed at the convent in Palermo during those years, until the death of the old Corleone suddenly changed the existence of her mother and brothers.

He died, as has been said, without much ceremony in a small hotel at Nice. He died childless and intestate, as well as ruined, so far as he knew at the time of his death. The news reached Camaldoli in the shape of a demand for money in payment of one of his just debts, from a money-lender in Palermo who was aware of the existence of the three Pagliuca brothers, and knew that they were the Prince's heirs-at-law.

It took a whole year to unravel the ruin of the dead man's estate. What he had not sold was mortgaged, and the mortgages had changed hands repeatedly during the tremendous financial crisis which began in 1888. There were debts of all kinds, just and unjust, and creditors by the hundred. The steward of the principal estate absconded with such cash as he happened to have in hand, as soon as he heard of Corleone's death. An obscure individual shot himself because the steward owed him money, and this also was talked of in the newspapers, and a good deal of printed abuse was heaped upon the dead rake. But one day Ferdinando Pagliuca entered the office of one of the papers in Palermo, struck the editor in the face, forced him into a duel, and ran him through the lungs the next morning. The editor ultimately recovered, but the Pagliuca had asserted themselves, and there was no more scurrilous talk in the press about poor dead Corleone.

Things turned out to be not quite so bad as he had imagined. Here and there, a little property had escaped, perhaps because he hardly knew of its existence. There was a small house in Rome, in the new quarter, which he had bought for a young person in whom he had been temporarily interested, and which, by some miracle, was not mortgaged. The mortgages on some of the principal estates in Sicily had found their way to the capacious desk of the Marchese di San Giacinto, whose name was Giovanni Saracinesca, and who represented a branch of that family. San Giacinto was enormously rich, and was a singular combination of old blood and modern instincts; a man of honour, but of terrible will and a good enemy; a man of very large views and of many great projects, some of which were already successfully carried out, some in course of execution, some as yet only planned. In the great crisis, he had neither lost much nor profited immediately by the disasters of others. No one called him grasping, and yet everything worth having that came within his long reach came sooner or later into his possession. When land and houses lost value and everything in the way of business was dull and dead, San Giacinto was steadily buying. When all had been excitement and mad speculation, he had quietly saved his money and waited. And in the course of his investments he had picked up the best of the Corleone mortgages, without troubling himself much as to whether the interest were very regularly paid or not. Before long he knew very well that it would not be paid at all, and that the lands would fall to him when Corleone should have completely ruined himself.

The Pagliuca family moved to Rome before the settlement of the inheritance was finished, and Vittoria was at last taken from the convent and accompanied her mother. Ferdinando alone remained at Camaldoli. The family established themselves in an apartment in the new quarter, and began to live well, if not extravagantly, on what was still a very uncertain income. Tebaldo, who managed all the business himself, succeeded in selling the house in Rome advantageously. Through San Giacinto he made acquaintance with a few Romans, who treated him courteously and regarded him with curiosity as the nephew of the notorious Prince Corleone. As for the title, San Giacinto advised him not to assume it at once, as it would not be of any especial advantage to him.

San Giacinto was on excellent terms with all his Saracinesca relations, and very naturally spoke to them about the d'Oriani. In his heart he did not like and did not trust Tebaldo, and thought his brother Francesco little better; but, in spite of this, he could not help feeling a sort of pity for the two young men, whose story reminded him of his own romantic beginnings. San Giacinto was a giant in strength and stature, and it is undoubtedly true that in all giants a tendency to good-nature and kindliness will sooner or later assert itself. He was advancing in years now, and the initial hardness of his rough nature had been tempered by years of success and of almost phenomenal domestic felicity. He was strong still, in body and mind, and not easily deceived; but he had grown kind. He pitied the Pagliuca tribe, and took his wife to see Donna Maria Carolina. He persuaded the Princess of Sant' Ilario to receive her and make acquaintance, and the Marchesa di San Giacinto brought her to the palace one afternoon with Vittoria.

Corona thought the mother pretentious, and guessed that she was at once bad-tempered and foolish; but she saw at a glance that the young girl was of a very different type, and a few kindly questions, while Donna Maria Carolina talked with the Marchesa, explained to Corona the mystery. Vittoria had never been at home, even for a visit, during the ten years which had elapsed since she had been placed at the convent, and her mother was almost a stranger to her. She was not exactly timid, as Corona could see, but her young grace was delicately nurtured and shrank and froze in the presence of her mother's coarse-grained self-assertion.

"Shall we marry her in Rome, do you think, Princess?" asked Donna Maria Carolina, nodding her head indicatively towards her daughter, while her eyes looked at Corona, and she smiled with much significance.

Vittoria's soft brown eyes grew suddenly bright and hard, and the blood sprang up in her face as though she had been struck, and her small hands tightened quietly on her parasol; but she said nothing, and looked down.

"I hope that your daughter may marry very happily," said Corona, with a kind intonation, for she saw the girl's embarrassment and understood it.

The Marchesa di San Giacinto laughed quite frankly. Her laughter was good-humoured, not noisy, and distinctly aristocratic, it is true; but Vittoria resented it, because she knew that it was elicited by her mother's remark, which had been in bad taste. Corona saw this also.

"You always laugh at the mention of marriage, Flavia," said the Princess, "and yet you are the most happily married woman I know."

"Oh, that is true!" answered the Marchesa. "My giant is good to me, even now that my hair is grey."

It was true that there were many silver threads in the thick and waving hair that grew low over her forehead, but her face had lost none of its freshness, and her eyes had all their old vivacity. She was of the type of women who generally live to a great age.

Donna Maria Carolina rose to go. In saying goodbye, Corona took Vittoria's hand.

"I am sorry that it is so late in the season, my dear," she said. "You will have little to amuse you until next year. But you must come to dinner with your mother. Will you come, and bring her?" she asked, turning to Donna Maria Carolina.

The Marchesa di San Giacinto stared in well-bred surprise, for Corona was not in the habit of asking people to dinner at first sight. Of course her invitation was accepted.

CHAPTER III

SAN GIACINTO and his wife came to the dinner, and two or three others, and the d'Oriani made a sort of formal entry into Roman society under the best possible auspices. In spite of Corona's good taste and womanly influence, festivities at the Palazzo Saracinesca always had an impressive and almost solemn character. Perhaps there were too many men in the family, and they were all too dark and grave, from the aged Prince to his youngest grandson, who was barely of age, and whose black eyebrows met over his Roman nose and seemed to shade his eyes too much. Ippolito, the exception in his family, as Vittoria d'Oriani was in hers, did not appear at table, but came into the drawing-room in the evening. The Prince himself sat at the head of the table, and rarely spoke. Corona could see that he was not pleased with the Pagliuca tribe, and she did her best to help on conversation and to make Flavia San Giacinto talk, as she could when she chose.

From time to time, she looked at Orsino, whose face that evening expressed nothing, but whose eyes were almost constantly turned towards Vittoria. It had happened naturally enough that he sat next to her, and it was an unusual experience for him. Of course, in the round of society, he occasionally found himself placed next to a young girl at dinner, and he generally was thoroughly bored on such occasions. It was either intentional or accidental on the part of his hosts, whoever they might be. If it was intentional, he had been made to sit next to some particularly desirable damsel of great birth and fortune, in the hope that he might fall in love with her and make her the future Princess Saracinesca. And he resented in gloomy silence every such attempt to capture him. If, on the other hand, he chanced to be accidentally set down beside a young girl, it happened according to the laws of precedence; and it was ten to one that the young lady had nothing to recommend her, either in the way of face, fortune, or conversation. But neither case occurred often.

The present occasion was altogether exceptional. Vittoria d'Oriani had never been to a dinner-party before, and everything was new to her. It was quite her first appearance in society, and Orsino Saracinesca was the first man who could be called young, except her brothers, with whom she had ever exchanged a dozen words. It was scarcely two months since she had left the convent, and during that time her mind had been constantly crowded with new impressions, and as constantly irritated by her mother's manner and conversation. Her education was undoubtedly very limited, though in this respect it only differed in a small degree from that of many young girls whom Orsino had met; but it was liberal as compared with her mother's, as her ideas upon religion were broad in comparison with Donna Maria Carolina's complicated system of superstition.

Vittoria's brown eyes were very wide open, as she sat quietly in her place, listening to what was said, and tasting a number of things which she had never seen before. She looked often at Corona, and wished that she might be like her some day, which was quite impossible. And she glanced at Orsino from time to time, and answered his remarks briefly and simply. She could not help seeing that he was watching her, and now and then the blood rose softly in her cheeks. On her other side sat Gianbattista Pietrasanta, whose wife was a Frangipani, and who was especially amused and interested by Vittoria's mother, his other neighbour, but paid little attention to the young girl herself.

A great writer has very truly said that psychological analysis, in a book, can never be more than a series of statements on the part of the author, telling what he himself fancies that he might have felt, could he have been placed in the position of the particular person whom he is analyzing. It is extremely doubtful whether any male writer can, by the greatest effort of imagination, clothe himself in the ingenuous purity of thought and intention which is the whole being of such a young girl as Vittoria d'Oriani when she first enters the world, after having spent ten years in a religious community of refined women.

The creature we imagine, when we try to understand such maiden innocence, is colourless and dull. Her mind and heart are white as snow, but blankly white, as the snow on a boundless plain, without so much as a fence or a tree to relieve the utter monotony. There is no beauty in such whiteness in nature, except when it blushes at dawn and sunset. Alone on snow, and with nothing but snow in sight, men often go mad; for snow-madness is a known and recognized form of insanity.

Evidently our imagination fails to evoke a true image in such a case. We are aware that maiden innocence is a state, and not a form of character. The difficulty lies in representing to ourselves a definite character in just that state. For to the word innocence we attach no narrow meaning; it extends to every question which touches humanity, to every motive in all dealings, and to every purpose which, in that blank state, a girl attributes to all human beings, living and dead. It is a magic window through which all good things appear clearly, though not often truly, and all bad things are either completely invisible, or seen in a dull, neutral, and totally uninteresting shadow of uniform misunderstanding. We judge that it must be so, from our observation. This is not analysis, but inspection.

Behind the blank lies, in the first place, the temperament, then the character, then the mind, and then that great, uncertain element of heredity, monstrous or god-like, which animates and moves all three in the gestation of unborn fate, and which is fate itself in later life, so far as there is any such thing as fatality.

Behind the blank there may be turbulent and passionate blood, there may be a character of iron and a man-ruling mind. But the blank is a blank, for all that. Catherine of Russia was once an innocent and quiet little German girl, with empty, wondering eyes, and school-girl sentimentalities. Goethe might have taken her for Werther's Charlotte. Good, bad, or indifferent, the future woman is at the magic window, and all that she is to be is within her already.

Vittoria d'Oriani was certainly not to be a Catherine, but there was no lack of conflicting heredities beneath her innocence. Orsino had thought more than most young men of his age, and he was aware of the fact, as he looked at her and talked with her, and carried on one of those apparently empty conversations, of which the recollection sometimes remains throughout a lifetime, while he quietly studied her face, and tried to find out the secret of its rare charm.

He began by treating her almost as a foreigner. He remembered long afterwards how he smiled as he asked her the first familiar question, as though she had been an English girl, or Miss Lizzie Slayback, the heiress from Nevada.

"How do you like Rome?"

"It is a great city," answered Vittoria.

"But you do not like it? You do not think it is beautiful?"

"Of course, it is not Palermo," said the young girl, quite naturally. "It has not the sea; it has not the mountains—"

"No mountains?" interrupted Orsino, smiling. "But there are mountains all round Rome."

"Not like Palermo," replied Vittoria, soberly. "And then it has not the beautiful streets."

"Poor Rome!" Orsino laughed a little. "Not even fine streets! Have you seen nothing that pleases you here?"

"Oh yes,—there are fine houses, and I have seen the Tiber, and the Queen, and—" she stopped short.

"And what else?" enquired Orsino, very much amused.

Vittoria turned her brown eyes full upon him, and paused a moment before she answered.

"You are making me say things which seem foolish to you, though they seem sensible to me," she said quietly.

"They seem original, not foolish. It is quite true that Palermo is a beautiful city, but we Romans forget it. And if you have never seen another river, the Tiber is interesting, I suppose. That is what you mean. No, it is quite reasonable."

Vittoria blushed a little, and looked down, only half reassured. It was her first attempt at conversation, and she had said what she thought, naturally and simply. She was not sure whether the great dark young man, who had eyes exactly like his mother's, was laughing at her or not. But he did not know that she had never been to a party in her life.

"Is the society in Palermo amusing?" he enquired carelessly.

"I do not know," she answered, again blushing, for she was a little ashamed of being so very young. "I left the convent on the day we started to come to Rome. And my mother did not live in Palermo," she added.

"No — I had forgotten that."

Orsino relapsed into silence for a while. He would willingly have given up the attempt at conversation, so far as concerned any hope of making it interesting. But he liked the sound of Vittoria's voice, and he wished she would speak again. On his right hand was Tebaldo, who, as the head of a family, and not a Roman, sat next to Corona. He seemed to be making her rather bold compliments. Orsino caught a phrase.

"You are certainly the most beautiful woman in Italy, Princess," the Sicilian was saying.

Orsino raised his head, and turned slowly towards the speaker. As he did so, he saw his mother's look. Her brows were a little contracted, which was unusual, but she was just turning away to speak to San Giacinto on her other side, with an otherwise perfectly indifferent expression. Orsino laughed.

"My mother has been the most beautiful woman in Europe since before I was born," he said, addressing Tebaldo rather pointedly, for the latter's remark had been perfectly audible to him.

Tebaldo had a thin face, with a square, narrow forehead, and heavy jaws that came to an over-pointed chin. His upper lip was very short, and his moustache was unusually small, black and glossy, and turned up at the ends in aggressive points. His upper teeth were sharp, long, and regular, and he showed them when he smiled. The smile did not extend upwards above the nostrils, and there was something almost sinister in the still black eyes. In the front view the lower part of the face was triangular, and the low forehead made the upper portion seem square. He was a man of bilious constitution, of an even, yellow-brown complexion, rather lank and bony in frame, but of a type which is often very enduring. Such men sometimes have violent and uncontrolled tempers, combined with great cunning, quickness of intelligence, and an extraordinary power of taking advantage of circumstances.

Tebaldo smiled at Orsino's remark, not at all acknowledging that it might be intended as a rebuke.

"It is hard to believe that she can be your mother," he said quietly, and with such frankness as completely disarmed resentment.

But Orsino in his thoughts contrasted Tebaldo's present tone with the sound of his voice when speaking to the Princess an instant earlier, and he forthwith disliked the man, and believed him to be false and double. Corona either had not heard, or pretended not to hear, and talked indifferently with San Giacinto, whose vast, lean frame seemed to fill two places at the table, while his energetic grey head towered high above everyone else. Orsino turned to Vittoria again.

"Should you be pleased if someone told you that you were the most beautiful young lady in Italy?" he enquired.

Vittoria looked at him wonderingly.

"No," she answered. "It would not be true. How should I be pleased?"

"But suppose, for the sake of argument, that it were true. I am imagining a case. Should you be pleased?"

"I do not know — I think —" She hesitated and paused.

"I am very curious to know what you think, said Orsino, pressing her for an answer.

"I think it would depend upon whether I liked the person who told me so." Again the blood rose softly in her face.

"That is exactly what I should think," answered Orsino, gravely. "Were you sorry to leave the convent?"

"Yes, I cried a great deal. It was my home for so many years, and I was so happy there."

The girl's eyes grew dreamy as she looked absently across the table at Guendalina Pietrasanta. She was evidently lost in her recollections of her life with the nuns. Orsino was almost amused at his own failure.

"Should you have liked to stay and be a nun yourself?" he enquired, with a smile.

"Yes, indeed! At least — when I came away I wished to stay."

"But you have changed your mind since? You find the world pleasanter than you expected? It is not a bad place, I daresay."

"They told me that it was very bad," said Vittoria, seriously. "Of course, they must know, but I do not quite understand what they mean. Can you tell me something about it, and why it is bad, and what all the wickedness is?"

Orsino looked at her quietly for a moment, realizing very clearly the whiteness of her life's unwritten page.

"Your nuns may be right," he said at last. "I am not in love with the world, but I do not believe that it is so very wicked. At least, there are many good people in it, and one can find them if one chooses. No doubt, we are all miserable sinners in a theological sense, but I am not a theologian. I have a brother who is a priest, and you will see him after dinner; but though he is a very good man, he does not give one the impression of believing that the world is absolutely bad. It is true that he is rather a dilettante priest."

Vittoria was evidently shocked, for her face grew extraordinarily grave and a shade paler. She looked at Orsino in a startled way and then at her plate.

"What is the matter?" he asked quickly. "Have I shocked you?"

"Yes," she answered, almost in a whisper and still looking down. "That is," she added with hesitation, "perhaps I did not quite understand you."

"No, you did not, if you are shocked. I merely meant that although my brother is a very good man, and a very religious man, and believes that he has a vocation, and does his best to be a good priest, he has other interests in life for which I am sure that he cares more, though he may not know it."

"What other interests?" asked Vittoria, rather timidly.

"Well, only one, perhaps,—music. He is a musician first, and a priest afterwards."

The young girl's face brightened instantly. She had expected something very terrible, perhaps, though quite undefined.

"He says mass in the morning," continued Orsino, "and it may take him an hour or so to read his breviary conscientiously in the afternoon. The rest of his time he spends over the piano."

"But it is not profane music?" asked Vittoria, growing anxious again.

"Oh no!" Orsino smiled. "He composes masses and symphonies and motetts."

"Well, there is no harm in that," said Vittoria, indifferently, being again reassured.

"Certainly not. I wish I had the talent and the interest in it to do it myself. I believe that the chief real wickedness is doing nothing at all."

"Sloth is one of the capital sins," observed Vittoria, who knew the names of all seven.

"It is also the most tiresome sin imaginable, especially when one is condemned to it for life, as I am."

The young girl looked at him anxiously, and there was a little pause.

"What do you mean?" she asked. "No one is obliged to be idle."

"Will you find me an occupation?" Orsino asked in his turn, and with some bitterness. "I shall be gratified."

"Is not doing good an occupation? I am sure that there must be plenty of opportunities for that."

She felt more sure of herself when upon such ground. Orsino did not smile.

"Yes. It might take up a man's whole life, but it is not a career —"

"It was the career of many of the saints!" interrupted Vittoria, cheerfully, for she was beginning to feel at her ease at last. "Saint Francis of Assisi — Saint Clare — Saint —"

"Pray for us!" exclaimed Orsino, as though he were responding in a litany.

Vittoria's face fell instantly, and he regretted the words as soon as he had spoken them. She was like a sensitive plant, he thought; and yet she had none of the appearance of an over-impressionable, nervous girl. It was doubtless her education.

"I have shocked you again," he said gravely. "I am sorry, but I am afraid that you will often be shocked, at first. Yes; I have no doubt that to the saints doing good was a career, and that a saint might make a career of it nowadays. But you see I am not one. What I should like would be to have a profession of some sort, and to work at it with all my might."

"What a strange idea!" Vittoria looked at him in surprise; for though her three brothers had been almost beggars for ten years, it had never struck them that they could possibly have a profession. "But you are a noble," she added thoughtfully. "You will be the Prince Saracinesca some day."

Orsino laughed.

"We do not think so much of those things as we did once," he answered. "I would be a doctor, if I could, or a lawyer, or a man of business. I do not think that I should like to be a shopkeeper, though it is only a matter of prejudice —"

"I should think not!" cried Vittoria, startled again.

"It would be much more interesting than the life I lead. Almost any life would be, for that matter. Of course, if I had my choice —" He stopped.

Vittoria waited, her eyes fixed earnestly on his face, but she said nothing. Somehow she was suddenly anxious to know what his choice would be. He felt that she was watching him, and turned towards her. Their eyes met in silence, and he smiled, but her face remained grave. He was thinking that this must certainly be one of the most absurd conversations in which he had ever been engaged, but that somehow it did not appear absurd to himself, and he wondered why.

"If I had my choice—" He paused again. "I would be a leader," he added suddenly.

He was still young, and there was ambition in him. His dark eyes flashed like his mother's, a warmer colour rose for one instant under his olive skin; the fine, firm mouth set itself.

"I think you could be," said Vittoria, almost under her breath and half unconsciously.

Then, all at once, she blushed scarlet, and turned her face away to hide her colour. If there is one thing in woman which more than any other attracts a misunderstood man, it is the conviction that she believes him capable of great deeds; and if there is one thing beyond others which leads a woman to love a man, it is her own certainty that he is really superior to those around him, and really needs woman's sympathy. Youth, beauty, charm, eloquence, are all second to these in their power to implant genuine love, or to maintain it, if they continue to exist as conditions.

It mattered little to Vittoria that she had as yet no means whatever of judging whether Orsino Saracinesca had any such extraordinary powers as might some day make him a leader among men. She had been hardly conscious of the strong impression she had received, and which had made her speak, and she was far too young and simple to argue with herself about it. And he, on his part, with a good deal of experience behind him and the memory of one older woman's absolute devotion and sacrifice, felt a keen and unexpected pleasure, quite different from anything he remembered to have felt before now. Nor did he reason about it at first, for he was not a great reasoner and his pleasures in life were really very few.

A moment or two after Vittoria had spoken, and when she had already turned away her face, Orsino shook his head almost imperceptibly, as though trying to throw something off which annoyed him. It was near the end of dinner before the two spoke to each other again, though Vittoria half turned towards him twice in the mean time, as though expecting him to speak, and then, disappointed, looked at her plate again.

"Are you going to stay in Rome, or shall you go back to Sicily?" he asked suddenly, not looking at her, but at the small white hand that touched the edge of the table beside him.

Vittoria started perceptibly at the sound of his voice, as though she had been in a reverie, and her hand disappeared at the same instant. Orsino found himself staring at the tablecloth, at the spot where it had lain.

"I think — I hope we shall stay in Rome," she

answered. "My brother has a great deal of business here."

"Yes. I know. He sees my cousin San Giacinto about it almost every day."

"Yes."

Her face grew thoughtful again, but not dreamily so as before, and she seemed to hesitate, as though she had more to say.

"What is it?" asked Orsino, encouraging her to go on.

"Perhaps I ought not to tell you. The Marchese wishes to buy Camaldoli of us."

"What is Camaldoli?"

"It is the old country house where my mother and my brothers lived so long, while I was in the convent, after my father died. There is a little land. It was all we had until now."

"Shall you be glad if it is sold, or sorry?" asked Orsino, thoughtfully, and watching her face.

"I shall be glad, I suppose," she answered. "It would have to be divided among us, they say. And it is half in ruins, and the land is worth nothing, and there are always brigands."

Orsino laughed.

"Yes. I should think you might be very glad to get rid of it. There is no difficulty about it, is there?"

"Only — I have another brother. He likes it and has remained there. His name is Ferdinando.

No one knows why he is so fond of the place. They need his consent, in order to sell it, and he will not agree."

"I understand. What sort of man is your brother Ferdinando?"

"I have not seen him for ten years. They are afraid of — I mean, he is afraid of nothing."

There was something odd, Orsino thought, about the way the young girl shut her lips when she checked herself in the middle of the sentence, but he had no idea what she had been about to say. Just then Corona nodded slightly to the aged Prince at the other end of the table, and dinner was over.

"I should think it would be necessary for San Giacinto to see this other brother of yours," observed Orsino, finishing the conversation as he rose and stood ready to take Vittoria out.

The little ungloved hand lay like a white butterfly on his black sleeve, and she had to raise her arm a little to take his, though she was not short. Just before them went San Giacinto, darkening the way like a figure of fate. Vittoria looked up at him, almost awe-struck at his mere size.

"How tall he is!" she exclaimed in a very low voice. "How very tall he is!" she said again.

"We are used to him," answered Orsino, with a short laugh. "But he has a big heart, though he looks so grim."

Half an hour later, when the men were smoking in a room by themselves, San Giacinto came and sat down by Orsino in the remote corner where the latter had established himself, with a cigarette. The giant, as ever of old, had a villainous looking black cigar between his teeth.

"Do you want something to do?" he asked bluntly.

"Yes."

"Do you care to live in Sicily for a time?"

"Anywhere — Japan, if you like."

"You are easily pleased. That means that you are not in love just at present, I suppose."

San Giacinto looked hard at his young cousin for some time, in silence. Orsino met his glance quietly, but with some curiosity.

"Do you ever go to see the Countess Del Ferice?" asked the big man at last.

Orsino straightened himself in his chair and frowned a little, and then looked away as he answered by a cross-question, knocking the ash off his cigarette upon a little rock crystal dish at his elbow.

"Why do you ask me that?" he enquired rather sternly.

"Because you were very much attracted by her once, and I wished to know whether you had kept up the acquaintance since her marriage."

"I have kept up the acquaintance — and no

more," answered Orsino, meeting his cousin's eyes again. "I go to see the Countess from time to time. I believe we are on very good terms."

"Will you go to Sicily with me if I need you, and stay there, and get an estate in order for me?"

"With pleasure. When?"

"I do not know yet. It may be in a week, or it may be in a month. It will be hot there, and you will have troublesome things to do."

"So much the better."

"There are brigands in the neighbourhood just now."

"That will be very amusing. I never saw one."

"You may tell Ippolito if you like, but please do not mention it to anyone else until we are ready to go. You know that your mother will be anxious about you, and your father is a conservative — and your grandfather is a firebrand, if he dislikes an idea. One would think that at his age his temper should have subsided."

"Not in the least!" Orsino smiled, for he loved the old man, and was proud of his great age.

"But you may tell Ippolito if you like, and if you warn him to be discreet. Ippolito would let himself be torn in pieces rather than betray a secret. He is by far the most discreet of you all."

"Yes. You are right, as usual. You have a good eye for a good man. What do you think of all these Pagliuca people, or Corleone, or d'Oriani

— or whatever they call themselves?" Orsino looked keenly at his cousin as he asked the question.

"Did you ever meet Corleone? I mean the one who married Norba's daughter, — the uncle of these boys."

"I met him once. From all accounts, he must have been a particularly disreputable personage."

"He was worse than that, I think. I never blamed his wife. Well — these boys are his nephews. I do not see that any comment is necessary." San Giacinto smiled thoughtfully.

"This young girl is also his niece," observed Orsino, rather sharply.

"Who knows what Tebaldo Pagliuca might have been if he had spent ten years amongst devout old women in a convent?" The big man's smile developed into an incredulous laugh, in which Orsino joined.

"There has certainly been a difference of education," he admitted. "I like her."

"You would confer a great benefit upon a distressed family, by falling in love with her," said San Giacinto. "That worthy mother of hers was watching you two behind Pietrasanta's head, during dinner."

"Another good reason for going to Sicily," answered Orsino. "The young lady is communicative. She told me, this evening, that you were trying to buy some place of theirs,— I forget the name,— and that one of her brothers objects."

"That is exactly the place I want you to manage. The name is Camaldoli."

"Then there is no secret about it," observed Orsino. "If she has told me, she may tell the next man she meets."

"Certainly. And mysteries are useless, as a rule. I do not wish to make any with you, at all events. Here are the facts. I am going to build a light railway connecting all those places; and I am anxious to get the land into my possession, without much talk. Do you understand? This place of the Corleone is directly in my line, and is one of the most important, because it is at a point through which I must pass, to make the railway at all, short of an expensive tunnel. Your management will simply consist in keeping things in order until the railway makes the land valuable. Then I shall sell it, of course."

"I see. Very well. Could you not give my old architect something to do? Andrea Contini is his name. The houses we built for Del Ferice have all turned out well, you know." Orsino laughed rather bitterly.

"Remind me of him at the proper time," said San Giacinto. "Tell him to learn something about building small railway stations. There will be between fifteen and twenty, altogether."

"I will. But — do you expect that a railway in Sicily will ever pay you?"

"No. I am not an idiot."

"Then why do you build one, if that is not an indiscreet question?"

"The rise in the value of all the land I buy will make it worth while, several times over. It is quite simple."

"It must take an enormous capital," said Orsino, thoughtfully.

"It needs a large sum of ready money. But the lands are generally mortgaged for long periods, and almost to two-thirds of their selling value. The holders of the mortgages do not care who owns the land. So I pay about one-third in cash."

"What becomes of the value of a whole country, when all the land is mortgaged for two-thirds of what it is worth?" asked Orsino, carelessly, and half laughing.

But San Giacinto did not laugh.

"I have thought about that," he answered gravely. "When the yield of the land is not enough to pay the interest on the mortgages, the taxes to the government, and some income to the owners, they starve outright, or emigrate. There is a good deal of starvation nowadays, and a good deal of emigration in search of bread."

"And yet they say that the value of land is

increasing almost all over the country," objected Orsino. "You count on it yourself."

"The value rises wherever railways and roads are built."

"And what pays for the railways?"

"The taxes."

"And the people pay the taxes."

"Exactly. And the taxes are enormous. The people in places remote from the projected railway are ruined by them, but the people who own land where the railways pass are indirectly very much enriched by the result. Sometimes a private individual like myself builds a light road. I think that is a source of wealth, in the end, to everyone. But the building of the government roads, like the one down the west coast of Calabria, seems to destroy the balance of wealth and increase emigration. It is a necessary evil."

"There are a good many necessary evils in our country," said Orsino. "There are too many."

"*Per aspera ad astra.* I never knew much Latin, but I believe that means something. There are also unnecessary evils, such as brigandage in Sicily, for instance. You can amuse yourself by fighting that one, if you please; though I have no doubt that the brigands will often travel by my railway — and they will certainly go in the first class."

The big man laughed and rose, leaving Orsino to meditate upon the prospect of occupation which was opened to him.

CHAPTER IV

ORSINO remained in his corner a few minutes, after San Giacinto had left him, and then rose to go into the drawing-room. As he went he passed the other men who were seated and standing, all near together and not far from the empty fireplace, listening to Tebaldo Pagliuca, who was talking about Sicily with a very strong Sicilian accent. Orsino paused a moment to hear what he was saying. He was telling the story of a frightful murder committed in the outskirts of Palermo not many weeks earlier, and about which there had been much talk. But Tebaldo was on his own ground and knew much more about it than had appeared in the newspapers. His voice was not unpleasant. It was smooth, though his words were broken here and there by gutturals which he had certainly not learned on his own side of the island. There was a sort of reserve in the tones which contrasted with the vividness of the language. Orsino watched him and looked at him more keenly than he had done as yet. He was struck by the stillness of the deep eyes, which were slightly bloodshot, like those of some Arabs, and at the same time by the mobility and changing expression of the lower part of the face. Tebaldo made gestures, too, which had a singular directness. Yet the whole impression given was that he was a good actor rather than a man of continued, honest action, and that he could have performed any other part as well. Near him stood his brother Francesco. There was doubtless a family resemblance between the two, but the difference of constitution was apparent to the most unpractised eye. The younger man was stouter, more sanguine, less nervous. The red blood glowed with strong health under his brown skin, his lips were scarlet and full, his dark moustache was soft and silky like his short, smooth hair, and his eyes were soft, too, and moistly bright, very long, with heavy drooping lids that were whiter than the skin of the rest of the face. Francesco was no more like his sister than was Tebaldo.

Orsino found himself by his father as he paused in passing, and he suddenly realized how immeasurably nearer he was to this strong, iron-grey, middle-sized, silent man beside him, than to any other one of all the men in the room, including his own brothers. Sant' Ilario had perhaps never understood his eldest son; or perhaps there was between them the insurmountable barrier of his own solid happiness. For it is sorrow that draws men together. Happiness needs no sympathy;

happiness is not easily disturbed; happiness that is solidly founded is itself a most negative source of the most all-pervading virtue, without the least charity for unhappiness' sins; happiness suffices to itself; happiness is a lantern to its own feet; it is all things to one man and nothing to all the rest; it is an impenetrable wall between him who has it and mankind. And Sant' Ilario had been happy for nearly thirty years. In appearance, as was to be anticipated, he had turned out to be like his father, as the latter had been at the same age. In temper, he was different, as the conditions of his life had been of another sort. The ancient head of the house had lost his Spanish wife when very young, and had lived many years alone with his only son. Giovanni had met with no such misfortune. His wife was alive and still beautiful at an age when many women have forgotten the taste of flattery; and his four sons were all grown men, straight and tall, so that he looked up to their faces when they stood beside him. Strong, peaceable, honest, rather hard-faced young men, they were, excepting Ippolito, the second of them, who had talent and a lovable disposition in place of strength and hardness of character.

They were fond of their father, no doubt, and there was great solidarity in the family. But what they felt for Sant' Ilario was perhaps more like an allegiance than an affection, and they looked to him as the principal person of importance in the family, because their grandfather was such a very old man. They were accustomed to take it for granted that he was infallible when he expressed himself definitely in a family matter, whereas they had no very high opinion of his judgment in topics and questions of the day; for they had received a modern education, and were to some extent imbued with those modern prejudices compared with which the views of our fathers hardly deserved the name of a passing caprice.

Orsino thought that there was something at once cunning and ferocious about Tebaldo's way of telling the story. He had a fine smile of appreciation for the secrecy and patience of the two young men who had sought occasion against their sister's lover, and there was a squaring of the angular jaws and a quick forward movement of the head, as of a snake when striking, to accompany his description of the death-blow. Orsino listened to the end and then went quietly out and returned to the drawing-room.

Vittoria d'Oriani was seated near Corona, who was talking to her in a low tone. The other ladies were standing together before a famous old picture. The Marchesa di San Giacinto was smoking a cigarette. Orsino sat down by his mother, who looked at him quietly and smiled, and then went on speaking. The young girl glanced at Orsino.

She was leaning forward, one elbow on her knee, and her chin supported in her hand, her lips a little parted as she listened with deep interest to what the elder woman said. Corona was telling her of Rome many years earlier, of the life in those days, of Pius the Ninth, and of the coming of the Italians.

"How can you remember things that happened when you were so young!" exclaimed Vittoria, watching the calm and beautiful face.

"I was older than you even then," answered Corona, with a smile. "And I married very young," she added thoughtfully. "I was married at your age, I think. How old are you, my dear?"

"I am eighteen — just eighteen," replied Vittoria.

"I was married when I was scarcely seventeen. It was too young."

"But you have always been so happy. Why do you say that?"

"What makes you think that I have always been happy?" asked the Princess.

"Your face, I think. One or two of the nuns were very happy, too. But it was different. They had quite another look on their faces."

"I daresay," answered Corona, and she smiled again, and looked proudly at Orsino.

She rose and crossed the room, feeling that she was neglecting her older guests for the young girl, who was thus left with Orsino again. He did not see Donna Maria Carolina's quick glance as she discovered the fact, and made sure of it, looking again and again at the two while she joined a little in the conversation which was going on around her. She was very happy, just then, poor lady, and almost forgot to struggle against the accumulated provincialisms of twenty years, or to be anxious lest her new friends should discover that her pearls were false. For the passion for ornament, false or real, had not diminished with the improvement in her fortunes.

But Orsino was not at all interested in Vittoria's mother, and he had seen too much to care whether women wore real jewelry or not. He had almost forgotten the young girl after dinner when he had sat down in the corner of the smoking-room, but San Giacinto's remark had vividly recalled her face to his memory, with a strong desire to see her again at once. Nothing was easier than to satisfy such a wish, and he found himself by her side.

Once there, he did not trouble himself to speak to her for several moments. Vittoria showed considerable outward self-possession, though it was something of an ordeal to sit in silence, almost touching him and not daring to speak, while he was apparently making up his mind what to say. It had been much easier during dinner, she thought, because she had been put in her place without being consulted, and was expected to be there, without the least idea of attracting attention. Now, she felt a little dizzy for a moment, as though the room were swaying; and she was afraid that she was going to blush, which would have been ridiculous.

Now, he was looking at her, while she looked down at her little white fan that lay on the white stuff of her frock, quite straight, between her two small, white-gloved hands. The nuns had not told her what to do in any such situation. Still Orsino did not speak. Two minutes had crawled by, like two hours, and she felt a fluttering in her throat.

It was absurd, she thought. There was no reason for being so miserable. Very probably, he was not thinking of her at all. But it was of no use to tell herself such things, for her embarrassment grew apace, till she felt that she must spring from her seat and run from the room without looking at him. The fluttering became almost convulsive, and her hands pressed the little fan on each side, clenching themselves tightly. Still he did not speak.

In utter despair she began to recite inwardly the litany of the saints, biting her lips lest they should move and he should guess what she was doing. In her suppressed excitement the holy personages raced and tumbled over each other at a most unseemly rate, till the procession was violently checked by the gravely indifferent tones of

Orsino's voice. Her hands relaxed, and she turned a little pale.

"Have you been to Saint Peter's?" he enquired calmly.

He was certainly not embarrassed, but he could think of nothing better to say to a young girl. On the first occasion, at dinner, he had asked her how she liked Rome. At all events it had opened the conversation. He remembered well enough the half dozen earnest words they had exchanged; and there was something more than mere memory, for he knew that he half wished they might reach the same point again. Perhaps, if the wish had been stronger and if Vittoria had been a little older, it might have been easier.

"Yes," she said. "My mother took me as soon as we came. She was very anxious that we should pay our devotion to the patron saint."

Orsino smiled a little.

"Saint Peter is not the patron of Rome," he observed. "Our protector is San Filippo Neri."

Vittoria looked up in genuine surprise.

"Saint Peter is not the patron saint of Rome!" she exclaimed. "But — I always thought — "

"Naturally enough. All sorts of things in Rome seem to be what they are not. We seem to be alive, for instance. We are not. Six or seven years ago we were all in a frantic state of excitement over our greatness. We have turned out to be nothing but a set of embalmed specimens in glass cases. Do not look so much surprised, signorina — or shocked — which is it?"

He laughed a little.

"I cannot help it," answered Vittoria, simply, her brown eyes still fixed on him in wonder. "It is — it is all so different from what I expected — the things people say — " She hesitated and stopped short, turning her eyes from him.

The light was strong in the room, for the aged Prince hated the modern fashion of shading lamps almost to a dusk. Orsino watched Vittoria's profile, and the graceful turn of her young throat as she looked away, and the fine growth of silky hair from the temples and behind the curving little ear. The room was warm, and he sat silently watching her for a moment. She was no longer embarrassed, for she was not thinking of herself, and she did not know how he was thinking of her just then.

"I wonder what you expected us to be like," he said at last. "And what you expected us to say," he added as an afterthought.

It crossed his mind that if she had been a married woman three or four years older, he might have found her very amusing in conversation. He could certainly not have been talking in detached and almost idiotic phrases, as he was actually doing. But if she had been a young married woman, her charm would have been different, and of a kind not new to him. There was a novelty about Vittoria, and it attracted him strongly. There was real freshness and untried youth in her; she had that sort of delicacy which some flowers have, and which is not fragility, the bloom of a precious thing fresh broken from the mould and not yet breathed upon. He wondered whether all young girls had this inexpressible something, and if so, why he had never noticed it.

"I am not quite sure," answered Vittoria, blushing a little at the thought that she could have had a preconceived idea of Orsino Saracinesca.

The reply left everything to be desired in the way of brilliancy, but the voice was soft and expectant, as some women's voices are, that seem just upon the point of vibrating to a harmonic while yielding the fundamental tone in all its roundness. There are rare voices that seem to possess a distinct living individuality, apart from the women to whom they belong, a sort of extra-natural musical life, of which the woman herself cannot control nor calculate the power. It is not the 'golden voice' which some great actresses have. One recognizes that at the first hearing; one admits its beauty; one hears it three or four times, and one knows it by heart. It will pronounce certain phrases in a certain way, inevitably; it will soften and swell and ring with mathematical precision at the same verse, at the identical word, night after night, year after year, while it lasts. Vittoria's voice was not like that. It had the spontaneity of independent life which a passion itself has when it takes possession of a man or a woman. Orsino felt it, and was conscious of a new sensitiveness in himself.

On the whole, to make a very wide statement of a general truth, Italian men are moved by sense and Italian women are stirred by passion. Between passion and sense there is all the difference that exists between the object and the idea. Sense appreciates, passion idealizes; sense desires all things, passion hungers for one; sense is material, though ever so æsthetized and refined, but passion clothes fact with unearthly attributes; sense is singly selfish, passion would make a single self of two. The sensual man says, 'To have seen much and to have little is to have rich eyes and poor hands'; the passionate man or woman will 'put it to the test, to win or lose it all,' like Montrose. Sense is vulgar when it is not monstrous in strength, or hysterical to madness. Passion is always noble, even in its sins and crimes. Sense can be satisfied, and its satisfaction is a low sort of happiness; but passion's finer strings can quiver with immortal pain, and ring with the transcendent harmony that wakes the hero even in a coward's heart.

Vittoria first touched Orsino by her outward

charm, by her voice, by her grace. But it was his personality, or her spontaneous imagination of it, which made an indelible impression upon her mind before the first evening of their acquaintance was over. The woman who falls in love with a man for his looks alone is not of a very high type, but the best and bravest men that ever lived have fallen victims to mere beauty, often without much intelligence, or faith, or honour.

Orsino was probably not aware that he was falling in love at first sight. Very few men are, and yet very many people certainly begin to fall in love at a first meeting, who would scout the idea as an absurdity. For love's beginnings are most exceedingly small in the greatest number of instances. Were they greater, a man might guard himself more easily against his fate.

CHAPTER V

AT that time a young Sicilian singer had lately made her first appearance in Rome and had been received with great favour. She was probably not destined ever to become one of the chief artists of the age, but she possessed exactly the qualifications necessary to fascinate a Roman audience. She was very young, she was undeniably beautiful, and she had what Romans called a 'sympathetic' voice. They think more of that latter quality in Italy than elsewhere. It is what in English we might call charm, and to have it is to have the certainty of success with an Italian public.

Aliandra Basili was the daughter of a respectable notary in the ancient town of Randazzo, which lies on the western slope of Mount Etna, on the high road from Piedimonte to Bronte and Catania, within two hours' ride of Camaldoli, the Corleone place. It is a solemn old walled town, built of almost black tufo, though many of the houses on the main street have now been stuccoed and painted; and it has a very beautiful Saracen-Norman cathedral.

Aliandra's life had been very like that of any

other provincial girl of the middle class. She had been educated in a small convent, while her excellent father, whose wife was dead, laboured to accumulate a little dowry for his only child. At fifteen years of age, she had returned to live with him, and he had entertained good hopes of marrying her off before she was seventeen. In fact, he thought that he had only to choose among a number of young men, of whom any one would be delighted to become her husband.

Then, one day, Tebaldo and Francesco Pagliuca came riding down from Camaldoli, and stopped at the notary's house to get a small lease drawn up; and while they were there, in the dusty office, doing their best to be sure of what old Basili's legal language meant, they heard Aliandra singing to herself upstairs. After that they came to Randazzo again, both separately and together, and at last they persuaded old Basili that his daughter had a fortune in her voice and should be allowed to become a singer. He consented after a long struggle, and sent her to Messina to live with a widowed sister of his, and to be taught by an old master of great reputation who had taken up his abode there. Very possibly Basili agreed to this step with a view to removing the girl to a distance from the two brothers, who made small secret of their admiration for her, or about their jealousy of each other; and he reflected that she could be better watched and guarded by his sister, who would have nothing else to do, than by himself. For he was a busy man, and obliged to spend his days either in his office, or in visits to distant clients, so that the motherless girl was thrown far too much upon her own resources.

Tebaldo, on the other hand, realized that so long as she lived in Randazzo, he should have but a small chance of seeing her alone. He could not come and spend a week at a time in the town, but he could find an excuse for being longer than that in Messina, and he trusted to his ingenuity to elude the vigilance of the aunt with whom she was to live. In Messina, too, he should not have his brother at his elbow, trying to outdo him at every turn, and evidently attracting the young girl to a certain extent.

To tell the truth, Aliandra's head was turned by the attentions of the two young noblemen, though her father never lost an opportunity of telling her that they were a pair of penniless good-for-nothings and otherwise dangerous characters, supposed to be on good terms with the brigands of the interior, and typical 'maffeusi' through and through. But such warnings were much more calculated to excite the girl's interest than to frighten her. She had an artist's nature and instincts, and the two young gentlemen were very romantic characters in her eyes, when they rode down from their dilapidated stronghold, on their compact little horses, their beautiful Winchester rifles slung over their shoulders, their velvet coats catching the sunlight, their spurs gleaming, and their broad hats shading their dark eyes. Had there been but one of them, her mind would soon have been made up to make him marry her, and she might have succeeded without much difficulty. But she found it hard to decide between the two. They were too different for comparison, and yet too much alike for preference. Tebaldo was a born tyrant, and Francesco a born coward. She was dominated by the one and she ruled the other, but she was not in love with either, and she could not make up her mind whether it would on the whole be more agreeable to love her master or her slave.

Meanwhile she made rapid progress in her singing, appeared at the opera in Palermo, and almost immediately obtained an engagement in Rome. To her father, the sum offered her appeared enormous, and her aunt was delighted by the prospect of going to Rome with her during the winter. Aliandra had been successful from the first, and she seemed to be on the high road to fame. The young idlers of rich Palermo intrigued to be introduced to her and threw enormous nosegays to her at the end of every act. She found that there were scores of men far handsomer and richer than the Pagliuca brothers, ready to fall in love with her, and she began to reflect seriously upon her position. Artist though she was, by one side of her nature, there was in her a touch of her father's sensible legal instinct, together with that extraordinary self-preserving force which usually distinguishes the young girl of southern Italy.

She soon understood that no one of her new admirers would ever think of asking her to be his wife, whereas she was convinced that she could marry either Tebaldo or Francesco, at her choice and pleasure. They were poor, indeed, but of as good nobility as any of the rich young noblemen of Palermo, and she was beginning to find out what fortunes were sometimes made by great singers. She dreamed of buying back the old Corleone estates and of being some day the Princess of Corleone herself. That meant that she must choose Tebaldo, since he was to get the title. And here she hesitated again. She did not realize that Francesco was actually a physical coward and rather a contemptible character altogether; to her he merely seemed gentle and winning, and she thought him much ill used by his despotic elder brother. As for the third brother, Ferdinando, of whom mention has been made, she had rarely seen him. He was probably the best of the family, which was not saying much, and he was also by far the least civilized. He was undoubtedly in close communication with the brigands, and when he was occasionally absent from home, he was not spending his time in Messina or Randazzo.

Time went on, and in the late autumn Aliandra and her aunt went to Rome for the season. As has been seen, it pleased fortune that the Pagliuca brothers should be there also, with their mother and sister, Ferdinando remaining in Sicily. When the question of selling Camaldoli to San Giacinto arose, Ferdinando at first flatly refused to give his consent. Thereupon Tebaldo wrote him a singularly temperate and logical letter, in which he very quietly proposed to inform the government of Ferdinando's complicity with the brigands, unless he at once agreed to the sale. Ferdinando might have laughed at the threat had it come from anyone else, but he knew that Tebaldo's thorough acquaintance with the country and with the outlaws' habits would give him a terrible advantage. Tebaldo, if he gave information, could of course never return to Sicily, for his life would not be safe, even in broad daylight, in the Macqueda of Palermo, and it was quite possible that the mafia might reach him even in Rome. But he was undoubtedly able to help the government in a raid in which many of Ferdinando's friends must perish or be taken prisoners. For their sakes

Ferdinando signed his consent to the sale, before old Basili in Randazzo, and sent the paper to Rome; but that night he swore that no Roman should ever get possession of Camaldoli while he was alive, and half a dozen of the boldest among the outlaws swore that they would stand by him in his resolution.

Aliandra knew nothing of all this, for Tebaldo was far too wise to tell anyone how he had forced his brother's consent. She would certainly have been disgusted with him, had she known the truth, for she was morally as far superior to him and to Francesco as an innocent girl brought up by honest folks can be better than a pair of exceedingly corrupt young adventurers. But they both had in a high degree the power of keeping up appearances and of imposing upon their surroundings. Tebaldo was indeed subject to rare fits of anger in which he completely lost control of himself, and when he was capable of going to any length of violence; but these were very unusual, and as a general rule he was reticent in the extreme. Francesco possessed the skill and gentle duplicity of a born coward and a born ladies' man. They both deceived Aliandra, in spite of her father's early warning and her old aunt's anxious advice.

Aliandra was successful beyond anyone's expectations during her first engagement in Rome, and she was wise enough to gain herself the reputation of being unapproachable to her many admirers. Only Tebaldo and Francesco, whom she now considered as old friends of her family, were ever admitted to her room at the theatre, or received at the quiet apartment where she lived with her aunt.

On the night of the dinner-party at the Palazzo Saracinesca, Aliandra was to sing in Lucia for the first time in Rome. Both the brothers had wished that they could have been in the theatre to hear her, instead of spending the evening in the society of those very stiff and mighty Romans, and both made up their minds separately that they would see her before she left the Argentina that night. Tebaldo, as usual, took the lead of events, and peremptorily ordered Francesco to go home with their mother and sister in the carriage.

When the Corleone party left the palace, therefore, Francesco got into the carriage, but Tebaldo said that he preferred to walk, and went out alone from under the great gate. He was not yet very familiar with the streets of Rome, but he believed that he knew the exact situation of the palace, and could easily find his way from it to the Argentina theatre, which was not very far distant.

The old part of the city puzzled him, however. He found himself threading unfamiliar ways, dark lanes, and winding streets which emerged suddenly upon small squares from which three or four other streets led in different directions. Instinctively he looked behind him from time to time, and felt in his pocket for the pistol which, like a true provincial, he thought it as necessary to carry in Rome as in his Sicilian home. Presently he looked at his watch, saw that it was eleven o'clock, and made up his mind to find a cab if he could. But that was not an easy matter either, in that part of the city, and it was twenty minutes past eleven when he at last drew up to the stage entrance at the back of the Argentina. A weary, grey, unshaven, and very dirty old man admitted him, looked at his face, took the flimsy currency note which Tebaldo held out, and let him pass without a word. The young man knew his way much better within the building than out in the streets. In a few moments he stopped before a dingy little door, the last on the left in a narrow corridor dimly lit by a single flame of gas, which was turned low for economy's sake. He knocked sharply and opened the door without waiting for an answer.

There were three persons in the small, low dressing-room, and all three faced Tebaldo rather anxiously. Aliandra Basili, the young Sicilian prima donna who had lately made her first appearance in Rome, was seated before a dim mirror which stood on a low table covered with appliances for theatrical dressing. Her maid was arranging a white veil on her head, and beside her, very near to her, and drawing back from her as Tebaldo entered, sat Francesco.

Tebaldo's lips moved uneasily, as he stood still for a moment, gazing at the little group, his hand on the door. Then he closed it quickly behind him, and came forward with a smile.

"Good evening," he said. "I lost my way in the streets and am a little late. I thought the curtain would be up for the last act."

"They have called me once," answered Aliandra. "I said that I was not ready, for I knew you would come."

She was really very handsome and very young, but the mask of paint and powder changed her face and expression almost beyond recognition. Even her bright, gold-brown eyes were made to look black and exaggerated by the deep shadows painted with antimony below them, and on the lids. The young hand she held out to Tebaldo was whitened with a chalky mixture to the tips of the fingers. She was dressed in the flowing white robe which Lucia wears in the mad scene, and the flaring gaslights on each side of the mirror made her face and wig look terribly artificial. Tebaldo thought so as he looked at her, and remembered the calm simplicity of Corona Saracinesca's mature beauty. But he had known Aliandra long, and his imagination saw her own face through her paint.

"It was good of you to wait for me," he said.

"I daresay my brother helped the time to pass pleasantly."

"I have only just come," said Francesco, quickly. "I took our mother home — it is far."

"I did not know that you were coming at all," replied Tebaldo, coldly. "How is it going?" he asked, sitting down by Aliandra. "Another ovation?"

"No. They are waiting for the mad scene, of course — and my voice is as heavy as lead to-night. I shall not please anyone — and it is the first time I have sung Lucia in Rome. My nerves are in a state —"

"You are not frightened? You — of all people?"

"I am half dead with fright. I am white under my rouge. I can feel it."

"Poor child!" exclaimed Francesco, softly, and his eyes lightened as he watched her.

"Bah!" Tebaldo shrugged his shoulders and smiled. "She always says that!"

"And sometimes it is true," answered Aliandra, with a sharp sigh.

A double rap at the door interrupted the conversation.

"Signorina Basili! Are you ready?" asked a gruff voice outside.

"Yes!" replied the young girl, rising with an effort.

Francesco seized her left hand and kissed it.

Tebaldo said nothing, but folded his arms and stood aside. He saw on his brother's dark moustache a few grains of the chalky dust which whitened Aliandra's fingers.

"Do not wait for me when it is over," she said. "My aunt is in the house, and will take me home. Good night."

"Goodbye," said Tebaldo, looking intently into her face as he opened the door.

She started in surprise, and perhaps her face would have betrayed her pain, but the terribly artificial rouge and powder hid the change.

"Come and see me to-morrow," she said to Tebaldo, in a low voice, when she was already in the doorway.

He did not answer, but kept his eyes steadily on her face.

"Signorina Basili! You will miss your cue!" cried the gruff voice in the corridor.

Aliandra hesitated an instant, glancing out and then looking again at Tebaldo.

"To-morrow," she said suddenly, stepping out into the passage. "To-morrow," she repeated, as she went swiftly towards the stage.

She looked back just before she disappeared, but there was little light, and Tebaldo could no longer see her eyes.

He stood still by the door. Then his brother passed him.

"I am going to hear this act," said Francesco, quietly, as though unaware that anything unusual had happened.

Before he was out of the door, he felt Tebaldo's hand on his shoulder, gripping him hard and shaking him a little. He turned his head, and his face was suddenly pale. Tebaldo kept his hand on his brother's shoulder and pushed him back against the wall of the passage, under the solitary gaslight.

"What do you mean by coming here?" he asked. "How do you dare?"

Francesco was badly frightened, for he knew Tebaldo's ungovernable temper.

"Why not?" he tried to ask. "I have often been here —"

"Because I warned you not to come again. Because I am in earnest. Because I will do you some harm, if you thrust yourself into my way with her."

"I shall call for help now, unless you let me go," answered Francesco, with white lips. Tebaldo laughed savagely.

"What a coward you are!" he cried, giving his brother a final shake and then letting him go. "And what a fool I am to care!" he added, laughing again.

"Brute!" exclaimed Francesco, adjusting his collar and smoothing his coat.

"I warned you," retorted Tebaldo, watching him. "And now I have warned you again," he added. "This is the second time. Are there no women in the world besides Aliandra Basili?"

"I knew her first," objected the younger man, beginning to recover some courage.

"You knew her first? When she was a mere child in Randazzo,— when we went to her father about a lease, we both heard her singing,— but what has that to do with it? That was six years ago, and you have hardly seen her since."

"How do you know?" asked Francesco, scornfully.

He had gradually edged past Tebaldo towards the open end of the passage.

"How do you know that I did not often see her alone before she went to Messina, and since then, too?" He smiled as he renewed the question.

"I do not know," said Tebaldo, calmly. "You are a coward. You are also a most accomplished liar. It is impossible to believe a word you say, good or bad. I should not believe you if you were dying, and if you swore upon the holy sacraments that you were telling me the truth."

"Thank you," answered Francesco, apparently unmoved by the insult. "But you would probably believe Aliandra, would you not?"

"Why should I? She is only a woman."

Tebaldo turned angrily as he spoke, and his eyelids drooped at the corners, like a vulture's.

"You two are not made to be believed," he said, growing more cold. "I sometimes forget, but you soon remind me of the fact again. You said distinctly this evening that you would go home with our mother —"

"So I did," interrupted Francesco. "I did not promise to stay there —"

"I will not argue with you —"

"No. It would be useless, as you are in the wrong. I am going to hear the act. Good night."

Francesco walked quickly down the passage. He did not turn to look behind him, but it was not until he was at the back of the stage, groping his way amidst lumber and dust towards the other side, that he felt safe from any further violence.

Tebaldo had no intention of following. He stood quite still under the gaslight for a few seconds, and then opened the door of the dressing-room again. He knew that the maid was there alone.

"How long was my brother here before I came?" he asked sharply.

The woman was setting things in order, packing the tinsel-trimmed gown which the singer had worn in the previous scene. She looked up nervously, for she was afraid of Tebaldo.

"A moment, only a moment," she answered,

not pausing in her work, and speaking in a scared tone.

Tebaldo looked at her, and saw that she was frightened. He was not in the humour to believe anyone just then, and after a moment's silence, he turned on his heel and went out.

CHAPTER VI

"WHAT strange people there are in the world," said Corona Saracinesca to her husband, on the morning after the dinner at which the Corleone family had been present.

Giovanni was reading a newspaper, leaning back in his own especial chair in his wife's morning room. It was raining, and she was looking out of the window. There are not many half-unconscious actions which betray so much of the general character and momentary temper, as an idle pause before closed window panes, and a careless glance down into the street or up at the sky. The fact has not been noticed, but deserves to be. Many a man or woman, at an anxious crisis, turns to the window, with the sensation of being alone for a moment, away from the complications created by the other person or persons in the room, free, for an instant, to let the features relax, the eye darken, or the lips smile, as the case may be — off the stage, indeed, as a comedian in the side scenes. Or again, when there is no anxiety, one goes from one's work, to take a look at the outside world, not caring to see it, but glad to be away from the task and to give the mind a breathing space. And then, also, the expression of the features changes, and if one stops to think of it, one is aware that the face is momentarily rested. Another, who has forgotten trouble and pain for a while, in conversation or in pleasant reading, goes to the window. And the grief, or the pain, or the fear, comes back with a rush and clouds the eyes and bends the brow, till he who suffers turns with something like fear from the contemplation of the outer world and takes up his book, or his talk, or his work, or anything which can help him to forget. With almost all people, there is a sudden change of sensation in first looking out of the window. One drums impatiently on the panes, another bites his lip, a third grows very still and grave, and one, perhaps, smiles suddenly, and then glances back to the room, fearing lest his inward lightness of heart may have betrayed itself.

Corona had nothing to conceal from Giovanni nor from herself. She had realized the rarest and highest form of lasting human happiness, which is to live unparted from the single being loved, with no screen of secret to cast a shadow on either side. Such a life can have but few emotions, yet the possibility of the very deepest emotion is always present in it, as the ocean is not rigid when it is quiet, as the strong man asleep is not past waking, nor the singer mute when silent.

Corona had been moving quietly about the room, giving life to it by her touch, where mechanical hands had done their daily work of dull neatness. She loosened the flowers in a vase, moved the books on the table, pulled the long lace curtains a little out from under the heavy ones, turned a chair here and a knickknack there, set the little calendar on the writing-table, and moved the curtains again. Then at last she paused before the window. Her lids drooped thoughtfully and her mouth relaxed, as she made the remark which caused Giovanni to look up from his paper.

"What strange people there are in the world!" she exclaimed.

"It is fortunate that they are not all like us," answered Giovanni.

"Why?"

"The world would stop, I fancy. People would all be happy, as we are, and would shut themselves up, and there would be universal peace, the millennium, and a general cessation of business. Then would come the end of all things. Of whom are you thinking?"

"Of those people who came to dinner last night, and of our boys."

"Of Orsino, I suppose. Yes — I know —" He paused.

"Yes," said Corona, thoughtfully.

Both were silent for a moment. They thought

together, having long been unaccustomed to think apart. At last Giovanni laughed quietly.

"Our children cannot be exactly like us," he said. "They must live their own lives, as we live ours. One cannot make lives for other people, you know."

"Orsino is so apathetic," said Corona. "He opens his eyes for a moment and looks at things as though he were going to be interested. Then he closes them again, and does not care what happens. He has no enthusiasm like Ippolito. Nothing interests him, nothing amuses him. He is not happy, and he is not unhappy. You could not surprise him. I sometimes think that you could not hurt him, either. He is young, yet he acts like a man who has seen everything, done everything, heard everything, and tasted everything. He does not even fall in love."

Corona smiled as she spoke the last words, but her eyes were thoughtful. In her heart, no thoroughly feminine woman can understand that a young man may not be in love for a long time, and may yet be normally sensible.

"I was older than he when you and I met," observed Giovanni.

"Yes — but you were different. Orsino is not at all like you."

"Nor Ippolito either."

"There is more of you in him than you think,

Giovanni, though he is so gentle and quiet, and fond of music."

"The artistic temperament, my dear,—very little like me."

"There is a curious tenacity under all that."

"No one has ever thwarted him," objected Giovanni. "Or, rather, he has never thwarted anybody. That is a better way of putting it."

"I believe he has more strength of character than the other three together. Of course, you will say that he is my favourite."

"No, dear. You are very just. But you are more drawn to him."

"Yes — strangely more — and for something in him which no one sees. It is his likeness to you, I think."

"Together with a certain feminility."

Giovanni did not speak contemptuously, but he had always resented Ippolito's gentle grace a little. He himself and his other three sons had the strongly masculine temperament of the Saracinesca family. He often thought that Ippolito should have been a girl.

"Do not say that, Giovanni," answered his wife. "He is not rugged, but he is strong-hearted. The artistic temperament has a certain feminine quality on the surface, by which it feels; but the crude creative force by which it acts is purely masculine."

"That sounds clever," laughed Giovanni.

"Well, there is dear old Gausche, whom we have known all our lives. He is an instance. You used to think he had a certain feminility, too."

"So he had."

"But he fought like a man at Mentana; and he thinks like a man, and he certainly paints like a man."

"Yes; that is true. Only we never had any artists in the family. It seems odd that our son should have such tendencies. None of the family were ever particularly clever in any way."

"You are not stupid, at all events."

Corona smiled at her husband. For all the world, she would not have had him at all different from his present self.

"Besides," she added, "you need not think of him as an artist. You can look upon him as a priest."

"Yes, I know," answered Giovanni, without much enthusiasm. "We never were a priest-breeding family either. We have done better at farming than at praying or playing the piano. Ippolito does not know a plough from a harrow, nor a thoroughbred colt from a cart-horse. For my part I do not see the strength you find in him, though I daresay you are right, my dear. You generally are. At all events, he helps the harmony of the family, for he worships Orsino, and the two younger ones always pair together."

"I suppose he will never be put into any position which can show his real character," said Corona, "but I know I am right."

They were silent for a few minutes. Presently Giovanni took up his paper again, and Corona sat down at her table to write a note. The rain pattered against the window, cheerfully, as it does outside a room in which two happy people are together.

"That d'Oriani girl is charming," said Corona, after writing a line or two, but not looking round.

"Perhaps Orsino will fall in love with her," observed her husband, his eyes on the newspaper.

"I hope not!" exclaimed Corona, turning in her chair, and speaking with far more energy than she had yet shown. "It is bad blood, Giovanni — as bad as any blood in Italy, and though the girl is charming, those brothers — well, you saw them."

"Bad faces, both of them. And rather doubtful manners."

"Never mind their manners! But their faces! They are nephews of poor Bianca Corleone's husband, are they not?"

"Yes. They are his brother's children. And they are their grandfather's grandchildren."

"What did he do?"

"He was chiefly concerned in the betrayal of Gaeta — and took money for the deed, too. They have always been traitors. There was a Pagliuca who received all sorts of offices and honours from Joaquin Murat and then advised King Ferdinand to have him shot when he was caught at Pizzo in Calabria. There was a Pagliuca who betrayed his brother to save his own life in the last century. It is a promising stock."

"What an inheritance! I have often heard of them, but I have never met any of them excepting Bianca's husband, whom we all hated for her sake."

"He was not the worst of them, by any means. But I never blamed her much, poor child — and Pietro Ghisleri knew how to turn any woman's head in those days."

"Why did we ask those people to dinner, after all?" enquired Corona, thoughtfully.

"Because San Giacinto wished it, I suppose. We shall probably know why in two or three years. He never does anything without a reason."

"And he keeps his reasons to himself."

"It is a strange thing," said Giovanni. "That man is the most reticent human being I ever knew, and one of the deepest. Yet we are all sure that he is absolutely honest and honourable. We know that he is always scheming, and yet we feel that he is never plotting. There is a difference."

"Of course there is — the difference between strategy and treachery. But I am sorry that his plans should have involved bringing the Corleone family into our house. They are not nice people, excepting the girl."

"My father remarked that the elder of those brothers was like an old engraving he has of Cæsar Borgia."

"That is a promising resemblance! Fortunately, the times, at least, are changed."

"In Sicily, everything is possible."

The remark was characteristic of Giovanni, of a Roman, and of modern times. But there was, and is, some truth in it. Many things are possible to-day in Sicily which have not been possible anywhere else in Europe for at least two centuries, and the few foreigners who know the island well can tell tales of Sicilians which the world at large would hardly accept even as fiction.

CHAPTER VII

DURING the ensuing weeks Orsino saw Vittoria d'Oriani repeatedly, at first by accident, and afterwards because he was attracted by her, and took pains to learn where she and her mother were going, in order to meet her.

It was spring. Easter had come very early, and as happens in such cases, there was a revival of gaiety after Lent. There were garden parties, a recent importation in Rome, there were great picnics to the hills, and there were races out at the Capannelle; moreover, there were dances at which the windows were kept open all night, until the daylight began to steal in and tell tales of unpleasant truth, so that even fair women drew lace things over their tired faces as they hurried into their carriages in the cold dawn, glad to remember that they had still looked passably well in the candle-light.

At one of these balls, late in the season, Orsino knew that he should meet Vittoria. It was in a vast old palace, from the back of which two graceful bridges crossed the street below to a garden beyond, where there were fountains, and palms, and statues, and walks hedged with box in the old Italian manner. There were no very magnificent preparations for the dance, which was rather a small and intimate affair, but there was the magnificent luxury of well-proportioned space, which belonged to an older age, there was the gentle light of several hundred wax candles instead of the cold glare of electricity or the pestilent flame of gas, and all night long there was April moonlight outside, in the old garden, whence the smell of the box, and the myrtle, and of violets, was borne in fitfully through the open windows with each breath of moving air.

There was also, that night, a general feeling of being at home and in a measure free from the oppression of social tyranny, and from the disturbing presence of the rich social recruit, who was sown in wealth, so to say, in the middle of the century, and who is now plentifully reaped in vulgarity.

"It is more like the old times than anything I remember for years," said Corona to Gianforte Campodonico, as they walked slowly through the rooms together.

"It must be the wax candles and the smell of the flowers from the garden," he answered, not exactly comprehending, for he was not a sensitive man, and was, moreover, considerably younger than Corona.

But Corona was silent, and wished that she were

walking with her husband, or sitting alone with him in some quiet corner, for something in the air reminded her of a ball in the Frangipani palace, many years ago, when Giovanni had spoken to her in a conservatory, and many things had happened in consequence. The wax candles and the smell of open-air flowers, and the glimpses of moonlight through vast windows may have had something to do with it; but surely there are times and hours, when love is in the air, when every sound is tuneful, and all silence is softly alive, when young voices seek each the other's tone caressingly, and the stealing hand steals nearer to the hand that waits.

There was no one to prevent Orsino Saracinesca from persuading Vittoria to go and sit down in one of the less frequented rooms, if he could do so. Her mother would be delighted, her brothers were not at the ball, and Orsino was responsible to no one for his actions. She had learned many things since she had come to Rome, but she did not understand more than half of them, and what she understood least of all was the absolute power which Orsino exerted over her when he was present. He haunted her thoughts at other times, too, and she had acquired a sort of conviction that she could not escape from him, which was greatly strengthened by the fact that she did not wish to be free.

On his part, his mind was less easy, for he was

well aware that he was making love to the girl with her mother's consent, whereas he was not by any means inclined to think that he wished to marry her. Such a position might not seem strange to a youth of Anglo-Saxon traditions; for there is a sort of tacit understanding among the English-speaking races to the effect that young people are never to count on each other till each has got the other up the steps of the altar, that there is nothing disgraceful in breaking an engagement, and that love-making at large, without any intention of marriage, is a harmless pastime especially designed for the very young. The Italian view is very different, however, and Orsino was well aware that unless he meant to make Vittoria d'Oriani his wife, he was doing wrong in his own eyes, and in the eyes of the world, in doing his best to be often with her.

One result of his conduct was that he frightened away other men. They took it for granted that he wished to marry her, dowerless as she was, and they kept out of his way. The girl was not neglected, however. San Giacinto had his own reasons for wishing to be on good terms with her brothers, and he made his wife introduce partners to Vittoria at dances, and send men to talk to her at parties. But as soon as Orsino came upon the scene, Vittoria's companion disappeared, whoever he happened to be at the time.

The Italian, even when very young, has a good deal of social philosophy when he is not under the influence of an emotion from which he cannot escape. He will avoid falling in love with the wrong person, if he can.

"For what?" he asks. "In order to be unhappy? Why?"

And he systematically keeps out of the way of temptation, well knowing his own weakness in love matters.

But Orsino was attracted by the girl and yielded to the attraction, though his manner of yielding was a domination over her whenever they met. His only actual experience of real love had been in his affair with the Countess del Ferice, before her second marriage. She was a mature woman of strong character and devoted nature, who had resisted him and had sacrificed herself for him, not to him. He had been accustomed to find that resistance in her. But Vittoria offered none at all, a fact which gave his rather despotic nature a sudden development, while the absence of opposition made him look upon his disinclination to decide the question of marriage as something he ought to have been ashamed of. At the same time, there was the fact that he had grown somewhat cynical and cold of late years, and if not positively selfish, at least negatively careless of others, when anything pleased him, which was not often. It is bad to have strength and not to use it, to possess power and not to exert it, to know that one is a personage without caring much what sort of person one may be. That had been Orsino's position for years, and it had not improved his character.

On this particular evening he was conscious of something much more like emotion than he had felt for a long time. San Giacinto had lain in wait for him near the door, and had told him that matters were settled at last and that they were to leave Rome within the week to take possession of the Corleone lands. The deeds had been signed and the money had been paid. There were no further formalities, and it was time to go to work. Orsino nodded, said he was ready, and went off to find Vittoria in the ballroom. But there was a little more colour than usual under his dark skin, and his eyes were restless and hungry.

He was passing his mother without seeing her, when she touched him on the sleeve, and dropped Campodonico's arm. He started a little impatiently, and then stood still, waiting for her to speak.

"Has anything happened?" she asked rather anxiously.

"No, mother, nothing—that is—" He hesitated, glancing at Campodonico. "I am going to Sicily with San Giacinto," he added in a low voice.

Corona could not have explained what she felt

just then, but she might have described it as a disagreeable chilliness creeping over her strong frame from head to foot. An hour later she remembered it, and the next day, and for many days afterwards, and she tried to account for it by telling herself that the journey was to make a great change in her son's life, or by arguing that she had half unconsciously supposed him about to engage himself to Vittoria. But neither explanation was at all satisfactory. She was not imaginative to that extent, as she well knew, and she at last made up her mind that it was an idle coincidence of the kind which some people call a warning, and remember afterwards when anything especial happens, though if nothing particular follows, they forget it altogether.

"Why are you going? Has it anything to do with the Corleone?" she asked, and she was surprised at the unsteadiness of her own voice.

"Yes. I will tell you some other time."

"Will you?"

"Yes, certainly."

She looked into his eyes a moment, and then took Campodonico's arm again. Orsino moved on quickly and disappeared in the ballroom they had left, wondering inwardly at his mother's manner as much as she was then wondering herself, and attributing it to her anxiety about his position with regard to Vittoria. Thinking of that, he stopped short in his walk just as he caught sight of the young girl in the distance, standing beside her mother. A man was before her, evidently just asking her to dance. Orsino watched them while he tried to get hold of himself and decide what he ought to do.

Vittoria came forward and swept out with her partner into the middle of the room. Orsino slipped back a little behind a group of people, so that she should not easily see him, but he watched her face keenly. Her eyes were restless, and she was evidently looking for him, and not thinking of her partner at all. As they came round to his side, Orsino felt the blood rise in his throat, and felt that his face was warm; and then, as they swung off to the other side of the big ballroom, he grew cool again, and asked himself what he should do, repeating the question rather helplessly. She came round once more, and just as he felt the same heat of the blood again, he saw that her eyes had caught his. In a flash her expression changed, and the colour blushed in her face. A moment later she stopped, and remained standing with her partner so that Orsino could see the back of her head. She half turned towards him two or three times, instinctively; but she would not turn quite round so as to look at him. She knew that she must finish the dance before he could come to her.

But he, deeply stirred, and, at the same time,

profoundly discontented with himself, suddenly left the room and went on till he stood all alone, out on one of the bridges which crossed the street to the garden at the back of the palace. The bridge was in the shadow, but the white moonlight fell full upon the fountain and the walks beyond; and moonlight has an extraordinary effect on people who do not habitually live in camps, or out of doors, at night. The sun shows us what is, but the moon makes us see what might be.

Orsino leaned against the stone parapet in the shadow, and made one of those attempts at self-examination which every honourable man has made at least once in his life, and which, with nine men out of ten, lead to no result, because at such times the mind is in no state to examine anything, least of all itself. Indeed, no healthy-minded man resorts to that sort of introspection unless he is in a most complicated situation, since such a man is normally always perfectly conscious of what is honourable and right, without any self-analysis, or picking to pieces of his own conscience.

But Orsino Saracinesca was in great difficulty. He did not question the fact that he was very much in love with Vittoria, and that this love for a young girl was something which he had never felt before. That was plain enough, by this time. The real question was, whether he should marry her, or whether he should go away to Sicily with San Giacinto and try to avoid her in future until he should have more or less forgotten her.

He was old enough and sensible enough to foresee the probable consequences of marrying into such a family, and they were such as to check him at the outset. He knew all about the Pagliuca people, as his father did, and the phrase 'the worst blood in Italy' was familiar to his thoughts. Vittoria's mother was, indeed, a harmless soul, provincial and of unusual manners, but not vulgar in the ordinary sense of the word. Vittoria's father was said to have been a very good kind of man, who had been outrageously treated by his elder brother. But the strain was bad. There were hideous stories of treachery, such as Giovanni had quoted to his wife, which were alone enough to make Orsino hesitate. And then, there were Vittoria's brothers, for whom he felt the strongest repulsion and distrust. In many ways it would have been wiser for him to marry a girl of the people, a child of Trastevere, rather than Vittoria d'Oriani.

He did not believe that any of the taint was on herself, that in her character there was the smallest shade of deceit or unfaithfulness. He found it hard to believe that she was really a Corleone at all. His arguments began from a premiss which assumed her practically perfect.

Had he been alone in the world, he would not have hesitated long, for he could have married her and taken her away for ever — he was enough in love for that.

But such a marriage meant that he should bring her brothers intimately into his father's house; that he and his own family must accept Tebaldo and Francesco Pagliuca, and possibly the third brother, whom he did not know, as near relations, to be called, by himself at least, 'thee' and 'thou,' and by their baptismal names. Lastly, it meant that Vittoria's mother and his own should come into close terms of intimacy, for Maria Carolina would make the most of the connexion with the Saracinesca. That thought was the most repugnant of all to the young man, who looked upon his mother as a being apart from the ordinary world and entitled to a sort of veneration. Maria Carolina would not venerate anybody, he thought.

On the other side, there was his honour. He did not care what the young men might think, but he had certainly led the girl herself to believe that he meant to marry her. And he was in love. Compared with giving up Vittoria, and with doing something which seemed dishonourable, the accumulated wickedness of generations of the Corleone shrank into insignificance. There was a sort of shock in his mind, as he brought up this side of the question.

Had there been any difficulty to be overcome in winning Vittoria's own consent, it would have been easier to decide. But he knew that he had but a word to say, and his future would be sealed irrevocably in a promise which he never would break. And in a day or two he was to leave Rome for a long time. It was clear that he ought to decide at once, this very night.

His nature rejected the idea of taking advice, and, generally, of confiding in anyone. Otherwise, he might have laid the matter before his mother, in the certainty that her counsel would be good and honourable. Or he might have told his favourite brother the whole story, and Ippolito would assuredly have told him what was right. But Orsino was not of those who get help from the judgment or the conscience of another.

It seemed to him that he stayed a long time on the bridge, thinking of all these things, for the necessity of finally weighing them had come upon him suddenly, since San Giacinto had given him warning to get ready for the journey. But presently he was aware that the distant music had changed, that the waltz during which he had watched Vittoria was over, and that a square dance had begun. He smiled rather grimly to himself as he reflected that he might stand there till morning, without getting any nearer to a conclusion. He turned his back on the moonlight impatiently and went back into the palace. In the distance, through an open door, he saw faces familiar to him all his life, moving to and fro rapidly in a quadrille. He watched them as he walked straight on towards the ballroom, through the rather dimly lighted chamber with which the bridge communicated.

He was startled by the sound of Vittoria d'Oriani's voice, close beside him, calling him softly but rather anxiously.

"Don Orsino! Don Orsino!"

She was all alone, pale, and standing half hidden by the heavy curtain on one side of the door opening to the ballroom. Orsino stood still a moment, in great surprise at seeing her thus left to herself in an empty room. Then he went close to her, holding out his hand.

"What is the matter?" he asked in a low voice, for several men were standing about on the other side of the open door, watching the dance.

"Nothing — nothing," she repeated nervously, as he drew her aside.

"Who left you here alone?" asked Orsino, in displeasure at some unknown person.

"I — I came here — " she faltered. "I slipped out — it was hot, in there."

Orsino laughed softly.

"You must not get isolated in this way," he said. "It is not done here, you know. People would think it strange. You are always supposed to be with someone — your partner, or your mother. But I am glad, since I have found you."

"Yes, I have found you," she said softly, repeating his words. "I mean —" she corrected herself hurriedly — "I mean you have found me."

Orsino looked down to her averted face, and in the dim light he saw the blush at her mistake — too great a mistake in speech not to have come from a strong impulse within. Yet he could hardly believe that she had seen him go out that way alone, and had followed in the hope of finding him.

They sat down together, not far from the door opening upon the bridge. The colour had faded again from Vittoria's face, and she was pale. During some moments neither spoke, and the music of the quadrille irritated Orsino as he listened to it. Seeing that he was silent, Vittoria looked up sideways and met his eyes.

"It was really very warm in the ballroom," she said, to say something.

"Yes," he answered absently, his eyes fixed on hers. "Yes — I daresay it was."

Again there was a pause.

"What is the matter?" asked Vittoria at last, and her tone sank with each word.

"I am going away," said Orsino, slowly, with fixed eyes.

She did not start nor show any surprise, but the

colour began to leave her lips. The irritating quadrille went pounding on in the distance, through the hackneyed turns of the familiar figures, accompanied by the sound of many voices talking and of broken laughter now and then.

"You knew it?" asked Orsino. "How?"

"No one told me; but I knew it — I guessed it."

Orsino looked away, and then turned to her again, his glance drawn back to her by something he could not resist.

"Vittoria," he began in a very low tone.

He had never called her by that name before. The quadrille was very noisy, and she did not understand. She leaned forward anxiously towards him when she spoke.

"What did you say? I did not hear. The music makes such a noise!"

The man was more than ever irritated at the sound; and as she bent over to him, he could almost feel her breath on his cheek. The blood rose in him, and he sprang to his feet impatiently.

"Come!" he said. "Come outside! We cannot even hear each other here."

Vittoria rose, too, without a word, and went with him, walking close beside him, and glancing at his face. She was excessively pale now; and all the golden light seemed to have faded at once, even from her hair and eyes, till she looked delicate and almost fragile beside the big dark man.

"Out of doors?" she asked timidly, at the threshold.

"Yes — it is very warm," answered Orsino, in a voice that was a little hoarse.

Once out on the bridge, in the shadow, over the dark street, he stopped, and instantly his hand found hers and closed all round it, covering it altogether.

Vittoria could not have spoken just then, for she was trembling from head to foot. The air was full of strange sounds, and the trees were whirling round one another like mad black ghosts in the moonlight. When she looked up, she could see Orsino's eyes, bright in the shadow. She turned away, and came back to them more than once; then their glances did not part any more, and his face came nearer to hers.

"We love each other," he said; and his voice was warm and alive again.

She felt that she saw his soul in his face, but she could not speak. Her eyes looking up to his, she slowly bent her little head twice, while her lips parted like an opening flower, and faintly smiled at the sweetness of an unspoken word.

He bent nearer still, and she did not draw back. His blood was hot and singing in his ears. Then, all at once, something in her appealed to him, her young delicacy, her dawn-like purity, her exquisite fresh maidenhood. It seemed a crime to touch her lips as though she had been a mature woman. He dropped her hand, and his long arms brought her tenderly and softly up to his breast; and as her head fell back, and her lids drooped, he kissed her eyes with infinite gentleness, first the one and then the other, again and again, till she smiled in the dark, and hid her face against his coat, and he found only her silky hair to kiss again.

"I love you — say it, too," he whispered in her ear.

"Ah, yes! so much, so dearly!" came her low answer.

Then he took her hand again, and brought it up to his lips close to her face; and his lips pressed the small fingers passionately, almost roughly, very longingly.

"Come," he said. "We must be alone — come into the garden."

He led her across the bridge, and suddenly they were in the clear moonlight; but he went on quickly, lest they should be noticed through the open door from within. The air was warm and still and dry, as it often is in spring after the evening chill has passed.

"We could not go back into the ballroom, could we?" he asked, as he drew her away along a gravel walk between high box hedges.

"No. How could we — now?" Her hand tightened a little on his arm.

They stopped before a statue at the end of the walk, full in the light, a statue that had perhaps been a Daphne, injured ages ago, and stone-grey where it was not very white, with flying draperies broken off short in the folds, and a small, frightened face that seemed between laughing and crying. One fingerless hand pointed at the moon.

Orsino leaned back against the pedestal, and lovingly held Vittoria before him, and looked at her, and she smiled, her lips parting again, and just glistening darkly in the light as a dewy rose does in moonlight. The music was very far away now, but the plashing of the fountain was near.

"I love you!" said Orsino once more, as though no other words would do.

A deep sigh of happiness said more than the words could, and the stillness that followed meant most of all, while Vittoria gently took his two hands and nestled closer to him, fearlessly, like a child or a young animal.

"But you will not go away — now?" she asked pleadingly.

Orsino's face changed a little, as he remembered the rest of his life, and all he had undertaken to do. He had dreamily hoped that he might forget it.

"We will not talk of that," he answered.

"How can I help it, if it is true? You will not go — say you will not go!"

"I have promised. But there is time — or, at

least, I shall soon come back. It is not so far to Sicily —"

"Sicily? You are going to Sicily?" She seemed surprised.

"I thought you knew where I was going —" he began.

"No — I guessed; I was not sure. Tell me! Why must you go?"

"I must go because I have promised. San Giacinto would think it very strange if I changed my mind."

"It is stranger that you should go — and with him! Yes — I see — you are going to take possession of our old place —"

Her voice suddenly expressed the utmost anxiety, as she sprang from one conclusion to another without a mistake. She pressed his hands tightly, and her face grew pale again with fear for him.

"Oh please, please, stay here!" she cried. "If it were anywhere else — if it were to do anything else —"

"Why?" he asked, in surprise. "I thought you did not care much for the old place. If I had known that it would hurt you —"

"Me? No! It is not that — it is for you! They will kill you. Oh, do not go! Do not go!" She spoke in the greatest distress.

Orsino was suddenly inclined to laugh, but he saw how much in earnest she was.

"Who will kill me?" he asked, as though humouring her. "What do you mean?"

Vittoria was more than in earnest; she was almost in terror for him. Her small hands clung to his arm nervously, catching him and then loosing their hold. But she said nothing, though she seemed to be hesitating in some sort of struggle. Though she loved him with all the whole-hearted impulses of her nature, it was not easy to tell him what she meant. The Sicilian blood revolted at the thought of betraying her wild brother, who had joined the outlaws, and would be in waiting for Orsino and his cousin when they should try to take possession of the lands.

"You must not go!" she cried, suddenly throwing her arms round his neck as though she could keep him by force. "You shall not go — oh, no, no, no!"

"Vittoria — you have got some mad idea in your head — it is absurd — who should try to kill me? Why? I have no enemies. As for the brigands, everyone laughs at that sort of thing nowadays. They belong to the comic opera!" He let himself laugh a little at last, for the idea really amused him.

But Vittoria straightened herself beside him and grew calmer, for she was sensible and saw that he thought her foolishly afraid.

"In Rome the outlaws belong to the comic opera

—yes," she answered gravely. "But in Sicily they are a reality. I am a Sicilian, and I know. People are killed by them almost every day, and the mafia protects them. They are better armed than the soldiers, for they carry Winchester rifles —"

"What do you know about Winchester rifles?" asked Orsino, smiling.

"My brothers have them," she said quietly. "And the outlaws almost all have them."

"I daresay. But why should they wish to kill me? They do not know me."

Vittoria was silent a moment, making up her mind what she should tell him. She was not positively sure of anything, but she had heard Francesco say lately that Camaldoli was a place easier to buy than to hold while Ferdinando was alive, and she knew what that meant, when coupled with the occasional comments upon Ferdinando's mode of life, which escaped in Francesco's incautious conversation at home. To a Sicilian, the meaning of the whole situation was not hard to guess. At the same time Vittoria was both desperately anxious for Orsino and afraid that he might laugh at her fears, as he had done already.

"This is it," she said at last in a low and earnest voice. "It has nothing to do with you or your cousin, personally, nor with your taking possession of Camaldoli, so far as I am concerned. But it is a wild and desolate place, and all through this year a large band of outlaws have been in the forests on the other side of the valley. They would never have hurt my brothers, who are Sicilians and poor, and who did not trouble them either. But you and your cousin are great people, and rich, and not Sicilians, and the mafia will be against you, and will support the brigands if they prevent you from taking possession of Camaldoli. You would be opposed to the mafia; you would bring soldiers there to fight the outlaws. Therefore they will kill you. It is certain. No one ever escapes them. Do you understand? Now you will not go, of course, since I have explained it all."

Orsino was somewhat puzzled, though it all seemed so clear to her.

"This mafia — what is it?" he asked. "We hear it spoken of, but we do not any of us really know who is the head of it, nor what it can do."

"It has no head," answered the young girl. "Perhaps it is hard to explain, because you are not a Sicilian. The mafia is not a band, nor anything of that sort. It is the resistance which the whole Sicilian people opposes to all kinds of government and authority. It is, how shall I say? A sentiment, a feeling, a sort of wild love of our country, that is a secret, and will do anything. With us, everybody knows what it is, and evil comes to everyone who opposes it — generally death."

"We are not much afraid of it, since we have the law on our side," said Orsino, rather incredulously.

"You are not afraid because you do not understand," answered Vittoria, her voice beginning to express her anxiety again. "If you knew what it is, as we know, you would be very much afraid."

She spoke so simply and naturally that it did not occur to Orsino to be offended at the slight upon his courage.

"We shall take an escort of soldiers, to please you," he said, smiling, and drawing her to him again, as though the discussion were over.

But her terror for him broke out again. She had not told him all she knew, still less all she suspected.

"But I am in earnest!" she cried, holding herself back from him so that he could see her eyes. "It is true earnest, deadly earnest. They mean to kill you — in the end, they will! Oh, tell me that you will not go!"

"San Giacinto has bought the place—"

"Let him go, and be killed, then, and perhaps they will be satisfied! What do I care for anyone but you? Is it nothing, that I love you so? That we have told each other? That you say you love me? Is it all nothing but words, mere words, empty words?"

"No, it is my whole life, dear—"

"Then your life is mine, and you have no right to throw it away, just to please your cousin. Let him get a regiment of soldiers sent there by the government to live in Santa Vittoria. Then after three or four years the brigands will be all gone."

"Three or four years!" Orsino laughed, in spite of himself.

"Ah, you do not know!" exclaimed Vittoria, sadly. "You do not know our country, nor our people! You think it is like Rome, all shopkeepers and policemen, and sixty noble families, with no mafia! You laugh now — but when they have killed you I shall not live to laugh again. Am I your life? Then you are mine. What will there be without you, when they have killed you? And the Winchester rifles shoot so far, and the outlaws aim so straight! How can you be saved? Do you think it is nothing that I should know that you are going to your death?"

"It is an exaggeration," said Orsino, trying to soothe her. "Such things are not done in a civilized country, in the nineteenth century."

"Such things? Ah, and worse, far worse! Last year they buried a man up to his neck in the earth, alive, and left him there to die, in the woods not far from Camaldoli, because they thought he was a spy! And one betrayed some of the band last summer, and they did not kill him at once, but caught him and tortured him, so that it took him three days to die. You do not know. You laugh, but you do not know what people there are in Sicily, nor what Sicilians will do when they are roused. Promise me that you will not go!"

"Even if all you tell me were true, I should go," answered Orsino.

"Will nothing keep you from going?" asked the girl, piteously.

"You will laugh at all this when I come back to you. You will wonder how you could have tried to frighten me with such tales."

She looked at him a long time in silence, and then her lip quivered, so that she quickly raised one hand to her mouth to hide it.

"It would have been better if I had never left the convent," she said in a broken voice. "When they have killed you, I shall go back and die there."

"When I come back, we shall be married, love—"

"Oh, no — not if you go to Camaldoli — we shall never be married in this world."

The slight and graceful girl shook all over for a moment, and then seemed to grow smaller, as though something crushed her. But there were no tears in her eyes, though she pressed her fingers on her lips as though to force back a sob.

"Let us go back," she said. "I want to go home — I can pray for you, if I cannot save you.

God will hear me, though you do not, and God knows that it will be your death."

He put his arm about her and tried to comfort her, but she would not again lift her face, and he kissed her hair once more, when they were again in the shadow on the bridge. Then they waited till no one was passing through the small room, and went in silently to find her mother. She stopped him at the door of the ballroom.

"Promise me that you will not speak to my mother, nor my brothers, about — about us," she said in a low voice.

"Very well. Not till I come back, if you wish it," he answered.

And they went in, amongst the people, unnoticed.

CHAPTER VIII

VITTORIA realized that it was beyond her power to keep Orsino in Rome, and she was in great trouble. She had begged him not to speak of their betrothal, scarcely knowing why she made the request, but she was afterwards very glad that she had done so. To her, he was a condemned man, and her betrothal was a solemn binding of herself to keep faith with a beloved being who must soon be dead. She did not believe that she could really outlive him, but if Heaven should be so unkind to her, she had already made up her mind to return to the convent where she had been educated, and to end her days as a nun. The acute melancholy which belongs to the people of the far south, as well as of the far north, of Norway and of Sicily or Egypt alike, at once asserted itself and took possession of her. The next time Orsino saw her he was amazed at the change. The colour was all gone from her face, her lips were tightly set, and her brown eyes followed him with a perpetual, mute anxiety. Her radiance was veiled, and her beauty was grievously diminished.

It was at a garden party, in a great, old villa beyond the walls, two days after the dance. Orsino had not been able to see her in the meantime, and had wisely abstained from visiting her mother, lest, in any way, he should betray their joint secret. She was already in the garden when he arrived with Corona, who caught sight of Vittoria from a distance and noted the change in her face.

"Vittoria d'Oriani looks ill," said the Princess, and she went towards her at once.

She was too tactful to ask the girl what was the matter, but she saw how Vittoria's eyes could not keep from Orsino, and she half guessed the truth, though her son's face was impenetrable just then. An old friend came up and spoke to her, and she left the two alone.

They quietly moved away from the more crowded part of the garden, walking silently side by side, till they came to a long walk covered by the interlacing branches of ilex trees. Another couple was walking at some distance before them. Orsino glanced down at Vittoria, and tried to say something, but it was not easy. He had not realized how the mere sight of her stirred him, until he found himself speechless when he wished to say many things.

"You are suffering," he said softly, at last. "What is it?"

"You know," she answered. "What is the use of talking about it? I have said all — but tell me only when you are going."

"To-morrow morning. I shall be back in a fortnight."

"You will never come back," said Vittoria, in a dull and hopeless tone.

She spoke with such conviction that Orsino was silent for a moment. He had not the smallest belief in any danger, but he did not know how to argue with her.

"I have thought it all over," she went on. "If you try to live there, you will certainly be killed. But if you only go once, there is a chance — a poor, miserable, little chance. Let them think that you are coming up from Piedimonte, by way of Randazzo. It is above Randazzo that the black lands begin, all lava and ashes, with deep furrows in which a man can lie hidden to shoot. That is where they will try to kill you. Go the other way, round by Catania; it is longer, but they will not expect you, and you can get a guide. They may not find out that you have changed your plan. If they should know it, they could kill you even more easily on that side, in the narrow valley; but they need not know it."

"Nothing will happen to me on either side," said Orsino, carelessly.

Vittoria bent her head and walked on in silence beside him.

"I did not wish to talk about all that," he continued. "There are much more important things. When I come back we must be married soon—"

"We shall never be married if you go to Sicily," answered Vittoria, in the same dull voice.

It was a fixed idea, and Orsino felt the hopelessness of trying to influence her, together with a pardonable impatience. The couple ahead of them reached the end of the walk, turned, met them, and passed them with a greeting, for they were acquaintances. Where the little avenue ended there was a great fountain of travertine stone, behind which, in the wide arch of the opening trees, they could see the Campagna and the Sabine mountains to the eastward.

Vittoria stopped when they reached the other side of the basin, which was moss-grown but full of clear water that trickled down an almost shapeless stone triton. The statue and the fountain hid them from anyone who might be coming up the walk, and at their feet lay the broad green Campagna. They were quite alone.

The young girl raised her eyes, and she looked already as though she had been in an illness.

"We cannot stay more than a moment," she said. "If people see us going off together, they will guess. I want it to be all my secret. I

want to say goodbye to you — for the last time.
I shall remember you always as you are now,
with the light on your face."

She looked at him long, and her eyes slowly
filled with tears, which did not break nor run
over, but little by little subsided again, taking
her grief back to her heart. Orsino's brows
frowned with pain, for he saw how profoundly
she believed that she was never to see him again,
and it hurt him that for him she should be so
hurt, most of all because he was convinced that
there was no cause.

"We go to-morrow," he said. "We shall be in
Messina the next day. On the day after that go
and see my mother, and she will tell you that
she has had news of our safe arrival. What more
can I say? I am sure of it."

But Vittoria only looked long and earnestly into
his face.

"I want to remember," she said, in a low voice.

"For a fortnight?" Orsino smiled lovingly, and
took her hand.

"For ever," she answered very gravely, and her
fingers clutched his suddenly and hard.

He still smiled, for he could find nothing to say
against such possession of presentiment. Common
sense never has anything effectual to oppose to
conviction.

"Goodbye," she said softly. "Goodbye, Orsino."

She had not called him by his name yet, and it sounded like an enchantment to him, though it was a rough name in itself. The breeze stirred the ilex leaves overhead in the spring afternoon, and the water trickled down, with a pleasant murmur, into the big basin. It was all lovely and peaceful and soft, except the look in her despairing eyes. That disturbed him as he met it and saw no change in it, but always the same hopeless pain.

"Come," he said quietly, "this is not sensible. Do I look like a man who is going to be killed like a dog in the street, without doing something to help myself?"

Her eyes filled again.

"Oh, pray — please — do not speak like that! Say goodbye to me — I cannot bear it any longer — and yet it kills me to let you go!"

She turned from him and covered her eyes with her hands for a moment, while he put his arm round her reassuringly. Then, all at once, she looked up.

"I will be brave — goodbye!" she said quickly.

It was a silent leave-taking after that, for he could not say much. His only answer to her must be his safe return, but as they went back along the walk, she felt that she was with him for the last time. It was like going with him to execution.

Orsino walked back to the city alone, thinking over her words and her face, and wondering whether there could be anything in presentiments of evil. He had never had any himself, that he could remember, and he had never seen anybody so thoroughly under the influence of one as Vittoria seemed to be.

Before dinner he went to see San Giacinto, whom he found alone in his big study, sitting in his huge chair before his enormous table. He was so large that he had his own private furniture made to suit his own dimensions. The table was covered with note books and papers, very neatly arranged, and the grey-haired giant was writing a letter. He looked up as Orsino entered and uttered a sort of inarticulate exclamation of satisfaction. Then he went on writing, while Orsino sat down and watched him.

"Do you happen to have a gun license?" asked San Giacinto, without looking up.

"Of course."

"Put it in your pocket for the journey," was the answer, as the pen went on steadily.

"Is there any game about Camaldoli?" enquired Orsino, after a pause.

"Brigands," replied San Giacinto, laconically, and still writing.

He would have said 'woodcock' in the same tone, being a plain man and not given to dramatic emphasis. Orsino laughed a little incredulously, but said nothing, as he sat waiting for his kinsman to finish his letter. His eyes wandered about the room, and presently they fell on a stout sole-leather bag which stood by a chair near the window. On the chair itself lay two leathern gun-cases obviously containing modern rifles, as their shape and size showed. With a man's natural instinct for arms, Orsino rose and took one of the weapons out of its case, and examined it.

"Winchesters," said San Giacinto, still driving his pen.

"I see," answered Orsino, feeling the weight, and raising the rifle to his shoulder as though to try the length of the stock.

"Most people prefer them in Sicily," observed San Giacinto, who had signed his name and was folding his note carefully.

"What do you want them for?" asked the younger man, still incredulous.

"It is the custom of the country to carry them down there," said the other. "Besides, there are brigands about. I told you so, just now."

San Giacinto did not like to repeat explanations.

"I thought you were joking," remarked Orsino.

"I never did that. I suppose we shall not have the luck to fall in with any of those fellows, but there has been a good deal of trouble lately, and we shall not be particularly popular as Romans going to take possession of Sicilian lands. We should be worth a ransom too, and by this time the whole country knows that we are coming."

"Then we may really have some excitement," said Orsino, more surprised than he would show at his cousin's confirmation of much that Vittoria had said. "How about the mafia?" he asked by way of leading San Giacinto into conversation. "How will it look at us?"

"The mafia is not a man," answered San Giacinto, bluntly. "The mafia is the Sicilian character — Sicilian honour, Sicilian principles. It is an idea, not an institution. It is what makes it impossible to govern Sicily."

"Or to live there," suggested Orsino.

"Except with considerable tact. You will find out something about it very soon, if you try to manage that place. But if you are nervous, you had better not try."

"I am not nervous, I believe."

"No, it is of no use to be. It is better to be a fatalist. Fatalism gives you your own soul, and leaves your body to the chemistry of the universe, where it belongs. If your body comes into contact with something that does not agree with it, you die. That is all."

There was an admirable directness in San Giacinto's philosophy, as Orsino knew. They made a final agreement about meeting at the station on the following morning, and Orsino went home a good deal less inclined to treat Vittoria's presentiments lightly. It had been characteristic of San Giacinto that he had hitherto simply forgotten to mention that there might be real danger in the expedition to Camaldoli, and it was equally in accordance with Orsino's character to take the prospect of it simply and gravely. There was a strong resemblance between the two kinsmen, and Orsino understood his cousin better than his father or any of his brothers.

He had already explained to his mother what he was going to do, and she had been glad to learn that he had found something to interest him. Both Corona and Sant' Ilario had the prevailing impression that the Sicilian difficulties were more or less imaginary. That is what most Romans think, and the conviction is general in the north of Italy. As Orsino said nothing about his conversation with San Giacinto on that last evening, his father and mother had not the slightest idea that there was danger before him, and as they had both noticed his liking for Vittoria, they were very glad that he should go away just then, and forget her.

The old Prince bade him goodbye that night.

"Whatever you do, my boy," he said, shaking his snowy old head energetically, "do not marry a Sicilian girl."

The piece of advice was so unexpected that Orsino started slightly, and then laughed, as he took his grandfather's hand. It was oddly smooth, as the hands of very old men are, but it was warm still, and not so feeble as might have been expected.

"And if you should get into trouble down there," said the head of the house, who had known Sicily seventy years earlier, "shoot first. Never wait to be shot at."

"It is not likely that there will be much shooting nowadays," laughed Sant' Ilario.

"That does not make my advice bad, does it?" asked old Saracinesca, turning upon his son, for the least approach to contradiction still roused his anger instantly.

"Oh, no!" answered Giovanni. "It is very good advice."

"Of course it is," growled the old gentleman, discontentedly. "I never gave anyone bad advice in my life. But you boys are always contradicting me."

Giovanni smiled rather sadly. It was not in the nature of things that men over ninety years old should live much longer, but he felt what a break in the household's life the old man's death must one day make, when the vast vitality should be at last worn out.

CHAPTER IX

ORSINO travelled down to Naples with San Giacinto in that peculiar state of mind in which an unsentimental but passionate man finds himself when he is leaving the woman he loves in order to go and do something which he knows must be done, which he wishes to do, and which involves danger and difficulty.

San Giacinto did not say much more about brigands, or the mafia, but he talked freely of the steps to be taken on arriving in Messina, in order to get a proper escort of soldiers from Piedimonte to Camaldoli, and it was perfectly clear that he anticipated trouble. Orsino was surprised to find that he expected to have four or five carabineers permanently quartered at Camaldoli, by way of protection, and that he had already applied in the proper quarter to have the men sent to meet him. Then he began to talk of the projected railway and of the questions of engineering involved.

Orsino felt lonely in his society, and it was a sensation to which he was not accustomed. It was long since he had known what it was to miss a woman's eyes and a woman's voice, and he had not thought that he should know it again. As the train ran on, hour after hour, he grew more silent, not wondering at himself, but accepting quite simply the fact that it hurt him to leave Vittoria far behind, and that he longed for her presence more and more. He could not help thinking how easy it would be for him to refuse to go on, and to take the next train back from Naples to Rome, and to see her to-morrow. He would not have done such a thing for the world, but he could not escape from the rather contemptible pleasure of thinking about it.

Late in the afternoon the steamer that was to take them to Messina got under way, — an old-fashioned, uncomfortable boat, crowded with people of all kinds, for the vessel was to go on to Malta on the next day. At the bad dinner in the dim cabin the tables were full, and many of the people were talking in the Maltese dialect, which is an astonishing compound of Italian and Arabic, perfectly incomprehensible both to Arabs and Italians. They stared at San Giacinto because he was a giant, and evidently talked about him in their own language, which irritated Orsino, though the big man seemed perfectly indifferent. Neither cared to speak, and they got through their abominable dinner in silence and went up to smoke on deck.

Orsino leaned upon the rail and gazed longingly

at the looming mountains, behind which the full moon was rising. He was not sentimental, for Italian men rarely are, but like all his fellow-countrymen he was alive to the sensuous suggestions of nature at certain times, and the shadowy land, the rising moon, the gleaming ripple of the water, and the evening breeze on his face, brought Vittoria more vividly than ever to his mind. He looked up at San Giacinto, and even the latter's massive and gloomy features seemed to be softened by the gentle light and the enchantment of the southern sea. Unconsciously he was more closely drawn to the man of his own blood, after being jostled in the crowd of doubtful passengers who filled the steamer.

It was not in his nature to make confidences, but he wished that his friend and kinsman knew that he was in love with Vittoria and meant to marry her. It would have made the journey less desolate and lonely. He was still young, as San Giacinto would have told him, with grim indifference, if Orsino had unburdened his heart at that moment. But he did not mean to do that. He leaned over the rail and smoked in silence, looking from the moon to the rippling water and back again, and wishing that the night were not before him, but that he were already in Messina with something active to do. To be doing the thing would be to get nearer to Vittoria, since he could return with a clear conscience as soon as it should be done. At last he spoke, in a careless tone.

"My grandfather gave me some advice last night," he said. "Never to marry a Sicilian girl, and always to shoot first if there were any shooting to be done."

"Provided that you do not marry the Corleone girl, I do not see why you should not take a Sicilian wife if you please," answered San Giacinto, calmly.

"Why should a man not marry Vittoria d'Oriani?" enquired Orsino, startled to find himself so suddenly speaking of what filled him.

"I did not say 'a man' in general. I meant you. It would be a bad match. It would draw you into relationship with the worst blood in the country, and that is a great objection to it. Then she is a niece, and her brothers are nephews, of that old villain Corleone who married one of the Campodonico women. She died of unhappiness, I believe, and I do not wonder. Have you noticed that none of the Campodonico will have anything to do with them? Even old Donna Francesca — you know? — the saint who lives in the Palazzetto Borgia — she told your mother that she hoped never to know a Corleone by sight again. They are disliked in Rome. But you would never be such an arrant fool as to go and fall in love with the girl, I suppose, though she is charming, and I can see that you admire her. Not very clever, I fancy, — brought up by a museum of old Sicilian ladies in a Palermo convent, — but very charming."

It was an unexpectedly long speech, on an unexpected theme, and it was fortunate that it contained nothing which could wound Orsino's feelings through Vittoria; for, in that case, he would have quarrelled with his cousin forthwith, not being of a patient disposition. As it was, the young man glanced up sharply from time to time, looking out for some depreciatory expression. He was glad when San Giacinto had finished speaking.

"If I wished to marry her," said Orsino, "I should not care who her relations might be."

"You would find yourself caring a great deal afterwards, if they made trouble with your own people. But I admit that the girl has charm and some beauty, and it is only fools who need clever wives to think for them. Good night. We may have a long day to-morrow, and we shall land about seven in the morning. I am going to bed."

Orsino watched the huge figure as it bent low and disappeared down the companion, and he was glad that San Giacinto had taken himself off without talking any more about Vittoria. He stayed on deck another hour, watching the light on the water, and then went below. He and his cousin had a cabin together, and he found the old giant asleep on the sofa, wrapped in a cloak, with his long legs resting on a portmanteau and extending half across the available space, while he had widened the transom for his vast shoulders by the help of a camp stool. He slept soundly, almost solemnly, under the small swinging oil-lamp, and there was something grand and soldier-like about his perfect indifference to discomfort. In a corner of the cabin, among a quantity of traps, the two rifles stood upright in their leathern cases. It was long before Orsino fell asleep.

He was glad when they got ashore at last in the early morning. Messina has the reputation of being the dirtiest city in all Italy, and it has the disagreeable peculiarity of not possessing a decent inn of any sort. San Giacinto and Orsino sat down in a shabby and dirty room to drink certain vile coffee which was brought up to them on little brass trays from a café at the corner of the street. San Giacinto produced a silver flask and poured a dose of spirits into his cup, and offered Orsino some; but the younger man had not been bred in the country and had never acquired the common Italian habit of strengthening bad coffee with alcohol. So he consoled his taste with cigarettes.

San Giacinto found that it would be impossible to proceed to Camaldoli till the following day, and the two men spent the morning and most of the afternoon in making the necessary arrangements. It was indispensable to see the officer in command of the carabineers and the prefect of the province, and San Giacinto knew that it would be wiser to send certain supplies up from Messina.

"I suppose that someone is there to hand the place over?" said Orsino.

"Tebaldo Pagliuca said that we should make enquiries of an old notary called Basili, in Randazzo, as his brother, being displeased with the sale, would probably refuse to meet us. Basili is to have the keys and will send a man with us. We shall have to rough it for a day or two."

"Do you mean to say that they have locked the place up and left it without even a servant in charge?" asked Orsino.

"Apparently. We shall know when we get there. I daresay that we may have to make our own coffee and cook our own food. It is rather a lonely neighbourhood, and the people whom Ferdinando Pagliuca employed have probably all left."

"It sounds a little vague," observed Orsino. "I suppose we shall find horses to take us up?"

"That is all arranged. We shall go up in a carriage, with four or five mounted carabineers, who will stay with us till they are relieved by others. They will all be waiting at the town of Piedimonte, above the station. I daresay that ruffian has carried off the furniture, too, and we may have to sleep on the floor in our cloaks."

"It would have been sensible to have brought a servant with us."

"No. Servants get into the way when there is trouble."

Orsino lighted another cigarette and said nothing. He was beginning to think that the whole thing sounded like an expedition into an enemy's country. They were dining in a queer little restaurant built over the water, at the end of the town towards the Faro. It was evidently the fashionable resort at that time of year, and Orsino studied the faces of the guests at the other tables. He thought that many of them were like Tebaldo Pagliuca, though with less malignity in their faces; but now and then he heard words spoken with the unmistakable Neapolitan accent, showing that all were not Sicilians.

"They killed a carabineer close to Camaldoli last week," said San Giacinto, thoughtfully dividing a large slice of sword-fish, which is the local delicacy. "One of them put on the dead soldier's uniform, passed himself off for a carabineer, and arrested the bailiff of the Duca di Fornasco that night, and marched him out of the village. They carried him off to the woods, and he has not been heard of since. He had given some information against them in the winter, so they will probably take some pains to kill him slowly, and send his head back to his relations in a basket of tomatoes in a day or two."

"Are those things positively true?" asked Orsino, incredulous even now.

"The story was in the paper this morning, and I asked the prefect. He said it was quite exact. You see the rifles may be useful, after all, and the carabineers are rather more indispensable than food and drink."

Again Orsino though of all Vittoria had told him, and he realized that whether the wild tales were literally true or not, she was not the only person who believed them. Just then a long fishing-boat ran past the little pier, close to the place where he was sitting at table. Six men were sending her along with her sharp stern foremost, as they generally do, standing to their long oars and throwing their whole strength into the work, for they were late, and the current would turn against them when the moon rose, as everyone knows who lives in Messina. Orsino did not remember that he had ever seen just such types of men, bare-headed, dark as Arabs, square-jawed, sinewy, fierce-eyed, with grave, thin lips, every one of them a fighting match for three or four Neapolitans. They were probably the first genuine Sicilians of the people whom he had ever seen, and they were not like any other

Italians. San Giacinto watched them too, and he smiled a little, as though the sight gave him satisfaction.

"That is the reason why there is no salt-tax in Sicily," he said. "That is also the reason why Italy is ruled by a single Sicilian, by Crispi. Good or bad, he is a man, at all events — and those fellows are men. I would rather have one of those fishermen at my elbow in danger, than twenty bragging Piedmontese, or a hundred civilized Tuscans."

"But they are treacherous," observed Orsino.

"No, they are not," answered the older man, thoughtfully. "They hate authority and rebel against it, and the mafia idea keeps them together like one man. Successful revolution is always called patriotism, and unsuccessful rebellion is always branded as treachery or treason. I have heard that somewhere, and it is true. But what we want in Italy is men, not ideas; action, not talk; honesty, not policy."

"We shall never get those things," said Orsino, who was naturally pessimistic. "Italian unity has come too late for a renascence, and too soon for a new birth."

San Giacinto smiled rather contemptuously.

"You are an aristocrat, my dear boy," he answered. "You want the **clear wine without the filthy, fermenting must.**"

"I think we have the same name, you and I," observed Orsino.

"Yes, but I should be what I am, if I had been called Moscetti."

"And I?" enquired Orsino, his eyes kindling a little at the implied contrast of powers.

"If you had been plain Signor Moscetti, you would have been a very different kind of man. You would have worked hard at architecture, I suppose, and you would have acquired an individuality. As it is, you have not much more than the individuality of your class, and very little of your own. You are a product, whereas I was forced to become a producer when I was very young — a worker, in other words. Socially, I am a Saracinesca, like you; morally and actually, I have been a man of the people all my life, because I began among the people. I have made myself what I am. You were made what you are by somebody who lived in the twelfth century. I do not blame you, and I do not boast about myself. We like each other, but we are fundamentally different, and we emphatically do not like the same things. We are different kinds of animals that happen to be called by the same name."

"I tried to work once," said Orsino, thoughtfully.

"A man cannot do that sort of work against the odds of sixty-four quarterings and an unlimited fortune. But you had the instinct, just as I have it. You and I have more in common with those fishermen who just went by, than we have with most of our friends in Rome. We are men, at all events, as I said of Crispi."

Orsino was silent, for he was not in the humour to argue about anything, and he saw the truth of much that his cousin had said, and felt a hopelessness about doing anything in the world with which he had long been familiar.

The sun had gone down, leaving a deep glow on the Calabrian mountains, on the other side of the straits, and the water rippled with the current like purple silk. To the left, the heights above Scilla were soft and dreamy in a wine-coloured haze, and the great lighthouse shot out its white ray through the gathering dusk. To the right, the royal yards and top-gallant rigging of the vessels in the harbour made a dark lace against the high, white houses that caught the departing twilight. It was near moonrise, and the breeze had almost died away. The lights of the city began to shine out, one by one, then quickly, by scores, and under the little jetty, where the two men sat, the swirling water was all at once black and gleaming as flowing ink. Far off, a boat was moving, and the oars swung against the single tholes with an even, monotonous knocking that was pleasant to hear.

Orsino poured out another glass of the strong black wine and drank it, for the air was growing chilly. San Giacinto did the same and lighted a cigar. They sat almost an hour in silence, and then went slowly back to their squalid hotel on the quay.

CHAPTER X

On the following day Orsino and San Giacinto descended from the train at the little station of Piedimonte d'Etna, 'the foot of Mount Etna,' as it would be translated. It is a small, well-kept station near the sea, surrounded by gardens of oranges and lemons, and orchards of fruit trees, and gay with vines and flowers, penetrated by the intense southern light. The sky was perfectly cloudless, the sea of a gem-like blue, the peach blossoms were out by thousands, and the red pomegranate flowers had lately burst out of the bud, in splendid contrast with the deep, sheeny green of the smooth orange leaves. The trees had an air of belonging to pleasure gardens rather than to business-like orchards, and the whole colouring was almost artificially magnificent. It was late spring in the far south, and Orsino had never seen it. He had been on the Riviera, and in Sorrento, when the orange blossoms were all out, scenting the sea more than a mile from land, and he had seen the spring in England, which, once in every four or five years, is worth seeing; but he had not dreamt of such dazzling glories of colour as filled the earth and sky and sea of Sicily. It was not tropical, for there was nothing uncultivated nor unfruitful in sight; it seemed as though the little belt of gardens he saw around him must be the richest in the whole world, and as though neither man nor beast nor flower nor fruit could die in the fluid life of the fragrant air. It was very unexpected. San Giacinto was not the kind of man to give enthusiastic descriptions of views, and the conversation on the previous evening had prepared Orsino's mind for the wild hill country above, but not for the belt of glory which Sicily wears like a jewelled baldric round her breast, hidden here and there as it were, or obliterated, by great crags running far out into the sea, but coming into sight again instantly as each point is passed.

In the heap of traps and belongings that lay at his feet on the little platform, the two repeating rifles in their leathern cases were very good reminders of what the two men had before them on that day and for days and weeks afterwards.

"Winchesters," observed the porter who took the things to the carriage behind the station.

"How did you know that?" asked Orsino, surprised at the man's remark.

"As if they were the first I have carried!" exclaimed the man, with a grin. "Almost all the signori have them nowadays. People say they will kill at half a kilometre."

"Put them inside," said San Giacinto, as they were arranging the things. "Put them on the back seat with that case."

"Yes, the cartridges," said the porter, knowingly, as he felt the weight of the package.

"And God send you no need of them!" exclaimed the coachman, a big dark man with a stubbly chin, a broad hat, and a shabby velvet jacket.

"Amen!" ejaculated the porter.

"Are you going with us all the way?" asked San Giacinto of the coachman, looking at him keenly.

"No, signore. The master will drive you up from Piedimonte. He is known up there, but I am of Messina. It is always better to be known — or else it is much worse. But the master is a much respected man."

"Since he has come back," put in the porter, his shaven mouth stretching itself in a grim smile.

"Has he been in America?" asked Orsino, idly, knowing how many of the people made the journey to work, earn money, and return within a few years.

"He has been to the other America, which they call Ponza," answered the man.

The coachman scowled at him, and poked him in the back with the stock of his whip, but San

Giacinto laughed. Ponza is a small island off the Roman coast, used as a penitentiary and penal settlement.

"Did he kill his man?" enquired San Giacinto, coolly.

"No, signore," said the coachman, quickly. "He only gave him a salutation with the knife. It was a bad knife," he added, anxious for his employer's reputation. "But for that — the master is a good man! He only got the knife a little way into the other's throat — so much — " he marked the second joint of his middle finger with the end of his whip — "and then it would not cut," he concluded, with an apologetic air.

"The Romans always stab upwards under the ribs," said San Giacinto.

"One knows that!" answered the man. "So do we, of course. But it was only a pocket knife and would not have gone through the clothes, and the man was fat. That is why the master put it into his throat."

Orsino laughed, and San Giacinto smiled. Then they got into the carriage and settled themselves for the long drive. In twenty minutes they had left behind them the beautiful garden down by the sea, and the lumbering vehicle drawn by three skinny horses was crawling up a steep but well-built road, on which the yellow dust lay two inches thick. The coachman cracked his long whip of twisted cord with a noise like a quick succession of pistol shots, the lean animals kicked themselves uphill, as it were, the bells jingling spasmodically at each effort, and the dust rose in thick puffs in the windless air, under the blazing sun, uniting in a long low cloud over the road behind.

San Giacinto smoked in silence, and Orsino kept his mouth shut and his eyes half closed against the suffocating dust. After the first half-mile, the horses settled down to a straining walk, and the coachman stopped cracking his whip, sinking into himself, round-shouldered, as southern coachmen do when it is hot and a hill is steep. From time to time he swore at the skinny beasts in a sort of patient, half-contemptuous way.

"May they slay you!" he said. "May your vitals be torn out! May you be blinded! Curse you! Curse your fathers and mothers, and whoever made you! Curse the souls of your dead, your double-dead and your extra-dead, and the souls of all the horses that are yet to be born!"

There was a long pause between each imprecation, not as though the man were thinking over the next, but as if to give the poor beasts time to understand what he said. It was a kind of litany of southern abuse, but uttered in a perfunctory and indifferent manner, as many litanies are.

"Do you think your horses are Christians, that you revile them in that way?" asked Orsino, speaking from the back of the carriage, without moving.

The man's head turned upon his slouching shoulders, and he eyed Orsino with curiosity.

"We speak to them in this manner," he said. "They understand. In your country, how do you speak to them?"

"We feed them better, and they go faster."

"Every country has its customs," returned the man, stolidly. "It is true that these beasts are not mine. I should feed them better, if I had the money. But these animals consist of a little straw and water. This they eat, and this they are. How can they draw a heavy carriage uphill? It is a miracle. The Madonna attends to it. If I beat them, what do I beat? Bones and air. Why should I fatigue myself? There are their souls, so I speak to them, and they understand. Do you see? Now that I talk with you, they stop."

He turned as the carriage stood still, and addressed the spider-like animals again, in a dull, monotonous tone, that had something business-like in it.

"Ugly beasts! May you have apoplexy! May you be eaten alive!" And he went on with a whole string of similar expressions, till the unhappy brutes strained and threw themselves forward and began to kick themselves uphill again spasmodically, as before.

It seemed very long before they reached the town, dusty and white under the broad clear sun, and decidedly clean; spotless, indeed, compared with a Neapolitan or Calabrian village. Here and there among the whitewashed houses there were others built of almost black tufo, and some with old bits of effective carving in a bastard style of Norman-Saracen ornament.

The equine spiders entered the town at a jog-trot. Orsino fancied that but for the noise of the bells and the wheels he could have heard their bones rattle as their skeleton legs swung under them. They turned two or three corners and stopped suddenly before their stable.

"This is the master," said the coachman as he got down, indicating a square-built, bony man of medium height who stood before the door, dressed in a clean white shirt and a decent brown velveteen jacket. He had a dark red carnation in his buttonhole and wore his soft black hat a little on one side.

In the shadow of the street near the door stood five carabineers in their oddly old-fashioned yet oddly imposing uniforms and cocked hats, each with a big army revolver and a cartridge case at his belt, and a heavy cavalry sabre by his side. They were tall, quiet-eyed, sober-looking men, and they saluted San Giacinto and Orsino gravely, while one, who was the sergeant, came forward, holding out a note, which San Giacinto read, and put into his pocket.

"I am San Giacinto," he said, "and this gentleman is my cousin, Don Orsino Saracinesca, who goes with us."

"Shall we saddle at once, Signor Marchese?" asked the sergeant, and as San Giacinto assented, he turned to his men and gave the necessary order in a low voice.

The phantom horses were taken out of the carriage, and the two gentlemen got out to stretch their legs while the others were put in. The carabineers had all disappeared, their quarters and stables being close by; so near, indeed, that the clattering of their big chargers' hoofs and the clanking of accoutrements could be plainly heard.

"The master is to drive us up to Camaldoli," observed Orsino, lighting a cigarette.

"Yes," replied his companion. "He is a smart-looking fellow, but for my part I prefer the other man's face. Stupidity is always a necessary quality in servants. The master looks to me like a type of a 'maffeuso.'"

"With five carabineers at our heels, I imagine that we are pretty safe."

"For to-day, of course. I was thinking of our future relations. This is the only man who can furnish carriages between Camaldoli and the station. One is in his power."

"Why should we not have carriages and horses of our own?" asked Orsino.

"It is a useless expense at present," answered San Giacinto, who never wasted money, though he never spared it. "We shall see. In a day or two we shall find out whether you can have them at all. If it turns out to be possible, it will be because you find yourself on good terms with the people of the neighbourhood."

"And turn 'maffeuso' myself," suggested Orsino, with a laugh.

"Not exactly, but the people may tolerate you. That is the most you can expect, and it is much."

"And if not, I am never to move without a squad of carabineers to take care of me, I suppose."

"You had better go armed, at all events," said San Giacinto, quietly. "Have your revolver always in your pocket and take a rifle when you go out of the house. The sight of firearms has a salutary effect upon all these people."

The fresh horses had been put in, very different from the wretched creatures that had dragged the carriage up from the station, for they were lean indeed, but young and active. San Giacinto looked at them and remarked upon the fact as he got in.

"Of course!" answered the philosophical coachman; "the road is long and you must drive up as high as paradise. Those old pianos could never get any higher than purgatory."

"Pianos?"

"Eh — they have but three legs each, and they are of wood, like a piano," answered the man, without a smile. "You also heard the music they made with their bones, as we came along."

The master mounted to his seat, and at the same moment the carabineers came round the corner, already in the saddle, each with his canvas bread-bag over his shoulder and his rifle slung by his stirrup. They were mounted on powerful black chargers, well-fed, good-tempered animals, extremely well kept, and evidently accustomed to long marches. The carabineers, foot and horse, are by far the finest corps in the Italian army, and are, indeed, one of the finest and best equipped bodies of men in the world. They are selected with the greatest care, and every man has to prove that neither he nor his father has ever been in jail, even for the slightest misdemeanour. The troopers and the men of the foot corps rank as corporals of the regular army, and many of them have been sergeants. In the same way each degree of rank is reckoned as equal to the next higher in the army, and the whole corps is commanded by a colonel. There are now about twenty-five thousand in the whole country, quartered in every town and village in squads from four or five, to twenty or thirty strong. The whole of Italy is patrolled by them, day and night, both by high roads and bridle-paths, and on the mainland they have effectually stamped out brigandage and highway robbery. But in Sicily they are pitted against very different odds.

The road rises rapidly beyond Piedimonte, winding up through endless vinelands to the enormous yoke which unites Etna with the inland mountains. Orsino leaned back silently in his place, gazing at the snow-covered dome of the volcano, from the summit of which rose a thin wreath of perfectly white smoke. From time to time San Giacinto pointed out to his companion the proposed direction of his light railway, which was to follow the same general direction as the carriage road. The country, though still cultivated, was lonely, and the barren heights of Etna, visible always, gave the landscape a singular character. To the westward rose the wooded hills, stretching far away inland, dark and mysterious.

They halted again in the high street of a long, clean village, called Linguaglossa, and some of the carabineers dismounted and drank from a fountain, being half choked with the dust. The master of the vehicle got down and dived into a quiet-looking house, returning presently with a big, painted earthenware jug full of wine, and a couple of solid glasses, which he filled and held out, without a word, to San Giacinto and Orsino. The wine was almost black, very heavy and strong. They quenched their thirst, and then the man swallowed two glasses in succession. San Giacinto held out some small change to him to pay for the drink. But he laughed a little.

"One does not pay for wine in our country," he said. "They sell a pitcher like this for three sous at the wineshops, but this is the house of a very rich signore, who makes at least a thousand barrels every year. What should one pay? One sou? That is as much as it is worth. A man can get drunk for five sous here."

"I should think so! It is as strong as spirits," said Orsino.

"But the people are very sober," answered San Giacinto. "They have strong heads, too."

They were soon off again, along the endless road. Gradually, the vinelands began to be broken by patches of arid ground, where dark stone cropped up, and the dry soil seemed to produce nothing but the poisonous yellow spurge.

It was long past noon when the dark walls and the cathedral spire of Randazzo came into sight. They found Basili's house, and the notary, whose daughter was already famous in Rome, was at work in his dingy study, with a sheet of governmental stamped paper before him. He was a curious compound of a provincial and a man of law, with regular features and extremely black eyebrows, the rest of his hair being white. Orsino thought that he must have been handsome in his youth.

Everything was prepared according to the orders San Giacinto had written. Basili handed over a big bunch of keys, most of which were rusty, while two of them were bright, as though they had been recently much used. He hardly spoke at all, but looked at his visitors attentively, and with evident curiosity. He called a man who was in readiness to go with them.

"Shall we find anybody at the house?" enquired Orsino.

"Not unless someone has been locked in," was the answer. "Nevertheless, it might be safer not to go straight to the door, but to get under the wall, and come up to it in that way. One never knows what may be behind a door until it is open."

San Giacinto laughed rather dryly, and Orsino looked hard at Basili to discover a smile.

"But, indeed," continued the notary, "there are too many bushes about the house. If I might be so bold as to offer my advice, I should say that you had better cut down the bushes at once. You will have time to begin this evening, for the days are long."

"Are they unhealthy?" enquired Orsino, not understanding in the least.

"Unhealthy? Oh, no. But they are convenient for hiding, and there are people of bad intentions everywhere. I do not speak of Don Ferdinando Pagliuca, believe me. But there are persons of no conscience, who do not esteem life as anything. But I do not mean to signify Don Ferdinando Pagliuca, I assure you. Gentlemen, I wish you a pleasant journey, and every satisfaction, and the fulfilment of your desires."

He bowed them out, being evidently not inclined to continue the conversation, and they drove on again, the man whom he had sent with them being beside the padrone on the box. He had a long old-fashioned gun slung over his shoulder, evidently loaded, for there was a percussion cap on the nipple of the lock.

Orsino thought Randazzo a grim and gloomy town in spite of its beautiful carved stone balconies and gates, and its Saracen-Norman cathedral, and he was glad when they were out in the country again, winding up through the beginning of the black lands. San Giacinto looked about him, and then began to get out one of the Winchesters, without making any remark. Orsino watched him as he dropped the cartridges one by one into the repeater and then examined the action again, to see that all was in working order.

"You understand them, I suppose?" he asked of Orsino.

"Yes, of course."

"Then you had better load the other," said the big man, quietly.

"As you please," answered Orsino, evidently considering the precaution superfluous, and he got out the other rifle with great deliberation.

They were going slowly up a steep hill, and the carabineers were riding close behind them at a foot pace. The two gentlemen could, of course, not see the road in front. The padrone and Basili's man were talking in a low tone in the Sicilian dialect.

Suddenly, with a clanging and clattering, two of the troopers passed the carriage at a full gallop up the hill. The sergeant trotted up to San Giacinto's side, looking sharply ahead of him. Basili's man slipped the sling of his gun over his head in an instant, and laid the weapon across his knees, and Orsino distinctly heard him cock the old-fashioned hammer. San Giacinto still had his rifle in his hand, and he leaned out over the carriage to see what was ahead.

There was nothing to be seen but the two carabineers charging up the steep road at a gallop.

"There was a man on horseback waiting at the crest of the hill," said the sergeant. "As soon as he saw us he wheeled and galloped on. He is out of sight now. They will not catch him, for he had a good horse."

"Have you had much trouble lately?" asked San Giacinto.

"They killed one of my men last week and used his uniform for a disguise," answered the soldier, gravely. "That fellow was waiting there to warn somebody that we were coming."

The troopers halted when they reached the top of the hill, looked about, and made a sign to the sergeant, signifying that they could not catch the man. The sergeant answered by a gesture which bade them wait.

"Touch your horses, Tatò," he said to the padrone, who had neither moved nor looked round during the excitement, but who immediately obeyed.

The carriage moved quickly up the hill, till it overtook the carabineers. Then San Giacinto saw that the road descended rapidly by a sharp curve to the left, following a spur of the mountain. No one was in sight, nor was there any sound of hoofs in the distance. To the right, below the road, the land was much broken, and there was shelter from sight for a man and his horse almost anywhere for a mile ahead.

When Orsino had finished loading the rifle, he looked about him, and saw for the first time the black lands of which Vittoria had spoken, realizing the truth of what she had said about the possibility of a man hiding himself in the fissures of the lava, to fire upon a traveller in perfect security. With such an escort he and his companion were perfectly safe, of course, but he began to understand what was meant by the common practice of carrying firearms.

It is impossible to imagine anything more hideously desolate and sombrely wild than the high ground behind Mount Etna. The huge eruptions of former and recent times have for ages sent down rivers of liquid stone and immeasurable clouds of fine black ashes, which have all hardened roughly into a conformation which is rugged but not wholly irregular, for the fissures mostly follow the downward direction of the slope, westward from the volcano. All over the broad black surface the spurge grows in patches during the spring, and somehow the vivid yellow of the flowers makes the dark stone and hardened ash look still darker and more desolate. Here and there, every two or three miles, there are groups of deserted huts built of black tufo, doorless and windowless, and almost always on the edge of some bit of arable land that stretches westward between two old lava beds. The distances are so great that the peasants move out in a body to cultivate these outlying fields at certain times of the year, and sleep in the improvised villages until the work is done, when they go back to the towns, leaving the crops to take care of themselves until harvest time. In the guerilla warfare which breaks out periodically between the carabineers and the outlaws, the stone huts are important points of vantage, and once or twice have been the scene of hard-fought battles. Being of stone, though roughly built, and being pierced with mere holes for windows, they are easily defended from within by men armed with repeaters and plentiful ammunition.

After the little excitement caused by the pursuit of the unknown rider, two of the troopers rode before the carriage, and three followed it, while all got their rifles across their saddle-bows, ready for action. They knew well enough that as long as they kept together, even a large band of brigands would not attack them on the open road, but there were plenty of narrow places where the earth was high on each side, and where a single well-directed volley might easily have killed many of the party. Since the outlaws' latest invention of shooting the carabineers in order to disguise themselves in their uniforms, the troopers were more than ever cautious and on the alert against a surprise.

But nothing happened. The single horseman had disappeared altogether, having probably taken to the broken land for greater safety, and the carriage jogged steadily on across the high land, towards its destination, with a regular jingling of harness bells, and an equally rhythmic clanking of sabres.

"A little quicker, Tatò," said the sergeant to the

padrone, from time to time, but no one else said anything.

Both San Giacinto and Orsino were weary of the long drive when, at an abrupt curve of the road, the horses slackened speed, to turn out of the highway, to the right.

"There is Camaldoli," said Tatò, turning round to speak to them for the first time since they had started. "You can see the Druse's tower above the trees, and the river is below."

So far as the two gentlemen could see there was not another habitation in sight, though it was no very great distance to the village of Santa Vittoria, beyond the next spur of Etna. The ancient building, of which only the top of one square black tower appeared, was concealed by a dense mass of foliage of every kind. Below, to the right and towards the mountain stream which Tatò called a river, the land was covered with wild pear trees, their white blossoms all out and reflecting the lowering sun. Nearer the building, the pink bloom of the flowering peaches formed a low cloud of exquisite colour, and the fresh green of the taller trees of all kinds made a feathery screen above and a compact mass of dark shadow lower down. The narrow drive was thickly hedged with quantities of sweetbrier and sweet hawthorn, which increased as the road descended, till it filled everything up to a man's height and higher. The way was so narrow that when the carabineers tried to ride on each side of the carriage, they found it impossible to do so without being driven into the tangle of thorns at every step. The whole party moved forward at a quick trot, and Orsino understood what Basili the notary had said about the bushes, so that even he laid his rifle across his knees and peered into the brambles from time to time, half expecting to see the muzzle of a gun sticking through the green leaves and white flowers.

The avenue seemed to be about half a mile long. In the middle of it the trees were so thick as to make it almost gloomy, even in the broad afternoon daylight. The road was rough and stony.

Suddenly the horse of one of the carabineers ahead stumbled and fell heavily, and the other trooper threw his horse back on its haunches with an exclamation. Almost at the same instant, the sharp crack of a rifle rang through the trees on the right; and the bullet, singing overhead, cut through the branches just above the carriage, so that a twig with its leaves dropped upon Orsino's knees. Another shot, fired very low down, struck a spoke of one of the carriage wheels, and sent the splinters flying, burying itself somewhere in the body of the vehicle. Another and another followed, all fired either far too high or much too low to strike any of the party. As the shots all came from the same side, however, the sergeant of carabineers sprang to the ground and plunged into the brush on that side, his rifle in his hand, calling to his men to follow him. San Giacinto stood up and knelt on the cushion of the carriage, though he knew that he could not fire in the direction taken by the carabineers, lest he should hit one of them by accident.

"Keep a lookout on your side, too!" he cried to Orsino. "Shoot anybody you see, and do not miss. They may be on both sides, but I think not."

Strangely enough, from the moment the soldiers entered the brush, not another shot was fired. Clearly the assailants were beating a hasty retreat.

At that moment something black stirred in the bushes on Orsino's side. Instantly his rifle was at his shoulder, and he fired. San Giacinto started and turned round, bringing up his own weapon at the same time.

"I believe I heard something fall," said Orsino, opening the door of the carriage. Tatò had disappeared. Basili's man had followed the soldiers into the brush.

In an instant both the gentlemen were in the thicket, Orsino leading, as he followed the direction of his shot.

CHAPTER XI

Orsino's gloved hand trembled violently as he pushed aside the tangle of sweetbrier, trying to reach the place where the man upon whom he had fired had fallen.

"Let me go first," said San Giacinto. "I am bigger and my gloves are thicker."

But Orsino pushed on, his heart beating so hard that he felt the pulse in his throat and his eyes. He had been cool enough when the bullets had been flying across the carriage, and his hand had been quite steady when he had aimed at the black something moving stealthily in the bushes. But the sensation of having killed a man, and in such a way, was horrible to him. He pushed on, scratching his face and his wrists above his gloves, in the sharp thorns. The bushes were more than breast high, even to his tall figure, but San Giacinto could see over his head.

"There!" exclaimed the giant, suddenly. "There he is — to your right — I can see him!"

Orsino pushed on, and in another moment his foot struck something hard that moved a little, but was not a stone. It was the dead man's foot in a heavy shooting-boot.

They found him quite dead, not fallen to the ground, but half sitting and half lying in the thorns. He had fallen straight backwards, shot through the temples. The eyes were wide open, but without light, the handsome face perfectly colourless, and the silky, brown moustache hid the relaxed mouth. His rifle stood upright in the bush as it had fallen from his hand. His soft hat was still firmly planted on the back of his head.

Orsino was stupefied with horror and stood quite still, gazing at the dead man's face. San Giacinto looked down over his shoulders.

"He looks like a gentleman," he said, in a low voice.

The chill of a terrible presentiment froze about Orsino's heart. As he looked, the handsome features became familiar, all at once, as though he had often seen them before.

"We had better get him out to the road," said San Giacinto. "The carabineers may identify him. The sooner, the better, though you were perfectly justified in shooting him."

He laid his hand upon Orsino's shoulder to make him move a little, and the young man started. Then he bit his trembling lip and stooped to try and lift the body. As he touched the velveteen coat, the head fell suddenly to one side, and

Orsino uttered an involuntary exclamation. He had never moved a dead man before.

"It is nothing," said San Giacinto, quietly. "He is quite dead. Take his feet."

He pushed past Orsino and lifted the head and shoulders, beginning to move towards the road at once, walking backwards and breaking down the bushes with his big shoulders. They got him out upon the road. The carriage horses were standing quite still, with their heads hanging down, as though nothing had happened. They had plunged a little at first. In the road before them stood the trooper who had been thrown, holding his own and another charger by the bridle. The cause of the accident was clear enough. A pit had been treacherously dug across the road and covered with sticks and wood, so as to be invisible. Fortunately the horse had escaped injury. The others were tethered by their bridles to the back of the carriage. In the brush, far to the right, the tall bushes were moving, showing where the other four carabineers were searching for the outlaws who had fired, if, indeed, there had been more than one.

They laid the dead man in the middle of the road, on the other side of the ditch, out of reach of the horses' feet, and the trooper watched them without speaking, though with a satisfied look of approval.

"Do you know him?" asked San Giacinto, addressing the soldier.

"No, Signor Marchese. But I have not been long on this station. The brigadiere will know him, and will be glad. I came to take the place of the man they killed last week."

Orsino looked curiously at the young carabineer, who took matters so quietly, when he himself was struggling hard to seem calm. He would not have believed that he could ever have felt such inward weakness and horror as filled him, and he could not trust himself to speak, yet he had no reason to doubt that he had saved his own life or San Giacinto's by firing in time.

"I see why the other ones fired so wildly," said San Giacinto. "They were afraid of hitting their friend, who was to do the real work alone, while they led the carabineers off on a false scent on the other side. This fellow felt quite safe. He thought he could creep up to the carriage and make sure of us at close quarters. He did not expect that one of us would be on the lookout."

"That is a common trick," said the soldier. "I have seen it done at Noto. It must have been a single person that fired, and this man was also alone. If he had been with a companion, the gentleman's shot would have been answered, and one of you would have been killed."

"Then it was the other man who was waiting

on horseback in the road to warn this one of our coming?"

"Evidently, Signor Marchese."

Still Orsino stood quite still, gazing down into the dead man's face, and feeling very unsteady. Just then nothing else seemed to have any existence for him, and he was unaware of all outward things excepting that one thing that lay there, limp and helpless, killed by his hand in the flash of an instant. And as he gazed, he fancied that the young features in their death pallor grew more and more familiar, and at his own heart there was a freezing and a stiffening, as though he were turning into ice from within.

The sergeant and the troopers came back, covered with brambles, hot and grim, and empty-handed.

"Did any of you fire that other shot?" he asked, as soon as he was in the road.

"I did," said Orsino. "I killed this man."

The sergeant sprang forward, and his men pressed after him to see. The sergeant bent down and examined the dead face attentively. Then he looked up.

"You have killed rather an important person," he said gravely. "This is Ferdinando Pagliuca. We knew that he was on good terms with the outlaws, but we could not prove it against him."

"Oh, yes," said Tatò, the padrone, suddenly appearing again. "That is Don Ferdinando. I know him very well, for I have often driven him. Who would have thought it?"

Orsino had heard nothing after the sergeant had pronounced the name. He almost reeled against San Giacinto, and gripped the latter's arm desperately, his face almost as white as the dead man's. Even San Giacinto started in surprise. Then Orsino made a great effort and straightened himself, and walked away a few paces.

"This is a bad business," said San Giacinto, in a preoccupied tone. "We shall have the whole mafia against us for this. Has the other man escaped?"

"Clean gone," said the sergeant. "You had better luck than we, for we never saw him. He must have fired his shots from his horse and bolted instantly. We could not have got through the brush with our horses."

Orsino went and leaned against the carriage, shading his eyes with his hands, while San Giacinto and the soldiers talked over what had happened. The sergeant set a couple of men to work on the brambles with their sabres, to cut a way for the carriage on one side of the pitfall that covered the road.

"Put the body into the carriage," said San Giacinto. "We can walk. It is not far." He roused Orsino, who seemed to be half stunned.

"Come, my boy!" he said, drawing him away

from the carriage as the soldiers were about to lay the body in it. "Of course it is not pleasant, but it cannot be helped, and you have rendered the government a service, though you have got us into an awkward position with the Corleone."

"Awkward!" Orsino's voice was hoarse and broken. "You do not know!" he added.

San Giacinto did not understand, but made him fall back behind the carriage, which jolted horribly with its dead occupant, as Tatò forced his horses to drag it round the end of the ditch. The carabineers, still distrustful of the thick trees and the underbrush, carried their rifles and led their horses, and the whole party proceeded slowly along the drive towards the ancient house. It might have been a quarter of a mile distant. Orsino walked the whole way in silence, with bent head and set lips.

They emerged upon a wide open space, overgrown with grass, wild flowers, and rank weeds, through which a narrow path led straight up to the main door. There had been a carriage road once, following a wide curve, but it had long been disused, and even the path was not much trodden, and the grass was beginning to grow in it.

The front of the house presented a broad, rough-plastered surface, broken by but few windows, all of which were high above the ground. The tower was not visible from this side. From the back, the sound of water came up with a steady, low roar. The door was, in fact, a great oak gate, studded with big rusty nails, paintless, grey, and weather-beaten. Regardless of old Basili's advice, San Giacinto walked straight up to it, followed by the notary's man with the bunch of keys.

The loneliness of it all was beyond description, and was, if possible, enhanced by the roar of the water. The air was damp, too, from the torrent bed, and near one end of the house there were great patches of moss. At the other side, towards the sun, the remains of what had been a vegetable garden were visible, rank broccoli and cabbages thrusting up their bunches of pale green leaves, broken trellises of cane, half fallen in, and overgrown with tomato vines and wild creeping plants. A breath of air brought a smell of rotting vegetables and damp earth to San Giacinto's nostrils, as he tried one key after another in the lock.

They got in at last, and entered under a gloomy archway, beyond which there was a broad courtyard, where the grass grew between the flagstones. In the middle was an ancient well, on the right a magnificently carved doorway led into the old chapel of the monastery. On the left, opposite the chapel, a long row of windows, with closed shutters in fairly good condition, showed the position of the habitable rooms.

"Is that a church?" asked San Giacinto of

Basili's man. "Take the dead man in and leave him there," he added, as the man nodded and began to look for the key on the bunch.

They took Ferdinando Pagliuca's body from the carriage, which stood in the middle of the courtyard, and carried it in and laid it down on the uppermost step of one of the side altars, of which there were three. Orsino followed them.

It was a very dilapidated place. There had once been a few frescoes, which were falling from the walls with age and dampness. High up, through the open windows from which the glass had long since disappeared, the swallows shot in and out, bringing a dark gleam of sunshine on their sharp, black wings. Although the outer air had free access, there was a heavy, death-like smell of mould in the place. The altars were dismantled and the grey dust lay thick upon them, with fragments of plaster here and there. Only on the high altar a half-broken wooden candlestick, once silvered, stood bending over, and a little glazed frame still contained a mouldering printed copy of the Canon of the Mass. In the middle of the floor a round slab of marble, with two greenish bolts of brass, bore the inscription, 'Ossa R R. P P.' covering the pit wherein lay the bones of the departed monks who had once dwelt in the monastery.

The troopers laid Ferdinando's body upon the

stone steps in silence, and then went away, for there was much to be done. Orsino stayed behind, alone, for his cousin had not even entered the church. He knelt down for a few moments on the lowest step. It seemed a sort of act of reverence to the man whom he had killed. Mechanically he said a prayer for the dead.

But his thoughts were of the living. The man who lay there was Vittoria d'Oriani's brother, the brother of his future wife, of the being he held most dear in the world. Between him and her there was her own blood, shed by his hand. The shot had done more than kill Ferdinando Pagliuca; it had mortally wounded his own life.

He asked himself whether Vittoria, or any woman, could marry the man who had killed her brother. In time, she might forgive, indeed, but she could not forget. No one could. And there were her other brothers, and her mother, and they were Sicilians, revengeful and long pursuing in their revenge. Never, under any imaginable circumstances, would they give their consent to his marriage with Vittoria, even supposing that she herself, in the course of years, could blot out the memory of the dead. He might as well make up his mind that she was lost to him.

But that was hard to do, for the roots of growing love had struck deep and burrowed themselves in under his heart almost unawares, from week to week since he had known her, and to tear them up was to tear out the heart itself.

He went to the other side of the dim chapel and rested his dark forehead against the mouldering walls. It was as though he were going mad then and there. He drew himself up and said, almost aloud, that he was a man and must act like a man. No one had ever accused him of being unmanly, and he could not tamely bear the accusation from himself.

All the old hackneyed phrases of cynical people he had known came back to him. 'Only one woman, and the world was full of them'—and much to that same effect. And all the time he knew that such words could never fit his lips, and that though the world was full of women, there was only one for him, and between her and him lay the barrier of her own brother's blood.

He turned as he stood, and saw the straight, dark figure, with its folded hands, lying on the steps of the altar opposite—the outward fact, as his love for Vittoria was the inward truth.

The horror of it all came over him again like a surging wave, roaring in his ears and deafening him. It could have been but one degree worse if Vittoria's brother had been his friend, instead of his enemy, and if he had killed him in anger.

He remembered that he had expected to send his

mother a long and reassuring telegram on this day, and that he had told Vittoria that she should go to the Palazzo Saracinesca and hear news of him. There was a telegraph station at Santa Vittoria, three-quarters of a mile from Camaldoli, but he was confronted by the difficulty of sending any clear message which should not contain an allusion to Ferdinando Pagliuca's death, since the carabineers would be obliged to report the fact at once, and it would be in the Roman papers on the following morning.

That was a new and terrible thought. There would be the short telegraphic account of how Don Orsino Saracinesca had been attacked by brigands in a narrow road and had shot one of the number, who turned out to be Ferdinando Corleone. Her mother, who always read the papers, would read that, too. Then her brothers — then Vittoria. And his own mother would see it — his head seemed bursting. And there lay the fact, the source of these inevitable things, cold and calm, with the death smile already stealing over its white face.

San Giacinto stalked in, looking about him, and the sound of his tread roused Orsino.

"Come," he said, rather sternly. "There is much to be done. I could not find you. The man is dead; you did right in killing him, and we must think of our own safety."

"What do you mean?" asked Orsino, in a dull voice. "We are safe enough, it seems to me."

"The sergeant does not seem to think so," answered San Giacinto. "Before night it will be known that Ferdinando Pagliuca is dead, and we may have half the population of Santa Vittoria about our ears. Fortunately this place will stand a siege. Two of the troopers have gone to the village to try and get a reinforcement, and to bring the doctor to report the death, so that we can bury the man. Come — come with me! We will shut the church up till the doctor comes, and think no more about it."

He saw that Orsino was strangely moved by what had happened, and he drew him out into the air. The carriage was being unloaded by Tatò and the notary's man, and the horses had all disappeared. The sergeant and the two remaining troopers were busy clearing out a big room which opened upon the court, with the intention of turning it into a guardroom. Orsino looked at them indifferently. A renewed danger would have roused him, but nothing else could. San Giacinto led him away to show him the buildings.

"Your nerves have been shaken," said the older man. "But you will soon get over that. I remember once upon a time being a good deal upset myself, when a man whom I had caught in mischief suddenly killed himself almost in my hands."

"I shall get over it, as you say," answered Orsino. "Give me one of those strong cigars of yours, will you?"

He would have given a good deal to have been able to confide in San Giacinto and tell him the real trouble. Had he been sure that any immediate good could come of it, he would have spoken; but it seemed to him, on the contrary, that to speak of Vittoria might make matters worse. They wandered over the dark old place for half an hour. At the back, over the torrent, there was one long wall with a rampart, terminating in the evil-looking Druse's tower. The trees grew thick over the stream, and there was only one opening in the wall, closed by double low doors with heavy bolts. The whole building was, in reality, a tolerably strong fortress, built round the four sides of a single great courtyard, to which there was but one entrance,— besides the little postern over the river.

"I should like to send a telegram to Rome," said Orsino, suddenly. "It is not too late for them to get it to-night."

"You can send it to Santa Vittoria by the doctor, when he goes back."

Orsino went down into the court and got a writing-case out of his bag. It seemed convenient to write on the seat of the carriage, but just as he was going to place his writing things there, he saw that there were dark wet spots on the cushions. He shuddered and turned away in disgust, and wrote his message, leaning on the stone brink of the well.

He telegraphed that San Giacinto and he had arrived and were well, that they had met with an attack, and that he himself had killed a man. But he did not write Ferdinando's name. That seemed useless.

The doctor arrived, and the carabineers brought a couple of men of the foot brigade to strengthen the little garrison. As they entered, San Giacinto saw that four rough-looking peasants were standing outside the gate, conversing and looking up to the windows; grim, clean-shaven, black-browed men of the poorer class, for they had no guns and wore battered hats and threadbare blue cloaks. San Giacinto handed the doctor over to the sergeant and went outside at once. The men stared in silence at the gigantic figure that faced them. In his rough dark clothes and big soft hat, San Giacinto looked more vast than ever, and his bold and sombre features and stern black eyes completed the impression he made on the hill men. He looked as though he might have been the chief of all the outlaws in Sicily.

"Listen!" he said, stepping up to them. "This place is mine now, for I have bought it and paid for it, and I mean to keep it. Your friend Ferdinando Pagliuca is dead. After consenting to the sale, he dug a pitfall in the carriage road to stop us, and he and a friend of his attacked us. We shot him, and you can go and look at his body in the chapel, in there, if you have curiosity about him. There are eleven men of us here, seven being carabineers, and we have plenty of ammunition, so that it will not be well for anyone who troubles us. Tell your friends so. This is going to be a barrack, and there will be a company of infantry here before long, and there will be a railway before two years. Tell your friends that also. I suppose you are men from the Camaldoli farms."

Two of the peasants nodded, but said nothing.

"If you want work, begin and clear away those bushes. You will know where there are tools. Here is money, if you will begin at once. If you do not want money, say what you do want. But if you want nothing, go, or I shall shoot you."

He suddenly had a big army revolver in one hand, and he pulled out a loose bank note with the other.

"But I prefer that we should be good friends," he concluded, "for I have much work for everybody, and plenty of money to pay for it."

The men were not cowards, but they were taken unawares by San Giacinto's singular speech. They looked at each other, and at the bushes. One of them threw his head back a little, thrusting out his chin, which signifies a negation. The shortest of the four, a broad-shouldered, tough-looking fellow stepped before the rest.

"We will work for you, but we will not cut down the bushes. We will do any other work than that. You will not find anybody here who will cut down the bushes."

"Why not?" asked San Giacinto.

"Eh — it is so," said the man, with a peculiar expression.

The other three shrugged their shoulders and nodded silently, but kept their eyes on San Giacinto's revolver.

"We are good people," continued the man. "We wish to be friends with everyone, and since you have bought the estate, and own the land on which we live, we shall pay our rent, when we have anything wherewith to pay, and when we have not, God will provide. But as for the bushes, we cannot cut them down. We wish to be friends with everyone. But as for that, signore, if you have no axes nor hedging knives, we have them. We will bring them, and then we will go away and do any other work for you. Thus we shall not cut down the bushes, but perhaps the bushes will be cut down."

San Giacinto laughed a little, and the big revolver went back into his pocket.

"I see that we shall be friends, then," he said.
"When you have brought the hatchets, then you can come inside and help to clean the house. Then I will give you this money for your work this evening and to-morrow."

The men spoke rapidly together in dialect, so that San Giacinto could not understand them. Then the spokesman addressed him again.

"Signore," he said, "we will bring the hatchets to the door, but it is late to clean the house this evening. We do not want the money to-night. We will return in the morning and work for you."

"There are three hours of daylight yet," observed San Giacinto. "You could do something in that time, I should think."

"An hour and a half," replied the man. "It is late," he added. "It is very late."

The other three nodded. San Giacinto understood perfectly that there was some other reason, but did not insist. He fancied that they were suspicious of his own intentions with regard to them, and he let them go without further words.

As he turned back, the village doctor appeared under the arch, leading his mule. He was a pale young fellow from Messina, who had been three or four years at Santa Vittoria. San Giacinto offered him an escort back to the village, but he refused.

"If I could not go about alone, my usefulness

would be over," he said. "It is quite safe now. They will probably kill me the next time there is a cholera season."

"Why?"

"They are convinced that the government sends them the cholera through the doctors, to thin the population," answered the young man, with a dreary smile.

"What a country! It is worse than Naples."

"In some ways, far worse. In others, much better."

"In what way is it better?" asked San Giacinto, with some curiosity.

"They are terrible enemies," said the doctor, "but they can be very devoted friends, too."

"Oh — we have had a taste of their enmity first. I hope we may see something of their friendship before long."

"I doubt it, Signor Marchese. You will have the people against you from first to last, and your position is dangerous. Ferdinando Corleone was popular, and he had the outlaws on his side. I have no doubt that many of the band have been hidden here. It is a lonely and desolate house, full of queer hiding-places. By the bye, are you going to bury that poor man here? Shall I send people down from Santa Vittoria with a coffin, to carry him up to the cemetery?"

"You know the country. What should you

advise me to do? We must give him Christian burial, I suppose."

"I should be inclined to lift up the slab in the church and quietly drop him down among the monks," said the doctor. "That would be Christian burial enough for him. But you had better consult the sergeant about it. If he is taken up to Santa Vittoria, there will be a great public funeral, and all the population will follow, as though he were a martyr. If you bury him without a priest, they will say that you not only murdered him treacherously, but got rid of his body by stealth. Consult the sergeant, Signor Marchese. That is best."

The doctor mounted his mule and rode away. San Giacinto closed and barred the great gate himself before he went back into the court. He found Orsino in the midst of a discussion with the sergeant, regarding the same question of the disposal of the body.

"I know his family," Orsino was saying. "Some of them are friends of mine. He must be decently buried by a priest. I insist upon it."

The sergeant repeated what the doctor had said, namely, that a public funeral would produce something like a popular demonstration.

"I should not care if it produced a revolution," answered Orsino. "I killed the man like a dog, not knowing who he was, but I will not have him buried like one. If you are afraid of the village, let them send their priest down here, dig a grave under the floor of the church, and bury him there. But he shall not be dropped into a hole like a dead rat without a blessing. Besides, it is not legal— there are all sorts of severe regulations—"

"There is one against burying anyone within a church," observed the sergeant. "But the worst that could happen would be that you might have to pay a fine. It shall be as you please, signore. In the morning we will get a priest and a coffin, and bury him under the church. I have the doctor's certificate in my pocket."

Orsino was satisfied, and went away to be alone again, not caring where. But San Giacinto and the carabineers proceeded to turn the great court into something like a camp. There were all sorts of offices, kitchens, bake-houses, oil-presses, and storerooms, which opened directly upon the paved space. The men collected old wood and kindling stuff to make a fire, and prepared to cook some of the provisions which San Giacinto had brought for the night, while he and the sergeant determined on the best positions for sentries.

Orsino wandered about the great rooms upstairs. They were half dismantled and much dilapidated, but not altogether unfurnished. Ferdinando had retired some days previously to the village and had taken what he needed for his own use, but had left the rest. There was a tolerably furnished room immediately above the great gate. Orsino opened the window wide, and leaned out, breathing the outer air with a certain sense of relief from oppression. Watching the swallows that darted down from under the eaves to the weed-grown lawn, and up again with meteor speed, and catching in his face the last reflexions of the sun, which was sinking fast between two distant hills, he could almost believe that it had all been a bad dream. He could at least try to believe it for a little while.

But the sun went down quickly, though it still blazed full on the enormous snowy dome of Etna, opposite the window; and the chill of evening came on while it was yet day, and with it came back the memory of the coldly smiling, handsome face of dead Ferdinando Pagliuca, and the terrible suggestion of a likeness to Vittoria, which had struck at Orsino's heart when he had found him in the bushes, shot through the head. It all came back with a sudden, drowning rush that was overwhelming. He turned from the window, and, to occupy himself, he went and got his belongings and tried to make the room habitable. He knew that it was in a good position for the night, since it was not likely that he should sleep much, and he could watch the gate from the window, for his share of the defence.

CHAPTER XII

As was perhaps to be expected, considering the precautions taken, the friends of Ferdinando Pagliuca gave no sign during the night. The carabineers, when they are actually present anywhere, impose respect, though their existence is forgotten as soon as they are obliged to move on.

Orsino lay down upon a dusty mattress in the room he had chosen. He had been down to the court again, where San Giacinto ate his supper from the soldiers' improvised kitchen, by the light of a fire of brush and scraps of broken wood, which one of the men replenished from time to time. But Orsino was not hungry, and presently he had gone upstairs again. About the middle of the night, San Giacinto, carrying a lantern, opened his door, and found him reading by the light of a solitary candle.

"Has all been quiet on this side?" asked the big man.

"All quiet," answered Orsino.

San Giacinto nodded, shut the door, and went off, knowing that the young man would rather be alone. An hour later, Orsino's book dropped from his hand, and he dozed a little, in a broken way. Outside, the waning moon had risen high above the shoulders of Etna, not a breath was stirring, and only the distant roar of the water came steadily up from the other side of the old monastery. Orsino dreamed strange, shapeless dreams of vast desolateness and empty darkness, in which he had no perception by sight, and heard only the unbroken rush of water far away. Then, in the extreme blackness of nothing, a dead face appeared, with wide and sightless eyes that stared at him, and he woke and turned upon his side with a shudder, to doze again, and dream again, and wake again. It was a horrible night.

Towards morning the dream changed. In the darkness, together with the sub-bass of the torrent, a voice came to him, in a low, long-drawn lamentation. It was Vittoria's voice, and yet unlike hers. He could hear the words:

"Me l' hanno ammazzato! Me l' hanno ammazzato!"

It was Vittoria d'Oriani wailing over her brother's body. Orsino heard the words and the voice distinctly. She was outside his door. She had dragged the corpse up from the church in the dark, all the long, winding way, to bring it to him and reproach him, and to weep over it. He refused to allow himself to awake, as one sometimes can in a dream, for he knew, somehow, that he was not altogether dreaming. There was an element of reality in the two sounds of the river and the voice, interfering with each other, and the voice came irregularly, always repeating the same words, but the river roared on without a break. Then there was a sound of moaning without words, and then the words began again, always the same.

Orsino started and sat up, wide awake. He was sure that he was awake now, for he could see that the light outside the window was grey. The dawn was beginning to drink the moonlight out of the air. He heard the voice distinctly.

"Me l' hanno ammazzato!" it moaned, but much less loudly than he had heard it in his dream. "They have killed him for me," is the meaning of the words.

Orsino sprang from the bed, and opened the door, which was opposite the window. The long corridor was dark and quiet, and he turned back and opened the casement, and looked out.

The words were half spoken again, but suddenly ceased as he threw the window open. In the dim grey dawn he saw a muffled figure crouching on the stones by the gate, slowly swaying forwards and backwards. The wail began again, very soft and low, and as though the woman half feared to be heard and yet could not control herself.

Orsino watched her intently for a few moments, and then understood. It was some woman who had loved Ferdinando Pagliuca, and who came in the simple old way to mourn at the door of the house wherein he lay dead. Her head was covered with a black shawl, and her skirts were black, too, but her hands were clasped about her knees, and visible, and looked white in the dawn.

The young man drew back softly from the window, and sat down upon the edge of the bed. He, of all men, had no right to silence the woman. She did no harm, wailing for the dead man out there in the cold dawn. She was not the only one who was to mourn him on that day. In a few hours his sister would know, his mother, his brothers, and all the world besides, though the rest of the world mattered little enough to Orsino. But this woman's grief was a sort of foretaste of Vittoria's. She was but a peasant woman, perhaps, or at most a girl of the small farmers' class, but she had loved him, and would hate for ever the man who had killed him. How much more should the slayer be hated by the dead man's own flesh and blood!

The light grew less grey by quick degrees, and there were heavy footsteps in the corridor. Then came a knock at the door, and a trooper appeared in his forage cap.

"We have made the coffee, signore," he said, on the threshold.

He held out a bright tin pannikin from which

the steam rose in fragrant clouds. The physical impression of the aromatic smell was the first pleasant sensation which Orsino had experienced since he had pulled the trigger of his rifle on the previous afternoon. If we could but look at things as they are, we should see that there is neither love nor hate, neither joy nor grief, nor hope nor fear, that will not at last efface itself for a moment before hunger and thirst; so effectually can this dying body mask and screen the undying essence.

Orsino drank the hot coffee with keen physical delight, though the woman's wailing came up to his ears through the open window, and though he had known a moment earlier that the stealing dawn was the beginning of a day which might end in a broken heart.

But the trooper heard the voice, and went to the window and looked out, while Orsino drank.

"Ho, there!" he cried roughly. "Will you go or not?" He turned to Orsino. "She has been there since two o'clock," he explained. "We heard her through the closed gate."

"Let her alone," said Orsino, authoritatively. "She is only a woman, and can do no harm; and she has a right to her mourning, God knows."

"There will be a hundred before the sun has been up an hour, signore," answered the soldier. "The people will collect about her, for they will come out of curiosity, from many miles away. It will be better to get rid of them as fast as they come."

"You might let that poor woman in," suggested Orsino. "After all, I have killed her lover—she has a right to see his body."

"As you wish, signore," answered the trooper, taking the empty pannikin.

Orsino got up and looked out again, as the man went away. The girl had risen to her feet, and stood looking up to the window. Her shawl had fallen back upon her shoulders, and disclosed a young and dishevelled but beautiful head, of the Greek type, though the eyes were somewhat long and almond-shaped. There was no colour in the olive-pale cheeks, and little in the parted lips; and the hand that gathered the shawl to the bosom was singularly white. The regular features were set in a tragic mask of grief, such as one very rarely sees in the modern world.

When she saw Orsino, she suddenly raised both hands to him, like a suppliant of old.

"They have killed him!" she cried. "They have killed my bridegroom! Let me see him! let me kiss him! Are they Christians, and will not let me see him?"

"You shall see him," answered Orsino. "I will let you in myself."

"God will render it to you, signore. And God will render also to his murderer a bad death."

She sat down upon the stones, thinking, perhaps, that it would be long before the gate was opened; and she began her low moan again.

"They have killed him! They have murdered him!"

But Orsino had already left the window and the room. He had understood clearly from her words and face that she was no light creature, for whom Ferdinando had conceived a passing fancy. He had meant to marry her, perhaps within a few days. There was in her face the high stamp of innocence, and her voice rang fearless and true. Ferdinando had never been like his brothers. He had meant to marry this girl, doubtless a small farmer's daughter, from her dress; and he would have lived happily with her, sinking, perhaps, to a lower social level, but morally rising far higher than his scheming brothers. Orsino had guessed from his dead face, and from what he had heard, that Ferdinando had been the best of the family; and in a semi-barbarous country like the interior of Sicily, the young Roman did not blame him overmuch for having tried to resist the new owners of his father's house when they came to take possession.

San Giacinto and the sergeant objected on principle to admitting the girl, but Orsino insisted, and at last opened the gate himself. She had covered her head and face again, and followed him swiftly and noiselessly across the court to the door of the church. As though by instinct she turned directly to her lover's body, where it lay before the side altar, and with a low wail like a wounded animal, she fell beside it, with clasped hands. Orsino left her there alone, closing the door softly, and came out into the court, where it was almost broad daylight. The men had drunk their coffee and were grooming their black chargers tethered to rusty rings in the wall. The old stables were between the court and the rampart. The two foot-carabineers were despatched to Santa Vittoria to get a coffin for the dead man and a priest to come and bury him.

From the church came every now and then the piteous echo of the girl's lamentations. Then there was a knocking at the gate, and someone called from without. One of the troopers looked out through the narrow slit in the stone, made just wide enough to let the barrel of a gun pass. Half a dozen peasants were outside, and the soldiers could see two more coming down the drive towards the house. He asked what they wanted.

"We wish to speak with the master," said one, and two or three repeated the words.

They were the men who had brought the tools on the previous evening, with a number of others, the small tenants of the little estate. San Giacinto went and spoke with them, assuring them that he would be a better landlord than they had ever had, if they would treat him well, but that if he met with any treachery, he would send every man of them to the galleys for life. It was his way of making acquaintance, and they seemed to understand it.

While he was speaking a number of men and women appeared in the drive, headed by the two soldiers who had gone to the village. Close behind them, swaying with the walk of the woman who carried the load upon her head, a white deal coffin caught the morning light. Then more people, and always more, came in sight, up the drive. Amongst them walked a young priest in his short white 'cotta' over his shabby cassock, and beside him came a big boy bearing a silver basin with holy water, and the little broom for sprinkling it. The two trudged along in a business-like way, and all the people were talking loudly. It seemed to San Giacinto that half the population of the village must have turned out. He stepped back and called to the troopers to keep the gate, and prevent the crowd from entering. Then he waited outside. The people became silent as they came near, and he looked at them, scrutinizing their faces. Some of the men had their guns slung over their shoulders, but many were only labourers and had none.

Many scowling glances were turned on San Giacinto as the crowd came up to the gate, and he began to anticipate trouble of some sort. The troopers had their rifles in their hands as they formed up behind him. The tenants of Camaldoli mixed with the crowd, evidently not wishing to identify themselves with their new landlord.

"What do you want?" asked San Giacinto, in a harsh, commanding voice.

The priest came close to him, and bowed and smiled, as though the occasion of meeting were a pleasant one. Then he stood aside a little, and a strapping woman who carried the coffin on her head marched in under the gate between the soldiers, who made way for her. And behind her came her husband, a crooked little carpenter, carrying a leathern bag from which protruded the worn and blackened handle of a big hammer. The third comer was stopped by the sergeant. He was a ghastly pale old man, with a three-days beard on his pointed chin, and he was dressed in dingy black.

"Who are you?" asked the sergeant, sharply.

"I am one without whom people are not buried," answered the old man, in a cracked voice. "You have a carpenter and a priest, but there is a third — I am he, the servant of the dead, who give no orders."

The sergeant understood that the man was the parish undertaker, and let him pass also. Meanwhile San Giacinto repeated his question.

"What do you all want?" he asked in a thundering tone, for he was annoyed.

"If it please you, Signor Marchese," said the priest, "these, my parishioners, desire the body of Don Ferdinando Corleone, in order to bury it in holy ground, for he was beloved of many. Pray do not be angry, Excellency, for they come in peace, having heard that Don Ferdinando had been killed by an accident. Grant their request, which is a proper one, and they shall depart quickly. I answer for them."

As he spoke the last words in a tone which all could hear, he turned to the crowd, as though for their assent.

"He answers for us," said many of them, in a breath. "Good, Don Niccola! You answer for us. We are Christians. We wish to bury Don Ferdinando properly."

"I have not the slightest objection," said San Giacinto. "On the contrary, I respect your wish, and I only regret that I have not the means of doing more honour to your friend. You must attend to that. Be kind enough to wait here while the priest blesses the body."

The priest and the boy with the holy water passed in, and the gate closed upon the crowd. While they had been talking, the carpenter and his wife had entered the court. Basili's man led them to the door of the church and opened it. The woman marched in with her swinging stride, and one hand on her hips, while the other steadied the deal coffin.

"Where is he?" she asked in a loud, good-natured voice, for the church seemed very dark after the morning light outside.

She was answered by a low cry from the steps of the side altar, where the unhappy girl lay half across her lover's body, looking round towards the door, in a new horror.

The woman uttered an exclamation of surprise, and then slowly swung her burden round so that she could see her husband.

"Help me, Ciccio," she said, in a matter-of-fact way. "They are always inconvenient things."

The man held up his hands and took the foot, while his wife raised her hands also and shifted the weight towards him little by little, until she got hold of the head. The loose lid rattled as they set the thing down on the floor. Then the woman took the rolled towel on which she had carried the weight, from her head, undid it, wiped her brow with it, and looked at the girl in some perplexity.

"It is the apothecary's Concetta," she said, suddenly recognizing the white features in the gloom. "Oh, poor child! Poor child!" she cried, going forward quickly, while her husband took the lid from the coffin and began to fumble in his leathern bag for his nails.

As the woman approached the step, Concetta threw her arms wildly over her head, stiffened her limbs straight out, and rolled over and over upon the damp pavement, in one of those strange fainting fits which sometimes seize women in moments of intense grief. The carpenter's wife tried to lift her, and to bend her arms, so as to get hold of her; but the girl was as rigid as though she were in a cataleptic trance.

"Poor child! Poor Concetta!" exclaimed the carpenter's wife, softly.

Then, bending her broad back, she raised the girl up by main strength, getting first one arm round her and then the other, till she got her weight up and could carry her. Her crooked little husband paid no attention to her. Women were women's business at such times. The big woman got the girl out into the morning sunshine in the court, meeting the eccentric undertaker and the priest, who were talking together outside. San Giacinto came forward instantly, followed by Orsino, who had been wandering about the rampart over the river when the crowd had come. San Giacinto took the unconscious girl's body from the woman, with ease.

"Come," he said, carrying her before him on his arms. "Get some water."

He entered the room where the men had slept on some straw and laid Concetta down, her arms still stiffened above her head. One of the troopers brought water in a pannikin. San Giacinto dashed the cold drops upon the white face, and the features quivered nervously.

"Take care of her," he said to the woman.

"Who is she?"

"She is Concetta, the daughter of Don Atanasio, the apothecary. She was to marry Don Ferdinando next week. But now that they have killed him, she will marry someone else."

"Poor girl!" exclaimed San Giacinto, compassionately, and he turned and went out.

Orsino was standing by the door, looking in, and he had heard what the woman had said. It confirmed what he had guessed from the girl's own words. He wondered how it was possible that the action of one second could really cause such terrible trouble in the world.

From the open door of the church came the sound of the regular blows of a hammer. The work had been quickly done, and the carpenter was nailing down the lid of the coffin. The priest, who had stayed in the early sunshine for warmth, hung a shabby little stole round his neck, and took the holy water basin and the little broom from the boy, and entered the church to bless the body before it was taken away.

As it was not advisable to let in the crowd, the six soldiers lifted the coffin and bore it out of the gate. Then the peasants laid it on a bier which had been brought after them and covered it with a rusty black pall. The priest walked before it, and began to recite the psalms for the dead. The women covered their heads, and some of the men uncovered theirs, and a few joined in the priest's monotonous recitations. A quarter of an hour later, San Giacinto, watching from the gate, saw the last of the people disappear up the drive. But the carpenter's wife had stayed with Concetta.

"It is a bad business," said the old giant to himself, as he turned and went in.

CHAPTER XIII

THE taking possession of Camaldoli had turned out much more difficult and dangerous than even San Giacinto had anticipated, for the catastrophe of Ferdinando Pagliuca's death had at once aroused the anger and revengeful resentment of the whole neighbourhood. He made up his mind that it would be necessary for himself or Orsino to return to Rome at once, both in order to see the Minister of the Interior, with a view to obtaining special protection from the government, and to see the Pagliuca family, in the hope of pacifying them.

The latter mission would not be an easy nor an agreeable one, and San Giacinto would gladly have undertaken it himself. On the other hand, he did not trust Orsino's wisdom in managing matters in Sicily. The young man was courageous and determined, but he had not the knowledge of the southern character which was indispensable. Moreover, he was not the real owner of the lands, and would not feel that he had authority to act independently in all cases. It was, therefore, decided that Orsino should go back to Rome at once, while San Giacinto remained at Camaldoli to get matters into a better shape.

It was a dreary journey for Orsino. He telegraphed that he was coming, found that there was no steamer from Messina, crossed to Reggio, and travelled all night and all the next day by the railway, reaching Rome at night, jaded and worn.

He found, as he had expected, that all Rome was talking of his adventure with the brigands, and of the death of Ferdinando Pagliuca, and of the probable consequences. But he learned to his surprise how Tebaldo had been heard to say at the club on the previous afternoon that Ferdinando was no relation of his, and that it was a mere coincidence of names.

"Nevertheless," said Sant' Ilario, "we all believe that you have killed his brother. Tebaldo Pagliuca has no mind to have it said that his brother was a brigand and died like a dog. He says he is not in Sicily, but left some time ago. As no one in Rome ever saw him, most people will accept the statement for the girl's sake, if not for the rest of the family."

Orsino looked down thoughtfully while his father was speaking. He understood at once that the story being passably discreditable to the d'Oriani, he had better seem to fall in with their view of the case, by holding his peace when he could. His father and mother, as well as the old Prince, insisted upon hearing a detailed account of the affair in the woods, however, and he was obliged to tell them all that had happened, though he said nothing about the fancied resemblance of Ferdinando to Vittoria, and as little as possible about the way in which the people had carried off the man's body with a public demonstration of sorrow. After all, no one had told him that Ferdinando was the brother of Tebaldo. He had taken it for granted, and it was barely possible that he might have been mistaken.

"There may be others of the name," he said, as he concluded his story.

His mother looked at him keenly. Half an hour later he was alone with her in her own sitting-room.

"Why did you say that there might be others of the name?" she asked gravely. "Why did you wish to imply that the unfortunate man may not have been the brother of Don Tebaldo and Donna Vittoria?"

Orsino was silent for a moment. There was reproach in Corona's tone, for she herself had not the slightest doubt in the matter. He came and stood before her, for he was a truthful man.

"It seemed to me," he said, "that I might let him have the benefit of any doubt there may be, though I have none myself. The story will be a terrible injury to the family."

"You are certainly not called upon to tell it to

everyone," said Corona. "I only wished to know what you really thought."

"I am sorry to say that I feel sure of the man's identity, mother. And I want you to help me," he added suddenly. "I wish to see Donna Vittoria alone. You can manage it."

Corona did not answer at once, but looked long and earnestly at her eldest son.

"What is it, mother?" he asked, at last.

"It is a very terrible thing," she answered slowly. "You love the girl, you wish to marry her, and you have killed her brother. Is not that the truth?"

"Yes, that is the truth," said Orsino. "Help me to see her. No one else can."

"Does anyone know? Did you speak about it to her mother, or her brothers, before you left? Does Ippolito know?"

"No one knows. Will you help me, mother?"

"I will do my best," said Corona, thoughtfully. "Not that I wish you to marry into that family," she added. "They have a bad name."

"But she is not like them. It is not her fault."

"No, it is not her fault, and she has not their faults. But for her brothers — well, we need not talk of that. For the sake of what there has been between you two, already, you have a sort of right to see Vittoria."

"I must see her."

"I went there yesterday, after we read the news in the papers," said Corona. "Her mother was ill. Later your father came in and said he had seen Don Tebaldo at the club. You heard what he said. They mean to deny the relationship. In fact, they have done so. I can therefore propose to take Vittoria to drive to-morrow afternoon, and I can bring her here to tea, in my own sitting-room. Then you may come here and see her, and I will leave you alone for a little while. Yes — you have a right to see her and to defend yourself to her, and explain to her how you killed that poor man, not knowing who he was."

"Thank you — you are very good to me. Mother —" he hesitated a moment — "if my father had killed your brother by accident, would you have married him?"

He fixed his eyes on Corona's. She was silent for a moment.

"Yes," she answered presently. "The love of an honest woman for an honest man can go farther than that."

She turned her beautiful face from Orsino as she spoke, and her splendid eyes grew dreamy and soft, as she leaned back in her chair beside her writing-table. He watched her, and a wave of hope rose slowly to his heart. But all women were not like his mother.

Early on the following morning she wrote a note

to Vittoria. The answer came back after a long time, and the man sent up word that he had been kept waiting three-quarters of an hour for it. It was written in a tremulous hand, and badly worded, but it said that Vittoria would be ready at the appointed time. Her mother, she added, was ill, but wished her to accept the Princess's invitation.

Vittoria had grown thin and pale, and there was a sort of haunted look in her young eyes as she sat beside Corona in the big carriage. Corona herself hesitated as to what she should say, for the girl was evidently in a condition to faint, or break down with tears, at any sudden shock. Yet it was necessary to tell her that Orsino was waiting for her, and it might be necessary also to use some persuasion in inducing her to meet him.

"My dear," said Corona, after a little while, "I want you to come home with me when we have had a little drive. Do you mind? We will have tea together in my little room."

"Yes — of course — I should like it very much," answered Vittoria.

"We shall not be quite alone," Corona continued. "I hope you will not mind."

Corona Saracinesca had many good qualities, but she was not remarkably clever, and when she wished to be tactful she often found herself in conflict with the singular directness of her own character. At the same time, she feared to let the girl at her side see how much she knew. Vittoria looked so pale and nervous that she might faint. Corona had never fainted. The girl naturally supposed that Orsino was still in Sicily.

They were near the Porta Salaria, and there was a long stretch of lonely road between high walls, just beyond it. Corona waited till they had passed the gate.

"My dear," she began again, taking Vittoria's hand kindly, "do not be surprised at what I am going to tell you. My son Orsino — "

Vittoria started, and her hand shook in her companion's hold.

"Yes — my son Orsino has come back unexpectedly and wishes very much to see you."

Vittoria leaned back suddenly and closed her eyes. Corona thought that the fainting fit had certainly come, and tried to put her arm round the slight young figure. But as she looked into Vittoria's face, she saw that the soft colour was suddenly blushing in her cheeks. In a moment her eyes opened again, and there was light in them for a moment.

"I did not know how you would take it," said Corona, simply, "but I see that you are glad."

"For him — that he is safe," answered the young girl, in a low voice. "But — "

She stopped, and gradually the colour sank away from her face again, and her eyes grew heavy once more. The trouble was greater than the gladness.

"Will you see him, in my own room?" asked the elder woman, after a pause.

"Oh, yes — yes! Indeed I will — I must see him. How kind you are!"

Corona leaned forward and spoke to the footman at once, and the carriage turned back towards the city. She knew well enough how desperately hard it would be for Vittoria to wait for the meeting. She knew also, not by instinct of tact, but by a woman's inborn charity, that it would be kind of her to speak of other things, now that she had said what was necessary, and not to force upon Vittoria the fact that Orsino had revealed his secret, still less to ask her any questions about her true relationship to Ferdinando Pagliuca, which might put her in the awkward position of contradicting Tebaldo's public statement. But as they swept down the crowded streets, amongst the many carriages, Vittoria looked round into Corona's face almost shyly, for she was very grateful.

"How good you are to me!" she exclaimed softly. "I shall not forget it."

Corona smiled, but said nothing, and ten minutes later the carriage thundered under the archway of the gate. Corona took Vittoria through the state apartments, where they were sure of meeting no one at that time, and into her bedroom by a door she seldom used. Then she pointed to another at the other side.

"That is the way to my sitting-room, my dear," she said. "Orsino is there alone."

With a sudden impulse, she kissed her on both cheeks and pushed her towards the door.

CHAPTER XIV

ORSINO heard the door of his mother's bedroom open, and rose to his feet, expecting to see Corona. He started as Vittoria entered, and he touched the writing-table with his hand as though he were unsteady. The young girl came forward towards him quickly, and the colour rose visibly in her face while she crossed the little room. Orsino was white and did not hold out his hand, not knowing what to expect, for it was the hand that had killed her brother but two days ago.

Vittoria had not thought of what she should do or say, for it had been impossible to think. But as she came near, both her hands went out instinctively, to touch him. Almost instinctively, too, he drew back from her touch a little. But she did not see the movement, and her eyes sought his, as she laid her fingers lightly upon his shoulders and looked up to him. Then the sadness in his face, that had been almost like fear of her, relaxed toward a change, and his eyes opened wide in a sort of hesitating surprise. Two words, low and earnest, trembled upon Vittoria's lips.

"Thank God!"

In an instant he knew that she loved him in spite of all. Yet, arguing against his senses that it was impossible, he would not take her at her word. He took both her hands from his shoulders and held them, so that they crossed.

"Was he really your brother?" he asked slowly.

"Yes," she answered faintly, and looked down.

Perhaps it seemed to her that she should be ashamed of forgiving, before he had said one word of defence or uttered one expression of sorrow for what he had done. But she loved him, and since she had been a little child she had not seen her brother Ferdinando half a dozen times. It was true that when she had seen him she had been drawn to him, as she was not drawn to the two that were left, for he had not been like the others. She knew that she should have trusted Ferdinando if she had known him better.

Orsino began his defence.

"We were fired upon several times," he said. Her hands started in his, as she thought of his danger. "I saw a man's coat moving in the brush," he continued, "and I aimed at it. I never saw the man's face till we found him lying dead. It was not an accident, for bullets cut the trees overhead and struck the carriage." Again her hands quivered. "It was a fight, and I meant to kill the man. But I could not see his face."

She did not speak for a moment. Then, for the first time, she shrank a little, and withdrew her hands from his.

"I know — yes — it is terrible," she said in broken tones; and she glanced at him, and looked down again. "Do not speak of it," she added suddenly, and she was surprised at her own words.

It was the woman's impulse to dissociate the man she loved from the deed, for which she could not but feel horror. She would have given the world to sit down beside him and talk of other things. But he wished the situation to be cleared for ever, as any courageous man would.

"I must speak of it," he answered. "Perhaps we shall never have the chance again — "

"Never? What do you mean?" she asked quickly. "Why not?"

"You may forgive me," he answered earnestly. "You know that I would have let him shoot me ten times over rather than have hurt you — "

"Orsino — " She touched his arm nervously, trying to stop him.

"Yes — I wish I were in his grave to-day! You may forgive, but you cannot forget — how can you?"

"How? If — if you still love me, I can forget — "

Orsino's eyes were suddenly moist. It seemed as though something broke, and let in the light.

"I shall always love you," he said simply; as

men sometimes do when they are very much in earnest.

"And I—"

She did not finish the sentence in words, but her hand and face said the rest.

"Sit down," she said, after a little silence.

They went to a little sofa and sat down together, opposite the window.

"Do you think that anything you could do could make me not love you?" she asked, looking into his face. "Are you surprised? Did you think that I should turn upon you and accuse you of my brother's death, and say that I hated you? You should not have judged me so — it was unkind!"

"It has all been so horrible that I did not know what to expect," he said. "I have not been able to think sensibly until now. And even now — no, I have not judged you, as you call it, dear. But I expected that you would judge me, as God knows you have the right."

"Why should I judge you?" asked Vittoria, softly and lovingly. "If you had lain in wait for him and killed him treacherously, as he meant to kill you, it would have been different. If he had killed you, as he was there to kill you — as he might have killed you if you had not been first — I — well, I am only a girl, but even these little hands would have had some strength! But as it is, God willed it. Whom shall I judge? God? That would be wrong. God protected you, and my brother died in his treachery. Do you think that if I had been there, and had been a man, and the guns firing, and the bullets flying, I should not have done as you did, and shot my own brother? It would have been much more horrible even than it is, but of course I should have done it. Then why are you in such distress? Why did you think that I should not love you any more?"

"I did not dare to think it," answered Orsino.

"You see, as I said, God willed it — not you. You were but the instrument, unconscious and innocent. It is only a little child that will strike the senseless thing that hurts it."

"You are eloquent, darling. You will make me think as you do."

"I wish you would, indeed I wish you would! I am sorry, I am grieved, I shall mourn poor Ferdinando, though I scarcely knew him. But you — I shall love you always, and for me, as I see it, you were no more the willing cause of his death than the senseless gun you held in your hand. Do you believe me?"

She took his hand again, as though to feel that he understood. And understanding, he drew her close to him and kissed her young eyes, as he had done that first time, out on the bridge over the street.

"You have my life," he said tenderly. "I give you my life and soul, dear."

She put up her face suddenly, and kissed his cheek, and instantly the colour filled her own, and she shrank back, and spoke in a different tone.

"We will put away that dreadful thing," she said, drawing a little towards her own end of the sofa. "We will never speak of it again, for you understand."

"But your mother, your brothers," answered Orsino. "What of them? I hear that they do not acknowledge—" he stopped, puzzled as to how he should speak.

"My mother is ill with grief, for Ferdinando was her favourite. But Tebaldo and Francesco have determined that they will act as though he were no relation of ours. They say that it would ruin us all to have it said that our brother had been with the brigands. That is true, is it not?"

"It would be a great injury to you," answered Orsino.

"Yes. That is what they say. And Tebaldo will not let us wear mourning, for fear that people should not believe what he says. This morning when the Princess's note came, Tebaldo insisted that I should accept, but my mother said that I should not come to the house. They had a long discussion, and she submitted at last. What can she do? He rules everybody—and he is bad, bad in his heart, bad in his soul! Francesco is only weak, but Tebaldo is bad. Beware of him, for though he says that Ferdinando was not his brother, he will not forgive you. But you will not go back to Sicily?"

"Yes, I must go. I cannot leave San Giacinto alone, since I have created so much trouble."

"Since poor Ferdinando is dead, you will be safer — I mean —" she hesitated. "Orsino!" she suddenly exclaimed, "I knew that he would try to kill you — that is why I wanted to keep you here. I did not dare tell you — but I begged so hard — I thought that for my sake, perhaps, you would not go. Tebaldo would kill me if he knew that I were telling you the truth now. He knew that Ferdinando had friends among the outlaws, and that he sometimes lived with them for weeks. And Ferdinando wrote to Tebaldo, and warned him that although he had signed the deed, no one should ever enter the gate of Camaldoli while he was alive. And no one did, for he died. But the Romans would think that he was a common brigand; and I suppose that Tebaldo is right, for it would injure us very much. But between you and me there must be nothing but the truth, so I have told you all. And now beware of Tebaldo; for, in spite of what he says, he will some day try to avenge his brother."

"I understand it all much better now," said

Orsino, thoughtfully. "I am glad you have told me. But the question is, whether your mother and your brothers will ever consent to our marriage, Vittoria. That is what I want to know."

"My mother — never! Tebaldo might, for interest. He is very scheming. But my mother will never consent. She will never see you again, if she can help it."

"What are we to do?" asked Orsino, speaking rather to himself than to Vittoria.

"I do not know," she answered, in a tone of perplexity. "We must wait, I suppose. Perhaps she will change, and see it all differently. We can afford to wait — we are young. We love each other, and we can meet. Is it so hard to wait awhile before being married?"

"Yes," said Orsino. "It is hard to wait for you."

"I will do anything you like," answered Vittoria. "Only wait a little while, and see whether my mother does not change. Only a little while!"

"We must, I suppose," said Orsino, reluctantly. "But I do not see why your mother should not always think of me as she does to-day. I can do nothing to improve matters."

"Let us be satisfied with to-day," replied Vittoria, rather anxiously, and as though to break off the conversation. "I was miserably unhappy this evening, and I thought you were in Sicily; and instead, we have met. It is enough for one day — it is a thousand times more than I had hoped."

"Or I," said Orsino, bending down and kissing her hand more than once.

The handle of Corona's door turned very audibly just then, and a moment later the Princess entered the room. Without seeming to scrutinize the faces of the two, she understood at a glance that Vittoria had accepted the tragic situation, as she herself would have done; and that if there had been any discussion, it was over.

Vittoria coloured a little, when she met Corona's eyes, realizing how the older woman had, as it were, arranged a lovers' meeting for her. But Corona herself did not know whether to be glad or sorry for what had happened.

Nor was it easy for anyone to foresee the consequences of the present situation. It was only too clear that the young people loved each other with all their hearts; and Corona herself was very fond of Vittoria, and believed her to be quite unlike her family. Yet at best she was an exception in a race that had a bad name; and Corona knew how her husband and his father would oppose the marriage, even though she herself should consent to it. She guessed, too, that Vittoria's mother would refuse to hear of it. Altogether Orsino had fallen in love very unfortunately, and Corona could see no possible happy termination to the affair.

Therefore, against her own nature and her affection for her son, she was conscious of a certain disappointment when she saw that the love between the two was undiminished, even by the terrible catastrophe of Ferdinando's death. It would have been so much simpler if Vittoria had bidden goodbye for ever to the man who had killed her brother.

CHAPTER XV

IPPOLITO SARACINESCA was, perhaps, of all the household the most glad to see his favourite brother at home again so soon. He missed the companionship which had always been a large element in his life.

"I shall go with you when you return," he said, sitting on the edge of Orsino's table, and swinging his priestly legs in an undignified fashion.

"Are you in earnest?" asked Orsino, with a laugh.

"Yes. Why not? You say that there is a church on the place, or a chapel. I will say mass there for the household on Sundays, and keep you company on week-days. You will be lonely when San Giacinto comes back. Besides, after what has happened, I hate to think that you are down there alone among strangers."

"Have you nothing to keep you in Rome?" asked Orsino, much tempted by the offer.

"Nothing in the world."

"There will be no piano at Camaldoli."

"I suppose there is an organ in your church, is there not?"

"No. There is probably one in the church of Santa Vittoria. You could go and play on it."

"How far is it?"

"Three-quarters of a mile, I was told."

"As far as from the Piazza di Venezia to the Piazza del Popolo."

"Less. That is a mile, they always used to say, when the loose horses ran the race in carnival."

"It would be just a pleasant walk, then," said Ippolito, already planning his future occupations at Camaldoli. "I could go over in the afternoon, when the church is closed, and play on the organ an hour or two whenever I pleased."

"I have no idea what sort of thing the Santa Vittoria organ will turn out to be," answered Orsino. "It is probably falling to pieces, and has not been tuned since the beginning of the century."

"I will mend it and tune it," said Ippolito, confidently.

"You?" Orsino looked at his brother's delicate hands and laughed.

"Of course. Every musician knows something about the instruments he plays. I know how an organ is tuned, and I understand the mechanism. The old-fashioned ones are simple things enough.

When a note goes wrong you can generally mend the tracker with a bit of wire, or a stick, as the case may be — or if it is the wind chest — "

"It is not of the slightest use to talk to me about that sort of thing," interrupted Orsino, "for I understand nothing about organs, nor about music either, for that matter."

"I will take some tools with me, and some kid, and a supply of fine glue," said Ippolito, still full of his idea. "How about the rooms? Is there any decent furniture?"

Orsino gave him a general idea of the state of Camaldoli, not calculated to encourage him in his intention, but the young priest was both very fond of his brother, and he was in love with the novelty of his idea.

"I daresay that they have not too many priests in that part of the country," he said. "I may be of some use."

"We got one without difficulty to bury that poor man," answered Orsino. "But you may be right. You may be the means of redeeming Sicily." He laughed.

He was, indeed, inclined to laugh rather unexpectedly, since his interview with Vittoria. He was far too manly and strong to be saddened for any length of time by the fact of having taken the life of a man who had, undoubtedly, attempted to murder him by stealth. He had been oppressed by the certainty that the deed had raised an insurmountable barrier between Vittoria and himself. Since he had found that he had been mistaken, he was frankly glad that he had killed Ferdinando Pagliuca, for the very plain reason that if he had not done so, Ferdinando Pagliuca would have certainly killed him, or San Giacinto, or both. He had no more mawkish sentiment about the horror of shedding human blood than had embarrassed his own forefathers in wilder times. If men turned brigands and dug pitfalls, and tried to murder honest folk by treachery, they deserved to be killed; and though the first impression he had received, when he had been sure that he had killed his man, had been painful, because he was young and inexperienced in actual fighting, he now realized that but for the relationship of the dead man, it had been not only excusable, but wise, to shoot him like a wild beast. His own people thought so too.

It was natural, therefore, that his spirits should rise after his interview with Vittoria. On that day he had already been busy in carrying out San Giacinto's directions, and on the following morning he went to work with increased energy.

Corona watched him when they met, and the presentiment of evil which had seized her when he had first spoken of going to Sicily became more oppressive. She told herself that the worst had happened which could happen, but she answered herself with old tales of Sicilian revenge after long-nourished hatred. She was shocked when Ippolito announced his intention of accompanying his brother. Ippolito was almost indispensable to her. The old Prince used to tell her that her priest son answered the purpose of a daughter with none of the latter's disadvantages, at which Ippolito himself was the first to laugh good-naturedly, being well aware that he had as good stuff in him as his rough-cast brothers. But Corona really loved him more as a daughter than a son, and because he was less strong than the others, she was not so easily persuaded that he was safe when he was away from her, and she half resented the old gentleman's jest. She especially dreaded anything like physical exposure or physical danger for him. She was a brave and strong woman in almost every way, and would have sent her other three sons out to fight for their country or their honour without fear or hesitation. But Ippolito was different. Orsino might face the brigands if he chose. She could be momentarily anxious about him, but the belief prevailed with her that he could help himself and would come back safe and sound. One of the reasons, an unacknowledged one, why she had been so ready to let Ippolito follow his inclination for the church, was that priests are less exposed to all sorts of danger than other men. San Giacinto's Sicilian schemes suddenly seemed to her quite mad since Ippolito wished to accompany his brother and share in any danger which might present itself.

But Ippolito was one of those gently obstinate persons whom it is hard to move and almost impossible to stop when they are moving. He had made up his mind that he would go to Camaldoli, and he met his mother's objections with gentle but quite unanswerable arguments.

Had there ever been an instance of a priest being attacked by brigands? Corona was obliged to admit that she could remember none. Was he, Ippolito, accomplishing anything in the world, so long as he stayed quietly in Rome? Might he not do some good in the half-civilized country about Camaldoli and Santa Vittoria? He could at least try, and would. There was no answer to this either. Was not Orsino, who was melancholic by nature, sure to be wretchedly lonely down there after San Giacinto left? This was undoubtedly true.

"But the malaria," Corona objected at last. "There is the fever there, all summer, I am sure. You are not so strong as Orsino. You will catch it."

"I am much stronger than anybody supposes," answered Ippolito. "And if I were not, it is not always the strong people that escape the fever. Besides, there can be none before June or July, and Orsino does not expect to stay all summer."

He had his way, of course, and made his preparations. Orsino was glad for his own sake, and he also believed that the change of existence would do his brother good. He himself was not present when these discussions took place. Ippolito told him about them.

Orsino wished to see Vittoria again before leaving Rome, but Corona refused to help him any further.

"I cannot," she said. "You had a right to see her that once. At least, I thought so. It seemed to be a sort of moral right. But I cannot arrange meetings for you. I cannot put myself in such a position towards that family. One may do in a desperate situation what one would absolutely refuse to do every day and in ordinary circumstances."

"Going away, not knowing when I may come back, does not strike me as an ordinary circumstance," said Orsino, discontentedly.

"You must see that for me to cheat Vittoria's mother and brothers by bringing her here to see you secretly, is to sacrifice all idea of dignity," answered Corona.

"I had not looked at it in that light, nor called it by that name."

"But I had, and I do. I am perfectly frank with you, and I always have been. I like the girl very much, but I do not wish you to marry her, on account of her family. It is one thing to object to a marriage on the score of birth or fortune. You know that I should not, though I hope you will marry in your own class. Happiness is, perhaps, independent of the details of taste which make up daily life, but it runs on them, as a train runs on rails — and if a bad jolting is not unhappiness, it is certainly discomfort."

"You are wise, mother. I never doubted that. But this is different —"

"Very different. That is what I meant to say. There would, perhaps, be no question of that sort of moral discomfort with Vittoria; she has been well brought up in a convent of ladies, like most of the young girls you meet in the world, like me, like all the rest of us. It is different. It is her family — they are impossible, not socially, for they are as good as anybody in the way of descent. Bianca Campodonico married Vittoria's uncle, and no one thought it a bad match until it turned out badly. But that is just it. They are all people who turn out badly. Tebaldo Pagliuca has the face of a criminal, and his brother makes one think of a satyr. Their mother is a nonentity and does not count. Vittoria is charming. I suppose she is like someone on her mother's side, for she has not the smallest resemblance to any of the others. But all the charm in the world will not compensate you for the rest of them. And now you have had the frightful misfortune to kill their brother. Did you never hear of a vendetta? The southern people are revengeful. The Corleone will never acknowledge to the world that Ferdinando was one of them, but they will not forget it, against you and yours, and your children. I meet those young men in the street, and they bow as though nothing had happened, but I know well enough that if they could destroy every one of us, they would. Can I put myself in the position of cheating such people by bringing Vittoria here to see you secretly? It is impossible. You must see it yourself."

"Yes," answered Orsino. "I suppose I must admit it. It would be undignified."

"Yes, very. The word is not strong enough. You must help yourself. I do not propose any solution of the difficulty. You love the girl. Heaven forbid that I should stand in the way of honest love between honest man and woman. But frankly, I wish that you did not love her, and that she did not love you. And I cannot help you any more, because I will not humiliate myself to deceive people who hate me, and you, and all of us, even to our name."

"Do you think they do? Would they not be

glad to see Vittoria married to me? After all, I am a great match for a ruined family's only daughter, and if Tebaldo Pagliuca is anything, he is grasping, I am sure."

"Yes, but he is more revengeful than grasping, and more cunning than revengeful — a dangerous enemy. That is why I hate to see Ippolito go with you to the south. Some harm will come to him, I am sure. The Corleone have the whole country with them."

"I will answer for him," said Orsino, smiling. "Nothing shall happen to him."

"How can you answer for him? How can you pledge yourself that he shall be safe? It is impossible. You cannot spend your life in protecting him."

"I can provide people who will," answered the young man. "But you are wrong to be so timid about him. No one ever touches a priest, in the first place, and before he has been there a fortnight, all the people will like him, as everybody always does. It is impossible not to like Ippolito. Besides, Tebaldo Pagliuca has no reason for going to Sicily now that the place is sold. Why in the world should he go? Little by little we shall gain influence there, and before long we shall be much more popular than the Corleone ever were. San Giacinto has written to me already. He says that everything is perfectly quiet already, — that was twenty-four hours after I left, — that he had twenty men from the village at work on the house, making repairs, and that they worked cheerfully and seemed to like his way of doing things. Since Ferdinando is dead there is no one to lead an opposition. They are all very poor and very glad to earn money."

"It may be as you say," said Corona, only partially reassured. "I do not understand the condition of life there, of course, and I know that when you promise to answer for Ippolito you are in earnest, and will keep your word. But I am anxious — very anxious."

"I am sorry, mother," replied Orsino. "I am very sorry. But you will soon see that you have no reason to be anxious. That is all I can say. I will answer for him with my life."

"That is a mere phrase, Orsino," said Corona, gravely, "like a great many things one says when one is very much in earnest. If anything happened to him, your life would be still more precious to me than it is, if that were possible. You all think that because I am often anxious about him, he is my favourite. You do not understand me, any of you. I love you all equally, but I am not equally anxious about you all, and my love shows itself most for the one who seems the least strong and able to fight the world."

"For that matter, mother, Ippolito is as able to

fight his own battles as the strongest of us. He is obstinate to a degree hardly anyone can understand. He has the quiet, sound, uncompromising obstinacy of the Christian martyrs. People who have that sort of character are not weak, and they are generally very well able to take care of themselves."

"Yes, I know he is obstinate. That is, when he insists upon going with you."

Corona was very far from being satisfied, and Orsino felt that in spite of what she had said she was in reality laying upon him the responsibility for his brother's safety. He himself felt no anxiety on that score, however. In Rome, many hundreds of miles away from Camaldoli, even the things which had really happened during his brief stay in Sicily got an air of improbability and distance which made further complications of the same sort seem almost impossible. Besides, he had the promise of the Minister of the Interior that a company of infantry should shortly be quartered at Santa Vittoria, which would materially increase the safety of the whole neighbourhood.

Orsino's principal preoccupation was to see Vittoria again, alone, before he left. In the hope of meeting her he went to a garden party, and in the evening to two houses where she had gone frequently during the winter with her mother. But she did not appear. Her mother was ill, and Vittoria stayed at home with her. Her brothers, on the contrary, were everywhere, always smiling and apparently well satisfied with the world.

It was said that Tebaldo was trying to marry an American heiress, and Orsino twice saw him talking with the young stranger, who was reported to have untold millions, and was travelling with an aunt, who seemed to have as many more of her own. He looked at the girl without much curiosity, for the type has become familiar in Europe of late years.

Miss Lizzie Slayback — for that was her name — was undeniably pretty, though emphatically not beautiful. She was refined in appearance, too, but not distinguished. One could not have said that she was 'nobody,' as the phrase goes, yet no one would have said, at first sight, that she was 'somebody.' Yet she had an individuality of her own, which was particularly apparent in her present surroundings, a sort of national individuality, which contrasted with the extremely de-nationalized appearance and manner of Roman society. For the Romans of the great houses have for generations intermarried with foreigners from all parts of Europe, until such strongly Latin types as the Saracinesca are rare.

Miss Slayback was neither tall nor short, and she had that sort of generally satisfactory figure which has no particular faults and which is extremely easy to dress well. Her feet were exquisite, her hands small, but not pretty. She had beautiful teeth, but all her features lacked modelling, though they were all in very good proportion. Her head was of a good shape, and her hair was of a glossy brown, and either waved naturally or was made to wave by some very skilful hand. She had dark blue eyes with strong dark lashes, which atoned in a measure for a certain uninteresting flatness and absence of character about the brows and temples, and especially below the eyes themselves and at the angles, where lies a principal seat of facial expression. She spoke French fluently but with a limited and uninteresting vocabulary, so that she often made exactly the same remarks about very different subjects. Yet her point of view being quite different from that of Romans, they listened to what she said with surprise, and sometimes with interest.

Her aunt was not really her aunt, but her uncle's wife, Mrs. Benjamin Slayback, whose maiden name had been Charlotte Lauderdale — a fact which meant a great deal in New York and nothing at all in Rome. She was an ambitious woman, well born and well educated, and her husband had been a member of Congress and was now a senator for Nevada. He was fabulously rich, and his wife, who had married him for his money, having been brought up poor, had lately inherited a vast fortune of her own. Miss Lizzie Slayback was the only daughter of Senator Slayback's elder brother.

Orsino was told a great many of these facts, and they did not interest him in the least, for he had never thought of marrying a foreign heiress. But he was quite sure from the first that Tebaldo had made up his mind to get the girl if he could. The Slaybacks had been in Rome about a month, but Orsino had not chanced to see them, and did not know how long Tebaldo might have known them. It was said that they did not mean to stay much longer, and Tebaldo was doing his best to make good his running in the short time that remained.

It chanced that the first time Orsino came face to face with Tebaldo was when the latter had just been talking with Miss Slayback and was flattering himself that he had made an unusually good impression upon her. He was, therefore, in a singularly good humour, for a man whose temper was rarely good and was often very bad indeed. The two men met in a crowded room. Without hesitation Tebaldo held out his hand cordially to Orsino.

"I am very glad to see you safely back," he said, with a great appearance of frankness. "You are the hero of the hour, you know."

For a moment even Orsino was confused by

the man's easy manner. Even the eyes did not betray resentment. He said something by way of greeting.

"I have had some difficulty in making out who the brigand was whom you shot," continued Tebaldo. "It is an odd coincidence. We think it must have been one of the Pagliuca di Bauso. There is a distant branch of the family — rather down in the world, I believe — it must have been one of them."

"I am glad it was no nearer relation," answered Orsino, not knowing what to say.

"No near relative of mine would have been likely to be in such company," answered the Sicilian, rather stiffly, for he was a good actor when not angry.

"No — of course not — I did not mean to suggest such a thing. It was an odd coincidence, of course." Orsino tried not to look incredulous.

Tebaldo was about to pass on, when an idea presented itself to Orsino's mind, of which he had not thought before now. Slow men sometimes make up their minds suddenly, and not having the experience of habitually acting upon impulses, they are much more apt to make mistakes, on the rare occasions when they are carried away by an idea, and do so. It seemed to him that if he were ever to speak to either of Vittoria's brothers about marrying her, this was the moment to do so. It would be impossible for Tebaldo, in an instant, to deny what he had just now said, and it would be hard for him to find a pretext for refusing to give his sister to such a man. The whole thing might be carried through by a surprise, and Orsino would take the consequences afterwards, and laugh at them, if he were once safely married.

Tebaldo had already turned away to speak to someone else, and Orsino went after him and called him back.

"There is a matter about which I should like to speak to you, Don Tebaldo," he said. "Can we get out of this crowd?"

Tebaldo looked at him quickly and sharply, before he answered by a nod. The two men moved away together to the outer rooms, of which there were three or four, stiffly furnished with pier tables and high-backed gilt chairs, as in most old Roman houses. When they were alone, Orsino stopped.

"It is an important matter," he said slowly. "I wish to speak with you, as being the head of your family."

"Yes," answered Tebaldo, and the lids drooped, vulture-like, at the corners of his eyes, as he met Orsino's look steadily. "By all means. We shall not be interrupted here. I am at your service."

"I wish to marry your sister, and I desire your consent," said Orsino. "That is the whole matter."

It would have been impossible to guess from the Sicilian's face whether he had ever anticipated such a proposition or not. There was absolutely no change in his expression.

"My sister is a very charming and desirable young girl," he said rather formally. "As there seems to be a good deal of liberty allowed to young girls in Rome, as compared with Sicily, you will certainly pardon me if I ask whether you have good reason to suppose that she prefers you in any way."

"I have good reason for supposing so," answered Orsino, but he felt the blood rising to his face as he spoke, for he did not like to answer such a question.

"I congratulate you," said Tebaldo, smiling a little, but not pleasantly. "Personally, I should also congratulate myself on the prospect of having such a brother-in-law. I presume you are aware that my sister has no dowry. We were ruined by my uncle Corleone."

"It is a matter of perfect indifference," replied Orsino.

"You are generous. I presume that you have inherited some private fortune of your own, have you not?"

"No. I am dependent on my father."

"Then — pardon my practical way of looking at the affair," said Tebaldo, accentuating his smile a little, "but, as a mere formality, I think that there must be some proposal from the head of your house. You see, you and Vittoria will be dependent on an allowance from your father, who, again, is doubtless dependent on your grandfather, Prince Saracinesca. As my poor sister has nothing, there must necessarily be some understanding about such an allowance."

"It is just," answered Orsino, but he bit his lip. "My father has an independent estate," he added, by way of correction. "And my mother has all the Astrardente property."

"There is no lack of fortune on your side, my dear Don Orsino. You are, of course, sure of your father's consent, so that an interview with him will be a mere formality. For myself, I give you my hand heartily and wish you well. I shall be happy to meet the Prince of Sant' Ilario at any time which may be agreeable to him."

Orsino felt that the man had got the better of him, but he had to take the proffered hand. Mentally he wondered what strange monster this Tebaldo Pagliuca could be within himself, to grasp the hand that had killed his brother less than a week ago, welcoming its owner as his brother-in-law. But he saw that the very simple and natural request for an interview with his father would probably prove a source of almost insurmountable difficulty.

"I had hoped," he said, "to have had the pleasure of seeing Donna Vittoria here this evening. I shall be obliged to return to Sicily in a day or two. May I see her at your house before I go?"

Tebaldo hesitated a moment.

"You will find her at home with my mother to-morrow afternoon," he answered almost immediately. "I see no reason why you should not call."

"But your mother —" Orsino stopped short.

"What were you going to say?" enquired Tebaldo, blandly.

"You will be kind enough to tell her that I am coming, will you not?" Orsino saw that he was getting into a terribly difficult situation.

"Oh, yes," Tebaldo answered. "I shall take great pleasure in announcing you. She is better, I am glad to say, and I have no doubt that this good news will completely restore her."

Orsino felt a vague danger circling about his heart, as a hawk sails in huge curves that narrow one by one until he strikes his prey. The man was subtle and ready to take advantage of the smallest circumstance with unerring foresight while wholly concealing his real intention.

"Come at three o'clock, if it is convenient," concluded Tebaldo. "And now —" he looked at his watch — "you will forgive me if I leave you. I have an engagement which I must keep."

He shook hands again with great cordiality, and they parted. Tebaldo went out directly, without returning to the inner rooms, but Orsino went back to stay half an hour longer. Out of curiosity he got a friend to introduce him to Miss Lizzie Slayback.

The girl looked up with a bright smile when she heard the great name.

"I have so much wanted to meet you," she said quickly. "You are the man who killed the brigand, are you not? Do tell me all about it!"

He was annoyed, for he could not escape, but he resigned himself and told the story in the fewest possible words.

"How interesting!" exclaimed Miss Slayback. "And we all thought he was the brother of Don Tebaldo. You know Don Tebaldo, of course? I think he is a perfect beauty, and so kind."

Orsino had never thought of Tebaldo Pagliuca as either kind or beautiful, and he said something that meant nothing, in reply.

"Oh, you are jealous of him!" cried the girl, laughing. "Of course! All the men are."

Orsino got away as soon as he could. As a necessary formality he was introduced to Mrs. Slayback. He asked her an idle question about how she liked Rome, such as all Romans ask all foreigners about whom they know nothing.

"How late is it safe to stay here?" she asked, with singular directness, by way of an answer.

"Rome becomes unhealthy in August," said Orsino. "The first rains bring the fever. Until then it is perfectly safe, and one can return in October without danger. The bad time lasts for six weeks to two months, at most."

"Thank you," answered Mrs. Slayback, with a little laugh. "We shall not stay till August, I think. It would be too hot. I suppose that it is hot in June."

"Yes," said Orsino, absently. "I suppose that you would find it hot in June."

He wanted to be alone, and he left her as soon as he could. He walked home in the warm night and reviewed his position, which had suddenly become complicated. It was clear that he must now speak to his father, since he had committed the folly of making his proposal to Tebaldo. It was almost certain that his father would refuse to hear of the marriage, on any consideration, and he knew that his mother disapproved of it. It was clear also that he could not avoid going to call upon Vittoria and her mother on the following afternoon, but he could not understand why Tebaldo had pretended to be so sure that he should be received, when he himself was tolerably certain that Maria Carolina would refuse to see him. That, however, was a simple matter. He should ask for her, and on being told that she could not receive, he should leave his card and go away. But that would not help him to see Vittoria, and it was in order to see her alone before he left that he had suddenly determined to make his proposal to Tebaldo.

He had got himself into a rather serious scrape, and he was not gifted with more tact than the rest of his bold but tactless race. He therefore decided upon the only course which is open to such a man, which was to take his difficulties, one by one, in their natural order and deal with each as best he could.

He had nothing more to hope from his mother's intervention. He knew her unchangeable nature and was well aware that she would now hold her position to the last. She would not oppose his wishes, and that was a great deal gained, but she would not help him either.

Early on the following morning he went to Sant' Ilario's own room, feeling that he had a struggle before him in which he was sure to be defeated, but which he could not possibly avoid. His father was reading the paper over his coffee by the open window, a square, iron-grey figure clad in a loose grey jacket. The room smelt of coffee and cigarettes. Sant' Ilario's perfect contentment and happiness in his surroundings made him a particularly difficult person to approach suddenly with a crucial question. His serene felicity made a sort of resisting shell around him, through which it was necessary to break before he himself could be reached.

He looked up and nodded as Orsino entered. Such visits from his sons were of daily occurrence, and he expected nothing unusual. It was of no use to beat about the bush, and Orsino attacked the main question at once.

"I wish to speak to you about a serious matter, father," he said, sitting down opposite Sant' Ilario.

"I wish Sicily were in China, and San Giacinto in Peru," was the answer.

"It has nothing to do with San Giacinto," said Orsino. "I want to be married."

Sant' Ilario looked up sharply, in surprise. His eldest son's marriage was certainly a serious matter.

"To whom?" he enquired.

"To Vittoria d'Oriani," said Orsino, squaring his naturally square jaw, in anticipation of trouble.

Sant' Ilario dropped the paper, took his cigarette from his lips, and crossed one leg over the other angrily.

"I was afraid so," he said. "You are a fool. Go back to Sicily and do not talk nonsense."

The Saracinesca men had never minced matters in telling each other what they thought.

"I expected that you would say something like that," answered Orsino.

"Then why the devil did you come to me at all?" enquired his father, his grey hair bristling and his eyebrows meeting.

But Orsino was not like him, being colder and slower in every way, and less inclined to anger.

"I came to you because I had no choice but to come," he answered quietly. "I love her, she loves me, and we are engaged to be married. It was absolutely necessary that I should speak to you."

"I do not see the necessity, since you knew very well that I should not consent."

"You must consent in the end, father —"

"I will not. That ends it. It is the worst blood in Italy, and some of the worst blood in Europe. Corleone was a scoundrel, his father was a traitor — "

"That does not affect Donna Vittoria so far as I can see," said Orsino, stubbornly.

"It affects the whole family. Besides, if they are decent people, they will not consent either. It is not a week since you killed Ferdinando Pagliuca — Vittoria's brother —"

"They deny it."

"They lie, I believe."

"That is their affair," said Orsino.

"The fact does not beautify their family character, either," retorted Sant' Ilario. "With the whole of Europe to choose from, excepting a dozen royalties, you must needs fall in love with the sister of a brigand, the niece of a scoundrel, the granddaughter of —"

"Yes — you have said all that. But I have promised to marry her, and that is a side of the question of which you cannot get rid so easily."

"You did not promise her my consent, I suppose. I will not give it. If you choose to marry without it, I cannot hinder you. You can take her and live on her dowry, if she has one."

"She has nothing."

"Then you may live by your wits. You shall have nothing more from me."

"If the wits of the family had ever been worth mentioning, I should ask nothing more," observed Orsino, coldly. "Unfortunately they are not a sufficient provision. You are forcing me into the position of breaking my word to a woman."

"If neither her parents nor yours will consent to your marriage, you are not breaking your engagement. They will not give her to you if you cannot support her. Of course, you can wait until I die. Judging from my father, and from my own state of health at present, it will be a long engagement."

Orsino was silent for a moment. He did not lose his temper even now, but he tried to devise some means of moving Sant' Ilario.

"I spoke to Tebaldo Pagliuca last night," he said, after a pause. "In spite of what you seem to expect, he accepted my proposition, so far as he could."

"Then he is an even greater villain than I had supposed him to be," returned Sant' Ilario.

"That is no reason why you should force me to humiliate myself to him —"

"Send him to me, if you are afraid to face him. I will explain the situation — I will —"

"You will simply quarrel with him, father. You would insult him in the first three words you spoke."

"That is very probable," said Sant' Ilario. "I should like to. He has been scheming to catch you for his sister ever since the evening they first dined here. But I did not think you were such a childish idiot as to be caught so easily."

"No one has caught me, as you call it. I love Vittoria d'Oriani, and she loves me. You have no right to keep us apart because you did not approve of her grandfather and uncle."

"No right? I have no right, you say? Then who has?"

"No one," answered Orsino, simply.

"I have the power, at all events," retorted his father. "I would not have you marry her — would not? I will not. It is materially impossible for you to marry with no money at all, and you shall have none. Talk no more about it, or I shall positively lose my temper."

It occurred to Orsino that it was positively lost already, but as he kept his own, he did not say so. He rose from his seat and calmly lighted a cigarette.

"Then there is nothing more to be said, I suppose," he observed.

"Nothing more on that subject," answered Sant' Ilario. "Not that I have the least objection to saying over again all I have said," he added.

"At all events, you do not pretend that you have any objection to Donna Vittoria herself, do you?"

"No — except that she has made a fool of you. Most women make fools of men, sooner or later."

"Perhaps, but you should be the last person to say so, I think."

"I married with my father's consent," replied Sant' Ilario, as though the fact were an unanswerable argument. "If I had made to him such a proposition as you are making to me, he would have answered in a very different way, my boy, I can tell you!"

"In what way?" asked Orsino.

"In what way? Why, he would have been furiously angry! He would have called me a fool and an idiot, and would have told me to go to the devil."

Orsino laughed in spite of himself.

"What are you laughing at?" enquired Sant' Ilario, sharply, growing hot again in a moment.

"Those are exactly the words you have been saying to me," answered Orsino.

"I? Have I? Well — that only proves that I am like my father, then. And a very good thing, too. It is a pity that you are not more like me than you are. We should understand each other better."

"We may yet understand each other," said Orsino, lingering in the vain hope of finding some new argument.

"No doubt. But not about this matter."

Seeing that it was useless to prolong the discussion, Orsino went away to think matters over. He had been quite sure of his father's answer, of course, but that did not improve the situation at all. It had been a necessity of conscience and honour to go to him, after speaking to Tebaldo on the previous evening, because it was not possible to take his answer for granted. But now it became equally a duty of honour and self-respect to communicate to Tebaldo what Sant' Ilario had said, and to do so was a most unpleasant humiliation. He cared nothing for the fact that his father's refusal might almost seem like an insult to Tebaldo Pagliuca, though he could not quite see how he could make the communication without giving offence. The real trouble was that he should be practically obliged to take back what he had said, and to say that after all, in the face of his family's objections, he could not marry Vittoria at present, and saw no prospect of being able to marry her in the future.

At the same time he wondered how much Tebaldo had told his mother. She also, according to Vittoria's statement, would oppose their marriage with all her power. Yet Tebaldo had professed himself quite certain that she would receive Orsino when he called. There was something mysterious about that.

Orsino made up his mind that he would ask for Tebaldo a quarter of an hour before the time named by the latter, and get over the disagreeable interview before making an attempt to have a word with Vittoria alone.

CHAPTER XVI

ORSINO reached the Corleone's house before three o'clock on that afternoon. They lived on the second floor of a large new building in the Via Venti Settembre, 'Twentieth of September Street,' as it would be in English, so named to commemorate the taking of Rome on that day in 1870.

A porter in livery asked Orsino whom he wished to see, rang an electric bell, spoke through a speaking-tube, took off his cocked hat in order to listen for the answer, and finally told Orsino that he would be received. There is always something mysterious to the looker-on about any such means of communication at a distance, when he does not hear the voice speaking from the other end.

It would not have surprised Orsino, if he had heard, as the porter did, that the answer came back in Tebaldo Pagliuca's voice; but he would then not have been so much surprised, either, at being admitted so readily. Tebaldo, in fact, had told the porter to send the visitor up, for he had been waiting for the porter's bell; but he then told his servant that a gentleman was coming upstairs to see him, who was to be shown into the drawing room at once, whither Tebaldo himself would presently come.

Tebaldo had been quite sure that his mother and sister would be at home at that hour, since the former was not yet well enough to go out; he had been equally sure that his mother would refuse to receive Orsino; he had, therefore, so arranged matters that Orsino should be ushered into her presence unexpectedly, and to accomplish this he had lain in wait in the neighbourhood of the speaking-tube, which came up into the hall of his apartment just inside the door opening upon the stairs.

So far the explanation of what happened is quite simple. It would be a different thing to unravel the complicated and passionate workings of Tebaldo's intricate thoughts. In the first place, in spite of his behaviour in public, he hated Orsino with all his heart for having unwittingly killed his brother, and important as the advantages would be, if Vittoria married the heir of the great house, they by no means outweighed his desire for revenge.

Tebaldo was not an inhuman monster, though a specialist might have said that he had a strong tendency to criminality. He was capable of affection in a certain degree, apart from mere passion. He was unscrupulous, treacherous, tortuous in his reasonings; but he was above all tenacious, and he was endowed with much boldness and daring, of the kind which cast a romantic glamour over crimes of violence. It had been one thing to threaten Ferdinando with the law, if he refused to sign the deed by which Camaldoli was to be sold. It was quite another matter to give his sister to the man who had shot Ferdinando like a wild animal. There the man's humanity had revolted, though Orsino had not guessed it, when they had met and talked together at the party on the previous evening.

On the other hand, his cunning bade him not to put himself in the position of refusing Orsino's request, seeing that he denied his own relationship with his dead brother. It was easy enough for him to bring Orsino and his mother unexpectedly face to face, and to let the young man hear from her lips what she thought of such a union, if indeed the interview should ever get so far as that. Tebaldo could then calmly intrench himself behind his mother's refusal, and yet maintain outward relations with Orsino, while waiting for an opportunity to avenge his brother, which was sure to present itself sooner or later.

Orsino mounted the stairs resolutely, squaring himself to meet Tebaldo and tell him of Sant' Ilario's refusal as briefly and courteously as he could. At the same time he was half painfully and half happily conscious of Vittoria's presence in the house. The pain and the pleasure were intermittent and uncertain.

A servant was waiting and holding the door ajar.

"Don Tebaldo said that he would see me," said Orsino, mechanically.

The man bowed in silence, shut the door upon the landing, and then led the way through the little hall and the antechamber beyond, opened a door, and stood aside to let Orsino pass.

As the door closed behind him, he heard a short and sharp cry in the room, like the warning note of certain fierce wild animals. It was followed instantly by an exclamation of terror in another voice. At the same instant he was aware that there were two women in the room, — Maria Carolina d'Oriani and her daughter.

The mother had been lying on a couch, and on seeing him had started up, supporting herself on her hand. The room was half darkened by the partly closed blinds.

Maria Carolina was dressed in a loose black gown with wide sleeves that showed her thin, bare arms, for the weather was warm. Her white face was thin and ghastly, and her dark eyes gleamed as they caught a little of the light from the window. Orsino stood still two paces from the door.

"Assassin!"

The one word — a word of the people, hissed

from her dry lips with such horror and hatred as Orsino had never heard. There was silence then. Vittoria, as white as her mother, and in an agony of terror, had risen, shrinking and convulsed, grasping with one hand the heavy inner curtain of the window.

Slowly the lean, dark woman left her seat, raising one thin arm, and pointing straight at Orsino's face, her head thrown back, her parched lips parted and showing her teeth.

"Murderer!" she cried. "You dare to show me your face — you dare to show me the hands that killed my son! You dare to stand there before God and me — to hear God's curse on you and mine — to answer for blood — "

Her lips and throat were dry, so that she could not speak, but choked, and swallowed convulsively, and her eyes grew visibly red. Orsino was riveted to the spot and speechless. For a moment he did not even think of Vittoria, cowering back against the curtain. The woman's worn face was changed in her immense wrath, and he could not take his eyes from her. She found her voice again, painfully, fighting against the fiery dryness that choked her.

"With his innocent blood on your hands, you come here — you come to face his very mother in her sacred grief — to see my tears, to tear out the last shreds of my heart, to revile my mother's soul

— to poison the air that breathes sorrow! But you think that I am weak, that I am only a woman. You think, perhaps, that I shall lose my senses and faint. It would be no shame, but I am not of such women."

Her voice gathered fulness but sank in tone as she went on. Still Orsino said nothing, for it was impossible to interrupt her. She must say her say, and curse her curse out, and he must listen, for he would not turn and go.

"You have come," she said, speaking quickly and with still rising fury. "I am here to meet you. I am here to demand blood of you for blood. I am here to curse you, and your name, and your race, your soul and their souls, dead and living, in the name of God, who made my son, of Christ, who died for him, of the Holy Saints, who could not save him from the devil you are — in the name of God, and of man, and of the whole world, I curse you! May your life be a century of cruel deaths, and when you die at last with a hundred years of agony in you, may your immortal soul be damned everlastingly a thousand fold! May you pray and not be heard, may you repent and not be forgiven, may you receive the Holy Sacraments to your damnation and the last Unction with fire in hell! May every living creature that bears your name come to an evil before your eyes, your father — your mother — the men and women of your house, and your unborn children! Blood — I would have blood! May your blood pay for mine, and your soul for my son's soul, who died unconfessed in his sins! Go, assassin! go, murderer of the innocent! go out into the world with my mother's curse on you, and may every evil thing in earth and hell be everlastingly with you and yours, living and dead! Blood! — blood! — blood!"

Her voice was suddenly and horribly extinguished in the last word, as an instrument that is strained too far cracks in a last discordant note and is silent. She stood one moment more, with outstretched hand and fingers that would still make the sign of one more unspoken curse, and then, without warning, she fell back in a heap towards the couch.

Simultaneously, Vittoria and Orsino sprang forward to catch her, but even before Vittoria could reach her she lay motionless on the floor, her head on the edge of the sofa, her hands stretched out on each side of her, her thin fingers twitching desperately at the carpet. A moment later, they were still, too, and she was unconscious, as the two began to lift her up.

For an instant neither looked at the other, but as Orsino laid the fainting woman upon the couch, he raised his eyes to Vittoria's. The girl was still overcome with fear at the whole situation, and trembling with horror at her mother's frightful outbreak of rage and hate. She shook her head in a frightened, hopeless way, as she bent down again and arranged a cushion for Maria Carolina.

"Why did you come — why did you come?" she almost moaned. "I told you—"

Orsino saw that if there was to be any explanation, he must seize the opportunity at once.

"I felt that I must see you before leaving," he answered. "Last night I told your brother Tebaldo that we were engaged to each other. He asked me to come at three o'clock, and said that your mother would receive me — I sent up word to ask — I was told to come up."

"We knew nothing of your coming. It must have been the servant's fault." She did not suspect her brother of having purposely brought about the meeting. "Now go!" she added quickly. "Go, before she comes to herself. Do not let her see you again. Go — please go!"

"Yes — I had better go," he answered. "Can I not see you again? Vittoria — I cannot go away like this—"

As he realized that it might be long before he saw her again, his voice trembled a little, and there was a pleading accent in his words which she had never heard.

"Yes — no — how can I see you?" she faltered. "There is no way — no place — when must you leave?" Maria Carolina stirred, and seemed about to open her eyes. "Go — please go!" repeated

Vittoria, desperately. "She will open her eyes and see you, and it will begin again! Oh, for Heaven's sake—"

Orsino kissed her suddenly while she was speaking, once, sharply, with all his heart breaking. Then he swiftly left the room without looking back, almost trying not to think of what he was doing.

He closed the door behind him. As he turned to look for the way out, in his confusion of mind, the door opposite, which was ajar, opened wide, and he was confronted by Tebaldo, who smiled sadly and apologetically. Orsino stared at him.

"I am afraid you have had an unpleasant scene," said the Sicilian, quickly. "It was a most unfortunate accident—a mistake of the servant, who took you for the doctor. The fact is, my mother seems to be out of her mind, and she will not be persuaded that Ferdinando is alive and well, till she sees him. She was so violent an hour ago that I sent for a doctor—a specialist for insanity. I am afraid I forgot that you were coming, in my anxiety about her. I hope you will forgive me. Of course, you have seen for yourself how she feels towards you at present, and in any case—at such a time—"

He had spoken so rapidly and plausibly that Orsino had not been able to put in a word. Now he paused as if expecting an answer.

"I regret to have been the cause of further disturbing your mother, who indeed seems to be very ill," said Orsino, gravely. "I hope that she will soon recover."

He moved towards the outer hall, and Tebaldo accompanied him to the door of the apartment.

"You will, of course, understand that at such a time it will be wiser not to broach so serious a matter as my sister's marriage," said Tebaldo. "Pray accept again my excuses for having accidentally brought you into so unpleasant a situation."

He timed his words so that he uttered the last when he was already holding the door open with one hand and stretching out the other to Orsino, who had no choice but to take it, as he said goodbye. Tebaldo closed the door and stood still a moment in thought before he went back. As he turned to go in, Vittoria came quickly towards him.

"How did it happen that Don Orsino was brought into the drawing-room?" she asked, still very pale and excited.

"I suppose the servant took him for the doctor," said Tebaldo, coolly, for he knew that she would not stoop to ask questions of the footman. "I am very sorry," he added.

He was going to pass on, but she stopped him.

"Tebaldo — I must speak to you — it will do as well here as anywhere. The nurse is with her," she said, looking towards the drawing-room. "She fainted. Don Orsino told me in two words, before he went away, that he had spoken to you last night, and that you had told him to come here to-day."

"That is perfectly exact, my dear. I have no doubt you have found out that your admirer, our brother's assassin, is a strictly truthful person. He insisted upon seeing you; it was impossible to talk at ease at a party, and I told him to come here, intending to see him myself. I told him to come at three o'clock — I daresay you know that, too?"

"Yes — he said it was to be at three o'clock."

Tebaldo took out his watch and looked at it.

"It is now only four minutes to three," he observed, "and he is already gone. He came a good deal before his time, or I should have been in the antechamber to receive him and take him into my room, out of harm's way, where I could have explained matters to him. As it is, I was obliged to show him out with some apology for the mistake."

"How false you are!" exclaimed Vittoria, her nostrils quivering.

"Because I refuse to ruin you, and our own future position here? I think I am wise, not false. Yes, I myself assured him last night that he did not kill our brother, but one of the Pagliuca di Bauso. I took the hand that did it, and shook it — to save your position in Roman society. You seem to forget that poor Ferdinando had turned himself into an outlaw — in plain language, he was a brigand."

"He was worth a score of his brothers," said Vittoria, who was not afraid of him. "You talk of saving my position. It is far more in order to save your own chance of marrying the American girl with her fortune."

"Oh, yes," answered Tebaldo, with perfect calm. "I include that in the general advantages to be got by what I say. I do not see that it is so very false. On the one hand, Ferdinando was my brother. I shall not forget that. On the other, to speak plainly, he was a criminal. You see I am perfectly logical. No one is obliged to acknowledge that he is related to a criminal—"

"No one is obliged to lie publicly, as you do," broke in Vittoria, rather irrelevantly. "As you make me lie — rather than let people know what kind of men my surviving brothers are."

"You are not obliged to say anything. You do not go out into the world just now, because you have to stay with our mother. I will wager that you have not once told the lie you think so degrading."

"No — I have not, so far. No one has forced me to."

"You need only hold your tongue, and leave the rest to me."

"You make me act a lie — even in not wearing mourning — "

"Of course, if you make morality and honesty depend upon the colour of your clothes," said Tebaldo, scornfully, "I have nothing more to say about it. But it is a great pity that you have fallen in love with that black Saracinesca, the assassin. It will be a source of considerable annoyance and even suffering to you, I daresay. It even annoyed me. It would have been hard to refuse so advantageous an offer without accusing him of Ferdinando's death, which is precisely what I will not do, for the sake of all of us. But you shall certainly not marry him, though you are inhuman enough to love him — a murderer — stained with your own blood."

"He is not a murderer, for it was an accident — and you know it. I am not ashamed of loving him — though I cared for Ferdinando more than any of you. And if you talk in that way — if you come between us —" she stopped.

"What will you do?" he asked contemptuously.

"I will tell the truth about Ferdinando," she said, fixing her eyes upon him.

"To whom, pray?"

"To Miss Slayback and her aunt," answered Vittoria, her gentle face growing fierce.

"Look here, Vittoria," said Tebaldo, more suavely. "Do you know that Orsino Saracinesca is going back to Camaldoli? Yes. And you know that Ferdinando had many friends there, and I have some in the neighbourhood. A letter from me may have a good deal to do with his safety or danger, as the case may be. It would be very thoughtless of you to irritate me by interfering with my plans. It might bring your own to a sudden and rather sad conclusion."

Vittoria turned pale again, for she believed him. He was playing on her fears for Orsino and on her ignorance of the real state of things at Camaldoli. But for the moment his words had the effect he desired. He instantly followed up his advantage.

"You can never marry him," he said. "But if you will not interfere with my own prospects of marriage, nothing shall happen to Saracinesca. Otherwise — " he stopped and waited significantly.

Exaggerating his power, she believed that it extended to giving warrant of death or safety for Orsino, and her imagination left her little choice. At all events, she would not have dared to risk her lover's life by crossing Tebaldo's schemes for himself.

"I am sorry for the American girl," she said. "I like her for her own sake, and I would gladly save her from being married to such a man as you. But if you threaten to murder Don Orsino if I tell her the truth, you have me in your power on that side."

"On all sides," said Tebaldo, scornfully, as he saw how deep an impression he had made on the girl. "I hold his life in my hand, so long as he is at Camaldoli, and while he is there you will obey me. After that, we shall see."

Vittoria met his eyes fiercely for an instant, and then, thinking of Orsino, she bent her head and went away, going back to her mother.

She found her conscious again, but exhausted, lying down on the couch and tended by the nurse, who had been in the house since the news of her son's death had prostrated Maria Carolina. She looked at Vittoria with a vague stare, not exactly recollecting whether the girl had been in the room during her outburst of rage against Orsino or not. Vittoria had been behind her all the time.

"Is he gone?" asked Maria Carolina, in a faint and hollow voice. "I am sorry — I could have cursed him much more — "

"Mother!" exclaimed Vittoria, softly and imploringly, and she glanced at the nurse. "You may go, now," she said to the latter, fearing a fresh outburst. "I will stay with my mother."

The nurse left the room, and the mother and daughter were alone together. They were almost strangers, as has been explained, Vittoria having been left for years at the convent in Palermo, unvisited by any of her family, until her uncle's death had changed their fortunes. It was impossible that there should be much sympathy between them.

There was, on the other hand, a sort of natural feeling of alliance between the two women of the household as against the two men. Maria Carolina was mentally degraded by many years of a semi-barbarous life at Camaldoli, which had destroyed some of her finer instincts altogether, and had almost effaced the effect of early education. She looked up to Vittoria as to a superior being, brought up by noble ladies, in considerable simplicity of life, but in the most extreme refinement of feeling on all essential points, and in an atmosphere of general cultivation and artistic taste, which had not been dreamed of in her mother's youth, though it might seem old-fashioned in some more modern countries. The girl had received an education which had been good of its kind, and very complete, and she was therefore intellectually her mother's superior by many degrees. She knew it, too, and would have despised her mother if she had been like her brothers. As it was, she pitied her, and suffered keenly when Maria Carolina did or said anything in public which showed more than usual ignorance or provinciality.

They had one chief characteristic in common,

and Ferdinando had possessed it also. They were naturally as frank and outspoken as the other two brothers were deceitful and treacherous. As often happens, two of the brothers had inherited more of their character from their father, while the third had been most like his mother. She, poor woman, felt that her daughter was the only one of the family whom she could trust, and looking up to her as she did, she constantly turned to her for help and comfort at home, and for advice as to her conduct in the world.

But since Ferdinando's death her mind, though not affected to the extent described by Tebaldo in speaking with Orsino, had been unbalanced. Nothing which Vittoria could say could make her understand how the catastrophe had happened, and though she had formerly liked Orsino, she was now persuaded that he had lain in wait for her son and had treacherously murdered him. Vittoria had soon found that the only possible means of keeping her quiet was to avoid the subject altogether, and to lead her away from it whenever she approached it. It would be harder than ever to accomplish this since she had seen Orsino.

She lay on her couch, moaning softly to herself, and now and then speaking articulate words.

"My son, my son! My handsome boy!" she cried, in a low voice. "Who will give him back to me? Who will find me one like him?"

Her lamentations were like the mourning of a woman of the people. Vittoria tried to soothe her. Suddenly she sat up and grasped the girl's arm, staring into her face.

"To think that we once thought he might marry you!" she cried wildly. "Curse him, Vittoria! Let me hear you curse him, too! Curse him for your soul's sake! That will do me good."

"Mother! mother!" cried the girl, softly pressing the hand that gripped her arm so roughly.

"What is the matter with you?" asked the half-mad creature fiercely, as her strength came back. "Why will you not curse him? Go down on your knees and pray that all the saints will curse him as I do!"

"For Heaven's sake, mother! Do not begin again!"

"Begin? Ah, I have not ended — I shall not end when I die, but always while he is alive my soul shall pursue him, day and night, and I will — " she broke off. "But you, too — you must wish him evil — you, all of us — then the evil will go with him always, if many of us cast it on him!"

She was like a terrible witch, with her pale face and dishevelled hair, and gaunt arms that made violent gestures.

"Speak, child!" she cried again. "Curse him for your dead brother!"

"No. I will never do that," said Vittoria.

A new light came into the raving woman's eyes.

"You love him!" she exclaimed, half choking. "I know you love him—"

With a vio'ent movement she pushed Vittoria away from her, almost throwing her to the ground. Then she fell back on the couch, and slowly turned her face away, covering her eyes with both her hands. Her whole body quivered, and then was still, then shook more violently, and then, all at once, she broke into a terrible sobbing, that went on and on as though it would never stop while she had breath and tears left.

Vittoria came back to her seat and waited patiently, for there was nothing else to be done. And the sound of the woman's weeping was so monotonous and regular that the girl did not always hear it, but looked across at tne half-closed blinds of the window and thought of her own life, and wondered at all its tragedy, being herself half stunned and dazed.

It was bad enough, as it appeared to her, but could she have known it all as it was to be, and all that she did not yet know of her brother Tebaldo's evil nature, she might, perhaps, have done like her mother, and covered her eyes with her hands, and sobbed aloud in terror and pain.

That might be said of very many lives, perhaps. And yet men do their best to tear the veil of the future, and to look through it into the darkened theatre which is each to-morrow. And many, if they knew the price and the struggle, would give up the prize beyond; but not knowing, and being in the fight, they go on to the end. And some of them win.

CHAPTER XVII

TEBALDO'S own affairs were by no means simple. He had made up his mind to get Miss Lizzie Slayback for his wife, and her fortune for himself; but he could not make up his mind to forget the beautiful Aliandra Basili. The consequence was that he was in constant fear lest either should hear of his devotion to the other, seeing that his brother Francesco was quite as much in love with the singer as he was himself, and but for native cowardice, as ready for any act of treachery which could secure his own ends. By that weakness Tebaldo held him, for the present, in actual bodily fear, which is more often an element even in modern life than is generally supposed. But how long that might be possible Tebaldo could not foresee. At any moment, by a turn of events, Francesco might get out of his power.

Aliandra's season in Rome had been a great success, and her career seemed secured, though she had not succeeded in obtaining an immediate engagement for the London season, which had been the height of her ambition. She had made her appearance too late for that, but the possibility of such a piece of good fortune was quite within her reach for the ensuing year. Being in reality a sensible and conscientious artist, therefore, and having at the same time always before her the rather vague hope of marrying one of the brothers, she had made up her mind to stay in Rome until July to study certain new parts with an excellent master she had found there. She therefore remained where she was, after giving a few performances in the short season after Lent, and she continued to live very quietly with her old aunt in the little apartment they had hired. A certain number of singers and other musicians, with whom she had been brought into more or less close acquaintance in her profession, came to see her constantly, but she absolutely refused to know any of the young men of society who had admired her and sent her flowers during the opera season. With all her beauty and youth and talent, she possessed a very fair share of her father's profound common sense.

Of the two, she very much preferred Francesco, who was gentler, gayer, and altogether a more pleasant companion; but she clearly saw the advantage of marrying the elder brother, who had a very genuine old title for which she could provide a fortune by her voice. There were two or three instances of such marriages which had turned out admirably, though several others had been failures.

She saw no reason why she should not succeed as well as anyone.

Tebaldo, on his part, had never had the smallest intention of marrying her, though he had hinted to her more than once, in moments of passion, that he might do so. Aliandra was as obstinate as he, and, as has been said, possessed the tenacious instinct of self-preservation and the keen appreciation of danger which especially characterize the young girl of the south. She was by no means a piece of perfection in all ways, and was quite capable of setting aside most scruples in the accomplishment of her end. But that desired end was marriage, and there was no probability at all that she should ever lose her head and commit an irrevocable mistake for either of the brothers.

She saw clearly that Tebaldo was in love with her, as he understood love. She could see how his eyes lighted up and how the warm blood mantled under his sallow brown skin when he was with her, and how his hand moved nervously when it held hers. She could not have mistaken those signs, even if her aunt, the excellent Signora Barbuzzi, had not taken a lively interest in the prospects of her niece's marriage, watching Tebaldo's face as an old sailor ashore watches the signs of the weather and names the strength of the wind, from a studding-sail breeze to a gale.

What most disturbed Aliandra's hopes was that

Tebaldo was cautious even in his passion, and seemed as well able to keep his head as she herself. His brother often told her that Tebaldo sometimes, though rarely, altogether lost control of himself for a moment, and became like a dangerous wild animal. But she did not believe the younger man, who was always doing his best to influence her against Tebaldo, and whom she rightly guessed to be a far more dangerous person where a woman was concerned.

Francesco had once frightened her, and she was really afraid to be alone with him. There was sometimes an expression which she dreaded in his satyr-like eyes and a smile on his red lips that chilled her. Once, and she could never forget it, he had managed to find her alone in her room at the theatre, and without warning he had seized her rudely and kissed her so cruelly while she struggled in his arms that her lips had been swollen and had hurt her all the next day. Her maid had opened the door suddenly, and he had disappeared at once without another word. She had never told Tebaldo of that.

Since then she had been very careful. Yet in reality she liked him better, for he could be very gentle and sympathetic, and he understood her moods and wishes as Tebaldo never did, for he was a woman's man, while Tebaldo was eminently what is called a man's man.

Aliandra was, as yet, in ignorance of Miss Slayback's existence, but she saw well enough that Tebaldo was concealing something from her. A woman's faculty for finding out that a man has a secret of some sort is generally far beyond her capacity for discovering what that secret is. He appeared to have engagements at unusual times, and there was a slight shade of preoccupation in his face when she least expected it. On the other hand, he seemed even more anxious to please her than formerly, when he was with her, and she even fancied that his manner expressed a sort of relief when he knew that he could spend an hour in her company uninterrupted.

When she questioned him, he said that he was in some anxiety about his affairs, and his engagements, according to his own account, were with men of business. But he never told what he was really doing. He had not even thought it necessary to inform her of the sale of Camaldoli. Though she was a native of the country, he told her precisely what he told everyone in regard to Ferdinando Pagliuca's death.

"Eh — you say so," she answered. "But as for me, I do not believe you. There never was but one Ferdinando Pagliuca, he was your brother, and he was a friend of all the brigands in Sicily. You may tell these Romans about the Pagliuca di Bauso, but I know better. Do you take me for a Roman? We of Randazzo know what a brigand is!"

"You should, at all events," answered Tebaldo, laughing, "for you are all related. It is one family. If you knew how many brigands have been called Basili, like you!"

"Then you and I are also related!" she laughed, too, though she watched his face. "But as for your brother, may the Lord have him in peace! He is dead, and Saracinesca killed him."

Tebaldo shrugged his shoulders, but showed no annoyance.

"As much as you please," he answered. "But my brother Ferdinando is alive and well in Palermo."

"So much the better, my dear friend. You need not wear mourning for him, as so many people are doing at Santa Vittoria."

"What do you mean?" asked Tebaldo, uneasily.

"Did you ever hear of Concetta, the beautiful daughter of Don Atanasio, the apothecary?" asked Aliandra, quietly smiling.

Tebaldo affected surprise and ignorance.

"It is strange," continued the singer, "for you admire beauty, and she is called everywhere the Fata del' Etna, — the Fairy of Etna, — and she is one of the most beautiful girls in the whole world. My father knows her father a little — of course, he is only an apothecary — " she shrugged her shoulders apologetically — "but in the country one knows everybody. So I have seen her sometimes, as at the fair of Randazzo, when she and her father have had a biscuit and a glass of wine at our house. But we could not ask them to dinner, because the mayor and his wife were coming, and the lieutenant of carabineers — an apothecary! You understand?"

"I understand nothing beyond what you say," said Tebaldo. "You did not consider the apothecary of Santa Vittoria good enough to be asked to meet the mayor of Randazzo. How does that affect me?"

"Oh, not at all!" laughed Aliandra. "But everything is known, sooner or later. Ferdinando, your brother, was at the fair, too — I remember what a beautiful black horse he had, as he rode by our house. But he did not come in, for he did not know us. Now, when Don Atanasio and Concetta went out, he was waiting a little way down the street, standing and holding his horse's bridle. I saw, for I looked through the chinks of the blinds to see which way Concetta and her father would go. And your brother bowed to the ground when they came near him. Fancy! To an apothecary's daughter! Just as I have seen you bow to the Princess of Sant' Ilario in the Villa Borghese. She is Saracinesca's mother, is she not? Very well. I tell you the truth when I tell you that Don Ferdinando took the two to dine with him in the best room at the inn. They say he thought nothing good enough for the apothecary's daughter, though he was of the blood of princes! But now Concetta wears mourning. Perhaps it is not for him? Eh?"

Aliandra had learned Italian very well when a child, and was even taking lessons in French, in order to be able to sing in Paris. But as she talked with Tebaldo she fell back into her natural dialect, which was as familiar to him as to herself. He loved the sound of it, though he took the greatest pains to overcome his own Sicilian accent in order not to seem provincial in Rome. But it was pleasant to hear it now and then in the midst of a life of which the restraints were all disagreeable to him, while many of them were almost intolerably irksome.

"How much better our language is than this stilted Roman!" he exclaimed, by way of suddenly turning the conversation. "I often wish you could sing your operas in Sicilian."

"I often sing you Sicilian songs," she answered. "But it is strange that Concetta should wear mourning, is it not?"

"Leave Concetta alone, and talk to me about yourself. I have never seen her — "

"Do not say such things!" laughed Aliandra. "I do not believe much that you say, but you will soon not let me believe anything at all. Everyone has seen Concetta. They sing songs about her even in Palermo — La Fata del' Etna — "

"Oh, I have heard of her, of course, by that name, but I never remember seeing her. At all events, you are ten times more beautiful than she — "

"I wish I were!" exclaimed the artist, simply. "But if you think so, that is much."

"It would be just the same if you were ugly," said Tebaldo, magnanimously. "I should love you just as I do — to distraction."

"To distraction?" she laughed again.

"You know it," he answered, with an air of conviction. "I love you, and everything that belongs to you — your lovely face, your angelic voice, your words, your silence — too much."

"Why too much?"

"Because I suffer."

"There is a remedy for that, my dear Tebaldo."

"Tell me!"

"Marry me. It is simple enough! Why should you suffer?".

Her laughter was musical and sunny, but there was a little irony in its readiness to follow the words.

"You know that we have often spoken of that," he answered, being taken unawares. "There are difficulties."

"So you always say. But then it would be wiser of you not to love me any more, but to marry where you do not find those difficulties. Surely it should be easy!"

She spoke now with a little scorn, while watching him; and as she saw the vulture-like droop of his eyelids she knew that she had touched him, though she could not quite tell how. She had never spoken so frankly to him before.

"Not so easy as you think," he replied, with a rather artificial laugh.

"Then you have tried?" she asked. "I had thought so! And you have failed? My condolences!"

"I? Tried to marry?" he cried, realizing how far she was leading him. "What are you making me say?"

"I am trying to make you tell the truth," she answered, with a change of tone. "But it is not easy, for you are clever at deceiving me, and I wonder that you cannot deceive the woman you wish to marry."

"I do not wish to marry anyone," he protested.

"No — not even me. Me, least of all, because I am not good enough to marry you, though you are good enough to pursue me with what you call your love. I am only an artist, and you must have a princess, of course. I have only my voice, and you want a solid fortune. I have only my honour, but you want honours through your wife for yourself, and you would tear mine to rags if I yielded a hair's-breadth. You make a mistake, Don Tebaldo Pagliuca. I am a Sicilian girl and I came of honest people. You may suffer as much as you please, but unless you will marry me, you may go on suffering, for you shall not ruin me."

She spoke strongly, with a strange mixture of theatrical and commonplace expressions; but she was in earnest, and he knew it, and in her momentary anger she was particularly fascinating to him. Yet her speech made no real impression upon his mind. He tried to take her hand, but she drew it away sharply.

"No," she said. "I have had enough of this love-making, this hand-taking, and this faith-breaking. You sometimes speak of marrying me, and then you bring up those terrible, unknown difficulties, which you never define. Yes, you are a prince — but there are hundreds of them in our Italy. Yes, I am only an artist, but some people say that I am a great artist — and there are very few in Italy, or anywhere else. If it is beneath your dignity to marry a singer, Signor Principe di Corleone, then go and take a wife of your own class. If you love me, Tebaldo Pagliuca, as an honest man loves an honest woman — and God knows I am that — then marry me, and I, with my voice, will make you a fortune and buy back your estates, besides being a faithful wife to you. But if you will not do that, go. You shall not harm my good name by being perpetually about me, and you shall not touch the tips of my fingers with your lips until you are my lawful husband. There, I have spoken. You shall know that a Sicilian girl is as good as a Roman lady — better, perhaps."

Tebaldo looked at her in some surprise, and his mind worked rapidly, remembering all she had said during the preceding quarter of an hour. She spoke with a good deal of natural dignity and force, and he was ready to admit that she was altogether in earnest. But his quick senses missed a certain note which should have been in her tones if this had been a perfectly spontaneous outburst. It was clear, as it always had been, that she wished to marry him. It was not at all clear that she loved him in the least. It struck him instantly that she must have heard something of his attention to the foreign heiress, and that she had planned this scene in order to bring matters to a crisis. He was too sensible not to understand that he himself was absurdly in love with her, in his own way, and that she knew it, as women generally do, and could exasperate him, perhaps, into some folly of which he might repent, by simply treating him coldly, as she threatened.

During the silence which followed, she sat with folded arms and half-closed eyes, looking at him defiantly from under her lids.

"You do me a great injustice," he said at last.

"I am sorry," she answered. "I have no choice. I value my good name as a woman, besides my reputation as an artist. You do not justify yourself in the only way in your power, by explaining clearly what the insuperable difficulties are in the way of our marriage."

The notary's daughter did not lack logic.

"I never said that they were insuperable —"

"Then overcome them, if you want me," answered Aliandra, implacably.

"I said that there were difficulties, and there are great ones. You speak of making a fortune by your voice, my dear Aliandra," he continued, his tones sweetening. "But you must understand that a man who is a gentleman does not like to be dependent on his wife's profession for his support."

"I do not see that it is more dignified to depend on his wife's money, because she has not earned it by hard work," retorted the singer, scornfully.

"It is honestly earned."

"The honour is entirely yours," said Tebaldo. "The world would grant me no share in it. Then there are my mother's objections, which are strong ones," he went on quickly. "She has, of course, a right to be consulted, and she does not even know you."

"It is in your power to introduce me to your mother whenever you please."

"She is too ill to see anyone—"

"She has not always been ill. You have either been afraid to bring an artist to your mother's house, which is not flattering to me, or else you never had the slightest intention of marrying me, in spite of much that you have said. Though I have heard you call your brother Francesco a coward, I think he is braver than you, for he would marry me to-morrow, if I would have him."

"And live on what you earn," retorted Tebaldo, with ready scorn.

"He has as much as you have," observed Aliandra. "Your uncle left no will, and you all shared the property equally—"

"You are not a notary's daughter for nothing," laughed Tebaldo. "That is true. But there was very little to share. Do you know what was left when the debts were paid? A bit of land here in Rome—that was all, besides Camaldoli. Both have been sold advantageously, and we have just enough to live decently all together. We should be paupers if we tried to separate."

"You are nothing if not plausible. But you will forgive me if I say that this difficulty has the air of being really insuperable. You absolutely refuse to share what I earn, and you are absolutely incapable of earning anything yourself. That being the case, the sooner you go away the better, for you can never marry me, on your own showing, and you are injuring my reputation in the meantime."

"I am engaged in speculations, in which I hope to make money," said Tebaldo. "I often tell you that I have appointments with men of business —"

"Yes, you often tell me so," interrupted Aliandra, incredulously.

"You are cold, and you are calculating," retorted Tebaldo, with a sudden change of manner, as though taking offence at last.

"It is fortunate for me that I am not hot-headed and foolish," replied Aliandra, coolly.

They parted on these terms. She believed that her coldness would bring him to her feet if anything could; but he was persuaded that his brother had betrayed him and had told her about the American heiress.

CHAPTER XVIII

ORSINO made his preparations for returning to Sicily with a heavy heart. His situation was desperate at present, for he had exhausted his ingenuity in trying to discover some means of seeing Vittoria a last time. To leave San Giacinto to do what he could with Camaldoli and refuse to go back at all, for the present, which seemed to be his only chance of a meeting with Vittoria, was a course against which his manliness revolted. Even if there had been no danger connected with the administration of the new estate, he would not have abandoned his cousin at such a time, after promising to help him, and indeed to undertake all work connected with the place. San Giacinto was a busy man, to whom any sacrifice of time might suddenly mean a corresponding loss of money, for which Orsino would hold himself responsible if he brought about the delay. But as it was, since the position he had promised to fill was a dangerous one, nothing could have induced him to withdraw from the undertaking. It would have seemed like running away from a fight.

It was a consolation to have his brother's company, as far as anything could console him, though he could not make up his mind for some time to confide in Ippolito, who had always laughed at him for not marrying, and who could probably not understand why he had now allowed himself to fall in love with one of the very few young women in the world whom he might be prevented from marrying. He was grave and silent as he put together a few books in his own room, vaguely wondering whether he should ever read them.

Ippolito was collecting a number of loose sheets of music that lay on the piano, on a chair beside it, on the table among Orsino's things, and even on the floor under the instrument. He had taken off his cassock, because it was warm, and he wore a grey silk jacket which contrasted oddly with his black silk stockings and clerical stock. From time to time, without taking his cigar from his lips, he hummed a few notes of a melody in the thin but tuneful voice which seems to belong to so many musicians and composers, interrupting himself presently and blowing a cloud of smoke into the air. Now and then he looked at Orsino as though expecting him to speak.

At last, having got his manuscript music into some sort of order, he sat down at the piano to rest himself by expressing an idea he had in his head.

"How glad you will be not to hear a piano at

Camaldoli," he said, stopping as suddenly as he had begun.

"It is a horrible instrument," Orsino said, "but it never disturbs me, and it seems to amuse you."

Ippolito laughed.

"That is what you always say, but I know you will be glad to be rid of it, and it will do me good to play the organ at Santa Vittoria for a change. As that is three-quarters of a mile away, it will not disturb you."

"Nothing disturbs me," replied Orsino, rather sadly.

Ippolito made up his mind to speak at last.

"Orsino," he began quietly, "I know all about you and Donna Vittoria. As we are going to be so much together, it is better that I should tell you so. I hate secrets, and I would rather not make a secret of knowing yours — if it is one."

Orsino had looked round sharply when the priest had first spoken, but had then gone back to what he was doing.

"I am glad you know," he said, "though I would not have told you. I have spoken to our father and mother about it. The one calls me a fool, and the other thinks me one. They are not very encouraging. As for her family, her mother curses me for having killed her favourite son, and her brothers pretend that she is mad and then intrench themselves behind her to say that it is impossible. I do not blame them much — Heaven knows, I do not blame her at all. All the same, Vittoria and I love each other. It is an impossible situation. I cannot even see her to say goodbye. I wish I could find a way out of it!" He laughed bitterly.

"I wish I could," echoed his brother. "But I am only a priest, and you call me a dilettante churchman, at that. Let us see. Let us argue the case as though we were in the theological school. No — I am serious — you need not frown. How many things can happen? Three, I think. There are three conceivable terminations. Either you part for ever and forget each other —"

"You may eliminate that," observed Orsino.

"Very well. Or else you continue to love each other, in which event you must either succeed in getting married, or not, and those are the other two cases."

"One does not need to be a theologian to see that. Similarly, a man must either live or die, and a door must be either open or shut, on pain of not being a door at all."

"I have not finished," objected Ippolito. "In fact, I have only begun. For the sake of argument, we will assume first that you continue to love each other, but cannot get married."

"That is the present position."

"It is not a position which usually lasts long. At the end of a certain time you will naturally cease to love each other, and we obtain a second time the case which you at first eliminated."

"Eliminate it again," said Orsino, gravely.

"Very well. There remains only one possible issue, after your eliminations. You must be married. On any other assumption you will forget each other. Now in such cases as yours, how do people act? You are a layman, and it is your business to know."

"When both are of age they 'respectfully require' their respective parents to give their consent. If it is refused, they marry and the law protects them."

"So does the church," said the priest. "But it does not provide them with an income afterwards, nor in any way guarantee them against the consequences of family quarrels. Those are subdivisions of the case which you can neither modify nor eliminate."

"Well," said Orsino, wearily, "what do you conclude for all this?"

Ippolito's gentle face grew suddenly grave, and seemed squarer and more like his brother's.

"From what I know of the world," he answered, "I conclude that men who mean to do things, do them, and let the consequences take care of themselves. If you mean to marry Vittoria d'Oriani, you will marry her, without any help and without anyone's advice. If you do not mean to marry her, you will not, because, under the circumstances, she can assuredly not marry you, as women have been known to marry husbands almost against their will."

"You have a singularly direct way of putting things," observed Orsino, thoughtfully.

"That is simply the result of your eliminations," answered the priest. "If you do not love her enough to take her in spite of everything and everybody, you must restore into the list of possibilities the certainty that before long you will not love her at all. For I conceive that half a love is no better as a basis of warfare than half a faith. I do not mean to breed war with our father and mother. That is a serious matter. I am only pursuing the matter to its logical conclusion and end, in words, as you will have to do in your acts, sooner or later."

"Meanwhile I am doing nothing," said Orsino. "And I am horribly conscious that I am doing nothing."

"You are going away," remarked Ippolito. "That is not inaction."

"It is worse than inaction — it is far worse than doing nothing at all."

"I am not so sure of that. It is sometimes a good thing to force an interval between events. In the first place, I often hear it said that a separation strengthens a great passion, but destroys a small one. All passions seem great when the object is present, but distance brings out the truth. By the time you have been a month at Camaldoli you will know whether it is essential to your happiness to marry Vittoria d'Oriani, or not."

"And suppose that it is? We come back to the same situation again."

"Yes — we come back to the eternal situation of force against force."

"And you mean that I should use force? That is — that I should marry her and take all the consequences, no matter what they may be?"

"I do not mean that you should. I distinguish. I mean that you will, that is all. I am not considering the moral ground of the action, but the human source of it. Your marriage may be the cause of great difficulties and complications, but if you are persuaded that it is quite necessary to your life to marry that young lady, you will marry her. It is by no means an impossible thing to accomplish, nor even a very difficult one."

"You do not tell me how far it is a matter of conscience to consider the consequences."

"It is of no use to tell courageous men that sort of thing," said the priest. "They take the consequences, that is all. No man who ever wanted a thing with his whole heart ever stopped to consider how his getting it would affect other people, unless the point of honour was involved."

"And there is no point of honour here, is there?" asked Orsino, as a man asks a question to which he knows the answer.

"You know what you have said to Donna Vittoria," answered Ippolito. "I do not."

"I have asked her to marry me, and she has consented." Orsino laughed a little dryly. "That is the way one puts it, I believe," he added.

"Then I should say that unless she, of her own accord, releases you from your word, the point of honour lies in not withdrawing it," replied the priest. "If you did, it would mean that you were not willing to take the risks involved in keeping it, would it not?"

"Of course it would. I wish you could make our father see that."

"People of the previous generation never see what happens in ours. They only infer what ought to happen if all their own prejudices had been canonical law for fifty years."

"That is sedition," laughed Orsino, whose spirits had risen suddenly.

"No, it is criticism, and criticism is only called sedition under despotic governments. There is no reason why grown men, like you and me, should not criticise their fathers and mothers up to a certain point, within limits of respect. We honour them, but they are not gods, that we should worship them. When we were little boys we supposed

that our father knew everything about everything.
We are aware, now, that we understand many
things which have grown up in our day much better
than he does. To go on supposing that he
knew everything, in spite of evidence, would be
a gross form of superstition. Superstition, I suppose,
means a survival, to wit, the survival of some
obsolete belief. That is exactly what it would be
in us to artificially maintain the belief of our
childhood in our parents' omniscience. Has your
love for Donna Vittoria anything to do with the
actual amount of her knowledge at any moment?
No. But love appears to be made up of passion
and affection. Therefore affection is independent
of any such knowledge in its object. Therefore
we love our parents quite independently of what
they know or do not know about life, or mathematics,
and we may, consequently, criticise such
knowledge in them on its own merits, without in
the least detracting from our affection for themselves."

"You are a very satisfactory brother," said Orsino,
smiling at his brother's speech. "But I am
not sure that you are a strictly orthodox priest on
the question of family relations."

"I give you a theory of such relations," answered
Ippolito. "In actual practice I believe that our
mother is one of the wisest women living, without
being in the smallest degree intellectual. It

is true that my experience of women is limited, but I hear a great deal of talk about them. She is fond of Donna Vittoria, I am sure."

"Yes — very. But she sees fifty reasons why I had better not marry her."

"So do I," said Ippolito, calmly.

"You? Why, you have been urging me to marry her in spite of everything!"

"Oh, no. I have only proved to you that if you love her enough, you will marry her in spite of everything. That is a very different thing."

"Priest!" laughed Orsino. "Sophist!"

"Anything you like," answered Ippolito, swinging round on the piano stool and striking a chord. "All the same, I hope you may marry her, and have no bad consequences to deal with, and I will help you if I can."

"Thank you," said Orsino; but his voice was drowned by a burst of loud and intricate music, as Ippolito's white fingers flew over the piano while he stared at the ceiling, his head thrown back, his cigar sticking up from between his teeth, he himself apparently unaware of what his hands were doing, and merely listening to the music.

Orsino was momentarily cheered and encouraged by all his brother had said, but the situation was not materially improved thereby. It was, indeed, almost as bad as it could be, and an older and wiser man than Orsino would have expected that something must occur before long, either to improve it, or to cut it short at once and for ever, for the simple reason that it could neither last, as it stood, nor be made more difficult by anything which could happen.

CHAPTER XIX

WHEN Orsino and Ippolito reached Camaldoli everything seemed to be quiet, and San Giacinto himself was greatly encouraged by the turn matters had taken. During the first day or two after Orsino's departure there had still been considerable curiosity among the people of Santa Vittoria, and more than once San Giacinto had made little speeches, in his direct manner, to the peasants and villagers who hung about in the neighbourhood of the big old house. But after that he had not been disturbed, and everything appeared to be progressing favourably. The year was one of abundance, the orange crop, which in Sicily is all gathered before May, had turned out well, the grapes promised an abundant vintage, and even the olives had blossomed plentifully, though it was still too early to make accurate predictions about the oil. On the whole the prospects for the year were unusually satisfactory, and San Giacinto congratulated himself on having chanced to buy the place in a good year. In an agricultural country like that part of Sicily, the temper of the people is profoundly affected by the harvest.

The outlaws had not been heard of in the neighbourhood since Ferdinando Pagliuca's death. They were said to be in the region about Noto, at some distance from Camaldoli, towards the southwest. San Giacinto was surprised at not having even received an anonymous letter from one of Ferdinando's friends. He did not suppose that the present pacific state of things could last forever, but he had been prepared to meet with a great deal more opposition in what he did.

On the other hand, he was hindered at every step by small difficulties which always seemed to be perfectly natural. If he wished to build a bit of wall, he found it impossible to obtain stone or quicklime, though there were plenty of masons professing themselves ready to work. He pointed to a quantity of slaked lime drying in a deep tank near the gate of Santa Vittoria.

"Eh," said the head mason, shaking his head, "that belongs to the mayor, and he will not sell it."

And, in fact, the mayor flatly refused to part with a single hodful of the lime, saying that he himself was going to repair his house.

The masons said that by and by it could be got from the lime-burners, who had sold their last burning to a man in Randazzo. Stone was to be had for the quarrying, in the black lands above Camaldoli, but there were no quarrymen in Santa

Vittoria, and the gang of them that lived higher up Etna had taken a large contract.

"Patience," said the head mason, gravely. "In time you will have all you want."

As the bit of wall was not a very important matter, San Giacinto did not care to go to the expense of bringing material from a great distance, and decided to wait. Meanwhile he hired certain men from Bronte to come and clear out all the bush and scrub from among the trees. They came without tools. He gave them tools that belonged to the tenants of Camaldoli, the same which the latter had lent him on the first day to make a clearing close to the house. The Bronte men worked for two hours and then came out of the brush and sat down quietly in the sun.

"The tools are not good for anything," they said gravely. " We cannot work with them."

"What is the matter with them?" asked San Giacinto.

"They are dull. They would not cut strings."

"Take them away and have them ground," said San Giacinto.

"Are there knife-grinders in this country?" asked the men. "Where are they? No. They come, they stay a day, perhaps two days, and they go away."

San Giacinto looked at the men thoughtfully a moment, then turned on his heel and left them to their own devices. He began to understand. The men neither wished to refuse to work for him, nor dared to do the work they undertook, when its execution would in any way improve the defensive conditions of Camaldoli. San Giacinto came back when the men were gone, with two or three of the soldiers, took a hatchet himself, and leading the way proceeded to cut away the thorns and brambles, systematically clearing the ground so as to leave no cover under which an armed man could approach the house unnoticed. He regularly devoted a part of each day to the work, until it was finished.

As soon as Ferdinando's body had been removed, there had been no difficulty in getting men to work indoors, and by the time Orsino arrived, considerable improvements had been effected. But the men would not have begun work in a house where an unburied dead person was still lying.

The three Saracinesca strolled up to Santa Vittoria late in the afternoon, San Giacinto and Orsino carrying their rifles, while Ippolito walked along with his hands behind him, just catching up his little silk mantle, staring hard at all the new sights of the road, and mentally wondering what sort of instrument he should find in the little church.

The place was a mere village without any mediæval wall, though there was a sort of archway at the principal entrance which was generally called the gate. Just beyond the shoulder of the mountain, away from Camaldoli, and about fifty yards from this gateway of the village, was a little white church with a tiled roof. It had a modern look, as though it had been lately restored. Then the village straggled down the rough descent towards the shallow valley beyond, having its own church in the little market place. It was distinctly clean, having decently paved streets and solid stone houses with massive mullions, and iron balconies painted red. There were a few small shops of the kind always seen in Italian villages. The apothecary's was in the market place, the general shop was in the main street, opposite a wine-seller's, the telegraph office — a very recent innovation — was over against the chemist's and was worked by the postmaster, and in what had once been a small convent, further on, at the outskirts of the town, the carabineers were lodged. At San Giacinto's request, fifty men of the line infantry had been quartered in the village within the last few days, the order having been telegraphed from Rome on Orsino's representations to the Minister of the Interior. The people treated the men and their two young officers civilly, but secretly resented their presence.

Nowadays, every Italian village has a walled cemetery at some distance from it. The burial ground of Santa Vittoria overlooked Camaldoli;

being situated a quarter of a mile from the little white church and on the other side of the hill, so that it was out of sight of the village. It was a grimly bare place. Four walls, six feet high, of rough tufo and unplastered, enclosed four or five acres of land. A painted iron gate opened upon the road, and against the opposite wall, inside, was built a small mortuary chapel. The cemetery had not been long in use, and there were not more than a score of black crosses sticking in the earth to mark as many graves. There was no pretence at cultivation. The clods were heaped up symmetrically at each grave, and a little rough grass grew on some of them. There was not a tree, nor a flower, nor a creeper to relieve the dusty dreariness of it, and the road itself was not more dry and arid. The little grass that grew had pushed itself up just in the gate-way, where few feet ever passed, and everyone knows what a desolate look a grass-grown entrance gives to any place, even to a churchyard. There were low, round curbstones on each side of the gate.

The three gentlemen strolled slowly up the hill in the warm afternoon sunshine, talking as they came. Ippolito was a little ahead of the others, for he was light on his feet, and walked easily.

"That is the cemetery," observed San Giacinto to Orsino, pointing at the hill. "That is where they buried your friend Ferdinando Corleone on the day you left. I suppose they will put up a monument to him."

"His brothers will not," answered Orsino. "They disown all connexion with him."

"Amiable race!" laughed San Giacinto. "There is a figure like a monument sitting outside the gate," he added. "Do you see it?"

"It is a woman in black," said Orsino. "She is sitting on something by the roadside."

They were still a long way off, but both had good eyes.

"She is probably resting and sitting on her bundle," observed San Giacinto.

"She is sitting on a stone,—on one of the curbstones," said Ippolito. "She has her head bent down."

"He sees better than either of us," said Orsino, with a laugh. "I wonder why nobody ever expects a priest to do anything particularly well except pray? Ippolito can walk as well as we can, he sees better, he could probably beat either of us with a pistol or a rifle if he tried, and I am sure he is far more clever in fifty ways than I am. Yet everyone in the family takes it for granted that he is no better than a girl at anything that men do. He was quite right about the woman. She is bending over—her face must be almost touching her knees. It is a strange attitude."

"Probably some woman who has a relation buried in the cemetery — her child, perhaps," suggested Ippolito. "She stops at the gate to say a prayer when she goes by."

"Then she would kneel, I should think," answered Orsino.

Almost unconsciously they all three quickened their pace a little, though the hill grew steeper just there. As they drew near, the outline of the woman in black became distinct against the dark tufo wall behind her, for the sunlight fell full upon her, where she sat. It was a beautiful outline, too, full of expression and simple tragedy. She sat very low, on the round curbstone, one small foot thrust forward and leading the folds of the loose black skirt, both white hands clasped about the higher knee, towards which the covered head bent low, so that the face could not be seen at all. Not a line nor fold stirred as the three men came up to her.

Orsino recognized Concetta, though he could not see her features. Her exceptional grace betrayed itself unmistakably, and he should have known anywhere the white hands that had been lifted up to him when he had stood at the window in the grey dawn. But he said nothing about it to San Giacinto, for he understood her grief, and he could not have spoken of her without being heard by her just then.

But Ippolito went up to her, before his brother

could hinder him. She was a lonely and unhappy creature, and he was one of those really charitable people who cannot pass by any suffering without trying to help it. He stood still beside her.

"What is your trouble?" he asked gently. "Can anyone help you?"

She did not move at first, but a voice of pain came with slow accents from under the black shawl that fell over her face, almost to her knee.

"God alone can help the dead," it answered.

"But you are alive, my child," said Ippolito, bending down a little.

The covered head moved slowly from side to side, denying.

"Who are you, that speak of life?" asked the sorrowful young voice. "Are you the Angel of the Resurrection? Go in peace, with Our Lady, for I am dead."

Ippolito thought that she must be mad, and that it might be better to leave her alone. His brother and cousin had gone on, up the road, and were waiting for him at a little distance.

"May you find peace and comfort," said the young priest, quietly, and he moved away.

But he turned to look back at her, for she seemed the saddest woman he had ever seen, and her voice was the saddest he had ever heard. Something in his own speech had stirred her a little, for when he looked again she had raised her head, and was lifting the black shawl so that she could see him. She was about to speak, and he stopped where he was, two paces from her, surprised by her extraordinary beauty and unnatural pallor.

"Who are you?" she asked slowly. "You are a stranger."

"I am Ippolito Saracinesca, a priest," answered the young man.

At the name, she started, and her sad eyes opened wide. Then she saw the other two men standing in the road a little way off. Slowly, and with perfect grace, she rose from her low seat.

"And those two — there — who are they?" she asked.

"They are also Saracinesca," said Ippolito. "The one is my brother, the other is my cousin. We are three of the same name."

He answered her question quite naturally, but he felt sure that she was mad. By this time San Giacinto was growing impatient, and he began to move a few steps nearer to call Ippolito. But the latter found it hard to turn away from the deep eyes and the pale face before him.

"Then there were three of you," said Concetta, in a tone in which scorn sharpened grief. "It is no wonder that you killed him between you."

"Whom?" asked Ippolito, very much surprised at the new turn of her speech.

"Whom?" All at once there was something

wild in her rising inflexion. "You ask of me who it was whom you killed down there in the woods? Of me, Concetta? Of me, his betrothed? Of me, who prayed to your brother, there, that I might be let in, to wash my love's face with my tears? But if I had known to whom I was praying, there would have been two dead men lying there in the chapel of Camaldoli — there would have been two black crosses in there, behind the gate — do you see? There it is! The last on the left. No one has died since, but if God were just, the next should be one of you, and the next another, and then another — ah, God! If I had something in these hands — "

She had pointed at Ferdinando's grave, throwing her arm backwards, while she kept her eyes on Ippolito. Now, with a gesture of the people, as she longed for a weapon, she thrust out her small white fists, tightly clenched, towards the priest's heart, then opened them suddenly, in a despairing way, and let her arms fall to her sides.

"Saracinesca, Saracinesca," she repeated slowly, her voice sinking; "three Saracinesca have made one widow! But one widow may yet make many widows, and many mourning mothers, and the justice of Heaven is not the justice of man."

San Giacinto and Orsino had gradually approached Ippolito, and now stood beside him, facing the beautiful, wild girl, in her desolation.

Grave and thoughtful, the three kinsmen stood side by side.

There was nothing theatrical nor unreal in the situation. One of themselves had killed the girl's betrothed husband, whom she had loved with all her soul. That was the plain fact, and Orsino had never ceased to realize it. Unhesitatingly, and in honourable self-defence, he had done a deed by which many were suffering greatly, and he was brought face to face with them in their grief. Somehow, it seemed unjust to him that the girl should accuse his brother and his cousin of Ferdinando's death.

As she paused, facing them, breathless with the wave of returning pain, rather than from speaking, Orsino moved forward, a little in front of Ippolito.

"I killed Ferdinando Corleone," he said, gravely. "Do not accuse us all three, nor curse us all three."

She turned her great eyes to his face, but her expression did not change. Possibly she did not believe him.

"The dead see," she answered slowly. "They know — they know — they see both you and me. And the dead do not forget."

A flying cloud passed over the sun, and the desolate land was suddenly all black and grey and stony, with the solemn vastness of the mountain behind. Concetta drew her shawl up over her head, as though she were cold, and turned from the three men with a simple dignity, and knelt down on the rough, broken stones, where the blades of coarse grass shot up between, close to the gate, and she clasped her hands together round one of the dusty, painted iron rails.

"Let us go," said San Giacinto's deep voice. "It is better to leave her, poor girl."

She did not look back at them as they walked quietly up the road. Her eyes were fixed on one point, and her lips moved quickly, forming whispered words.

"Maria Santissima, let there be three black crosses! Mother of God, three black crosses! Mother of Sorrows, three black crosses!"

And over and over again, she repeated the terrible little prayer.

CHAPTER XX

THE three men entered the village and walked through the main street. The low afternoon sun was shining brightly again, and only the people who lived on the shady side of the street had opened their windows. Many of them had little iron balconies in which quantities of magnificent dark carnations were blooming, planted in long, earthenware, trough-like pots, and hanging down by their long stalks that thrust themselves between the railings. Outside the windows of the poorer houses, too, great bunches of herbs were hung up to dry in the sun, and strings of scarlet peppers had already begun to appear, though it was early for them yet. Later, towards the autumn, the people hang up the canteloup melons of the south, in their rough green and grey rinds, by neatly made slings of twisted grass, but it was not time for them yet. In some of the houses the people were packing the last of the oranges to be sent down to Piedimonte and thence to Messina for England and America, passing each orange through a wooden ring to measure it, and rejecting those that were much too small or much too large, then wrapping each one separately in tissue paper, while other women packed them neatly in thin deal boxes. The air smelt of them and of the carnations in the balconies, for Santa Vittoria was a clean and sweet village. The cleanliness of the thoroughbred Oriental, a very different being from the filthy Levantine, begins in Sicily, and distinguishes the Sicilians of the hills from the Calabrians and from the Sicilians of such seaport towns as Messina. Moreover, there are no beggars in the hill towns.

San Giacinto had his pocket full of letters for the post office, and wished to see the lieutenant in command of the soldiers; but Orsino had nothing to do, and Ippolito had made up his mind not to return to Camaldoli without having seen the organ in the church. The two brothers went off in search of the sacristan, for the church was closed.

They found him, after some enquiry, helping to pack oranges in a great vaulted room that opened upon the street. He was a fat man, cross-eyed, with a sort of clerical expression.

"You wish to see the organ," he said, coming out into the street. "Truly you will see a fine thing! If you only do not hear it! It makes boom, boom, and wee, wee — and that is all it makes. I wager that not even ten cats could make a noise like our organ. Do you know that it is very aged? Surely, it remembers the ark of Noah, and Saint Paul must have brought it with him. But then, you shall see; and if you wish to hear it, I take no responsibility."

Ippolito was not greatly encouraged by such a prospect.

"But when you have a festival, what do you do?" he enquired.

"We help it, of course. How should one do? Don Atanasio, the apothecary, plays the clarinet. He is a professor! Him, indeed, you should hear when he plays at the elevation. You would think you heard the little angels whistling in Paradise! I, to serve you, play the double bass a little, and Don Ciccio, the carpenter, plays the drum. Being used to the hammer, he does it not badly. And all the time the organ makes boom, boom, and wee, wee. It is a fine concert, but there is much sentiment of devotion, and the women sing. It seems that thus it pleases the saints."

"Do not the men sing too?" asked Orsino, idly.

"Men? How could men sing in church? A man can sing a 'cantilena' in the fields, but in church it is the women who sing. They know all the words. God has made them so. There is that girl of the notary in Randazzo, for instance — you should hear her sing!"

"I have heard her in Rome," said Orsino. "But she sings in a theatre."

"A theatre? Who knows how a theatre is made? See how many things men have invented!"

They reached the door of the church.

"Signori, do you really wish to see this organ?" asked the sacristan. "There is a much better one in the little church outside the gate. But the day is hot, and if you only wish to see an organ, this one is nearer."

"Let me see the good one, by all means," said Ippolito. "I wish to play on it—not to see it! I have seen hundreds of organs."

"Hundreds of organs!" exclaimed the man to himself. "Capers! This stranger has travelled much! But if it is indeed not too hot for you," he said, addressing Ippolito, "we will go to Santa Vittoria."

"It is not hot at this hour," laughed Orsino. "We have walked up from Camaldoli."

"On foot!" The fat sacristan either was, or pretended to be, amazed. "Great signori like you, to come all that distance on foot!"

"What is there surprising in that?" enquired Ippolito. "We have legs."

"Birds also have legs," observed the man. "But they fly. It is only the chickens that walk, like poor people. I say that money is wings. If I were a great signore, like you, I would not even walk upstairs. I would be carried. Why should I walk? In order to be tired? It would be a folly, if I were rich. I, if you ask me, I like to eat well, to drink well, and then to sleep well. A man who could do these three things should be always happy. But the poor are always in thought."

"So are the rich," observed Ippolito.

"Yes, signore, for their souls, for we are all sinners; but not for their bodies, because they have always something to eat. What do I say? They eat meat every day, and so they are strong and have no thought for their bodies. But one of us, what does he eat? A little bread, a little salad, an onion, and with this in our bodies we have to move the earth. The world is thus made. Patience!"

Thus philosophizing, the fat man rolled unwieldily along beside the two gentlemen, swinging his keys in his hand.

"If I had made the world, it should be another thing," he continued, for he was a loquacious man. "In the first place, I would have made wine clear, like water, and I would have made water black, like wine. Thus if the wine-seller put water into his wine, we should all see it. Another thing I would have done. I would have made corn grow on trees, like olives. In that way, we should have planted it once in two hundred years, as we do the olive trees, and there would have been less fatigue. Is not that a good thought?"

"Very original," said Orsino. "It had never struck me."

"I would also have made men so that their hair should stand on end when they are telling lies, as a donkey lifts his tail when he brays. That would also have been good. But the Creator did not think of it in time. Patience! They say it will be different in Paradise. Hope costs little, but you cannot cook it."

"You are a philosopher," observed Ippolito.

"No, signore," answered the sacristan. "You have been misinformed. I am a grocer, or, to say it better, I am the brother of the grocer. When it is the season, after Santa Teresa's day, I kill the pigs and salt the hams and make the sausages. I am also the sacristan, but that yields me little; for although there is much devotion in our town at festivals, there is little of it among private persons. Sometimes an old woman brings a candle to the Madonna, and she gives a soldo to have it lighted. What is that? Can one live with a soldo now and then? But my brother, thanks be to Heaven, is well-to-do, and a widower. He makes me live with him. He had a son once, but, health to you, Christ and the sea took the boy when he was not yet twenty. Therefore I live with him, to divert him a little, and I kill the pigs, speaking with respect of your face."

"And what do you do during the rest of the

year?" enquired Orsino, as they neared the gate.

"Eh, I live so. According to the season, I pack oranges, I trim vines, I make the wine for my brother, and the oil, I take the honey and the wax from the bees, I graft good fruit upon the wild pear trees — what should I do? A little of everything, in order of eat."

"But your brother seems to be rich. Have you nothing?"

"Signore, to me money comes like a freshet in spring and runs away, and immediately I am dry. But to my brother it comes like water into a well, and it stays there. Men are thus made. The one gives, the other takes; the one shuts his hand, the other opens his. My mother, blessed soul, used to say to me, 'Take care, my son, for when you are old, you will go in rags!' But thanks be to Heaven, I have my brother, and I am as you see me."

They came to the little church with its freshly whitewashed walls and tiled roof.

"This is the chapel of Santa Vittoria," said the fat sacristan. "The church in the town is dedicated to Our Lady of Victories, but this is the chapel of the saint, and there is more devotion here, though it is small, and at the great feast of Santa Vittoria, the procession starts from here and goes to the church, and returns here."

"It looks new," observed Ippolito.

"Eh, if all things were what they seem!" The man chuckled as he turned the key in the lock. "You shall see inside whether it is new. It is older than Saint Peter's in Rome."

And so it was, by two or three centuries. It was a dark little building, of the Norman period, with low arches and solid little pillars terminating in curiously carved capitals. It had a little nave with intercommunicating side chapels, like aisles. Over the door was a small loft containing the organ, the object of Ippolito's visit. In the uneven floor there were slabs with deep cut but much worn figures of knights and prelates in stiff armour or long and equally stiff looking robes, their heads surrounded by almost illegible inscriptions. Over the principal altar there was a bad painting of Saint Vittoria, half covered with ex-voto offerings of silver hearts, while on each side of the picture were hung up scores of hollow wax models of arms, legs, and other parts of the human body, realistically coloured, all remembrances of recoveries from illness, accident, and disease, attributed to the beneficent intervention of the saint. But above, in the little vault of the apse, there were some very ancient and well preserved mosaics, magnificently rich in tone. There was, of course, no dome, and the dim light came in through low windows high up in the nave, above the lower side chapels. The church was clean and well kept, and on each side there were half a dozen benches painted with a vivid sky-blue colour.

The two brothers looked about, with some curiosity, while the fat sacristan slowly jingled his bunch of keys against his leg.

"Here the dead walk at night," he observed, cheerfully, as the two young men came up to him.

"What do you mean?" asked Orsino, who had been much amused by the man's conversation.

"The old Pagliuca walk. I have seen their souls running about the floor in the dark, like little candle flames. A little more, and I should have seen their bodies, too, but I ran away. Soul of my mother! I was frightened. It was on the eve of Santa Vittoria, five years ago. The candles for the festival had not come, though we had waited all day for the carrier from Piedimonte. Then he came at dark, for he had met a friend in Linguaglossa, and he was a drunkard, and the wine was new, so he slept on his cart all the way, and it was by the grace of the Madonna that he did not roll off into the ditch. But I considered that it was late, and that the office began early in the morning, and that many strangers came from Bronte and the hill village to our festa, and that it would be a scandal if they found us still dressing the church in the morning. So I took the box of candles on my back and came here, not thinking to bring a lantern, because there is always the lamp before the altar where the saint's bones are. Do you understand?"

"Perfectly. But what about the Pagliuca?"

"My brother said, 'You will see the Pagliuca' — for everyone says it. But I had a laugh at him, for I thought that a dead man in his grave must be as quiet as a handkerchief in a drawer. So I came, and I unlocked the door, thinking about the festival, and I came in, meaning to take a candle from the box and light it at the altar lamp, so that I might see well to stick the others into the candlesticks. But there was the flame of a candle burning on the floor. It ran away from me as I came in, and others ran after it, and round and round it. Then I knew that I saw the souls of the old Pagliuca, and I said to myself that presently I should see also their bodies — an evil thing, for they have been long dead. Then I made a movement — who knows how I did? I dropped the box and I heard it break, and all the candles rolled out upon the floor as though the dead Pagliuca were rattling their bones. But I counted neither one nor two, but jumped out into the road with one jump. Santa Vittoria helped me; and it was a bright moonlight night, but as I shut the door, I could see the souls of the Pagliuca jumping up and down on the pavement. I said within me, when the dead dance, the living go home. And my face was white. When I came home, my brother said, 'You have seen the Pagliuca.' And I said, 'I have seen them.' Then he gave me some rum, and I lay in a cold sweat till morning. From that time I will not come here at night. But in the daytime, it is different."

Orsino and Ippolito knew well enough that in old Italian churches, where many dead are buried under the pavement, it is not an uncommon thing to see a will-o'-the-wisp at night. But in the dim little church, with the dead Pagliuca lying under their feet, there was something gruesome about the man's graphic story, and they did not laugh.

"Let us hope that we may not see any ghosts," said Orsino.

"Amen," answered the sacristan, devoutly. "That is the organ," he said, pointing to the loft.

He led the way. On one side of the entrance a small arched door gave access to a narrow winding staircase in the thickness of the wall, lighted by narrow slits opening to the air. Though the loft had not appeared to be very high above the pavement, the staircase seemed very long. At last the three emerged upon the boarded floor, at the back of the instrument, where four greasy, knotted ropes hung out of worn holes in the cracked wood. The rose window over the door of the church threw a bright light into the little forest of dusty wooden and metal pipes above. The ropes were for working the old-fashioned bellows.

Ippolito went round and took the thin deal cover from the keyboard. He was surprised to find a double bank of keys, and an octave and a half of pedals, which is very uncommon in country organs. He was further unprepared to see the name of a once famous maker in Naples just above the keys, but when he looked up he understood, for on a gilded scroll, supported by two rickety cherubs above his head, he read the name of the donor.

'FERDINANDUS PALIUCA PRINCEPS CORLEONIS COMES SANCTAE VICTORIAE SICULUS DONAVIT A.D. MDCCCXXI.'

The instrument was, therefore, the gift of a Ferdinando Pagliuca, Prince of Corleone, Count of Santa Vittoria, probably of one of those Pagliuca whose souls the fat sacristan believed he had seen 'jumping up and down on the pavement.'

The sacristan tugged at the ropes that moved the bellows. Ippolito dusted the bench over which he had leaned to uncover the keys, slipped in, swinging his feet over the pedals, pulled out two or three stops, and struck a chord.

The tone was not bad, and had in it some of that richness which only old organs are supposed to possess, like old violins. He began to prelude softly, and then, one by one, he tried the other stops. Some were fair, but some were badly out of tune. The cornopean brayed hideously, and the hautboy made curious buzzing sounds. Ippolito promised himself that he would set the whole instrument in order in the course of a fortnight, and was delighted with his discovery. When he had finished, the fat sacristan came out from behind, mopping his forehead with a blue cotton handkerchief.

"Capers!" he exclaimed. "You are a professor. If Don Giacomo hears you, he will die of envy."

"Who is Don Giacomo?"

"Eh, Don Giacomo! He is the postmaster and the telegrapher, and he plays the old organ in the big church on Sundays. But when there is the festival here, a professor comes to play this one, from Catania. But he cannot play as you do."

Orsino had gone down again into the church while Ippolito had been playing. They found him bending very low over an inscription on a slab near the altar steps.

"There is a curious inscription here," he said, without looking up. "I cannot quite read it, but it seems to me that I see our name in it. It would be strange if one of our family had chanced to die and be buried here, ages ago."

Ippolito bent down, too, till his head touched his brother's.

"It is not Latin," he said presently. "It looks like Italian."

The fat sacristan jingled his keys rather impatiently, for it was growing late.

"Without troubling yourselves to read it, you may know what it is," he said. "It is the old prophecy about the Pagliuca. When the dead walk here at night they read it. It says, 'Esca Pagliuca pesca Saracen.' But it goes round a circle like a disk, so that you can read it, 'Saracen esca Pagliuca pesca'—either, Let Pagliuca go out, the Saracen is fishing, or, Let the Saracen go out, Pagliuca is fishing."

"' Or Saracinesca Pagliuca pesca'—Saracinesca fishes for Pagliuca," said Ippolito to Orsino, with a laugh at his own ingenuity.

"Who knows what it means!" exclaimed the sacristan. "But they say that when it comes true, the last Corleone shall die and the Pagliuca d'Oriani shall end. But whether they end or not, they will walk here till the Last Judgment. Signori, the twilight descends. If you do not wish to see the Pagliuca, let us go. But if you wish to see them, here are the keys. You are the masters, but I go home. This is an evil place at night."

The man was growing nervous, and moved away towards the door. The two brothers followed him.

"The place is consecrated," said Ippolito, as they reached the entrance. "What should you be afraid of?"

"Santa Vittoria is all alone here," answered the

man, "and the Pagliuca are more than fifty, when they come out and walk. What should a poor Christian do? He is better at home, with a pipe of tobacco."

The sun had set when they all came out upon the road, and the afterglow was purple on the snow of Etna.

END OF VOL. I

CORLEONE
VOL. II

Vol. 13—O

CORLEONE

CHAPTER XXI

VITTORIA D'ORIANI had very few companions. Corona Saracinesca really liked her, for her own sake, and was sorry for her because she belonged to the family which was so often described as the worst blood in Italy. Corona and San Giacinto's wife had together presented the Corleone tribe in Roman society, but they were both women of middle age, without daughters who might have been friends for Vittoria. On the other hand, though the Romans had accepted the family on the endorsement, as it were, of the whole Saracinesca family, there was a certain general disinclination to become intimate with them, due to the posthumous influence of their dead uncle, Corleone of evil fame. The Campodonico people were unwilling to have anything to do with them, even to the gentle and charitable Donna Francesca, who had been a Braccio, and might therefore, perhaps, have been expected to condone a great many shortcomings in other families. Pietro Ghisleri, who generally spent the winter in Rome, refused to know the d'Oriani, for poor dead Bianca Corleone's sake; and his English wife, who knew the old story, thought he was right. The great majority of the Romans received them, however, very much as they would have received foreigners who had what is called a right to be in society, with civility, but not with enthusiasm.

Vittoria had, therefore, met many Roman girls of her own age during the spring, but had not become intimate with any of them. It was natural that when her brother made the acquaintance of Mrs. and Miss Slayback, and when the young American took what is usually described in appalling English as a violent fancy to Vittoria, the latter should feel that sort of gratitude which sometimes expands into friendship.

They saw much of each other. It is needless to say that they had not an idea in common, and it would have been very surprising if they had. But on the other hand they had that sort of community of feeling which is a better foundation for intimacy than a similarity of ideas.

Miss Lizzie Slayback was not profound, but she was genuine. She had no inherited tendency to feel profound emotions nor to get into tragic situations, but she was full of innocent sentiment. Like many persons who do not lead romantic lives, she was in love with romance, and she believed that romance had a sort of perpetual existence somewhere, so that by taking some pains one could really find it and live in it. Her fortune would be useful in the search, although it was unromantic to be rich. She had not read 'Montecristo,' because she was told that Dumas was old-fashioned. She was not very gifted, but she was very clever in detail. She did not understand Tebaldo in the least, for she was no judge of human nature, but she knew perfectly well how to keep him at arm's length until she had decided to marry him. She was absolutely innocent, yet she had also the most absolute assurance, and bore herself in society with the independence of a married woman of thirty.

"It is our custom in my country," she said to Vittoria, who was sometimes startled by her friend's indifference to the smaller conventionalities.

The two young girls spoke French together, and understood each other, though a third person might not at first have known that they were speaking the same language. Vittoria spoke the French of an Italian convent, old-fashioned, stilted, pronounced with the rolling southern accent which only her beautiful voice could make bearable, and more or less wild as to gender. Lizzie Slayback, as has been said, spoke fluently and often said the same things because she had a small choice of language. Occasionally she used phrases that would have made a Frenchman's hair feel uneasy on his head, and her innocent use of which inspired disquieting doubts as to the previous existence of the person who had taught her.

"We think," she said, "that it is better to enjoy yourself while you are young, and be good when you grow old, but in Europe it seems to be the other way."

"No one can be good all the time," answered Vittoria. "One is good a little and one is bad a little, by turns, just as one can."

"That makes a variety," said Miss Slayback. "That is why you Italians are so romantic."

"I never can understand what you mean by romantic," observed Vittoria.

"Oh — everything you do is romantic, my dear. Your brother is the most romantic man I ever saw. That is why I think I shall marry him," she added, as though contemplating a new hat with a view to buying it, and almost sure that it would suit her.

"I do not think you will be happy with him," said Vittoria, rather timidly.

"Because he is romantic, and I am not? Well, I am not sure."

"There! You use the word again! What in the world do you mean by it?"

Miss Slayback was at a loss to furnish the required definition, especially in French.

"Your brother is romantic," she said, repeating herself. "I am sure he looks like Cæsar Borgia."

"I hope not!" exclaimed Vittoria. "Surely you would not marry —" she stopped.

"Cæsar Borgia?" enquired Lizzie Slayback, calmly. "Of all people, I should have liked to marry him! He was nice and wicked. He would never have been dull, even nowadays, when everybody is so proper, you know."

"No," laughed the Italian girl, "I do not think anybody would have called him dull. He generally murdered his friends before they were bored by his company."

Miss Lizzie laughed, for Vittoria seemed witty to her.

"If I had said that at a party," she answered, "everybody would have told me that I was so clever! I wish I had thought of it. May I say it, as if it were mine? Shall you not mind?"

"Why should I? I should certainly not say it myself, before people."

"Why not?"

"It would not be thought exactly — oh — what shall I say? We young girls are never expected to say anything like that. We look down, and hold our tongues."

"And think of all the sharp things you will say when you are married! That is just the difference. Now, in the West, where I come from, if a girl has anything clever to say, she says it, even if she is only ten years old. I must say, it seems to me much more sensible."

"Yes — but there are other things, besides being sensible," objected Vittoria.

"Then they must be senseless," retorted Miss Lizzie. "It follows."

"There are all sorts of customs and traditions in society that have not very much sense perhaps, but we are all used to them, and should feel uncomfortable without them. When the nuns taught me to do this, or that, to say certain things, and not to say certain other things, it was because all the other young girls I should meet would be sure to act in just the same way, and if I did not act as they do, I should make myself conspicuous."

"I never could see the harm in being conspicuous," said Miss Slayback. "Provided one is not vulgar," she added, by way of limitation.

"Do you not feel uncomfortable, when you feel that everyone is looking at you?"

"No, of course not, unless I am doing something ridiculous. I rather like to have people look at me. That makes me feel satisfied with myself."

"It always makes me feel dreadfully uncomfortable," said Vittoria.

"It should not, for you are beautiful, my dear. You really are. I only think I am, when I have good clothes and am not sunburnt or anything like that—I never really believe it, you know. But when people admire me, it helps the illusion. I wish I were beautiful, like you, Vittoria."

"I am not beautiful," said the Sicilian girl, colouring a little shyly. "But I wish I had your calmness. I am always blushing—it is so uncomfortable—or else I am very pale, and then I feel cold, as though my heart were going to stop beating. I think I should faint if I were to do the things you sometimes do."

"What, for instance?" laughed the American girl.

"Oh—I have seen you cross a ballroom alone, and drive alone in an open carriage—"

"What could happen to me in a carriage?"

"It is not that—it is—I hardly know! It is like a married woman."

"I shall be married some day, so I may as well get into the habit of it," observed Miss Lizzie, smiling and showing her beautiful teeth.

In spite of such inconclusive conversations, the two girls were really fond of each other. When Mrs. Slayback looked at Tebaldo's sharp features, her heart hardened; but when she looked at Vittoria, it softened again. She was a very intelligent woman, in her way, and, having originally married for his money a man whom she considered beneath her in social standing and cultivation, she wished to improve his family in her own and her friends' eyes by making a brilliant foreign marriage for his niece. 'Princess of Corleone' sounded a good deal better than 'Miss Lizzie Slayback,' and there was no denying the antiquity and validity of the title. There were few to be had as good as that, for the girl's religion was a terrible obstacle to her marrying the heir of any great house in Europe in which money was not a paramount necessity. But Tebaldo assured her that he attached no importance whatever to such matters. Lizzie was in love with him, and he took pains to seem to be in love with her.

Mrs. Slayback did not give more weight to her niece's inclinations and fancies than Tebaldo gave to his religious scruples. The girl was highly impressionable to a very small depth, skin deep, in fact, and below the shallow gauge of her impressions she suddenly became hard and obstinate like her uncle. She had an unfortunate way of liking people very much at first sight if she chanced to meet them when she was in a good humour, and quite regardless of what they might really be. She had said to herself that Tebaldo was 'romantic,' and as his life hitherto might certainly have been well described by some such word, he had no difficulty in keeping up the illusion for her.

He saw that she listened with wonder and delight to his tales of wild doings in Sicily, and he had not the slightest difficulty in finding as many of them to tell her as suited his purpose. He had been more intimately connected with one or two of his stories than he chose to tell her; but he was ready at turning a difficulty of that sort, and when he introduced himself he treated his own personality and actions with that artistic modesty which leaves vague beauties to the imagination. Never having had any actual experience of the rude deeds of unbridled humanity, Miss Lizzie liked revengeful people because they were 'romantic.' She liked to think of a man who could carry off his enemy's bride in the grey dawn of her wedding day, escape with her on board a ship, and be out of sight of land before night — because such deeds were 'romantic.' She liked to know that a band of thirty desperate men could bid defiance to the government and the army for months, and she loved to hear of Leone, the outlaw chief, who had killed a dozen soldiers with his own hand in twenty minutes, before he fell with twenty-seven bullets in him — that was indeed 'romantic.' And Tebaldo had seen Leone himself, many years ago, and remembered him and described him; and he had seen most of the people whose extraordinary adventures he detailed to the girl, and had known them and spoken with them, had shot with them for wagers, had drunk old wine of Etna at their weddings, and had followed some of them to their graves when they had been killed. A good many of his acquaintances had been killed in various 'romantic' affairs.

Everything he told her appealed strongly to Lizzie Slayback's imagination, and he had the advantage, if it were one, of being really a great deal like the people he described, daring, unscrupulous, physically brave and revengeful, very much the type which is so often spoken of in Calabria with bated breath, as 'a desperate man of Sicily.' For the Italian of the mainland is apt both to dread and respect the stronger man of the islands.

In addition to his accomplishments as a storyteller, Tebaldo possessed the power of seeming to be very much in love, without ever saying much about it. He flattered the girl, telling her that she was beautiful and witty and charming, and everything else which she wished to be; and when his eyelids were not drooping at the corners as they did when he was angry, he had a way of gazing with intense and meaning directness into Lizzie Slayback's dark-blue eyes, so that Vittoria would no longer have envied her, for she blushed and looked away, half pleased and half disturbed.

Aliandra Basili thought Francesco much more ready and apt to anticipate her small wishes and to understand her thoughts than his brother. But when he chose to take the trouble, with cool calculation, Tebaldo knew well enough how to make a woman believe that he was taking care of her, which is what many women most wish to feel. With Aliandra, whom he loved as much as he was capable of loving anyone, Tebaldo felt himself almost too much at his ease to disguise his own selfishness. But he gave himself endless trouble for Miss Slayback, and she was sometimes touched by little acts of his which showed how constantly she was in his mind—as indeed she was, much more than she knew.

In her moments of solitude, which were few, for she hated to be alone, she reflected more than once that her money must seem a great inducement to a poor Italian nobleman; but she was too much in love with the 'romantic' to believe that Tebaldo wished to marry her solely for her fortune. It was too hard to believe, when she looked at her own face in the mirror and saw how young, and pretty, and smiling she really was. Her dark lashes gave her blue eyes so much expression that she could not think herself not loved, a mere encumbrance to be taken with a fortune, but not without, in exchange for a title. She was fond of her refined but not very remarkable self, and it would have been hard to convince her that Tebaldo's silent looks and ever-ready service meant nothing but greed of money. Very possibly, she admitted, he could not have thought of marrying her if she had been poor, but she believed it equally certain that if she had been an ugly, rich, middle-aged old maid, he would never have thought of it either.

Besides, Tebaldo had watched with great satisfaction the growing intimacy between her and his sister, and he took care to play his comedy before Vittoria as carefully as before Miss Slayback herself. Vittoria, as he knew, was very truthful, and if her friend asked questions about him, she would repeat accurately what he had said in her presence, if she gave any information at all. To his face, Vittoria accused him of wishing to marry for money, but so long as he affirmed that he loved Miss Slayback, Vittoria would never accuse him behind his back, nor tell tales about his character which might injure his prospects. Though he knew that she rarely believed him and never trusted him, he knew that he could trust her. That fact alone might have sufficiently defined their respective characters.

CHAPTER XXII

TEBALDO had not been at all willing to believe that Aliandra Basili really meant to treat him differently after the meeting in which she had defined her position so clearly, but he soon discovered that she was in earnest. She was not a person to change her mind easily, and she had decided that it was time to end the situation in one way or the other. Tebaldo must either marry her, or cease to persecute her with his attentions. In the latter case she intended to marry Francesco.

Like most successful singers, and, indeed, like most people who succeed remarkably in any career, she possessed the extraordinary energy which ultimately makes the difference between success and failure in all struggles for preëminence. Many have the necessary talent and the other necessary gifts; few have, besides these things, the restless, untiring force to use them at all times to the extreme limit of possibility. People who have the requisite facility but not the indispensable energy find it so hard to realize this fact that they have inverted our modern use of the word 'genius' to account for their own failures. The ancients, and even the mediævals, when beaten in a fair fight by men more enduring than themselves, were always ready to account for their defeat on the ground of a supernatural intervention against them. Similarly the people who are clever enough to succeed, nowadays, but not strong enough, nor patient enough, attribute to the man who surpasses them some sort of supernatural inspiration, which they call genius, and against which they tell themselves that it is useless to strive. Socrates called his acute sense of right and wrong his familiar spirit, his dæmon; but in those days of the supremacy of the greatest art the world has ever seen, or ever will see, at a time when most people still believed in oracles, no one ever attributed any such familiar spirit to Sophocles, to Praxiteles, nor to Zeuxis, nor to any other poets, sculptors, or painters. The Muses had become mere names even then, and the stories about them were but superstitious fables.

That restless energy was part of the Sicilian singer's nature. Whether her other gifts were great enough for greatness remained to be seen, and the question had nothing to do with Tebaldo Pagliuca. Her singing gave him pleasure, but it was not what chiefly attracted him. He was in love with her in a commonplace and by no means elevated way, and artistic satisfaction did not enter into his passion as a component factor. There was nothing so elevated about it.

Aliandra's very womanly nature made her vaguely aware of this, and she had a physical suspicion, so to say, that if Tebaldo ever lost his head, he would be much more violent than his brother, who had frightened her so badly one evening at the theatre. She was inclined to think that it would not be safe to irritate Tebaldo too much; yet she was sure that it was of no use to prolong the present ambiguous situation, in which she was practically accepting and authorizing the love of a man who would not marry her if he could help it.

After she had finally told him what she meant to do, nothing could move her, and she entirely refused to see him alone. Hitherto she had used her privilege as an artist in this respect, and had often sent away her worthy aunt, the Signora Barbuzzi, during his visits. But now, when he came, the black-browed, grey-haired, thin-lipped old woman kept her place beside her niece on the little green sofa of the little hired drawing-room, her withered fingers steadily knitting black silk stockings. This was her only accomplishment, but it was an unusual one, and she was very proud of it, and of her wonderful eyes, which never needed glasses, and could count the minute black stitches even when the light was beginning to fail on a winter's afternoon.

Then Tebaldo sat uneasily on his chair, and

wished the old woman might fall dead in an apoplexy, and that he had the evil eye, and by mere wishing could bring her to destruction. And Aliandra leaned back in the other corner of the sofa, behind her aunt, and smiled coolly at what Tebaldo said, and answered indifferently, and looked at her nails critically but wearily when he said nothing, as if she wished he would go away. And he generally went at the end of half an hour, unable to bear the situation much longer than that, after he had discovered that the Signora Barbuzzi was in future always to sit through his visits.

"And now, my daughter," said the aunt one day when he had just gone, "the other will come in a quarter of an hour. The sun sets, the moon rises, as we say."

Which invariably happened. Francesco did not like being caught with Aliandra by his brother, as has been already seen. He had, therefore, hit upon the simple plan of spying upon him, following him at a distance until he entered Aliandra's house, and then sitting in a little third-rate café opposite until he came out. Tebaldo, who was extremely particular about the places he frequented, because he wished to behave altogether like a Roman gentleman, would never have entered any such place as Francesco made use of for his own purposes. Francesco knew that, and felt perfectly safe as he sat at his little marble table, with a glass of syrup and soda water, his eyes fixed on the big front door which he could see through the window from the place he regularly occupied. He was also quite sure that, as Tebaldo had always just left the house when he himself came, there was no danger of his elder brother's sudden appearance.

The Signora Barbuzzi was decidedly much more civilized than her brother, the notary of Randazzo, for she had been married to a notary of Messina, which meant that she had lived in much higher social surroundings. That, at least, was her opinion, and Aliandra was too wise to dispute with her. She had given the deceased Barbuzzi no children, and in return for her discretion he had left her a comfortable little income. Notaries are apt to marry the sisters and daughters of other notaries, and to associate with men of their own profession, for they generally have but little confidence in persons of other occupations. The Signora Barbuzzi might have been a notary herself, for she had the avidity of mind, the distrustfulness, the caution about details, and the supernormal acuteness about the intentions of other people which are the old-fashioned Italian notary's predominant characteristics. She looked like one, too.

"For my part, my daughter," she said to her niece, shaking her head twice towards the same side, as some old women frequently do when they are knitting a stocking, "for my part, I should send them both away for the present. They will not marry, for they have no money. Who marries without money? I see that you earn a great deal, but not a fortune. If you should marry Tebaldo or Francesco, and if you should not earn the fortune you expect, you would find yourself badly off. But if you can earn ten times, twenty times what you have earned this winter during the next four or five years, then you can marry either of them, because they will want your money as well as yourself."

Aliandra said nothing for some minutes, for she saw the truth of her aunt's advice. On the other hand, she was young and felt quite sure of success, and she did not feel sure that some unexpected turn of fortune might not suddenly bring about an advantageous marriage for one of the two men.

"I am not the Patti," she said thoughtfully. "I am not the Melba. I am only the little Basili yet, but I have a remarkable voice and I can work — "

"Voices are treacherous," observed the cautious old woman. "They sometimes break down. Then you will only be the daughter of Basili the notary again."

"My voice will not break down," answered Aliandra, confidently. "It is a natural voice, and I never make any effort. My master says it is the voices which are incomplete at first and have to be developed to equalize them, which break down sometimes."

"You may have an illness," suggested the Signora Barbuzzi. "Then you may lose your voice."

"Why should I have an illness? I am strong." The handsome girl leaned back on the sofa and raising her arms clasped her hands behind her head, resting them against the wall — a splendidly vital figure.

"We are mortal," observed the old woman, sententiously. "When God pleases to send us a fever, goodbye voice!"

"Have I some sin on my soul that Heaven should send me a fever?" asked Aliandra, rather indignantly. "What have I done?"

"Nothing, nothing, my daughter! Who accuses you? You are an angel, you are a crystal, you are a little saint. I have said nothing. But a fever is a fever for saints and sinners."

"I am not going to have a fever, and I am not going to lose my voice. I shall make a great reputation and earn a great deal of money."

"Heaven send it you thus!" answered the Signora Barbuzzi, devoutly.

"But I shall make Tebaldo jealous of Francesco, so that he will not be able to see out of his eyes for jealousy. Then he will marry me. But if not, I will marry the other, whom I like better."

"Indeed, jealousy is a weapon, my dear. A bad mule needs a good stick, as they say. But for my part, I am a notary's daughter, the widow of a notary — may the Lord preserve him in glory! — and the sister of a notary. I am out of place as the aunt of an artist. With us we have always said, who leaves the old road to take the new, knows what he leaves but not what he shall find. That is a good proverb. But your life is on a new road. You may find fortune, but no one knows. At least, you have bread, if you fail, and you risk nothing, if you remain a good girl."

"So far as that goes!" Aliandra laughed scornfully. "My head will not turn easily."

"Thank Heaven, no. There is the other one," added the old woman, as she heard the door-bell ring. "Shall I leave you alone with him, my daughter?"

"Why should you?", asked Aliandra, indifferently. "What have I to say to him?"

She was perhaps not quite as indifferent as she seemed, for Francesco attracted her. On the other hand, she did not wish to be attracted by him so long as there was a chance of marrying the other brother, and her aunt's presence was a sort of precaution against an improbable but vaguely possible folly which she distinguished in the future.

On his part, Francesco always did his best to make a favourable impression on the Signora

Barbuzzi, considering her friendship indispensable. He fancied that it must be a comparatively easy thing to please an old chaperon who got little attention from anyone, and he used to bring her bunches of violets from time to time, which he presented with a well-turned speech. He might as well have offered a nosegay to the deceased Barbuzzi himself, for all the impression he produced by his civilities to the hard-headed, masculine old woman.

He was not discouraged, however, and though he wished her anywhere but where she was, he bore her presence with equanimity and made himself as agreeable as he could. He was far too sharp-sighted himself not to see what Aliandra was doing, but he had no means of acting upon her feelings as she was trying to act upon Tebaldo's, and he had the low sort of philosophy which often belongs to sensual people, and which is perhaps not much higher than the patience of the cat that crouches before the mouse's hole, waiting for its victim to run into danger. He was no match, however, for the two women, and he very much overestimated the attraction he exercised upon Aliandra.

It was, in a manner, a sort of disturbing influence rather than an attraction, and Aliandra avoided it until she was forced to feel it, and when she felt it, she feared it. Yet she liked him, and was surprised at the contradiction, and distrusted herself in a general way. She was not much given to self-examination, and would probably not have understood what the word meant; but, like a young wild animal, she was at once aware of the presence of danger, and was tempted towards the cause of it, while her keen natural instinct of self-preservation made her draw back cautiously whenever the temptation to advance was particularly strong.

This was the situation of Aliandra with regard to the two brothers respectively. Her interest lay with the one, her inclination, so far as it was one, with the other, and she distrusted both in different ways, fearing the one that was a coward, but distrusting more the one who was the braver and more manly of the two, but also incomparably the more deceitful.

They, on their part, were both in love with her, and not in very different ways; but though Tebaldo was the bolder in character, he was the one more able to be cautious where a woman was concerned, while he was also capable of jealousy to a degree inconceivable to Francesco.

CHAPTER XXIII

THE world would go very well, but for the unforeseen. The fate of everyone in this story might have been very different if Gesualda, old Basili's maid of all work, had not stopped to eat an orange surreptitiously while she was sweeping down the stone stairs early in the morning, before the notary was dressed. She was an ugly girl, and had not many pleasures in life; Basili was old and stingy and fault-finding, and she had to do all the work of the house,—the scrubbing, the cooking, the serving, the washing, and the mending.

She did it very well; in the first place because she was strong, secondly because she was willing and sufficiently skilful, and lastly because she was very unusually ugly, and therefore had no distractions in the shape of love-making. She was also scrupulously honest and extremely careful not to waste things in the kitchen. But fruit was her weakness, and, being a Sicilian, she might have been capable of committing a crime for the sake of an orange, or a bunch of grapes, or a dozen little figs, if they had not been so plentiful that one could always have what one could eat for the mere asking. Her only shortcoming, therefore, was that she could not confine herself to eating her oranges in the kitchen. She always had one in her pocket. A cynical old lady once said that the only way to deal with temptation was to yield to it at once, and save oneself all further annoyance. Gesualda yielded to the temptation to eat the orange she had in her pocket, when she had resisted it just long enough to make the yielding a positive delight. She felt the orange through her skirt, she imagined how it looked, she thought how delicious it would be, and her lips were dry for it, and her soul longed for it. There was always a quiet corner at hand, for the notary lived alone. In an instant the orange was in her hands, her coarse fingers took the peel off in four pieces with astonishing skill, the said peel disappeared temporarily into the pocket again, and a moment later she was happy.

Her whole part in this history consisted in the eating of a single orange on the dark stone stairs, yet it was an important one, for out of all the thousands of oranges she had eaten during her life, that particular one was destined to be the first link in a long and tragic chain of circumstances.

Whether the orange was not quite ripe, so that the peel did not come away as easily as usual, or whether she was made a little nervous by the fact that her master might be expected to appear at any moment, a fact which enhanced the delight of the misdeed, neither she herself nor anyone else will ever know. As usual, she ran her sharp, strong thumb-nail twice round the fruit, crosswise, dug her fingers into the crossing cuts thus made, and stripped the peel off in a twinkling, thrusting the four dry pieces into her pocket. And as usual, in another moment, she was perfectly, blissfully happy, for it was a blood-orange, and particularly sweet and juicy, having no pips, for it had grown on a very old tree, and those are the best, as everyone knows in the orange country of the south.

But fate tore off a tiny fragment of the peel, a mere corner of one strip, thick, and the shiny side upwards, all slippery with its aromatic oil, and placed it cunningly just on the edge of one of the worn old stone steps, above her in the dark turning. Then fate went away, and waited quietly to see what should happen, and Gesualda also went away, down to her kitchen, to begin and prepare the vegetables which she had bought at daybreak of the vendor, a little way down the street. The bit of peel lay quite quietly in the dark, doing as fate had bidden it, and waiting likewise.

Now, fate had reckoned exactly how many paces Basili the notary would take from his room to the head of the stairs, in order to know with which foot he would take the first step downwards, and hence to calculate whether the bit of peel should be a little to the right or a little to the left. And it lay a little to the left; for the left foot, as fate is aware, is the unlucky foot, except for left-handed people. Basili was a right-handed man; and as he came downstairs in his great, flapping leathern slippers, he put the smoothest spot of the old sole exactly upon the shiny bit of peel. All of which shows the astonishing accuracy which fate can bring to bear at important moments. That was the beginning of the end of this history.

Basili fell, of course, and, as it seemed to him, he fell backwards, forwards, sideways, and upside down, all in a moment; and when he came to the bottom of the stairs, he had a broken leg. It was not a bad break, though any broken leg is bad, and the government surgeon was at home, because it was early in the morning, and came and set it very well, and Basili lay in a sunny room, with pots of carnations in the window, drinking syrup of tamarind with water, to cool his blood, and very much disturbed in his mind. Gesualda sat on the steps all the morning, moaning and beating her breast, for she had found the little piece of orange-peel, groping in the dark, and she knew that it had all been her fault. For penitence, she made a vow, at first, not to eat an orange till the master was recovered. Later in the day, she went to confession, in order to ease her soul of its burden, and she told her confessor that she could not possibly keep the vow, and that she had already twice undergone horrible temptation since the accident, at the mere sight of an orange. Thereupon the confessor, who was a wise little old man, commuted her self-imposed penance to abstinence from cheese, which she scrupulously practised for a whole month afterwards, until the notary was on his feet for the first time. But by that time a great many things had happened.

Basili lay in his sunny room, finding it difficult to understand exactly what had happened to him. He had never been ill in his life, excepting once when he had taken a little fever, as a mere boy. He was a tough man, not so old as he looked, and he had never thought it possible that he could be laid on his back and made perfectly helpless for a whole month. He had ground his teeth while they had been setting his leg, but in spite of the pain he had been thinking chiefly of the check to his business which must be the inevitable result of such a long confinement. He had a shabby little clerk who copied for him, and was not altogether stupid, but he trusted no one with the affairs of his clients, and he was a very important person in Randazzo. Moreover, a young notary from Catania had recently established himself in opposition to him, and he feared the competition.

He was very lonely, too, for the clerk, after presenting his condolences, had seized the opportunity of taking a holiday, and there was nobody but Gesualda in the house. In the afternoon she got her mother to take her place while she went to confession. Basili was very lonely indeed, for the doctor would not let him receive his clients who came on business, fearing fever for his patient. The day seemed very long. He called for paper and pen, and in spite of the surgeon's prohibition, he had himself propped up in bed, and wrote a letter to his daughter. He told her of his accident, and begged her to come to him, if she could do so without injuring the course of study she had undertaken.

Time was precious to Aliandra, for her master generally left Rome at the end of June, and she had only learned about half of Aïda, the opera she had undertaken to study, and which was a necessary one for her future career. But she made up her mind at once to go to her father, for a fortnight, after which time, in the ordinary course of things, he would probably be able to spare her. She was very fond of him, for her mother had died when she had been very young, and Basili had loved the child with the grim tenderness peculiar to certain stern characters; and afterwards, when once persuaded that she had both voice and talent for the stage, he had generously helped her in every way he could.

He had missed her terribly, for she had not been

in Sicily since the previous autumn, and it was natural that he should send for her to keep him company during his recovery. She, on her part, looked forward with pleasure to a taste of the old simple existence in which she had been so happy as a child. She left her maid in Rome, and her aunt stopped in Messina, intending to come up to Randazzo a few days later and pay her brother a visit.

Before leaving Rome Aliandra told both Tebaldo and Francesco where she was going, and that she intended to return in a fortnight in order to study with her teacher until he should leave Rome. She maintained her attitude of coldness towards Tebaldo to the last. He complained of it. For once, the Signora Barbuzzi had left the room unbidden, judging, no doubt, that before going away for some time Aliandra might wish to see Tebaldo alone, and possibly have some further explanation with him.

"Look here," he said roughly, "you have treated me in this way long enough, and I have borne it quietly. Be reasonable—"

"That is exactly what I am," answered Aliandra. "It is you who are unreasonable."

"Because I love you, you say that I am unreasonable!" he retorted, his patience giving way suddenly. "Because you burn me—bah! find words! I cannot. Give me your hand!"

"Only in one way. I have told you—"

"Give me your hand." He came quite close to her.

She held her hands behind her and looked at him defiantly, her head high, her eyes cold.

"If you want my hand — you must keep it," she said.

She was very handsome just then, and his heart beat faster. There was a tremor in his voice when he spoke again, and his fingers shook as he laid them lightly on her shoulder, barely touching her. There is a most tender vibration in any genuine passion under control, just before it breaks out. Aliandra saw it, but she distrusted him, and believed that he might be acting.

"I cannot bear this much longer," he said. "It is killing me."

"There is no reason why it should," she answered coldly. "You know what you have to do. I will marry you whenever you please."

He was silent. The vision of Miss Lizzie Slayback with her millions, and with all his own future, rose before him. He seemed to see it all behind the handsome head, on the ugly flowered paper of the wall. That stake was too heavy, and he could not afford to risk it. Yet, as he met Aliandra's hard eyes and cruelly set mouth, her resistance roused him as nothing ever had before.

"You hesitate still," she said scornfully. "I do not think your love will kill you."

"Yours for me will not hurt you, at all events," he answered rudely.

"Mine? Oh — you may think of that as you please."

She shrugged her shoulders like a woman of the people, and turned from him indifferently; leaving him standing near the door, growing pale by quick degrees, till his face was a faint yellow and his eyes were red.

"I believe you love my brother," he said hoarsely, as she moved away.

She stopped and turned her head, as she answered.

"His is by far the more lovable character," she said in a tone of contempt. "I should not blame any woman for preferring him to you."

"It will be better for him that you should not prefer him." His face was livid now. Aliandra laughed, and turned so that she could see him.

"Bah! I believe you are a coward after all. He need not fear you, I fancy."

"Do you really think me a coward?" asked Tebaldo, in a low voice, and his eyes began to frighten her.

"You behave like one," she answered. "You are afraid of the mere opinion of society. That is the reason why you hesitate. You say you love me, but you really love only that you call your position."

"No," he answered, not moving. "There are other reasons. And you are mistaken about me. I am not a coward. Do not say it again. Do you understand?"

Again she shrugged her shoulders, as though to say that it mattered little to her whether he were a coward or not. But she did not like the look in his eyes, though she did not believe that he would hurt her. She had heard of his occasional terrible outbreaks of anger, but had never seen him in one of them. He was beginning to look dangerous now, she thought. She wondered whether she had gone too far, but reflected that, after all, if she meant to exasperate him into a promise of marriage, she must risk something.

"Do not make me say it," she replied, more gently than she had spoken yet.

Few feminine retorts are more irritating than that one, of which most women know the full value, but in some way it acted upon Tebaldo as a counter-irritant to his real anger.

"No," said Tebaldo, and his eyelids suddenly drooped, "you shall say something else. As you are just going away, this is hardly the moment to fix a day for our marriage."

She started slightly at the words, and looked at him. His eyes were less red, and the natural brown colour was coming back in his cheeks. She thought the moment of danger past.

"I shall be back in a fortnight," she answered.

"There will be time enough when you come back," he said in his usual tone of voice. "Provided that you do not change your mind in the meantime," he added, with a tolerable easy smile. "Do not forget that you love Francesco." He laughed, for he was really a good actor.

She laughed, too, but uneasily, more to quiet herself than to make him think that she was in a good humour again.

"I never forget the people I love," she said lightly.

Then with a quick gesture and movement, as though wholly forgiving him, she kissed her fingers to him, laughed again, and was out of the room in a moment, leaving him where he was. He stood still for three or four seconds, looking at the door through which she had disappeared, longing for her — like a fool, as he said to himself. Then he went out.

It had been a singular parting, he thought, and if he had not been at her mercy by one side of his nature, he said to himself that he would never have spoken to such a woman again. There was a frankly cynical determination on her part to marry him, which might have repelled any man, and which, he admitted, precluded all idea of love on her side. In spite of it all, his hand trembled when he had touched her sleeve at her shoulder, and he had not been quite able to control his voice. In spite of it all, too, he hated his brother with all his heart, far more bitterly than ever before, for what Aliandra had said of him.

Something more would have happened on that day, if he had known that Francesco was sitting in the little third-rate café opposite Aliandra's house, waiting to see him come out. He would, however, have been momentarily reassured had he further known that the Signora Barbuzzi, for diplomatic reasons, returned to the sitting-room and was present during the whole of Francesco's visit.

Aliandra left Rome the next morning. She did not care to tire herself by travelling very fast, so she slept in Naples, and did not reach Randazzo until the third day, a week after her father's accident.

CHAPTER XXIV

TEBALDO felt a sort of relief when Aliandra was gone. He missed her, and he longed for her, and yet, every time that he thought of Lizzie Slayback, he was glad that Aliandra was in Sicily. He felt more free. It was easier to bear a separation from her than to be ever in fear of her crossing the heiress's path. That, indeed, might have seemed a remote danger, considering the difference that lay between the lives of the American girl and the singer. But Miss Slayback was restless and inquisitive; she liked of all things to meet people who were 'somebody' in any department of art; she had heard of Aliandra Basili and of the sensation her appearance had created during the winter, and she was quite capable of taking a fancy to know her. Miss Lizzie generally began her acquaintance with anyone by ascertaining who the acquaintance's acquaintances might be, as Tebaldo well knew, and if at any moment she chose to know the artist, it was probable that his secret would be out in a quarter of an hour.

Then, too, he saw that he must precipitate matters, for spring was advancing into summer, and if his engagement were suddenly announced while Aliandra was in Rome, he believed that she would very probably go straight to Miss Slayback and tell her own story, being, as he could see, determined to marry him at any cost. He was therefore very glad that she was gone.

But when the hour came round at which he had been accustomed to go and see her every day, he missed her horribly, and went and shut himself up in his room. It was not a sentimentality, for he was incapable of that weak but delicate infusion of sentiment and water from which the Anglo-Saxon race derives such keen delight. It was more like a sort of physical possession, from which he could not escape, and during which he would have found it hard to be decently civil to Miss Slayback, or indeed to any other woman. At that time his whole mind and senses were filled with Aliandra, as though she had been bodily present in the room, and her handsome head and vital figure rose distinctly in his eyes, till his pulse beat fast in his throat and his lips were dry.

Two days after Aliandra's departure, Tebaldo was in this state, pacing up and down in his room and really struggling against the intense desire to drive instantly to the railway station and follow Aliandra to Sicily. Without a knock the door opened, and Francesco entered.

"What do you want?" asked Tebaldo, almost brutally, as he stopped in his walk.

"What is the matter with you?" enquired the other, in some surprise, at his brother's tone.

"What do you want, I say?" Tebaldo tapped the floor impatiently with his foot. "Why do you come here?"

"Really, you seem to be in an extraordinary frame of mind," observed Francesco. "I had no intention of disturbing you. I often come to your room —"

"No. You do not come often. Again — what do you want? Money? You generally want that. Take it — there on the table!" He pointed to a little package of the small Italian notes.

Francesco took two or three and put them carefully into his pocket-book. Tebaldo watched him, hating him more than usual for having come at that moment. He hated the back of his neck as Francesco bent down; it looked so smooth and the short hair was so curly just above his collar. He wondered whether Aliandra liked to look at the back of Francesco's neck, and his eyes grew red.

"So Aliandra has gone," observed Francesco, carelessly, as he returned the purse to his pocket and turned to his brother.

"Have you come here to tell me so?" asked Tebaldo, growing rapidly angry.

"Oh, no! You must have known it before I

did. I merely made a remark — why are you so angry? She will come back. She will probably come just when you are ready to marry Miss Slayback."

"Will you leave my affairs to me, and go?" Tebaldo made a step forward.

"My dear Tebaldo, I wish you would not be so furious about nothing. I come in peace, and you receive me like a wild animal. I am anxious about your marriage. It will be the salvation of our family, and the sooner you can conclude the matter, the better it will be for all of us."

"I do not see what advantage you are likely to gain by my marriage."

"Think of the position! It is a great advantage to be the brother of a rich man."

"In order to borrow money of him. I see."

"Not necessarily. It will change our position very much. The danger is that your friend Aliandra may spoil everything, if she hears of Miss Slayback."

"Either go, or speak plainly," said Tebaldo, beginning to walk up and down in order to control the impulse that was driving him to strike his brother.

Francesco sat down upon the edge of the writing-table and lighted a cigarette.

"It is a pity that we should be always quarrelling," he said.

"If you had not come here, we should not have quarrelled now," observed Tebaldo, thrusting his hands into his pockets, lest they should do Francesco some harm.

"We should have quarrelled the next time we met," continued the latter. "We always do. I wish to propose a peace, a compromise that may settle matters for ever."

"What matters? There are no matters to settle. Let me alone, and I will let you alone."

"Of course, you really mean to marry Miss Slayback? Do you, or do you not?"

"What an absurd question! If I do not mean to marry her, why do you suppose I waste my time with her? Do you imagine that I am in love with her?" He laughed harshly.

"Exactly," answered Francesco, as though his brother's question seemed perfectly natural to him. "The only explanation of your conduct is that you wish to marry the girl and get her money. It is very wise. We are all delighted. Vittoria likes her for her own sake, and our mother will be very happy. It will console her for Ferdinando's death, which has been a great blow to her."

"Well? Are you satisfied? Is that all you wished to know?" Tebaldo stopped before him.

"No. Not by any means. You marry Miss Slayback, and you get your share. I want mine."

"And what do you consider your share, as you

call it?" enquired Tebaldo, with some curiosity, in spite of his ill temper.

"It does not seem likely that you mean to marry them both," said Francesco, swinging one leg slowly and blowing the smoke towards the window.

"Both — whom?"

"Both the American and Aliandra. Of course, you could marry Aliandra in church and the American by a civil marriage, and they might both be satisfied, if you could keep them apart — "

"What an infernal scoundrel you are," observed Tebaldo, slowly.

"You are certainly not the proper person to point out my moral shortcomings," retorted Francesco, coolly. "But I did not suppose that you meant to marry them both, and as you have very wisely decided to take the American girl, I really think you might leave Aliandra to me. If you marry the one, I do not see why I should not marry the other."

"If I ever find you making love to Aliandra Basili," said Tebaldo, with slow emphasis, "I will break every bone in your body."

But he still kept his hands in his pockets. Francesco laughed, for he did not believe that he was in present bodily danger. It was not the first time that Tebaldo had spoken in that way.

"You are ready to quarrel again! I am sure, I am perfectly reasonable. I wish to marry Aliandra

Basili. I have kept out of your way in that direction for a long time. I should not mention the matter now, unless I were sure that you had made up your mind."

"And—" Tebaldo came near to him, but hesitated. "And — excuse me — but what reason have you for supposing that Aliandra will marry you?"

"That is my affair," answered Francesco, but he shrank a little and slipped from his seat on the table to his feet, when he saw his brother's face.

"How do you mean that it is your affair?" asked Tebaldo, roughly. "How do you know that she will marry you? Have you asked her? Has she told you that she loves you?"

Francesco hesitated a moment. The temptation to say that he was loved by Aliandra, merely for the sake of giving his brother pain, was very great. But so was the danger, and that was upon him already, for Tebaldo mistook the meaning of his hesitation, and finally lost his temper.

His sinewy hands went right at his brother's throat, half strangling him in an instant, and then swinging him from side to side on his feet as a terrier shakes a rat. If Francesco had carried even a pocket knife, he would have had it out in an instant, and would have used it. But he had no weapon, and he was no match for Tebaldo in a fury. He struck out fiercely enough with his fists, but the other's hands were above his own, and he could do nothing. He could not even cry out, for he was half choked, and Tebaldo was quite silent in his rage. There would have been murder, had there been weapons within the reach of either.

When Tebaldo finally threw him off, Francesco fell heavily upon one knee against the door, but caught the handle with one hand, and regained his feet instantly.

"You shall pay me yet," he said in a low voice, his throat purple, but his face suddenly white.

"Yes. This is only something on account," said Tebaldo, with a sneer. "You shall have the rest of the payment some other time."

But Francesco was gone before the last words had passed his brother's lips. The door closed behind him, and Tebaldo heard his quick footsteps outside as he went off in the direction of his own room.

The angry man grew calmer when he was alone, but now and then, as he walked up and down, and backwards and forwards, he clenched his hands spasmodically, wishing that he still had his brother in his grip. Yet, when he reflected, as he began to do before long, upon what had really happened, he realized that he had not, after all, had much reason for taking his brother by the throat. It was the hesitation that had made his temper break out. But then, it might have meant so much. In his present state, the thought that perhaps Aliandra loved Francesco was like the bite of a horsefly in a raw wound, and he quivered under it. He could not get away from it. He fancied he saw Francesco kissing Aliandra's handsome mouth, and that her eyes smiled, and then her eyelids drooped with pleasure. His anger subsided a little, but his jealousy grew monstrously minute by minute, and his wrath smouldered beneath it. He remembered past days and meetings, and glances Aliandra had given his brother, such as she had never bestowed upon himself. She did not love him, though she wished to marry him, and was determined to do so, if it were possible. But it flashed upon him that she loved Francesco, and had loved him from the first. That was not quite the truth, though it was near it, and he saw a hundred things in the past to prove that it was the truth altogether.

He was human enough to feel the wound to his vanity, and the slight cast upon him by a comparison in which Francesco was preferred to him, as well as the hurt at his heart which came with it. He did not know of Francesco's daily visits, but he suspected them and exaggerated all he guessed. Doubtless Francesco had seen her again and again alone, quite lately, while Tebaldo had been made to endure day after day the presence of Aliandra's aunt in the room. Again the red-lipped vision of a kiss flashed in the shadow of the room, a living picture, and once more his eyes grew red, and his hands clenched themselves spasmodically, closing on nothing.

She had said that she preferred Francesco. She had almost admitted that she loved him, and he could remember how cold her eyes had been while she had been saying it. There had been another light in them for his brother, and she had not held her hands behind her back when Francesco had held out his. Or else she had, laughingly. And then she had put up her face, instead, for him to kiss. Tebaldo ground his teeth.

His jealousy got hold of him in the vitals and gnawed cruelly. Everything in his own room made him think of Aliandra, though there was not one object in a score that could possibly have any association with her, nor any right to remind him of her, as he tried to tell himself. But his watch, lying on the toilet table, made him think of her watch, a pretty little one he had given her. His gloves made him think of her gloves, his books recalled hers, his very chairs, as they chanced to stand about the room, revived the memory of how other chairs had stood when he had parted from her. The infinite pettiness of the details that irritated him did not shock his reason as would have happened at any other time. On the contrary, the more of them sprang up, the more they stung him. Instead of one gadfly, there were hundreds. And all the time there was the almost irresistible physical longing to go to her, and throw over everything else. He went out, for he could not bear his room any longer.

It was still hot in the streets in the early afternoon, and there was a fierce glare all through the new part of the city where there were many white houses in straight rows along smoothly paved streets. Tebaldo walked in the shade, and once or twice he took off his hat for a moment and let the dry, hot breeze blow upon his forehead. The strong light was somehow a relief as he grew accustomed to it, and his southern nature regained its balance in the penetrating warmth. He walked quickly, not heeding his direction, as he followed the line of broad shade and passed quickly through the blazing sunshine that filled the crossing of each side street.

He regained his normal state, and presently, being quite calm, he stopped and quietly lighted a cigar. Like many men of ardent and choleric temperament, he neither smoked nor drank much, but there were times, like the present, when smoking helped him to think quietly.

Before the cigar was half finished he was at the door of the hotel at which Miss Slayback and her aunt were staying. He was glad that he had decided to see her on that afternoon, and he attributed the good sense, as he would have called it,

which had ultimately brought him to her door, to
the soothing influence of the tobacco.

Miss Slayback was alone in the sitting-room.
The blinds were closed, but the windows were
open, and the warm breeze stirred the white curtains. It was an ordinary hotel sitting-room, like
hundreds of others, but Miss Lizzie had not been
satisfied with such mediocrity of surroundings, and
had taken much pains to give the room an inhabited
look. She had, of course, bought several hundred
objects of no particular value, as rich women who
visit Rome for the first time invariably do, and
most of them were in sight in her sitting-room.
There were photographs by the score, pinned to
the walls and standing on tables, and heaped
together in a corner. The photograph is the
unresistible temptation to women. There were
three or four clever water-colour studies of men
and women in costume, such as one sees everywhere
in Rome; there were half a dozen bronzes copied,
in the unfinished, wholesale manner, from the
antique; there was the inevitable old choir book
of the psalms, with the old musical notation that
is still used for plain chaunt, written on parchment
and opened at the page which presented the best
illuminated capital letter; there were three or
four pieces of old embroidered vestments, draped
over the backs of chairs, and there were several
vases containing fresh flowers and dry wild grasses

from the Campagna. And there was Miss Lizzie Slayback.

She was exceedingly pretty in a sort of nondescript dress, between a tea-gown and something else; for though it was adorned with ribbons and laces, after the manner of tea-gowns, it was short-skirted when she stood up. In fact, it was 'a little creation' of her own, as her dressmaker would have said, thereby disclaiming all responsibility for its eccentricity. But it was distinctly becoming, and Miss Lizzie knew it.

There is a great difference, morally, between being vain and being æsthetically aware of one's advantages and good points. Vanity is even more blind than love, but there is something really and healthily artistic in judicious and successful self-adornment. Vanity paints its eyes, and rouges its cheeks, and dyes its hair, and laces its waist till its ribs crack. Good taste cuts its clothes according to its figure and its age, instead of pinching its body to fit its clothes. Vanity is full of affectation; good taste presents the best it has to view, so far as it can, and hides what is less good, without attempting to distort it, because what is not good cannot be made to look good, by torture, to eyes that understand. The vain woman interprets the statement that she is clay, in a literal sense, and tries to violently model her clay into the Venus of her dreams. The woman of taste accepts the fact that she is not a goddess and makes the best of her mortality as she has received it.

Miss Slayback was very pretty, and even Tebaldo Pagliuca admitted the fact, though he was not in the least in love with her. She smiled and looked ten times prettier than before, as he entered the room.

"My aunt is supposed to be out," she said, as he sat down. "But she is in the next room. So it is quite proper."

She laughed a little at her own speech, for she was still amused by European ideas of propriety, and she would have been surprised if anyone had been shocked by her receiving Tebaldo alone, when Mrs. Slayback was really asleep in the next room, during the heat of the afternoon. Tebaldo smiled courteously, leaned back a little in his small, low armchair, and fixed his eyes upon her face in silence. His expression might have deceived an older and a wiser woman.

"I am very glad to find you alone," he said softly, after an emphatic pause of admiration. "Your aunt is one of the most charming women in the world, of course, but—"

"But she is not always necessary," interrupted Miss Slayback. "Do you want to see my new embroidery? I bought it this morning—"

"No. I do not care about your embroideries. I came to see you, not vestments."

"It is not a vestment. It is an altar cloth—"

"It is not you, at all events," said Tebaldo, fixing his eyes upon her again. "I want you and only you—to-day, to-morrow, and for ever." His voice was well modulated.

Miss Lizzie looked down, thoughtfully, but she did not blush. Tebaldo leaned forward a little, gazing earnestly into her face. But she looked down and said nothing, for she wished him to say more. It was pleasant to hear, and though her eyes were bent upon the carpet, she could really see his face quite distinctly.

"I think you see and understand that I love you devotedly," he said in soft tones.

It was not easy for him, with his ideas, to make the statement in cold blood, so to say. But that was evidently what she expected, and he did his best.

"You must have seen it," he continued. "You must have understood it. I have tried to express it to you with the most profound respect, with that respect which I have felt for you from the first, and shall always feel, and wish to feel, for my wife."

Possibly Miss Lizzie, not being a Latin, would have been willing to hear less about respect and more about love. But he managed to make his tone convey something of that also. She looked up, slowly raising her long black lashes, till her dark blue eyes met his.

"You know," she said, with an odd mixture of gentleness and wilfulness, "if I marry you, you must always let me do exactly as I please."

Tebaldo had known her long enough to be past the stage in which she could surprise him. The conception of American life which he had formed from her conversation was somewhat fantastic.

"You would not be so frank if you meant to misuse your liberty," he answered wisely.

"Do not be so sure!" laughed Miss Lizzie, gaily.

But Tebaldo wanted a more binding reply to his proposal.

"Please do not laugh," he said. "Your answer —your consent will transport me to paradise."

"I hope not," answered the girl, still laughing a little. "I prefer you on earth, if I am to marry you."

"You are adorable!" exclaimed Tebaldo, understanding that he must accept her jesting humour.

"Yes? Am I?" She smiled.

"But you see that I adore you, worship you— love you! Everyone does—"

"I do not want everyone—"

"But me? That is the question. Do you—"

"Oh, yes! I want you," she answered, interrupting him. "Please let me think a moment. I am making up my mind."

Thereupon Miss Lizzie got up from her seat. Tebaldo rose also, wondering what she might be going to do to help her mind in making itself up. He rather expected that she meant to go into the next room to consult her aunt before giving her final answer. But she had no intention of doing that. She went to the window, and looked through the slats of the closed blinds, into the hot glare outside. Tebaldo remained standing close to the chair in which he had been sitting. As has been said, she could no longer surprise him, but he watched the ways and manners of the American young girl with interest, even while he grew nervous as he thought of the magnitude of the stake he hoped to win.

Miss Lizzie stayed some time at the window, without moving. When she suddenly turned back into the room, and came straight up to Tebaldo, her face was a little paler than usual; but he could not see it, for the light was behind her. Her manner had quite changed now, and she spoke very gravely.

"I have not known you very long, and you are asking me to put my whole life in your hands," she said. "I like you very much. I care for you so much that I am going to trust you, though I know you so little. I am going to say yes."

She laid her hands in his trustfully, and looked up into his face. His lids half veiled his eyes, for the triumph in his look was not the triumph of love, and he knew it. No sane man is without some good impulse, be he ever so bad.

"I thank you with all my heart," he said, wisely choosing simple words now; and he pressed her hands gently. "I shall try to make you happy," he added.

It all seemed very strange to her. Possibly something warned her even then that he was very false, more false than she could have understood. She had expected, shyly and with a little not quite unpleasant trepidation, that he would suddenly catch her in his arms and kiss her a score of times, quickly, as no one had ever kissed her. Yet there he stood, quite calm, just pressing the tips of her fingers, as though he were afraid of hurting her, and saying that he meant to make her happy. She was disappointed, though she would not have admitted that she was.

She little guessed that the bad man had just then chanced to feel one of the few good impulses that ever disturbed him. At that moment it would have seemed considerably worse to him to act as she really expected that he would than it would have seemed to cut Francesco's throat in his sleep. Explain those things who can. There is good in human nature, even at its worst; and it comes to the surface unexpectedly. Francesco, whose character was on the whole far less evil and malevolent, would have had no such scruple. To him a woman was a woman, and nothing more. But Tebaldo either loved or did not love, and the woman he did not love was not a woman at all in his eyes. And since in this case she chanced to be an innocent girl, his manliness — for he was manly and physically brave — revolted at the idea of offending her innocence.

An old-fashioned theologian might say that a man who has no good in him is not properly fit to be damned. Such a man would have no free-will, and could not, therefore, logically be punished for anything he did. That was not Tebaldo Pagliuca's case, at all events.

Miss Lizzie stood still a moment, looking up to his face, after he had spoken; then she drew away her hands, and sat down again, feeling rather shy, for the first time since she had been a child. It seemed strange that it should all be over, and that she was to be married. Tebaldo began a little speech.

"You have made me very happy," he said; and he formed a number of fairly well turned phrases, in which to express his satisfaction, which was genuine, and his affection, which was not.

She did not hear him, for her own thoughts seemed louder than his smoothly spoken words. She was happy, and yet she was uncomfortable, in an undefined way, and did not know what was the matter. He did not seem to expect any response just then, and she let him talk on. Then she was aware that he was repeating a question.

"May I announce our engagement?" he was asking, for the second time.

"Of course!" she exclaimed, suddenly realizing the sense of his words. "It is not a thing to be concealed. I will tell my aunt at once. You must come and see her this evening — no, we are going somewhere — I forget where! Come to-morrow, please."

"And when — ?" He purposely left the sentence incomplete, filling the question with one of the long looks he had employed so often with such success.

"When what? Oh! You mean, when shall we be married? Let me see. It is May now. I shall have to go to Paris, of course. You will come, will you not?"

"Could we not be married first, and go to Paris afterwards?" enquired Tebaldo.

But Miss Lizzie had no intention of being hurried to the altar without having got the full amount of enjoyment out of buying beautiful clothes, and Tebaldo was obliged to content himself with a promise that the wedding should take place early in the autumn. She wished to be married in Rome by an archbishop, if not by a cardinal. Tebaldo agreed to the whole college of cardinals, if necessary.

When he went away, he walked more slowly. The sun was very low, and the air was growing cooler. He sauntered down towards the Corso, well pleased with his own prospects and thinking out the details of his future with intense satisfaction. Tebaldo was no spendthrift fool to waste his wife's fortune on absurd frivolities, or to gamble it away in mad speculations. He meant to build up the Corleone once more, and make his family far greater than it had ever been. He did not know exactly how rich Miss Slayback was, but his guessing was, if anything, under the truth, and he had seen enough of her to know that she desired to be a personage, and was attracted by the idea of rank. He knew that she and her aunt had taken pains to enquire into the validity of his titles. He smiled when he remembered how cheaply he had held them in the old days at Camaldoli, when he would have sold his birthright for a new rifle, and a title or two for a supply of ammunition; and he admired in himself the transformation from the rough country gentleman, hardly one step above the tenant farmer of the Sicilian hills, to the fashionable young nobleman, engaged to be married to a great heiress, and already on the point of restoring to his family all its ancient magnificence.

He walked the length of the Corso and back before he went home. He had hardly entered his room when there was a light knock at the door. Vittoria entered, looking pale and frightened.

"What was the matter between you and Francesco?" she asked as soon as she had shut the door behind her.

"The matter?" Tebaldo looked at her curiously, wondering whether she knew anything about Aliandra Basili. "We quarrelled, as usual," he said briefly.

"It must have been worse than usual," said Vittoria, in a low voice. "He is gone."

"Gone? Where? Gone out to dinner?" Tebaldo affected to laugh carelessly.

"No. I think he is gone to Sicily," answered the young girl.

Tebaldo uttered an exclamation of surprise, and his expression changed as he looked at his sister.

"Yes," she continued. "He made a terrible scene with me and our mother — not exactly a scene, perhaps — it was all about you. He said that he was going, that he could not live in the house any longer, that he should never come back again. He said —" she hesitated.

"What more did he say?"

"He was half mad, I think. He said it was better to be an outlaw than to live under such a brother as you, and that he would pay you for what you had done to him in the way you least expected."

"What makes you think that he is gone to Sicily?" asked Tebaldo, very quietly, while his lids drooped at the corners.

"He looked for the trains in the newspaper, and I heard him say 'Reggio' and 'Messina.' We tried to quiet him — we did what we could. But he packed a quantity of things in a hurry, and went off in a cab, looking at his watch, and saying that he had barely time. Mother fell into one of those terrible fits of crying that she has sometimes, and she is ill again. I thought it best to tell you."

"Certainly," said Tebaldo, thoughtfully. "And now that you have told me, please go away, for I must dress."

She was already turning, for she was used to his peremptory ways, but he stopped her.

"I may as well tell you, Vittoria," he said; "I am engaged to be married to your friend Miss Slayback. I hope that, as the marriage will be so advantageous to our family, you will not criticise me to her too much. I am not quite so bad as you sometimes think."

Vittoria looked at him in silence for three or four seconds before she spoke.

"I shall say nothing to injure you with her," she said slowly, and at once left the room.

CHAPTER XXV

ALIANDRA was received in Randazzo with that sort of ovation which only Italians accord to a successful artist; and her father's house was filled for a whole day with the respectable townsmen and their wives and daughters, who came to greet her and congratulate her. For the newspapers had informed them of her successes in Rome, and the Sicilian papers had exaggerated the original reports tenfold. The mayor and his wife, the municipal officers, the grey-haired lieutenant of carabineers with his pretty daughter, the rector, the curate, the young emigration agent of the big steamship company with his betrothed bride and her mother, the principal shopkeeper with his wife and children, the innkeeper — in short, all that represented the highest fashion in Randazzo, including Don Tolomeo Bellini, the most important tenant farmer on the great Fornasco estate as well as a small freeholder, whose ancestors had been privileged to bear arms, and who, therefore, ranked as a gentleman and stamped the cheeses from his dairy with a little five-pointed coronet. Basili had formerly hoped to get him for a son-in-law, and he would have been considered a very good match for the notary's daughter.

All Randazzo talked of the singer's return, and the poor people crowded the street to get a look at her. The mayor said she was an honour to the province and to Sicily, and the rector, who had baptized her, expressed his hope that she might be always as good as she was famous, for he distrusted the name of art, but wished the girl well for her father's sake and her own.

Don Atanasio, the apothecary of Santa Vittoria, tried to persuade his daughter to go with him down to Randazzo and pay Aliandra a visit.

"It will divert you a little from your sorrow, my daughter," he said, shaking his head.

Concetta's dark eyes turned slowly towards her father with a wondering look, as though she were amazed at his audacity and yet pitied his inability to measure her grief.

"The dead need no amusements," she said, gravely. "They are very quiet. They wait."

"Eh — but the living," objected Don Atanasio. "We are alive, you know."

Concetta did not heed what he said.

"The dead are very quiet. They wait for the Judgment and the Resurrection — the judgment of blood, and the resurrection of the innocent. Then they will be alive again."

Don Atanasio sighed, for his unhappy daughter

was no longer like other women. She was of those simple beings for whom life has but one purpose after love has taken possession, and from whom the loved one, dying, takes all purpose away for ever. The old man sighed and looked sideways at her, and a tear ran down his thin, straight nose, and fell upon the plaster he was spreading on the marble slab before him; but his daughter's dark eyes were dry. She was sitting on a little low stool behind one end of the counter, where she could not be seen by anyone who might chance to come into the shop. Her head was screened by the great old-fashioned marble mortar.

Don Atanasio laid down the broad mixing-knife he was using, pushed back the black broadcloth cap which Concetta had once embroidered with a design of green leaves, wiped his spectacles, turned away to blow his nose with a large coloured handkerchief, and turned back again to take a long look at the girl. He laid his hand gently on her head, pressing her forehead back until she looked up into his face.

"You wish to make me die also," he said slowly. "What have I done that you wish to make me die?"

She looked at him very sadly, and then quickly got hold of his other hand and kissed it with a sort of devotion. She was very fond of him. He patted the back of her head affectionately.

"In truth, my dear," he said gently, "if I see you always thus, I shall not live long, for I have only you in the world, and the rest does not matter. But it is not that, since I would die to make you happy. What should it be for me? I am old. I am of no use. They will have another apothecary in Santa Vittoria. That is nothing. My thoughts are for you."

"Do not think for me," answered the girl. "I sit here quietly. I do no harm. And then, when it is later, I go to see my dead one every day."

"But it is not good to do this always," objected Don Atanasio, coaxingly. "That is why I say come down with me to Randazzo to-morrow, and let us go and see the notary Basili, who has broken his leg, and his daughter, the great singer, who has come back from Rome to visit him. She is a good girl, and you can make a little conversation with her. It will be a diversion, a sober diversion, and the air will do you good, and the movement."

She kissed his hand again, then dropped it, and drew up her black shawl over her head, for she heard a step on the threshold. Don Atanasio heard it, too, and immediately took up his mixing-knife and went to work again at the plaster. The newcomer was the lieutenant who commanded the infantry men quartered in Santa Vittoria. He asked for six grains of quinine in three doses.

He was a quiet young fellow, scrupulously neat

in his close-fitting tunic with its turned-down velvet collar, his small red moustache, carefully trimmed, and his red hair parted behind and well brushed below his cap. He had singularly bright blue eyes with rough red eyebrows and a bright and healthy but much freckled complexion.

Don Atanasio proceeded to weigh out the little doses of the valuable drug, and the officer watched him as he cut the clean white paper into smaller sizes and neatly folded each package.

"Do you know all those Pagliuca brothers?" he asked suddenly.

The apothecary stopped in his work and looked at him keenly. The officer was a Piedmontese, and was, therefore, unpopular in the south.

"Eh!" ejaculated the apothecary. "They formerly lived here. I have seen them."

Concetta did not stir in her hiding-place at the end of the counter, behind the marble mortar. The officer was silent for a moment, and the apothecary hastily folded the last package, slipping one end of the doubled paper into the other, as chemists do, and taking up another sheet of paper in which to wrap the three doses together.

"One of them has suddenly returned here," said the officer. "He is in the neighbourhood, and is not here for any good purpose. Most probably he has come to do some injury to the gentleman who killed his brother, the brigand."

In spite of herself Concetta drew a sharp breath between her teeth. The officer's eyes turned inquisitively towards the corner where she sat.

"It is the cat," said Don Atanasio, calmly. "One lira and fifty centimes, Signor Lieutenant," he added, handing the officer the package across the counter.

"They say that it is Francesco Pagliuca who has come back, and that he was seen this morning in Randazzo," said the young man, while he counted out the money in big coppers; for, as usual in the south, there was a scarcity even of the flimsy little paper notes. "We do not know him by sight, you see," he continued, "and I should be very glad of any information, if you should see him in the village. One thirty — forty — fifty — there it is."

He laid the last copper on the marble slab.

"A thousand thanks, Signor Lieutenant," said Don Atanasio, collecting the coins.

"And you will let us know if you see the young man?" asked the officer.

"You shall be served," replied the apothecary, gravely.

The officer thanked him, nodded, and went out, with a little clattering of his light sabre. When he was gone, Don Atanasio's grave face relaxed in a smile.

"And those are the men who expect to rule us Sicilians," he said in a low voice, more to himself than to his daughter. "They wish to catch a man. What do they do? They warn his friends by asking questions. What can such people catch? A crab, as we say, that will bite their own fingers. Then they complain. They are like children. They do not even know what the mafia is, and they come to Sicily."

Concetta sat quite still in her corner, thinking. It seemed to her sure that Francesco Pagliuca had come to kill Orsino Saracinesca, for his brother's sake. That was what the officer thought, and all the soldiers would be looking out for Francesco, and on the smallest excuse he would be arrested on mere suspicion. It did not strike her that he could possibly have come for any other purpose, and her one desire was that Orsino should be killed. That was man's work, that killing, and she would leave it to the men. But if none of them would do it, she would some day take her father's gun and wait for Orsino at the cemetery, for he often passed that way. She was not afraid to kill him, but she considered it to be the duty and business of the Corleone men. They had prior rights, and, besides, they were men. A woman should not do any killing so long as there were men to do it, except in self-defence.

It was clearly her duty, she thought, to warn Francesco that the soldiers were aware of his presence in the neighbourhood. It would be much wiser of him, she reflected, to communicate with the outlaws who were about Noto, and get half a dozen resolute fellows to help him. She had no knowledge of his character, though she had often met him, and she supposed him to be like his brothers, bold and determined. So she wished to warn him, in order that he might safely accomplish what she supposed must be his purpose.

The difficulty lay in finding him. Her father might help her, perhaps, but it was doubtful. It was quite certain that he could not say or do anything which could thwart Francesco's plans, but, on the other hand, she knew that he would be careful not to seem to help him, for he had to keep on good terms with the authorities, for the simple reason that he held a government license as apothecary, which could easily be taken from him.

"Did you know that Francesco Pagliuca had come back?" she asked, after a long silence, during which the plaster had been finished, folded up, and laid aside ready to be called for.

"I knew," answered Don Atanasio, but he did not seem inclined to say anything more.

"Why did you not tell me, father?" asked the girl.

"It might have given you pain, my child. And then, one does not say everything one knows. One forgets many things. He slept at the house of Don Taddeo, the grocer."

"Where is he now? Is he still here?"

"Who shall say where he is? Heaven knows where he is. I cannot know everything."

He answered with a little irritation, for he understood that Concetta wished to see her dead lover's brother, and he could not understand how any good could come of the meeting.

Concetta rose slowly to her feet and came out from behind the counter. She had grown very thin, but she was not less beautiful. She drew her black shawl together under her chin, and it fell over her forehead to her eyes. There was no disguise in it, for everyone knew her, but she felt that it gave her some privacy in her grief, even in broad day and in the street.

"I go to breathe the air," she said quietly, moving towards the door.

"Go, my daughter, you need it," answered the apothecary.

He watched her sadly, and as she went out he moved to the entrance of the shop and looked after her. Tall, sad, and black, and graceful, she walked smoothly along the shady side of the street, which was deserted in the blazing noon. Don Atanasio did not go in again till she had turned the corner and was out of sight.

She found the grocer's brother, the fat and cross-eyed sacristan, eating dark brown beans out of an earthen bowl with an iron fork, in the open shop. No one else was there. It was a cool, vaulted place, with a floor of beaten cement and volcanic ashes, and a number of big presses, in a row behind a long walnut counter, black and polished with age. Hams and sides of bacon hung from the ceiling, and the air smelt of salt pork, cereals, and candles. The fat man sat on a bench, in his shirt sleeves, eating his beans with a sort of slow voracity. He looked up as Concetta's shadow darkened the door.

"Will you accept?" he asked, lifting his earthen bowl a little as he spoke.

"Thank you, and good appetite," answered the girl. "How are you?"

"Always to serve you, most gentle Concetta," said the man. "What do you need?"

"Eat," replied Concetta, sitting down upon a rush-bottom chair. "I do not come to disturb you. Are you all alone?" She peered into the shadows at the back of the shop.

"Eh, you know how it is? Taddeo eats and then goes to sleep, and while he sleeps I keep the shop. In truth, it needs no great merchant to do that, for no one comes at this hour."

"And you and your brother do not eat together?"

"Generally we do, but to-day, who knows how it was? He ate first and went to sleep. Then I brought my beans here for company. This is our conversation. I open my mouth, and before I can speak the beans answer me. This I call, indeed, conversation."

"And Francesco Pagliuca, with whom does he converse upstairs?" asked Concetta, lowering her voice.

The man looked up quickly, with his mouth full, as though to see whether she were in earnest and knew the truth. A glance convinced him that she did.

"He went to Randazzo at dawn," he said, almost in a whisper. "He makes love with the notary's daughter there."

Concetta did not believe that this could be the only reason for Francesco's return.

"Why does he not stay at Randazzo, then?" she enquired. "Why should he come here at all? It is a long way."

"Perhaps he is afraid of Basili's friends," suggested the fat man. "Or he prefers to sleep here because the air is better. He will certainly not tell us why he comes."

"Is he coming back this evening?"

"I think so, for he has a box here with his clothes, and other things. But for charity's sake, tell no one."

"I?" Concetta laughed in a cold way, without a smile. "I wish to warn him that the soldiers know he was in Randazzo yesterday, and are looking out for him."

She told the man of the lieutenant's visit to her father's shop, and he listened attentively.

"I could wait for him in the road," he said. "He thought that the soldiers would not know him here, because they are all new men. But they have seen him in Randazzo and have sent word. They think that he has come on account of the Saracinesca, but he has followed the notary's daughter from Rome. They cannot touch him so long as he does no harm."

"They may prevent him from doing it," said Concetta, looking steadily at the man.

"That would be a pity," he answered gravely. "I will wait for him in the road."

"But if he comes by the bridle path over the hills, you will miss him."

"I do not think he will do that, for it is a bad road, and he had my brother's best horse to ride."

"Go and wait in the bridle path," said Concetta.

"I will wait in the road, towards Camaldoli."

"He will not come before sunset," observed the sacristan. "That crazy priest of the Saracinesca, Don Ippolito, comes to play the organ in Santa Vittoria every day, and pays me to blow the bellows, and he never goes away till twenty-three o'clock."

Twenty-three of the clock is half an hour before the sun sets, at all times of the year, by the old reckoning, which is still in use in the south.

"You can send a boy to blow the bellows," suggested Concetta. "You cannot trust anyone to warn Francesco Pagliuca."

They both supposed that since enquiry was being made for him, he would be in imminent danger of arrest, with or without any legal grounds, an opinion sufficiently indicative of the state of the country. The man stared blankly at the wall for a few seconds after Concetta had last spoken, then nodded, and began to eat again.

The girl rose from her chair, and moved towards the door with her graceful, slowly cadenced step. She had done what she had come to do and was quite sure of the man, as indeed she had reason to be, for the mafia protects its own, and generally has its own way in the end, in spite of governments and soldiers. If Concetta and the fat sacristan asked no one to help them, it was because it was such a very simple matter to warn Francesco of danger, that they needed no assistance. But as they needed none, they told no one what they were going to do.

Concetta came home again to the quiet little shop, and Don Atanasio bolted the glass door, and they both went upstairs to dinner. The girl ate a little better than usual, and sipped half a glass of strong, black wine.

"The air did you good," observed her father, looking at her. "Eh, this human body! What is it? Who shall ever understand it? You go out every afternoon, when it is cool, for two hours, and it does you no good, and you eat no more than a bee takes from a flower. And to-day you go out for half an hour into a heat that would burn up paving-stones, and you come back with an appetite. So much the better. It is not I that should complain, if you ate the house and the walls, poor child."

"When the heart is thirsty for blood, the body is not hungry for meat," said the beautiful, white-faced girl, in her clear, low voice.

CHAPTER XXVI

IPPOLITO and Orsino had already acquired certain fixed habits in their several occupations, so that they rarely failed to meet at the same regular hours and then separate again, each doing the same or similar things day after day. Such regularity becomes a second nature in remote places where there is little chance that anything unexpected should happen.

Orsino had really not enough to do, after he had once familiarized himself with his surroundings. So long as San Giacinto had remained, it had been different, for he had great plans, and had spent much time in riding about the country with an engineer from Palermo who was to build the light railway round Etna. San Giacinto had now gone back to Rome, however, leaving his cousin in charge of Camaldoli, with directions to manage things with an easy hand, so as not to prejudice the people against the work of the railway when it should be begun. To do this meant, practically, to leave the tenants to their own devices, unless it were possible to help them in any way to which they should not object. At the same time, there were certain defensive measures which were always necessary, for no one knew when the brigands might grow weary of Noto and appear on the slopes of Etna again to avenge their friend, Ferdinando Pagliuca.

Orsino used to ride about a good deal, more for the sake of exercise than for anything he could accomplish, and he carried his rifle now as a matter of habit, but rarely took one or two of the carabineers with him. He began to believe that there were not really any outlaws at all, and that Ferdinando's unknown friend had left that part of the country. Ippolito, as a priest, went about unarmed, and, being naturally fearless, he rambled about as he pleased. Almost every day he walked to Santa Vittoria and spent an hour at the organ. Orsino accompanied him, when there was any reason for going to the village, but it did not amuse him to hear his brother's music. In fact, it was rather a relief to him not to hear the piano constantly at his elbow, as he heard it when Ippolito played in their joint sitting-room in Rome.

On the afternoon of the day on which Concetta had walked to the grocer's shop, Ippolito strolled up to the small church as usual. There was a little lame boy who had discovered the priest's habits, and used to hang about in the afternoon in the hope of earning a penny by calling the fat sacristan to come and blow the organ. He was not strong enough to blow it himself, and was content and glad to get a copper or two for limping into the village with his message. Ippolito now had a key of his own to the church, and went inside while the man was coming. Each day, during the twenty minutes or so which generally elapsed, he worked at the back of the instrument, repairing with bits of wire a number of trackers that ran from the pedals to a wooden stop set up on one side of the organ. At some former time the connexions had been repaired with waxed string, which the hungry church mice had gnawed to pieces. It was a troublesome job, requiring patience and some mechanical skill, as well as two or three simple tools which Ippolito had brought from Rome and now left in the organ until the work should be finished.

Instead of the sacristan, a big boy appeared on this particular day, the same who had carried the holy water for the priest who had come down to Camaldoli when Ferdinando had been killed. He explained that the sacristan had been sent on an errand to Bronte by his brother, the grocer, and had left him, the boy, to do duty at the bellows if needed. Ippolito thought nothing of the matter, and sat down to make music, as usual. The days were growing very long, and he generally regulated his stay in the church by the sun rather than by his watch. Sometimes the fat sacristan came round from behind, perspiring, and declaring that his brother needed him at home.

Meanwhile Concetta had gone down the road to the cemetery just beyond the shoulder of the hill, out of sight of the village and the little church in which Ippolito was playing the organ. It was her hour, and he had grown used to seeing her sitting on the curbstone by the churchyard gate every day when he went home just before sunset. When she passed the church and heard the music through the door that was left ajar, she knew also who was there, and her eyes darkened as she went by, and she drew her shawl more closely about her head. And she recognized the priest's light step when he came by the cemetery gate an hour later, and she always turned her face away, that she might not see him.

The people knew her, too, and most of them pitied her, and all respected her sorrow. Some of the labourers who came down from the hill farm, by the paths that turned into the main road just at the end of the churchyard, used to touch their hats when they passed her, and, when she chanced to be looking, she nodded gravely, acknowledging their greeting. They knew she was half mad, but the madness of a great sorrow has always been respected by simple folks who feel seldom, but keenly, and think little. The peasants generally passed about sunset on their way into the village.

To-day Concetta came to the gate as usual, and when she reached it Francesco was no longer uppermost in her thoughts. At the sight of the black cross that marked the last grave on the left, the whole world vanished again, and her sorrow came down like a darkness between her and all life. She stood with dry eyes and compressed lips, grasping the iron rails that were hot with the level sun, and out of the long, low mound rose the face and figure of the well-loved man.

There can be nothing intellectual in the spasm of a great sorrow, in the blind grasping upon emptiness for what is not, in the heart-famine that no living thing can satisfy. Such grief brings no thoughts, for it is the very contrary of thinking. It is only when each returning convulsion has subsided that thought comes back, and then it comes uncertainly like the sense of touching a small object through a heavy pall.

Concetta had no consciousness of the passing of time, as she stood at the gate, nor for a long while afterwards, when she had sat down upon the curbstone in her accustomed attitude, with her shawl drawn down over her face, shielding it from the low rays of the sinking sun, and from the sight of the world that was so desolate for her. As spring warmed to summer, no one passed that way who could help it, for the road was dusty and hot.

Two of the foot-carabineers passed her, returning to Santa Vittoria from their regular patrol of the high road, their carbines slung over their shoulders and their pipe-clayed cross-belts gleaming white in the sun. They knew her, too, and barely glanced at her as they went by. She did not even raise her head, though she remembered, now, that she had come to wait for Francesco Pagliuca, and she was glad that the patrol had marched up again, for he must be following them, and could thus not be met by them. She knew that he would come on horseback. As she strained her ears to catch the distant sound of hoofs, the savage longing for revenge began to burn again in her heart. Surely he must have come for that, and not really for love of Aliandra Basili. If he reached the cemetery in time, he could kill Ippolito, the priest, as he came down from the church. She would show him just where to stand with his gun, at the corner of the wall, and she would stand beside him; and then, if he were quick, he could get down half way to Camaldoli, near the crossroads and kill Orsino, too, when he came up hastily to see his dead brother. The vision of much blood reddened before her aching eyes, as she listened for the horse's hoofs. If only he could come before Ippolito, she thought, and she listened also for the priest's light step behind her.

Francesco came first. She saw him far down

the road before the first sound reached her. He was riding leisurely up the steep way, a broad hat drawn over his eyes, against the level sun, that gleamed like fire on the barrel of his rifle. She could see that from time to time he looked behind him quickly. He was warned already, she thought. So much the better. If only he would quicken his speed a little. Ippolito almost always passed the graveyard before the sun was quite down. Her heart beat very fast as she heard the clink of the horse's iron shoes against the stones, and then the rattle of the tiny pebbles that flew up and fell to right and left at every step.

She rose when he was within fifty yards of her, and threw the black shawl back from her splendid black hair. He knew her face and would stop when he recognized her. She remembered the sound of his voice, and how he had said in her hearing that she was very beautiful, and once when she had been alone in her father's shop, he had come in and had talked strangely, and she had been a little frightened, but Ferdinando had entered just then. She remembered it all distinctly. It did not matter, now, for he had come to avenge Ferdinando. The bullets that should do justice were already in the Winchester that gleamed so red in the setting sun.

She stood upright, with her head thrown back, that he might recognize her. He stopped beside her.

"Concetta!" he exclaimed, smiling, as he smiled at every pretty woman. "What brings you here? What are you doing out here in the road alone?" She hardly saw that he smiled, in her own earnestness.

"That brings me here," she said, pointing through the iron gate. "Do you see? It is the last one on the left, with the black cross."

Francesco looked.

"I see a grave," he said indifferently.

"It is your brother's grave," said the girl. "Ferdinando lies there."

"Oh — I understand."

The young man glanced up and down the road, and dismounted from his horse, passing his arm through the bridle. He advanced close to the gate, and looked through it in silence for several seconds.

"Poor fellow!" he exclaimed, turning away again, but without any very strong feeling in his tone.

Concetta grasped his arm roughly, to draw him after her, and spoke rapidly into his ear.

"The priest Saracinesca will be coming down the road from the village at any moment. Come quickly, come with me. Behind the corner of the wall. You can shoot him from there, and I will hold your horse." She dragged him along and the horse followed, led by his arm. "No one will come. When he is dead, mount quickly and ride down to the crossroads above Camaldoli, by the fields, and wait behind the shrine. I will run all the way, and tell the other Saracinesca that his brother is dead in the road. He will run out, — from behind the shrine you can kill him easily. Then ride for the woods of Noto. The brigands are there, and you will be safe."

Almost before he knew where she was leading him, he found himself behind the corner of the cemetery, on the side away from the village. In digging the foundations of the wall, the dark tufo had been broken out of the earth and piled high up at a short distance, so that there was a sort of deep trench between the wall and the heap of stones, out of which the poisonous yellow spurge grew in great bunches. It would have been impossible to select a better spot for an ambush in what was really an open country.

With the unconscious ease of a country-bred woman, Concetta, taking the bridle, backed the horse into the trench so as to leave room in front of him for herself and Francesco to be under cover of the wall. She had scarcely done speaking when they were already in position.

"Get your rifle ready!" she said in a whisper, at the same time taking hold of the leathern belt by which the Winchester was slung. "He may be here at any moment. Be quick!"

"But I do not wish to kill anybody," said Francesco, at last, with an uneasy laugh.

Concetta started and stared at him, too much astonished to despise him yet.

"You do not wish to kill the Saracinesca!" Her face expressed blank amazement. "But then, why have you come?"

"Not to murder anyone, at all events. You are quite mad."

"Mad? I? Mad? Is not the body of your murdered brother lying there, on the other side of that wall? Does not his blood cry out for the blood of those who killed him? Have you not come to do justice? Have I not brought you to a safe place? And you call me mad!"

"Quite mad," reiterated Francesco, coolly.

She stared at him a moment longer, and an immense contempt rose in her eyes.

"Give me your rifle," she said in a different tone. "I will kill him, since you are afraid."

"I am not in the least afraid," answered Francesco, with the too ready resentment against a woman's accusation of cowardice, which a real coward always shows. "Not that I see why I should risk being sent to penal servitude because my brother got himself killed in a foolish affair —"

"Foolish?" Concetta's black eyes blazed suddenly from contempt to anger.

"Foolish, yes! Ferdinando — I am sorry for him, of course — but he was a fool."

The back of one little white hand had struck him across the mouth, almost before the word was out.

"Infame!" she cried, using the strongest word in her language.

He did not care for the light blow, still less for the word. She was matchlessly beautiful in her anger, as the blood rose a little in her white cheeks, and her nostrils dilated with wrath. The shawl had fallen almost to the ground, and revealed her perfect throat and exquisitely graceful figure as she faced him. The colour rose in his face, and his lips reddened, and his eyes sparkled badly. Almost before the hand that had struck him had fallen to her side, he had caught her in his arms, and his lips were on hers, smothering her, hurting her, and he was forcing her backwards against the heap of stones — not twenty yards from his brother's grave.

She was lithe and strong, but she was no match for him. Yet, defending herself as she could, like a wild animal, she bit his lip half through, and as he started under the pain she wrenched her head aside and screamed with all her might, once, before he got one of his hands over her mouth.

But her scream had been heard. She had judged rightly that Ippolito Saracinesca would be coming along the road in a few moments, to meet his death, as she had hoped. Instead, he saved her, for at her cry, being but a few yards from the corner of the wall, he sprang forward, saw a woman struggling against a man, recognizing neither, leapt into the trench and had Francesco by the back of the collar in a moment, twisting the tough starched linen with all the might of his by no means weak white hands. As Orsino had always said, Ippolito was more of a man than anybody suspected, and there was the good blood of his good race in him, and all the fearlessness.

In an instant he had dragged Francesco backwards, half strangled, up the little declivity of the trench, and out into the middle of the road. So far he had done nothing more, perhaps, than was necessary to save the girl. But having got him out, the man's instinct against the wretch that does violence to a woman, took possession of him, and holding Francesco by the back of the collar in front of him with his right hand, he struck him half a dozen times quickly and violently on the side of the head with his left fist, till Francesco, stunned and choked, suddenly fell in a heap in the road.

Concetta had struggled to her feet at once, and stood leaning against the corner of the wall. With a mad horror she saw that she had been saved by the man she had wished to kill. The horse leisurely picked its way up through the stones and stood waiting in the road.

At that moment, four peasants coming home from the hill farm came down into the road from behind the other end of the long wall of the cemetery. They naturally glanced downwards before going up towards the village, and seeing the priest standing over a fallen man, they hurried to the spot. Francesco was already beginning to get to his feet. Ippolito drew back a little to be ready if he should be attacked, as he naturally expected. But a moment later the peasants had recognized Francesco, had helped him up, and were dusting his clothes, while they scowled at Ippolito.

"It is well that you come, friends," said Concetta's clear, low voice. "A moment later and another Saracinesca would have killed another Pagliuca."

Ippolito stared at her, dumbfounded by her speech, and then looked at the grim and angry faces of the lean brown men who surrounded Francesco. He could not conceive that a woman whom he had saved from worse than death but a moment earlier should turn upon him instantly, as she was doing.

But she could not help it, for she was half mad, and the idea of injuring the Saracinesca was always uppermost in her unsettled brain. She had come to warn Francesco of danger, because she had loved his brother, and loved the name; and she had done her best to make him do a murder then and there.

"Help Don Francesco to his horse," she said to the peasants. "Take him round to the back of Don Taddeo's house — not through the village — you will meet the carabineers, and he is bleeding. They would see; there would be questions. Go quickly — the patrol passed half an hour ago; the next will come out in half an hour more."

She foresaw everything. In a moment the men had helped Francesco to the saddle, and they were moving away. He had not uttered a word, surprised, bruised, and terrified as he was, and his lip was bleeding where Concetta had bitten it. His face was white with fear, and he held a handkerchief to his mouth, as he slowly rode away, leaving Concetta and Ippolito standing in the road together.

Ippolito faced the girl quietly enough, but he meant to ask for an explanation of some sort.

"Did you think that I should accuse him, though he is — what he is?" she asked, speaking first. "You saved me from that infamous beast — yes. I thank you, though you are my enemy. But do not think that I value myself higher than the blood of my bridegroom whom you killed. I would rather lose body and soul together than not hurt a Saracinesca if I could, kill you, if I could, give your bodies to dogs, if I could, send you unconfessed to hell, if I could. And you thought that I would turn and accuse a Corleone when I could accuse a Saracinesca? You do not know us."

She turned from him scornfully before he could answer a word. She had found her little shawl, and she drew it about her face as she moved away. He stood still a moment, looking after her in mute surprise. Then he shook his head and turned towards Camaldoli, not yet understanding that the beautiful girl was not quite sane, but speculating upon women in general, as good priests sometimes do in total ignorance of the subject.

Orsino looked grave when Ippolito told him at supper what had happened.

"The girl is mad," he said sadly, for he was himself the cause of her madness. "And she is a Sicilian. We understand these people very little, after all. I sometimes think we never shall."

"Nobody could possibly understand that kind of woman," observed Ippolito.

"No. Put such a scene as that on the stage, if it were possible, and the audience would hiss it, as a monstrous improbability. They would say that the girl would fall at the feet of her preserver, forget her hatred for ever, or possibly turn it all against the man from whom she had been saved. Unfortunately things are different in real life. Poor Concetta will hate us all the more because one of us has helped her in danger. It is true that she is mad. All the people say so."

"Because she sits half the day outside the cemetery? It is not a month since Ferdinando died. One need not be mad to feel a great sorrow for a whole month."

"No. Perhaps not. I should like to know what that fellow is here for. It means no good to anyone. I have no doubt that he is in communication with the outlaws, and she is quite capable of trying to help them to catch us."

"Then you really believe in the existence of the brigands, after all," said Ippolito, with a laugh, for Orsino did not often speak of the outlaws seriously.

"We all know that they exist. But we have trouble in realizing that they do. We know the names of many of them. Everybody does. But of course, with so many soldiers about, we feel safe. I wish you could carry a weapon, Ippolito."

"I? I am a priest. Nobody will touch me."

"Do not be too sure. There are even priests who wear a revolver under their cassocks down here."

"I could hardly carry a rifle," remarked Ippolito, laughing again. "And imagine carrying a knife in these days — one of us! It sounds like the last century."

"A knife is a very good weapon, nevertheless.

The peasants say that a knife has more shots in it than a revolver, and does not miss fire."

"I hate the idea of carrying a weapon."

"Yes, no doubt. But suppose that matters had turned out a little differently to-day, and that Francesco Pagliuca, instead of being an abject coward, had turned upon you and fought you for his life. What could you have done with your hands?"

"A priest has no business to be fighting," said Ippolito. "When he fights, he must take the consequences."

"But you could not escape it to-day. The cause was just and urgent. As a man, you could not have done otherwise."

"Certainly not. I admit that, and the fellow was scared. He had a Winchester rifle across his back. It got into the way when I twisted his collar, I remember. Do you know that I never struck anyone before? It was rather a curious sensation."

"You have struck me often enough," laughed Orsino. "You used to fight like a wildcat when we were little boys. It is a pity that you turned priest."

"I am very glad I did," said Ippolito. "Besides, I do not like fighting. It was different when we were children and pummelled each other."

"Look here," said Orsino. "I shall feel anxious

about you after this affair. Unless you will carry some weapon, I shall have you escorted to Santa Vittoria and back by a carabineer."

"How absurd!"

"I will, I assure you. If you were like that miserable Francesco Pagliuca, I should send four men with you. But I know that you could make a pretty good defence alone, if you had anything to fight with."

"Of course if you insist in that way, I must. I utterly refuse to be followed about by soldiers. It is too ridiculous. Have you got a knife? Something that is easy to carry—"

"Two or three," answered Orsino. "There is a very nice bowie knife—one of those American things made in England. It is convenient, for it has a cross-hilt and a leathern sheath."

He rose from the table and opened a drawer in an old-fashioned press, from which he produced the weapon in question.

"There is a saddler in Rome who gets these things," he observed, showing it to his brother. "You see it is really a dagger, for there is no spring. It is made solid and straight and would go through anything, I should think. Look at the thickness of the back of the blade, will you? And the point is extremely fine. You could engrave with it, and yet it is as strong as the rest."

Ippolito turned the knife over and over.

"At all events it will be useful in cutting up the bits of leather I use for mending the old organ," he observed. "My pocket knife is of hardly any use."

He sheathed the knife blade and dropped it into the deep side pocket of his cassock.

"Imagine me carrying a bowie knife!" he exclaimed, still inclined to laugh.

"Imagine the feelings of Francesco Pagliuca this afternoon, if he had thought you had one in your pocket, when you were behind him and twisting his collar." Orsino smiled grimly.

"My hands were good enough for such a beast," answered Ippolito, in a tone of disgust.

Thus it was that Ippolito began to go armed, much against his will, for he took his profession as a priest and a man of peace seriously. Orsino was not even then half satisfied, and intended before long to try and persuade him to carry a revolver instead of the knife.

But up at Santa Vittoria there was much talk of another sort on that evening. As generally happens in such cases in Sicily, the carabineers and the soldiers, though on the lookout for Francesco Pagliuca, were in profound ignorance of the fact that he was now lodging for the second night at the house of Taddeo the grocer, though there was now hardly a man in the village who did not know it. The soldiers in Sicily are matched as one to a thousand against a whole population of the most reticent people in the world, bound together by that singular but half-defined force, which is the mafia. Knowing the country perfectly and well acquainted with the unchanging hours of the regular patrols in the neighbourhood, Francesco might have stayed ten days in Santa Vittoria in spite of the soldiers, even if he had been guilty of the crimes which he did not at all mean to commit. Not a human being would have informed against him, and if anyone had betrayed him, the betrayer's own life would not have been worth much. They did not think any the better of him, nor any the worse, because he was innocent of any misdeed. He was a part of the idea of the mafia, a born Sicilian, who, somehow, had been obliged to give up his birthright to Romans, who were as much foreigners to the people of Santa Vittoria as Englishmen could have been. It was their duty, to a man, for Sicily's sake and their own, to stand by him as a Sicilian against all authority whatever. Besides, they knew him, the Romans had killed his brother, whom they had also known, and both he and his had always helped the outlaws against the government. The peasants remembered and told their children how the Corleone brothers had once led a dozen carabineers about the hills for two days in search of the brigands, taking good care not to catch them. It was not probable that the soldiers should ever get any information against such popular persons, except by stratagem or accident.

And now Francesco sat in a long upper room at the back of Taddeo's house, bathing his sore face with vinegar and water and telling his story to the grocer and his brother, in his own way. And in many humble little houses, the men were talking in low tones, telling each other how the 'priest of the Saracinesca' had fallen upon Francesco Pagliuca after they had quarrelled over Ferdinando's grave, and had treacherously twisted his collar and beaten him before he could get his gun into his hand. And they discussed the matter in whispers. And one man, who had loved Ferdinando, said nothing, but went out quietly from his house and walked down over the black lands and set fire to three haystacks on the Camaldoli estate, because the corn was not yet harvested, and there was nothing else to burn at that time of year. In the morning everyone heard of it and was glad, but no one ever knew who had set fire to the hay, for the man who did it did not tell his wife.

But neither did Concetta tell her father truly what had happened to her. She had been at the cemetery, she said, and the two gentlemen had met, the priest and the layman, and had quarrelled, she knew not about what, and the priest of the Saracinesca had caught Francesco Pagliuca unawares by the neck. So her story corresponded with that of the peasants and with that of Francesco.

For two reasons she could not tell her father the truth. If he had known it, he would never have allowed her to leave the village alone again. And he would most certainly have risen from the table, and would have gone straight to Taddeo's house, where Francesco was, to kill him at once, though Don Atanasio was an old man, having married very late in life. It was true that since it was all over, and she had cast the blame upon Ippolito, the hatred of her offended maidenhood for her cowardly assailant was slowly and surely waking; and her white cheeks blushed scarlet as though they had been struck, when she thought of it all. But it was better that her father should not know, and she held her peace. It was hardest of all to feel that she had almost had Francesco's rifle in her hands, and that if he had not assailed her, there might by this time have been one Saracinesca less in the world.

It would have done her good to see the haystacks flaming down in the valley, and it would have brought a smile of satisfaction to her tragic face to have heard what the peasants were whispering to one another in all the little houses of the village that night.

No one said that it was a shame for an armed man to have been beaten by an unarmed priest.

They felt personally injured by what they called the treachery of the latter in choking his antagonist, and they softly cursed the Romans, and vowed to hurt them if they could. Generations of their fathers had known generations of the Corleone, had been ground and rack-rented by them, and had resisted their extortions with a cunning that had often been successful. But now that the Pagliuca had lost their birthright, that was all forgotten in the fact that they were Sicilians, injured by Romans. No one said in defence of the Saracinesca that San Giacinto had paid the Pagliuca more than twice the actual value of Camaldoli. In the eyes of the peasants their old masters had been ignominiously ejected from their home by Romans, and Ferdinando had done a brave and honourable deed in trying to resist them. It was the duty of every good Sicilian to stand by the Pagliuca against the Romans and against the authorities, come what might. If this young Roman priest had the overbearing courage to beat a Pagliuca on the high road in broad daylight, what might not his tall, black-browed brother be expected to do, or what deed of violence might not follow at the hands of the grey-haired giant who had been at Camaldoli, and who had momentarily terrorized everyone? No one's life or property was safe while the Saracinesca remained in the country. And they meant to remain. They had cut down the brush around the house so that no one could creep up with a rifle under safe cover, and they had strengthened the gate and were restoring the tower. They had turned the monastery into a barrack for the carabineers, and had quartered a company of infantry in the village. Their power and their evident influence in Rome, since they had obtained troops for their protection, made them ten times more hateful to men who hated all authority. They wished that Ippolito had wounded Francesco slightly with some weapon. Then he might have been arrested, and there was not a man in the village who would have said a word in his favour. Many would have perjured themselves to testify against him, in the hope that he might really be sent to prison. The fact that he was a priest went for nothing. He was not their own priest, and more than one churchman had been in trouble in Sicily, before now.

CHAPTER XXVII

FRANCESCO was no more able to understand Concetta's conduct than Ippolito himself. He had expected a very different termination to the affair, for he knew well enough that if the four peasants had caught him as Ippolito had, they would very probably have torn him limb from limb, in the most literal and barbarous sense of the word, in spite of any sympathy they might have felt for his family until then. He vaguely understood that Concetta had saved him for his dead brother's sake, and out of hatred for the Saracinesca; but there was a sort of reckless self-sacrifice in her act which it was beyond his cowardice and selfishness to comprehend. He rarely addressed the saints, but he inwardly thanked them for his safety as he rode round the outskirts of the village and the back of Taddeo's house. He was still in a tremor of fear, but he knew that he could easily twist and exaggerate the story of the ignominious beating he had received, and thereby account for his pallor and his nervousness. He knew that anything would be believed against the Saracinesca.

It would be hard to give a single reason for his having chosen to come up to Santa Vittoria to find a lodging, when he had left Rome in order to see Aliandra in Randazzo. His timidity might have had something to do with his decision, making him prefer the village where he was sure of finding friends, whatever he might do, to the large town where there was no one upon whom he could count. He had also told Basili, when he had been to see him, that he had business in Santa Vittoria. Vaguely, too, he guessed that Tebaldo might know where he was and follow him. But he had not the slightest intention of doing any harm to the Saracinesca, of whom, in his heart, he had always been afraid.

As soon as Concetta had spoken, he had known that he was safe, though it was long before the effect of his fright had passed off. After what she had said, he knew that no one in Santa Vittoria would believe any statement which Ippolito might make about the encounter, and he set himself to enlarge upon the impression she had given so as to show himself in the most advantageous light possible.

He was not injured, and his bruises, though painful, had not disfigured him, for Ippolito had struck him on the side of the head. As for his lip, he told Taddeo that Ippolito had at first picked up a stone and wounded him in the mouth with it.

Taddeo was ready to believe anything, and so was his brother, the fat sacristan, who had waited for Francesco in the bridle path until a late hour, and grievously lamented having missed the fight, for in spite of his fat and his odd smile and the cast in his eye, he was fond of fighting for its own sake, and no coward, except in the presence of what he believed to be supernatural and therefore irresistible.

Having eaten his supper and refreshed his spirits and nerves with some of Taddeo's strongest wine, Francesco went to sleep in the great, old-fashioned trestle bed, in sheets that smelt of lavender, though they were of coarse linen. And early in the morning he got up, feeling almost quite himself, and rode down to Randazzo in the early dawn. An uncomfortable sensation assailed him as he passed the wall of the cemetery, but he looked away and rode on, thinking of Aliandra Basili, and concocting the story he should tell her to account for his wounded lip Of all things, he desired to make a good impression on her and her father, for he had come from Rome with the determination to marry her if he could.

It did not seem impossible, with Tebaldo out of the way, for she liked him, and Basili himself would think it a good thing for his daughter to marry a Pagliuca. Francesco's native cowardice had kept him out of the sort of daring mischief which gives a man a bad character. He did not gamble, he did not drink, and he could have a title, of course, according to the southern custom of distributing that sort of social distinction through all the members of a family. Aliandra might do far worse, Basili thought; and though he knew that she had made up her mind to get Tebaldo if she could, he also knew Tebaldo well enough to judge that, as the head of his family, he would try to make an ambitious and rich marriage. He frankly told Francesco that he had little influence with his daughter, but that so far as he himself was concerned, he approved of the marriage. Francesco had an equal share of the small family fortune with his brother and sister, and it had been increased by the addition of Ferdinando's, since the latter had left no will. In former times Basili had warned his daughter against the brothers, but their existence had changed since then. They now had a social position, and friends in Rome, and were altogether much more deserving of consideration.

Francesco found the notary's broken leg a distinct advantage in his courtship; for Basili was, of course, helpless to move, in his room upstairs, and when the young man had paid him a visit, he and Aliandra had the house to themselves without fear of interruption. Then the two could stay as long as they pleased in the sitting-room below, with the blinds half closed and hooked together, and it was a cool and quiet place just so high above the street that people could not look in as they passed along outside.

Aliandra had been flattered by the young man's pursuit, as was natural, but she had by no means given up the idea of marrying Tebaldo. She would have preferred that Francesco should not come all the way down from Santa Vittoria every day, but she could not refuse to see him when he came. She had temporarily returned, with a good deal of pleasure and amusement, to the primitive social state in which she had been brought up, and she was no longer able to tell a servant to say that she was not at home. Gesualda, the maid of all work, would not have understood any such order. Besides, Francesco always made a pretence of having come to see how Basili was doing, and invariably went upstairs to the latter's room, as soon as he entered the house. In the middle of the day he went to the inn for his dinner, because Aliandra dined with her father, but an hour later he returned and stayed until it was time for him to ride away in order to reach Santa Vittoria before dark. It was a long ride, and as he rode the same horse every day he saved his animal's strength as much as possible.

To-day, everything happened as usual. At the accustomed hour he appeared, put up his horse in

Basili's stable beside the notary's brown mare, flicked the dust from his boots and gaiters, and went in to see Aliandra and her father. The stable was in a little yard on one side of the house, entered by a wooden gate from the street, and accessible also from the house itself by a side door which led down three or four steps.

The notary was in a good humour, for the doctor said that he was doing well, and hoped to get him on his feet again in a shorter time than had at first been expected. He was beginning to like Francesco because the young man took some pains to amuse him, having an object to gain, and treated him with even more deference than the principal notary of a provincial town had a right to expect. It was amusing to be told about Rome, and to hear a great many things explained which had always been more or less a mystery to one who had never left the island. It was pleasant, too, to hear of his daughter's triumphs from one who had assisted at them all, and who now spoke with the authority of a man of the world, representing the opinion of the Roman aristocracy.

Now and then, when Francesco spoke of some especial passage in an opera by which Aliandra had raised a storm of enthusiasm, Basili would ask her what the music was like; and then, without effort or affectation, as though it was a pleasure to her, her splendid voice burst out, true and clear and fresh, and sang what the old man wished to hear. Then the peasants and people passing through the street would stop to listen, and even the ugly Gesualda, peeling potatoes or shelling pease in the kitchen, paused in her work and had a vision of something beautiful and far above her poor comprehension.

On this morning, Francesco did his best to be agreeable, though his head ached and his lip was swollen. He refused to say much about the latter. Aliandra was sure to hear, in a day or two, the story which the peasants would tell each other about the affair, and which would certainly redound to his credit. He said that he had met with a slight accident in going home, and when Aliandra pressed him for an account of it, he said that it was nothing worth mentioning and turned the subject quickly. He did not wish to let her know that he had been worsted by a Saracinesca. The peasants would be sure to concoct a story of treachery, much more to his own glory than anything he could put together, and which would probably contain a number of details that might not agree with those of his own invention.

Aliandra did not ask any more questions about it, even after they had gone downstairs and sat talking in the front room as usual. Her feeling for him had not changed at all. She was not in love with him any more than before she had left

Rome, but he still attracted her in the same rather unaccountable way, and she never felt quite sure of what he might do or say when they were alone together. Yet she felt safer in being with him in her father's house than she had felt in Rome, even under the protection of the Signora Barbuzzi.

He pressed her to marry him, at every meeting. Sometimes she laughed at him, sometimes she gave reasons why she could not accept him, sometimes she refused to listen altogether, and told him that he must go away if he could not talk more reasonably. But he was not easily discouraged; he knew how to make love better than Tebaldo, and after all, she liked him. Tebaldo, when with her, was apt to be either cross-tempered, or over-elated, and almost too much at his ease, for he was far too much moved by her mere presence, and by the atmosphere that surrounded her, to have control of his words and his looks, as he had when he was with Miss Slayback. He was often abrupt with Aliandra, and there are few outward faults which a woman dislikes more in a possible husband than abruptness. Yet Aliandra perpetually did her best to please Tebaldo. Francesco, on the other hand, used every means in his power to please her. It was no wonder that she liked him better than his brother. He had many of the ways which appeal to all women, and he was clever at hiding those weaknesses which they despise quite as heartily as men can. A born coward not only fears danger, but fears, above all things, to show that he is afraid, and is keenly aware of anything, even in conversation, which can show him in his true light. If he is skilful, as well as cowardly, he will often succeed in deceiving brave men, who are the least suspicious, into the belief that he is as fearless as they. He finds it far easier to deceive women, who always attach much more importance to mere words than men do.

It was a warm and sultry afternoon, for the wind was from the southeast and had in it something of the suffocating fumes of the volcano over which it blew. The blinds were drawn together and hooked, in the Italian way, so as to let in plenty of air and little light. Aliandra had established herself on the stiff, old-fashioned sofa, putting up her feet, to be more at her ease, and Francesco sat beside her, close to the window, smoking and talking to her. It was very quiet. Now and then footsteps passed along the street outside, and sometimes the sound of peasants' voices was heard, discussing prices or some bit of local gossip. Francesco had eaten his dinner at the inn and had come back, Basili was dozing upstairs on his couch, and Gesualda, the maid of all work, was probably eating oranges in the kitchen, or asleep in her chair, with the cat on her knees.

There is nothing so peaceful in the whole world as the calm that descends on all things in the far south after the midday meal.

"This is better than Rome," observed Francesco, looking at Aliandra's handsome profile.

"For a change — yes," answered the singer, idly. "I should not care for it always."

"I can imagine that it might be dull, if I were alone."

Aliandra turned her head slowly and looked at him gravely for a moment. Then she smiled.

"If you were alone here," she said, "you would not have the excitement of taking care of a father with a broken leg, as I have."

"Excitement!" Francesco laughed. "Yes. I imagined what your existence would be like, so I came all the way from Rome to help you pass the time."

"How merciful! But I am grateful, for though I love my father dearly, a broken leg as a subject of conversation, morning, noon, and night, leaves something to be desired."

"I suppose the old gentleman is anxious about himself and talks about his leg all the time."

"When you are not there, he generally does. You do him good, I am sure."

"And so you are grateful to me for coming? Really?"

"Yes. What did you expect?"

"I would rather have less gratitude and more — what shall I say?"

"Anything you like — within certain limits!" Aliandra laughed softly.

"I might say too much, and that might offend you. Or too little, and that would certainly bore you."

"Could you not say just enough? Sometimes you say it very well. You can be tactful when you like."

"If ɪ say that I should like more love, you will think it too much. If I say affection, it is too little, and must seem ridiculous."

Aliandra looked away from him, and rested her head against the hard back of the sofa for a moment.

"Why do you wish to marry me?" she asked suddenly, without turning to him. "You could do much better, I am sure."

"A man cannot do better than marry the woman he loves," said Francesco, softly.

"He can marry a woman who loves him," suggested Aliandra, laughing again.

"You cannot be serious very long," he retorted. "That is one reason why I love you. I hate serious people."

"I know you do, and that makes me doubt whether you can ever possibly be serious yourself. Now, to marry a man who is not serious —"

"Or a woman who is not," interrupted the young man.

"Is folly," said Aliandra, completing her sentence.

"Then neither you nor I should ever marry at all. That is the conclusion, evidently. But you began by asking me why I wish to marry you. I answered you. It is simple. I love you, and I have loved you almost since you were a child. You know something about my life in Rome, do you not? Have you ever heard that I cared for any other woman?"

"How should I hear? I am not of your world, and though you know how I live, I know nothing of what you do when you are not with me. How should I? Have I allowed any of the men in society to make my acquaintance? You speak as though I had friends who might be friends of yours, yet you know that I have none. What you say may be quite true, but I have no means of knowing."

"There is Tebaldo," said Francesco. "He knows all about me, and would not be likely to attribute to me any virtue which I do not possess. Has he ever told you that I was making love to anyone else?"

"No," answered Aliandra, thoughtfully. "That is true."

"And he hates me," observed Francesco. "He

would not lose a chance of abusing me, I am sure."

Aliandra made no answer at first, for what he said was quite true, though she did not care to admit it.

"You two are antipathetic to each other," she said at last, using the phrase because it was vague and implied no fault on either side. "You will never agree. I am sorry."

"Why should you care, whether we agree or not?"

"Because I like you both. I should wish you to be good friends."

"I am glad you include us both in one category," said Francesco. "You say that you like us both."

"Well — what of that?"

"There is a beautiful indifference about the expression. If Tebaldo is satisfied, I suppose that I should be. But I am not. I am made of different stuff. I cannot say, 'I love you' in one breath, and 'I will not marry you' in the next."

Aliandra started perceptibly and looked at him. He had a well-affected air of righteous contempt.

"I am in earnest," he continued, as she said nothing. "I do not know whether I could do better for myself, as you say, or not. I suppose you mean that I might marry the daughter of some Roman prince, with a dowry and sixteen quarterings. Perhaps I might, for I have a good name of my own and an equal share of the property. I do not know and I do not care, and I shall certainly never try to make any such marriage, because I will either marry you or no one. I will not, I could not — nothing could induce me, neither fortune, nor position, nor anything else in the world."

He had a very convincing way of speaking when he chose, and for the first time, perhaps, Aliandra hesitated and thought that she might do worse than accept him for a husband. She thought him handsome as he sat beside her, leaning forward a little and speaking earnestly, and she mistook his masculine vitality for real manliness, which is a common mistake with young women of little experience. Besides, he made no reservations, and Tebaldo made many. Yet it was hard to give up her dream of being a real princess, the wife of the head of an old family, for she was very ambitious in more ways than one. Francesco had said very much the same things before now, it was true, so that there was no novelty in them for her. But his importunity was beginning to make an impression upon her, as contrasted with his brother's determined avoidance of the question of marriage.

Still she said nothing, but her face betrayed her hesitation. He bent nearer to her, and spoke still more earnestly. There was no affectation in his speech now, for though his passions were evanescent, they had all the heat of his vital temperament as long as they lasted. The fact that he had carefully weighed the advantage to be got by marrying an artist who had youth, beauty, honesty, a small but solid inheritance to expect, and very possibly fame and fortune in the near future, did not make him cold nor calculating when he was close beside that beauty and youth which had at first attracted him. Her eyes softened dreamily from time to time as he spoke, and she made no attempt to withdraw the hand of which he had taken possession.

He spoke quickly, warmly, eloquently, and without reserve, for he had nothing to conceal, and nothing to fear but her refusal. The words were not carefully chosen, nor the phrases very carefully turned, but they had the accent of sincerity, for his whole being was moved, as he spoke. They had also the merit of not being too few nor too short; for that is often a merit in women's eyes. A woman loves to hear the whole tale of love, from the beginning to the end, and feels herself somehow cheated by the short and broken sentences which are often all that a strong man can command, though his hand trembles and his lips are white with emotion which the weak never feel.

In the tender shadow of the half-darkened room, his eyes filled hers till she could not look away, and his speech grew softer and was broken by little silences. Aliandra was falling under the spell of his voice, of the hour, of her own warm youth, and of his abundant vitality.

The blinds, hooked together against the bars, shook a little, perhaps with the sultry afternoon breeze, and all at once there was less light in the room. Aliandra moved a little, realizing that she was falling under the man's influence.

"But Tebaldo!" she exclaimed. "Tebaldo!" she repeated, still clinging to her long-cherished hope, as though she owed it a sort of allegiance for its own sake.

Francesco laughed softly, and pressed the hand he held.

"Tebaldo is going to marry the American girl with the great fortune," he said quietly. "You need not think of Tebaldo any more."

Again the blind creaked a little on its hinges. But Aliandra started at what Francesco said, and did not hear the window. She sat upright on the sofa.

"What American girl?" she asked. "I never heard of her. Has this been going on a long time?"

"About two months—" The blind creaked a third time, as he spoke.

"There is someone under the window!" cried Aliandra, lowering her voice and looking round.

"It is the wind," said Francesco, indifferently.

"The southeast wind blows up the street and shakes the blinds."

Aliandra leaned back again, and he took her hand once more.

"It is quite well known, in Rome," he continued. "The engagement is not actually announced, but it will be very soon. They say she has many millions, and she is very pretty — insignificant, fair with blue eyes, but pretty. He has done very well for himself."

Aliandra was silent. The news meant the absolute destruction of a project she had long hoped to realize, and with which she had grown familiar. But she knew, as it fell to pieces before her eyes, that she had never firmly believed in its success, and there was a sort of relief in feeling that she was freed from the task set her by her own ambition, while at the same time she was hurt by the disappointment of failure, and a sudden keen resentment against Tebaldo prompted her to yield to Francesco's entreaties on his own behalf. He held her hand and waited for her to speak.

The silence lasted long, for the notary's daughter was afraid of herself and of making up her mind hastily. The blind creaked again, more loudly than before, and she turned her head nervously.

"I am sure there is someone under the window!" she said. "I wish you would look!"

"I assure you it is only the wind," answered Francesco, as before.

"I know, but please look. I am nervous. The scirocco always makes me nervous."

"It is not the weather, Aliandra," he said softly, and smiling, with his eyes in hers. "You are not nervous, either. It is — it is — " he bent nearer to her face. "Do you know what it is?"

Though he was so near, forcing her with his eyes, he had no power over her now. She could not help looking anxiously over his shoulder at the hooked blinds. She was not listening to him.

"It is love," he said, and his red lips gave the word a sensuous sound, as they came nearer to her face.

She did not hear him. The rich colour in her face faded all at once, and then with a sharp cry she stood upright, pushing him away from her.

"I saw a hand on the window sill!" she exclaimed. "It is gone again."

Francesco rose also. He was annoyed at the untoward interruption, for he fancied that the hand must have belonged to some boy in the street, playing outside and climbing up a little way to jump down again, as boys do.

"It is ridiculous!" he said in a tone of irritation, and going to the window.

He looked down between the blinds that were ajar, expecting to see a peasant boy. Instead, there was Tebaldo Pagliuca's face, yellow in the sun, as though he had a fever, and Tebaldo's bloodshot eyes looking up to his, and the thin, twisted lips smiling dangerously.

"Come outside," said Tebaldo, in an odd voice. "I want to speak with you."

But Francesco only heard the first words. His abject terror of his brother overcame him in an instant, and he almost ran into Aliandra's arms as he sprang back.

"It is Tebaldo!" he whispered. "Let him in. Keep him here, while I go away through the stable yard!"

And before she could answer, or realize exactly what he meant, he had left her standing alone in the middle of the room. In ten seconds he had made sure that the gate of the stable yard was fast inside, and he was saddling his horse. It was done in less than a minute, somehow. Then he listened, coming close to the gate. He heard Aliandra speaking with Tebaldo at the open window, a moment later he heard the street door open and close, and he knew that Tebaldo was in the house.

Very softly and quickly he unbolted the yard gate. He swung it wide, reckless of the noise it made, and in an instant he was in the saddle and galloping for his life up the deserted street. It was well that he had known the house thoroughly, and that Aliandra had obeyed him and admitted Tebaldo at once.

She was braver than Francesco, by many degrees, though she was no heroine; but she was scared by the look in the man's face, as he entered without a word, and looked round the room slowly for his brother.

"Where is he?" he asked.

Before Aliandra could find any answer, the loud noise of clattering hoofs filled the room. Tebaldo was at the window almost before the sound had passed, and the thrust of his open hand smashed the fastenings so that the blinds flew wide open. He looked out and saw his brother galloping away.

He knew the house, too, for he had been in it many times, and he knew also that Basili's brown mare was a good beast, for the notary was a heavy man and often had to ride far. Without even glancing at Aliandra he turned to the door. But she was there before him, and held it closed, though she was frightened now.

"You shall not go," she tried to say.

"Shall not?" he laughed harshly, as his hands caught her.

He did not hurt her, for he loved her in his way, but a moment later she found herself turned round like a leaf in a storm, and the door had closed behind him. It seemed to her but a second more, and she had not been able to think what she should do, when the sound of flying hoofs passed the window again. She ran to look out, and she saw the brown mare already far up the street. Tebaldo could ride, and he had not wasted time in saddling. Bareback he rode the mare with her halter for a bridle, as he had found her. Aliandra realized that he had no rifle. At all events he would have to overtake his brother in order to kill him, and Francesco had the start of him by several minutes.

He knew it, but he guessed what Tebaldo would do, and he kept his horse at full speed as the road began to wind upward to the black lands. He glanced behind him just before each turning, expecting to see his pursuer. But a clear start of four minutes meant a mile, at the pace he had ridden out of the town. He kept the horse to it, for he was riding for the wager of his life. But the animal had been put to it too suddenly after his feed, without as much as a preliminary walk or trot to the foot of the hill, and even in his terror Francesco saw that it would be impossible to keep the pace much longer. But he could save distance, if he must slacken speed, if he followed the footpath by which the peasants had made short cuts between each bend of the road and the next. They were hard and safe in the heat, and his horse could trot along them fairly well, and even canter here and there. And then, when he was forced to take the high road for a few hundred yards, he could break once more into a stretching gallop. If he could but reach that turn, just beyond the high hill, where Ferdinando's friend had once waited for San Giacinto, he believed that he could elude Tebaldo in the black lands.

It was a terrible half-h , and he gasped and sweated with fear, as h .rged his horse up t at last long stretch of the road which could not be avoided. His heart beat with the hoof-falls, and the sweat ran down upon his velvet coat, while he felt his hands so cold that it was an effort not to drop the reins. But the beast had got his wind at last, and galloped steadily up the hill.

It was growing suddenly dark, and there was a feverish yellow light in the hot air. A vast thunderstorm was rolling over Etna, and another had risen to meet it from the west, hiding the lowering sun. Only overhead the air was calm and clear. The first clap of the thunder broke in the distance, and went rolling and echoing away from the volcano to the inland mountains. As he reached the top of the hill, Francesco felt the big drops of rain in his face like a refreshment, though they were warm. The thunder pealed out again from the mountain's side with a deafening explosion. He turned in his saddle and looked back.

The road was straight and long, and he could see far. Tebaldo was in sight at last, almost lying on the mare's bare back as she breasted the hills, his hand along her neck, his voice near her ear while she stretched her long brown body out at every stride.

Francesco's teeth chattered as he spurred his hoi e for another wild effort. He could break fro 1 the road now, just before the wide curve it ma le to the left, and he knew the bridle paths and all the short cuts and by-ways through the black lar ds, as few men knew them except that one man, his brother, who was behind him. In his haste to escape he had left his rifle in Basili's hall. It was so much the less weight for his horse to carry, but it left him defenceless, and he knew that Tebaldo must be armed.

The storm broke and the rain came down in torrents. His horse almost slipped in jumping the ditch to get off the main road, but recovered himself cleverly, and long before Tebaldo had reached the top of the hill Francesco was out of sight. He might have felt safe then, from almost any other pursuer. But he knew Tebaldo, and now and then his teeth chattered. He told himself that he was chilled by the drenching rain, but in his heart he knew it was fear. Death was behind him, gaining on him, overtaking him, and he felt a terrible weakness in all his bones, as though they were softened and limp like a skeleton made of ropes.

It was hard to think, and yet he had to use his

mind. Tebaldo was lighter than he, and he rode without saddle or bridle. To take the shortest way through the black lands was to be surely overtaken in the long run. It might be best to take the longest, and perhaps Tebaldo might get before him, and give him a chance to turn back to Randazzo.

But as he looked down at the path his heart sank. The heavy rain had already softened the ground in places and his horse's hoofs made fresh tracks. There was no mistaking them. There was only one way, then, and it must be a race, for only speed could save him. Whichever way he might turn in and out of the fissures and little hollows, he must leave a trail in the wet, black ashes, which anyone could follow.

Don Taddeo's best horse was one of the best horses in that part of the country, as Francesco knew, and more than a match for the notary's brown mare, had other things been alike. But there was the difference of weight against him, and, moreover, Tebaldo was the better rider.

There was less than three-quarters of a mile between them now, but if he could keep the pace, that would do. He followed the shortest path, which was also the best because it was naturally the one most used by travellers. The rain fell in torrents, and the air was dusky and lurid. Again and again the great forked lightnings flashed down the side of the mountain, and almost at the instant the terrible thunder crashed through the hissing rain. Francesco felt as though each peal struck him bodily in the back, between the shoulders, and his knees shook with terror as he tried to press them to the saddle, and he bent down as if to avoid a shot or a blow, while his ears strained unnaturally for the dreaded sound of hoofs behind. Yet he scarcely dared to turn and look back, lest while he looked his horse might hesitate, or turn aside to another path through the black wilderness. Under the lurid light the yellow spurge had a horribly vivid glow, growing everywhere in big bunches among the black stones and out of the blacker soil. It almost dazzled him, as he rode on, always watching the path lest he should make a mistake and be lost.

Then the wind changed in a moment and came up behind him in gusts, and brought to his ears the sound of terror, the irregular beat of a horse's hoofs, cantering, pacing, trotting, according to the ground. It was fearfully near, he thought. He had just then his choice of taking to the road again for half a mile or more, or of following the bridle path that turned off amongst the spurge and the stones. There was a broad, deep ditch, and the rain had made the edges slippery and there was a drop of several feet, and little space to take off. It was a dangerous leap, but the greater fear devoured the less, and Francesco did not hesitate, but put the good horse at it. It would be a relief to get a stretching gallop along the road again.

The horse cleared it well, and thundered up the highway, as glad as his rider to be out of the intricate paths again. Francesco breathed more freely, and presently turned in his saddle as he galloped, and looked back. He could see nothing, but every now and then a gust of wind brought the sound of hoofs to him. Just as he neared the end of the half-mile stretch he distinctly saw Tebaldo come up to the leap. The rain had ceased for a moment, and in the grey air he could see tolerably well how the brown mare took off. For an instant he gazed, absolutely breathless. Horse and rider disappeared into the ditch together, for the mare had not cleared it. She might be injured, she might be killed, and Tebaldo with her. With a wild welling up of hope, Francesco galloped along the road, already half sure that the race was won and that he could reach a safe place in time.

The highway was level now, for two or three miles, over the high yoke, below which, on the other side, Camaldoli lay among the trees. He settled down once more to a long and steady gallop, and the going was fairly good, for the volcanic stuff used in making the road drank up the rain thirstily and was just softened by it without turning to mud. His terror was subsiding a little.

But all at once from far behind came the regular

galloping, tramping tread of the horse his brother was riding. He turned as though he had been struck, and there, a mile behind him, was a dark, moving thing on the road. They had not been injured, they had not been killed, they were up and after him again. And again his teeth chattered and his hands grew cold on the reins.

The entrance to the avenue of Camaldoli was in sight, and he set his teeth to keep them still in his head. It was half a mile from the entrance to the house, and little more than that to Santa Vittoria. But if he turned into the entrance, Tebaldo would cut across the fields and might catch him under the trees, caring little who might be there to see. It was safer to make for Santa Vittoria.

He passed the turn of the road at a round pace, and the good horse breasted the hill bravely. But on the smooth highway, the difference in weight began to tell very soon. Tebaldo was clearly in sight again now, stretching himself along the mare's body, his head on her neck, his voice close to her ear, riding like vengeance in a whirlwind, gaining at every stride.

Francesco's horse was almost spent, and he knew it. He had spurs and used them cruelly, and the poor beast struggled to gallop still, while the lean brown mare gained on him. The sun was low among the lurid clouds, and sent a pale level glare across the desolate land.

Before the cemetery gate, her black clothes and her black shawl drenched with the thunderstorm and clinging to her, Concetta sat in her accustomed place, bent low. Francesco scarcely saw her, as he rode up the last stretch for his life. But, as he passed her, his horse stumbled a little. Francesco thought he shied at the black figure, but it was not that. Four, five, six strides more, and the brave beast stumbled again, staggered as Francesco sprang to the ground, and then rolled over, stone dead, in the middle of the road.

Francesco did not glance at him as he lay there, but ran like a deer up the last few yards of the hill. The little church was just on the other side, and it might be open. Tebaldo was not two hundred yards behind him, and had seen all and was ready, and the lean mare came tearing on. She took the dead horse's body in her desperate stride, just as Francesco burst into the church.

With all his strength he tried to force the bolt of the lock across the door inside, for the key was outside where Ippolito had left it when he had entered. He could not move it, and he heard the thunder of hoofs without. If Tebaldo had not seen him enter, the mare would gallop past the closed door to the gate of the town. In wild fear he waited the ten seconds that seemed an age. The clattering ceased suddenly, and someone was forcing the door in behind him. Francesco's lips moved, but he could not cry out. He ran from the door up the aisle.

When Tebaldo had killed him, on the steps of the altar, he sheathed the big knife, with which he had done the deed at one blow, and instantly dropped it through the old gilded grating under the altar itself, behind which the bones of the saint lay in a glass casket. No one would ever look for it there.

As though the fever that had burned him were suddenly quenched in the terrible satisfaction of murder, the natural colour returned to his face for a moment, and he grew cold. Then all at once he realized what he had done, and he knew that he must escape from the church before anyone surprised him. He turned away from the altar and found himself face to face with Ippolito Saracinesca, who had been at work at the back of the organ, while he was waiting for the fat sacristan as usual, and had come down the winding stairs as soon as he had heard the noise of running feet, without even going to the front of the loft to see who was there.

Tebaldo stood stock-still, facing the priest while one might have counted a score. He knew him well and was known to Ippolito. But Ippolito could not see who it was that lay dead across the steps, for the face was downwards. Tebaldo looked at the churchman's calm and fearless eyes and knew that he was lost, if he could not silence him. Before Ippolito spoke, for he was too much surprised and horror-struck to find anything to say, and was rather thinking of what he ought to do, the Sicilian was on his knees, grasping his sleeve with one hand and crossing himself with the other.

He began the words of the Confession. A moment more and he was confessing to Ippolito as to a priest, and under the sacred seal of silence, the crime of having slain his brother. Ippolito could not stop him, for he had a scruple. He could not know that the man did not at once truly repent of what he had done, and in that case, as a priest, he was bound to hear and to keep silence for ever. Tebaldo knew that, and went to the end, and said the last Latin words even while getting on his feet again.

"I cannot give you absolution," said the young priest. "The case is too grave for that. But your confession is safe with me."

Tebaldo nodded, and turned away. He walked firmly and quickly to the door, went out and closed it behind him. He had already made up his mind what to do. He met the fat sacristan less than twenty paces from the church. He had known him all his life, and he stopped him, asking him where he was going. The man explained.

"Don Ippolito will not need you to blow the organ to-day," said Tebaldo, gravely. "He has just killed my brother in the church. I have turned the key on him, and am going to fetch the carabineers."

The fearful lie was spoken with perfect directness and clearness. The man started, stared at Tebaldo, and grew pale with excitement, but he could not believe his ears till Tebaldo had repeated the words. Then he spoke.

"We thought he had killed him yesterday afternoon by the cemetery," he said. "And now he has really done it! Madonna! Madonna! And another of them killed Don Ferdinando!"

"What is that about the cemetery?" asked Tebaldo. "Tell me as we go, for I am in a hurry."

"It is better that I stay," said the man. "He knows the lock and he may be able to slip the bolt from the inside, for he is very strong. He almost killed Don Francesco last night with his hands and only a stone he picked up."

He told Tebaldo in a few words the story which the peasants had already invented.

"I am glad you have told me," said Tebaldo. "It explains this horrible murder. I will go for the carabineers at once. There is no more time to be lost. Stay here and watch the door."

He knew he could trust the man to do his worst

against a Roman, and he walked rapidly into the town.

Ippolito watched Tebaldo until the door closed behind him. He was a very honourable as well as a very good man, and though as a priest he felt that he must give the murderer the benefit of a doubt, he felt as a man that the doubt could not really exist, and that Tebaldo had intentionally put him under the seal of confession in order to destroy his power of testifying in the case. The clever treachery was revolting to him.

He turned to look at the dead man, suddenly hoping that there might be some life left in him after all. He went and knelt beside him on the step of the altar and turned his body over so that it lay on its back. He felt the sort of pitying repulsion for anything dead which every sensitively organized man or woman feels, but he told himself that it was his duty to make sure that Francesco was not alive.

There was no doubt about that. Even he, in his inexperience, could not mistake the look in the wide-open, sightless eyes. He shuddered when he remembered how only twenty-four hours ago he had struck the poor dead head again and again with all his might, and he thanked Heaven that he had not struck harder and more often. He looked for the wound. It was on the left side low down in the breast, and must have gone to the heart at once. There was blood on both his hands, but very little had run down upon the steps.

He got his handkerchief from the side pocket of his cassock, and started as he felt there the sheathed knife which Orsino had made him carry. There was no water in the church, except a little holy water, and he could not defile that, so he wiped his hands as well as he could on his handkerchief and put the latter back into his pocket.

Suddenly he realized that he ought to be doing something, and he stood up, and looked about in hesitation. He asked himself how far the secret of confession bound him, and whether it could be regarded as a betrayal to call the authorities at once. Someone might have seen Tebaldo leave the church, and to give the alarm at once might be to fasten suspicion upon him. The rule about the secrecy of confession is very strict.

The sacristan might be expected to appear at any moment, too. Ippolito looked at his watch and wondered why the man had not come already. He was in great difficulty, for the case was urgent. Being alone, too, he did not like to shut up the church, leaving the dead man there alone. But he was sure that the sacristan would come in a few moments. It was more than half an hour since he had sent the lame boy to find him. It was wiser to wait for him and send him for the doctor and the carabineers.

He paced up and down before the altar rail rather nervously, glancing every now and then at the dead man. But the sacristan did not come. He thought it would be charitable to straighten out the lifeless limbs and cross the hands upon the breast, and he went up the steps and did so. When it was finished, he found more blood on his hands, and again rubbed away as much as he could with his handkerchief. Once more he paced the stone floor. Then he remembered that in his excitement he had not even said a prayer, and he knelt awhile by the rail, repeating some of the psalms for the dead, in a low voice.

He rose and walked again, and his eyes fell on the queer words in worn, raised letters on the slab in the floor — 'Esca Pagliuca pesca Saracen' — and again he was struck by the way in which his own name, or something very like it, could be made out of the letters.

He walked down the church, intending to look out and see whether the sacristan were coming. He was surprised to find the door locked. Then, all at once, he heard the sound of many voices, speaking loudly and coming nearer. He could distinguish his own name, spoken again and again in angry tones by someone with a loud voice.

CHAPTER XXVIII

IPPOLITO moved a step backwards when he heard the key turned in the lock, for the door opened inwards. It swung wide, a moment later, and he faced a multitude of angry eyes. There was Tebaldo pointing to him with an evil smile on his thin lips, and his lids falling at the angles like those of a vulture that scents death. There was the young red-haired lieutenant of infantry, gazing sharply at him; there was a corporal, with three or four of the foot-carabineers in their forage-caps. These represented the law. But pressing upon them, around them, and past them, was also a throng of angry men, and with them half a dozen women, and some children, even little ones, and the lame boy who waited every day to call the sacristan, and the fat sacristan himself, with the disturbing cast in his eye. In the background, just within the door when all had entered, and leaning against the doorpost, stood Concetta, her shawl falling back from her head, her splendid eyes gleaming with insanity.

"Take him," said Tebaldo, harshly. "There lies

my brother, before the altar, and his blood is on this man's hands."

Then came a discordant chorus of cries and curses from the crowd.

"Take the priest of the Saracinesca! Handcuff him! Put him in chains! Curses on his soul and on the souls of his dead!"

"He tried to kill him with a stone yesterday!"

"He has done it to-day, the assassin!"

"Let us burn him alive! Let us tear him to pieces! Death to the Roman!"

"Let me get my hands upon his face!" screamed a dishevelled woman.

And a child, that stood near, spit at him.

Ippolito had stepped backwards before them and faced them, pale and staring in amazement and horror. He could not understand, at first. The hideous treachery was altogether beyond his belief. Yet Tebaldo's outstretched hand pointed at him, and it was Tebaldo's voice that was bidding the soldiers take him. Their faces were impenetrable. Only the young Piedmontese officer, used to another world in the civilized north, betrayed in his expression the sort of curiosity one sees in the looks of people who are watching wild beasts in a cage.

"You had better clear the church," he said to the carabineers. "This confusion is unseemly."

He was not their officer, but they at once began

to obey him. The crowd resisted a little, when the big men pushed them back with outstretched arms, as one gathers canes in the brake, to bind them together before cutting them off at the roots.

"They will let him go, like his brother," growled an old man, fiercely.

"They will send him to Rome, and then let him go free, because he is a Roman," said the crooked little carpenter.

And the little boy spat at Ippolito again, and dodged the hand of one of the soldiers and ran out. With protesting cries, and with many curses and many evil threats, the people allowed themselves to be pushed out without any violence.

"I am the sacristan," said the fat man, objecting; and they let him stay.

"I am Concetta," said the dark girl, gravely.

"Let her stay," advised the sacristan. "She saw the priest beat him yesterday."

Ippolito had not spoken a word. He had folded his arms, and stood waiting for the confusion to end. He was fearless, but he could not realize, at first, that he might be seriously accused of the murder, and he believed that he should be set free very soon. He understood the treachery now, however, and his clear eyes fixed themselves on Tebaldo's face.

When the church was cleared, and the door fastened, the corporal stepped up to him. Two of his men had gone to examine the body, and to search for the weapon.

"You are accused of having killed that gentleman," said the corporal, quietly. "He is quite dead, and you are in the church with him. There is blood on both your hands. What have you to say?"

"I did not kill him," said Ippolito, simply. "When I saw that he was lying before the altar, I examined him, to see if he were dead. That is how I soiled my hands."

The two men came back from the altar. They had ascertained that Francesco had been killed by a knife-thrust, but had not found the knife.

"I regret that I must search you," said the corporal, in his quiet, determined voice.

"You will find a knife in my pocket," answered Ippolito, very pale, for he saw how all evidence must go against him.

The corporal looked up sharply, for he himself was surprised. Ippolito emptied his pockets, not wishing to submit to the indignity of being searched. He at once produced the sheathed bowie knife and the handkerchief, which was deeply dyed with blood and not yet dry. Some of it had stained the yellow leathern sheath in several places. The corporal drew out the weapon, which was bright and spotless, returned it to its sheath, and then held up the handkerchief by two corners. It is very easy to wipe blood from burnished steel, provided it is done instantly, and the corporal had a wide experience of such matters. He concluded that Ippolito might have cleaned the knife with the pocket handkerchief. He handed both objects to one of his men.

Tebaldo's lids had quivered and his lips had moved a little as he looked on. It seemed as though some supernatural power were conspiring in his favour against his enemy. But he said nothing. The young officer opened his blue eyes very wide, and thoughtfully twisted his small, red moustache.

Ippolito emptied the other pocket of his cassock, and produced a small volume of the Breviary, containing the offices for the spring, a little flexible morocco pocket-book, containing a few bank-notes, and an ivory-handled penknife.

"It is enough," said the corporal. "These things do not interest us. Your name," he added, taking out his note-book and pencil.

"Ippolito Saracinesca."

"Son of whom?"

"Of Don Giovanni Saracinesca, Prince of Sant' Ilario, of Rome."

"Age?"

"Twenty-seven years."

"Your occupation?"

"A priest."

"Present residence?"

"Rome. I am staying with my brother at Camaldoli."

The corporal noted the answers rapidly in his book, and returned it to his pocket, buttoning his tunic again. Then he was silent for a moment.

"You have already given your account of the affair," he said presently to Tebaldo. "It is not necessary to repeat it. But this girl — what has she to say?" He turned to Concetta.

Gravely, but with gleaming eyes, the pale and beautiful girl came forward and faced Ippolito.

"Yesterday at sunset I was at the gate of the cemetery," she said. "This man's brother, who lives at Camaldoli, shot this Don Tebaldo's brother, to whom I was betrothed, and he is buried in the cemetery. Therefore, I go every day to the gate, to visit him. Yesterday Don Francesco came up the road and was speaking to me. He who lies there dead was talking with me but yesterday. God give his soul peace and rest. Then this priest, coming down from Santa Vittoria, fell upon him from behind treacherously, and choked him by the collar, and beat him upon the head, so that he fell down fainting. But certain peasants came by that way and lifted him up and took him into our village, but the priest went down to Camaldoli. This I saw, and this I tell you. And now two Saracinesca have killed two Pagliuca."

She ceased speaking, and her white hands drew her shawl over her head, for she was in church, where a woman's head should be covered.

"Do you admit the truth of what this girl says?" asked the corporal, turning to Ippolito.

"It is true that I beat Francesco Pagliuca with my hands yesterday afternoon."

"Do you not admit also that you killed him to-day, in this church, with that knife? Don Tebaldo testifies that he saw you do it."

The young priest drew himself up to his height, and his clear gaze riveted itself on Tebaldo's half-veiled eyes. The good man faced the bad silently for many seconds.

"Did you testify that you saw me kill your brother?" asked Ippolito, at last.

"I did, and I shall repeat my testimony at the proper time," answered Tebaldo, steadily.

But under the clear, high innocence that silently gave him the lie, his eyelids drooped more and more, till he looked down.

"Do you admit that you killed him?" asked the corporal again.

"I did not kill him."

"But you must necessarily know who did, if you did not," said the soldier. "The sacristan says that you sent a boy for him some time ago. The man is only just dead, as my men have seen. You must have been in the church when he was killed, and you must have seen the man who did it."

Ippolito had not seen the deed done, but he had seen the murderer. It would be hard to answer on the one point and not on the other, and by the very smallest slip he might unintentionally say something which might end in the betrayal of the secret told him in confession. He therefore kept silent.

"You say nothing? You insist in saying nothing?" asked the corporal.

"I say nothing beyond what I have said. I did not do it."

"And you," continued the soldier, addressing Tebaldo, "you testify that you saw this man do it?"

"I do. Those things would bear evidence without me," added Tebaldo, pointing to the knife and the bloody handkerchief, which latter one of the soldiers held by a single corner in order not to soil his fingers. "Those things, and the man's hands," he added. "Moreover, his brother killed my other brother, as everyone knows, and he himself admits that he assaulted Francesco only last night. You can hardly hesitate about arresting him, corporal. The fact that he is a Roman and that we are Sicilians is hardly a sufficient defence, I think."

The corporal understood that he had no choice. He was a very sensible man and had seen much service in Sicily, and whenever there was bloodshed he was inclined to attribute the crime to a

Sicilian rather than to an Italian. He liked Ippolito's face and innocent eyes and would have given much to feel that he had a right to leave him at liberty. But he had to admit that the evidence was overpoweringly strong against the accused. At first sight, indeed, it seemed perfectly absurd to suppose that a young churchman of a sensitive organization and educated in a high state of civilization should suddenly, wilfully, and violently stab to death such a man as the carabineer believed Francesco Pagliuca to have been; a man against whom the authorities had been warned, as being likely on the contrary to do the Saracinesca some injury, if he could; a man who had grown up in a wild part of Sicily, imbued with the lawless ideas of the mafia; a man, in fact, who though a nobleman by birth was looked upon as a 'maffeuso,' and whose brother had certainly had friendly relations with outlaws. It was not to be denied that the carabineers and the soldiers were all strongly prejudiced in favour of the Saracinesca, as against the Corleone.

At the same time, the evidence was overwhelming, and was the more so because Ippolito was so obstinately silent and would say nothing in self-defence beyond making a general denial of the charge. In his difficulty the corporal turned to the officer of the line, both as his military superior and as a man of higher education than himself.

He wanted support. He begged the lieutenant to speak with him in private for a moment, and they moved away together to one of the side chapels.

Ippolito folded his arms and paced up and down before the carabineers, in profound and distressing perplexity. Tebaldo leaned against a pillar and watched him with evil satisfaction. Concetta went and knelt down, facing the altar, by a pillar on the opposite side, and the fat sacristan stood still in the background, watching everybody.

The lieutenant shook his head from time to time while the corporal went over the case.

"For my part," said the officer, at last, "I will wager my honour as a soldier that the priest did not kill him. But you will have to arrest him, not because of the feeling in the village, but simply because the evidence appears to be so strong. There is something here which we do not understand. But soldiers are not called upon to understand. It is always our duty to act to the best of our ability on what we can see. Understanding such things belongs to the law. I advise you to take him to your quarters and get him away from here to-night. He will make no resistance, of course."

The corporal was satisfied, though he did not like the duty, and he came back to Ippolito.

"It is my duty to arrest you," he said, in a tone which expressed some respect and much annoyance.

Ippolito had stopped in his walk and turned when he heard the soldier's footsteps behind him.

"You must do what you think right," he said calmly. "I am ready."

The corporal gave an order to his men and requested Ippolito to walk between them. Then he himself opened the door of the church.

A multitude of people had assembled outside, and there were now at least three times as many as had at first followed Tebaldo and the carabineers. Many more were hurrying down from the gate, and there was the confused sound of many voices, talking angrily. But when Ippolito appeared there was silence for a moment. Then, from far back in the crowd, came a single cry, loud, high, derisive, and full of hatred.

"Assassin!"

The word rang out, and was immediately taken up and repeated by a hundred men and women, with a sort of concentrated fury that hissed out the syllables, as though each were a curse.

Ippolito faced the people calmly enough, walking between the four carabineers, who marched two and two on each side of him, and the evening light shone full upon his clear-cut features and his innocent, brave eyes. He needed courage as well as innocence to bear him through the ordeal, for he knew that but for the handful of soldiers the crowd would have made short work of tearing him to pieces in their fury. For once, the soldiers were on their side against the hated Italians of the mainland. The people applauded them and their corporal, and the infantry officer, as they went by.

The children ran before, crying out to the people who were still coming down from the village.

"Here comes the priest of the Saracinesca!" they shouted. "Here comes the assassin!"

"Assassin! assassin!" Ippolito heard the word a thousand times in five minutes. And some of the people spoke to the soldiers and the corporal.

"Give him to us, Uncle Carabineer!" cried the crooked carpenter. "What has the law to do with him? Give him to us! We will serve him half roasted and half boiled!"

All the people who heard laughed at this and jeered at Ippolito.

"See the blood on his hands!" screamed the carpenter's big wife, suddenly catching sight of the red stains. "See the blood of Sicily on the priest's hands!"

A yell rose from all the multitude, for a hundred had heard the woman's high, shrill voice, and the rest took up the cry, so that the children who went before ran back to see what was the matter. One was the woman's child. She caught him in her strong arms and raised him up to see, as she marched along.

"See the good Sicilian blood!" she cried into the boy's ear.

"Curses upon the souls of his dead!" yelled the child, half mad with excitement.

All the people surged along together, running and jostling one another to keep the priest in sight. And the children whistled and made catcalls and strange noises, and the women screamed, and the men cursed him in their hard voices.

Bareheaded he walked between the soldiers, looking far ahead and not seeing or not wishing to see the people, nor to understand what they said. He had but one thought — not to break the faith of his priestly order by betraying the confession. Had he known that death was before him, he would not have yielded.

Suddenly something struck him on the shoulder, and he started, and his face changed. Someone had thrown a rotten orange at him, well aimed, and as it smashed upon his shoulder, some of the yellow juice spurted upon his cheek. For one moment the calm look was gone, and the clear features set themselves sternly, and the eyes flashed with human anger at the indignity of the insult. The crowd screamed with delight, and pushed the soldiers upon each other.

"Halt!" cried the carabineer corporal.

In a moment his great army revolver was in his hand, and all his men, watching him, had theirs ready.

"We are acting in the name of the law," he said, in a loud voice. "If anything more is thrown at us, we shall disperse you, and you must take the consequences."

"The orange was not thrown at you," cried the carpenter's wife.

"I have warned you," said the corporal. "Stand off, there! Fall back! Make way!" And he kept his revolver in his hand, as the people slunk away to right and left, cowed by the sight of the weapon.

After that there was less noise for a while, though he did not pretend to control that, nor to hinder them from saying what they pleased. And presently they began again, and the hissing words filled the air, and pierced the young priest's ears.

But he said nothing, and his face was cold and pale again, as he walked on, fearless and innocent, keeping the real murderer's secret for the sake of his own churchman's vow, and holding his head high amidst the insults and the jeers of the multitude.

It was a long way, for they had to march through the whole town to reach the quarters of the carabineers in the old convent on the other side. Ippolito would have marched a whole day's journey without wincing, if it had fallen to his lot, but he was glad when the wooden gates of the yard were loudly shut behind him, and he was at last free from his enemies. He looked round, and Tebaldo was gone, and Concetta, and the sacristan, as well as all the rest, except the carabineers. The officer of the line had gone home to write a despatch to his colonel, and Ippolito was alone with the carabineers.

Meanwhile the little lame boy whom Ippolito employed, and who had a sort of half-grateful, half-expectant attachment for the kind priest, had done a brave thing, considering his infirmity. Seeing what was happening at the church and hearing what all the people said, he quietly slipped away and limped down to Camaldoli to warn Orsino Saracinesca. It took him a long time to get there, for he was very lame, having one leg quite crooked from the knee, besides some natural deformity of the hip. But he got to the gate at last, and it chanced that Orsino had just come in from riding and was standing there, his rifle slung behind him, when the little boy came down.

At first Orsino could not understand, and when he partly understood, he could not at first believe, the story. The boy's account, however, was circumstantial, and could not possibly have been invented. Then, when he felt sure that his brother was accused of Francesco's murder, Orsino's face darkened, and he called for his horse again and mounted quickly. The little lame boy looked up to him wistfully, beginning to limp along, and

Orsino bent over in his saddle and picked him up with one hand by his clothes, and set him before him, though he was a dirty little fellow. Then he galloped off up the hill. But the boy begged to be let down to the ground at the cemetery, for he said that his mother would kill him if she knew that he had warned Orsino.

The crowd was still lingering in the streets as the big man on his big horse came thundering along the paved way, his rifle at his back and the holsters on his saddle, his face stern and set. It was as well that he did not meet Tebaldo Pagliuca just then. It was one thing to throw an orange at an unarmed priest, and to scream out curses at him; it was quite another to stand in the way of Orsino Saracinesca, with nearly thirty shots to dispose of, mounted on his strong horse, and in a bad temper. The people shrank aside in silence, and looked after the hated Roman as he galloped by towards the carabineers' quarters.

He struck the gate with his heavy boot by way of knocking, without dismounting. A man on duty inside asked who he was, for there were orders to keep the gate shut on account of the crowd.

"Saracinesca!" answered Orsino.

The gate swung back, and he rode in and asked for the corporal, dismounted, threw the bridle to the soldier, and went into the house. The corporal met him in the corridor.

"What is the meaning of this?" asked Orsino. "Is it true that you have arrested my brother?"

"I was obliged to do so," answered the corporal, quietly enough. "I consulted the lieutenant and he also advised it. I am sorry, but it was evidently my duty."

"Release him at once," said Orsino, in a tone of authority.

The corporal shook his head.

"I cannot do that," he answered. "You are at liberty to see him, but he is a prisoner."

"You are the best judge of your own conduct. You know what you are doing. I shall telegraph to the Ministry in Rome at once."

"The Minister will not order Don Ippolito's release," answered the corporal, with conviction.

Orsino stared at him, and laughed rather roughly.

"You are mad," he replied. "You will lose your stripes for this, if nothing worse happens to you. I advise you to let my brother out at once."

"Signor Don Orsino," said the corporal, gravely, "I am an old soldier. I am especially instructed to protect you and your interests here. Yet, in the execution of my duty, I have been absolutely obliged to arrest your brother, the Reverend Don Ippolito, for killing Don Francesco Pagliuca, in the church of Santa Vittoria, this afternoon. The evidence was such that I should have risked degradation and punishment, if I had refused to arrest him. It is not for me to judge of his possible guilt, which to me, personally, seems impossible. I could only act as a non-commissioned officer of carabineers is obliged to act by the terms of our general orders. I say this to you personally, but I am answerable for the act to my superiors, and they do not often overlook mistakes. If you will come with me into my private room, I will tell you all the details of the case, and show you the knife and the blood-stained handkerchief which we found in Don Ippolito's pocket. I and my men will do all in our power to serve you, as we are instructed to do; but to release Don Ippolito without further proceedings is absolutely out of the question."

Orsino's expression changed while the man was speaking, for he judged him to be what he was, an honourable soldier with a vast amount of common sense. He followed him into the little room which had been the parlour of the convent, and sat down beside the plain deal table on which lay several day-books and a heap of large ruled paper with printed headings over the columns, half filled with neat writing. A little lamp with a green shade was already burning.

Orsino sat down and listened patiently to all the corporal had to say. When the latter had finished, he had said more than enough to prove to any sane person that he had done his duty.

There was the fact of the quarrel on the previous day. It mattered little that Orsino knew the true cause of the scuffle in the road, and that the corporal had not known it till Orsino told him. The fact of violence remained. There was the singularly continuous chain of circumstantial evidence got in the church. And there was Ippolito's obstinate silence.

"I see," said Orsino, gravely. "I beg your pardon. You have done right. That Francesco Pagliuca was killed by his brother Tebaldo, I am convinced."

"By his own brother?" exclaimed the carabineer, incredulously.

"That is what I believe; but I have no evidence. I should like to see Don Ippolito, if you please."

"I am glad that you understand me," said the corporal, who was used to being misjudged.

He led the way to a door in the corridor, and opened it. It was not locked, and he simply closed it by the latch, after admitting Orsino.

The room was a large one, overlooking the ample courtyard, but the two windows were heavily barred, as indeed were all those on the lower floor of the old convent. On one side, against the wall, stood a low trestle bed, covered with one of the soldiers' brown blankets. There was a deal table that had been painted green, an iron washstand,

and half a dozen rush-bottomed chairs. On the table stood a small lamp, with a shade precisely like the corporal's own, and beside it there was a big jug of wine and a heavy glass tumbler into which nothing had as yet been poured. The corporal had brought the wine himself, supposing that Ippolito would need it. It was the soldier's idea of comfort and refreshment.

Ippolito sat by the other side of the table, and started to his feet as Orsino entered. He smiled rather sadly, for he knew that he was in a very terrible and dangerous situation. So far as he could see, he might be sent to penal servitude for Tebaldo's crime, for nothing could have induced him to break his vow and betray the secret.

Orsino grasped his outstretched hand.

"I knew you would come," said Ippolito, with a glad intonation. "Who called you? They all hate us here. You should have heard how they cursed me and all of us, in the street. Somebody threw a rotten orange at me, and hit my shoulder, but the carabineers kept them in order after that."

Orsino said something under his breath, and looked steadily into his brother's eyes. At last he spoke, and asked one question, quietly, coaxingly, as though only half hoping for an answer:

"Did Tebaldo kill him, or did he not?"

Ippolito's eyelids quivered at the suddenness of the question. His soul abhorred a lie, and most of all one to proclaim the innocence of such a man. To answer the truth was to betray the confession and to break his solemn vow before God, as a priest. Silence, perhaps, was equivalent to casting suspicion on the murderer.

But he kept silent, for he could do nothing else.

CHAPTER XXIX

IPPOLITO was silent, and he turned away from his brother, half fearing lest even his eyes should assent to the accusation against Tebaldo. He went towards the window, through which the afterglow of the sunset was still faintly visible, and then, as though changing his mind, he came back to the table and sat down, keeping his face from the lamp as much as possible. Orsino took another chair.

"It is not right to accuse anyone of such a crime without evidence," said Ippolito, slowly.

Orsino did not answer at once. He took two cigars from his pocket and silently offered one to his brother, and both began to smoke, without speaking. They were so much in sympathy, as a rule, that there would have been nothing surprising in their silence on any ordinary occasion. But the elder man now felt that there was a mystery of which Ippolito was making a secret; he knew his brother's extraordinary but perfectly quiet tenacity when he chose not to speak of anything, and he turned the whole situation over in his mind. He was in possession of all the details known to the carabineers, and of another piece of information which had not reached them, but which he was keeping to himself until it might be of use.

For one of his men had seen from a long way off how a man riding bareback had chased a man on a saddled horse up the long straight hill to the cemetery, and he had told Orsino of the fact before the lame boy had arrived, though he admitted that he had not been able to recognize the riders. Orsino himself had found Taddeo's horse lying dead in the road just beyond the gate of the graveyard, and his own horse had shied at it. He recognized the dead beast, which was well known as one of the best horses in the country, and he had seen in a flash that it was not injured, and had not been shot, whereat he had concluded that it had probably been ridden to death in the race his man had described. Ippolito had told him, after the scuffle on the previous evening, that Concetta had directed the peasants to take Francesco to Taddeo's house. Distrusting Tebaldo altogether, as Orsino did, it was not extraordinary that he should hit on something very near the truth, by a single guess founded on what he knew. He was in total ignorance of Aliandra's connexion with the story, and he had no idea why the one brother should have been chasing the other. But he had often heard of Tebaldo's fits of ungovernable fury. Vittoria herself had told Orsino that, at such times, Tebaldo was more dangerous than a wild beast, and she had also told him that her brothers often quarrelled.

Orsino guessed that such a quarrel had taken place to-day, somewhere on the road, and that it had ended in Francesco's killing his horse, reaching the church on foot, and being overtaken by his brother and stabbed a few seconds later, as had really happened.

Orsino was not very clever in the ordinary sense of the word, but his mind was direct and logical, when he exerted it. He went a step farther in his guessing, and concluded that Ippolito had not seen the murder, nor perhaps Tebaldo himself, but that Tebaldo had seen him. The priest had come down from the organ loft, had found the body lying on the steps, and had moved it, while Tebaldo had conceived the idea of accusing him of the deed. He explained Ippolito's silence by attributing to him, as a very conscientious man, the most extreme fear of bringing an accusation for which he had no ocular evidence. Though the train of thought is not easily expressed in words, it was a sufficiently reasonable one.

When he had followed it out, he knocked the ashes from his cigar, and looked at his brother.

"I am going to tell you what I think," he said, "for you are making a mystery of the truth out of some scruple of conscience."

Ippolito shaded his eyes with his hand, resting

his elbow on the table. He felt his brow moisten suddenly with anxiety, lest Orsino should somehow have guessed the secret, and his fears increased as his brother told him of the race, of the dead horse, and of the conclusions he had drawn.

In his painful position the young priest might have been forgiven for wishing that, altogether without his agency, Orsino might find out the truth. But he did not. As Orsino had once said of him, he had in him the stuff that sent martyrs to the stake in old days. He honestly hoped, with all his heart, that Orsino might not hit on the true story, and he was relieved when he heard the end of his brother's deductions. As a man, he was most anxious for his own immediate release, and he was willing that the murderer should be brought to justice. But as a priest, he felt horror at the thought that he, who had received the confession, might in any way whatever help to bring about such a result.

At that moment he wished that Orsino would go away, since he had not, at the first attempt, fathomed the secret. He might succeed the second time.

"I partly understand why you are silent," said Orsino. "It is not good to accuse a man who may be innocent. Neither you nor I should care to do that. But I am not the Attorney General. You can surely speak freely to me. You know that anything you say is safe with me, and it is not as though you should be suggesting to me a suspicion which I had not already formed by myself. Do you not trust me? It is hardly even a case of trust! What could I say? That you, the accused, have the same impression which I have. But I will not even say that. The point is this: You were on the spot, in the church. Your guess at the truth must be incomparably more valuable than mine. That is what I am trying to make you understand."

He gently patted the table with his hand, emphasizing the last words, while he leaned forward to see his brother's face. But the latter turned away and smoked towards the window.

"Is that all true, or not?" Orsino asked, in a tone of insistence.

"What?" asked Ippolito, fearing to commit himself.

"That you can trust me not to put you in the position of accusing an innocent man."

"Yes; of course it is true."

Orsino looked at him thoughtfully for a few seconds.

"When you asked me what was true, just now, before you answered me, you asked the question because you were afraid that your answer might include my guess as to what happened. I suppose my guess was not altogether right, since you were afraid of assenting to it. I wish you would look at me, Ippolito! What is all this? Is there to be no more confidence between us, because a mere look might mean that you suspect Tebaldo Pagliuca?"

Ippolito faced him, and smiled affectionately.

"If you, or our father, or any man like us, were in my position, you would act exactly as I am acting," he said slowly.

"You are perfectly innocent, and yet you act like a man who is afraid of incriminating himself!" said Orsino, growing impatient at last.

"I am perfectly innocent, at all events," answered Ippolito, with something like a laugh.

"I am glad that you are so light-hearted about it all. I am not. If we cannot catch the man who really killed Francesco before to-morrow morning, you will be taken down to Messina and imprisoned until we can bail you out, if bail is accepted at all, which I doubt. You run a good chance of being tried for murder. Do you realize that?"

"I cannot help it, if it comes to that," said Ippolito, quietly puffing at his cigar.

"You can at all events say something to help me in proving your innocence—"

"I am sorry to say that I cannot."

Orsino made an impatient movement, uncrossing and recrossing one knee over the other.

"You could if you chose," he said. "But there

is no more terrible obstacle to common sense than a morbidly scrupulous conscience. What do you suppose our people will think, in Rome?"

"They will not think me guilty, at all events," answered the priest. His manner changed. "I tell you frankly, Orsino," he said, his face growing square, as it sometimes did, "if I knew that I was to be sent to penal servitude for this, I would not say one word more than I have said already. It is quite useless to question me. Do your best to save me,—I know you will,—but do not count on me for one word more. Consider me to be a lay figure, deaf and dumb, if you please, mad, if you choose, an idiot, if it serves to save me, but do not expect me to say anything. I will not."

Orsino knew his brother well, and knew the manner and the tone. There was unchangeable resolution in every distinct syllable and in every quiet intonation. His own irritation disappeared, for he realized that Ippolito must have some great and honourable reason for keeping silence.

"So long as you are here, unless we find the murderer to-night, you will be shut up in this room," said Orsino, after a pause. "No preliminary examination can take place here, where there is not even an office of the Prefecture. They would naturally take you to Randazzo, but Messina would be better. We should have more chance of getting you out on bail at once if we went to headquarters."

"Randazzo is a cooler place," observed Ippolito, thoughtfully.

"What in the world has that to do with it?" asked Orsino, in surprise.

"Only that if I am to be kept in prison all summer, I should prefer a cool climate."

"Really — " Orsino almost laughed at his calmness. "That is absurd," he said. "We shall certainly have the power to get you out provisionally."

"I hope so. Let them take me to Messina, if you think it best."

"I will make the corporal telegraph for authority at once. It would be well if we could get off before morning and avoid the rabble in the street. Have you had supper?"

"No. They brought me some wine. There it is — but I do not want anything. Shall you telegraph to our people? It would be better. They might see it in the papers."

"Of course. I shall send them a full account, and shall send the same telegram to the Minister of Justice. I know him very well, and so does our father."

"Send me up some clothes and my dressing things by a trooper, will you?" said Ippolito.

They made a few more arrangements, but Orsino abstained from asking any more questions, and presently he left his brother alone, and after speaking with the corporal he mounted his horse and rode slowly out of the court into the street, towards the telegraph office. Half an hour later he was on his way down to Camaldoli. The people of the village had mostly gone into their houses, and the streets were almost deserted, for the short twilight was over, and it was already night.

He tried to see ahead of him in the gloom as he came near the cemetery, for he expected to find the grocer's horse still lying in the road. But it had been taken away already.

He had hesitated, at first, as to whether he should seek out Tebaldo and try to force the truth from him by sheer violence, but he had given up the idea at once as being absurd. If he failed, as he might fail, — for Tebaldo was desperately brave, — he should simply be creating fresh evidence of the hatred which existed between the two families, not to mention the fact that any such encounter might easily end in more bloodshed. Even to his unimaginative mind there seemed to be a strange fatality in the whole story. He had killed one brother in self-defence, or in what the law considered to be that, and now Ippolito was accused of murdering another of the brothers. It was wiser to leave the third alone, and to trust to the law to prove Ippolito's innocence. Orsino was not a man who instinctively loved violence and fighting, as some men do. He felt that if San Giacinto had been present he would somehow have managed to set Ippolito free and get Tebaldo imprisoned in his place, by sheer strength and the power of terror which he exerted over so many people, but which, to do him justice, he did not abuse. The giant was an extraordinary man, mentally and physically, and always put action before logic, and logic before sentiment. Orsino, on the contrary, generally wished to think out every matter to the end before acting, though he was neither slow nor timid when he had ultimately made up his mind.

So far as he could do so, he had decided and acted; and his thoughts reverted to the situation itself, and most directly, now, to his love for Vittoria. He had been looking forward to seeing her before long, for he had begun to understand that his presence in Camaldoli was not often necessary for many days at a time; and of late, during his lonely rides, he had given himself up to planning some means for meeting her during his next visit to Rome.

She was the principal and central being in his whole daily life. The separation was not one of distance only, for there were other and almost insuperable obstacles to his marriage. After Ferdinando's death, after Maria Carolina d'Oriani's terrible imprecations, after his own father's absolute refusal to listen to the proposal, it seemed almost impossible that he should ever really marry Vittoria. And now, as though to crush the last possibility out of existence, this new and terrible disaster had fallen like a thunderbolt from a clear sky.

Orsino was not very easily roused, but persistent opposition had the effect of slowly increasing the tension of his nature. Events had this effect upon him in a cumulative way. And his moral force slowly rose, as water in a huge embanked reservoir, into which, being empty, the little stream trickles idly, as though it had no force at all; but ever quietly flowing in from the source, it covers the bottom little by little, and still flows in, day by day, week by week; and the water rises slowly and very surely, gathering its terrible, incompressible weight into itself from the streamlet, till the body of it is deep and broad, and its weight is millions of tons, calm and still and ever rising; and then, one day, the freshet comes hissing down the bed of the stream, and the last rise in the reservoir is sudden and awful. The huge embankment quivers and rocks, and bursts at last; and the pent-up strength of the water is let loose in one moment, and sweeps howling and roaring down the valley, carrying death in its bosom and leaving utter desolation behind.

As he rode down through the silent night, the man wondered when he thought of the emptiness in which his life had once moved, of how little he had cared for anything, of the imperturbable indifference with which he had thought of all the world. For he was beginning to feel his strength in him, matched against the resistance of events.

A girl had wrought the change; and even in his great perplexity and trouble, his face softened in the dark as he thought of her. Yet he knew, as grown men do, that only half the secret was in her, and that the other half was in himself. For the strength of love is that it is the source of all existing life, and is a law which men and women obey, as atoms are subject to gravitation. That is the strength of it. But the beauty of love, and the happiness, and the nobility, are of a higher and finer essence, not suddenly to be seen, grasped, and taken, but distilled in life's alembic of that which was before life, and shall be afterwards, for ever.

Orsino was not imaginative, and his nature was not of that kind which is commonly called spiritual, which is given to contemplation, and delights in the beautiful traceries of the soul's guesswork. He vaguely understood that there was more between his father and mother and in their happiness than he would have called love, though there was nothing for which he might not hope. At present his love was that great natural law, from which, if one comes within the sphere of its attraction, there is no more escape than there is from hunger and thirst. He dignified it in his own person, by his inheritance of high manliness and honour. It did not dignify him. Vittoria lent it, by her being, the purity and loveliness of something half divine while wholly human, but it gave her nothing in return. Love can be coarse, brutal, violent, and yet still be love. According to the being it moves, we say that it is ennobled or debased.

Orsino saw the monster of impossibility rising between him and Vittoria, and though he said nothing to himself and formed no resolutions, he felt something within him rising to meet the impossible, and put it down. And beyond the obstacles he saw Vittoria's face clearly, with the light on it, watching him, and her eyes expecting him, and her lips moving to form words that should bid him come.

He rode slowly on through the blackness, for the road descended rapidly, and it was not safe to urge his horse. A deep, resentful melancholy settled upon him in the damp night air. There was nothing hopeless in it, for it was really the sensation of a new strength; and as the Greeks knew long ago, all great strength is grave and melancholic as Melancholia herself.

He thought of his brother sitting alone in the room where he was confined. He thought of Francesco's body lying in the little church, waiting to be buried, as Ferdinando's had lain, barely a month ago. He thought of the widowed mother, twice bereaved, half crazed with suffering already, destined to waken on the morrow to meet another death wound. He thought of Vittoria, alone with that mother, cut off from himself as he was cut off from her, mourning with horror, if not with grief, for the brother who had been nothing to her while he lived. Then he was glad that he had not sought out Tebaldo and tried to force the truth from him. Things were bad enough, without more violence to make them worse.

But most of all he wondered at Ippolito's silence, and afterwards when he had tasted his lonely supper he sat long in his place, staring at the empty chair opposite, and trying to force his intelligence to penetrate the mystery by sheer determination.

CHAPTER XXX

TEBALDO felt safe that night when he set his thirsty lips to a big jug of thin wine and water and drained the whole contents at a draught, while the fat sacristan stood waiting at the door of the room in the grocer's house. He had been giving the man directions about the disposal of the funeral. It was the room Francesco had occupied, and his things lay about in disorder, as he had left them early in the morning when he had ridden down to Randazzo for the last time.

The man who had killed him had been under a terrible physical and mental strain, ever since he had left Rome, in the insanity of his jealousy. Now that all was over, he fancied that he should be able to think connectedly and reason about the future. He sent the man away with the empty jug and sat down, feeling in his pocket for a cigar. He had none, and he rose again, and began to look among his brother's belongings for something to smoke.

A strange sensation came over him, all at once. It seemed as though Francesco could not be dead, after all. His things seemed to have his life in them. The leathern valise lay open on the floor, one side filled with fresh linen that had been disturbed in pulling something out, a heap of half-unfolded clothes in the other side, keeping up the flap that divided the two. A pair of black silk braces had fallen out upon the floor; a coat lay upon the chair close by; there was a clean handkerchief on the table, a smart note-book with a silver clasp, a small bottle of Eau de Lubin, a new novel in a paper cover, a crumpled newspaper two days old, and a pink pasteboard box of Egyptian cigarettes, open and less than half empty. Tebaldo took one and lighted it mechanically at the flame of the candle, wondering how it could be that Francesco would never want his cigarettes again. Surely he would come in, presently, and take one, and then would begin the old bickering and quarrelling that had gone on for years.

Now that it was all over, Tebaldo's first feeling among all these objects was that he missed his brother, whom he had always so utterly despised and whom he had bitterly hated with all his heart. He had not the sort of real timidity under a superficial recklessness which begins to feel the terror of remorse almost as soon as the irrevocable deed is done. But, little by little, as he turned over the things and puffed at the cigarette, a kind of stealing horror surrounded him, and would not leave him.

It had nothing to do with any suspicion of the supernatural, and he intended to lie down and try to sleep in the bed in which Francesco had slept on the previous night. It had nothing to do with fear of discovery, for he felt safe and was outwardly brave to recklessness. It was rather the horror of having done, almost unwittingly, what no power could undo, and of having utterly destroyed, at a blow, something to which he had been accustomed all his life. And this strangely piercing regret clashed continually with the expectation, arising out of long habit, of suddenly seeing Francesco appear in person where all his belongings were lying about, in the room he had last inhabited. He was reckless, unscrupulous, choleric, almost utterly bad, but he was human, as all but madmen are. He felt safe, but just then he would have risked any danger for the sake of seeing Francesco open the door and walk in.

He threw away his cigarette and sat down to think. His eyes fixed themselves, as his chin rested on his hand and his elbow on the table, and a long time passed before he moved. But when he got up, he had taken hold of himself again and was ready to begin his life once more. His weaknesses did not last long. Francesco was dead. If it had been to do over again, he would not have done it. He could not have done it at all, in cold blood. — perhaps no man could, — and there had been much to rouse him. But since it was done, Francesco could never again make love to Aliandra, and there was the evil satisfaction of having successfully thrown the guilt upon a Saracinesca, of all people, and so cleverly that the accused man would, in all probability, be condemned.

He had made up his mind at the instant as to what he should say, and he had said it all to the corporal of carabineers. He and his brother had met in Randazzo at Basili's house, and intending to come up to Santa Vittoria, had laid a wager, the one who first entered the little church to be the winner, and Tebaldo had agreed to ride bareback and allow his brother a start of five minutes. Francesco had killed his horse and had run for the church on foot, and Tebaldo had entered two or three minutes late. Doubtless, he had said, Francesco, in his haste to win the bet, had run against Ippolito, and in a moment the quarrel of the previous day had been renewed more violently. Francesco was unarmed, and the priest had stabbed him instantly, just as Tebaldo came in. The wager had been a reckless and foolish one, no doubt, but there was nothing impossible in the story, which perfectly accounted for the wild riding, in case, as had really happened, anyone had seen the two men on the road. No one but Aliandra Basili knew how they had left her father's house, and she, for her own sake, and certainly for Francesco's, would not tell what she knew. She was sure to say that Tebaldo had borrowed the horse, and she would not let her father know that the brothers were quarrelling about her. Nevertheless, she knew that much, and would guess the rest, and being a woman, there was a possibility that she might volunteer her evidence when she should hear that the innocent priest was upon his trial.

It was necessary to see Aliandra at once. The crude cynicism which was at the root of the man's strange character came to the surface again, as he followed out his train of thought and discovered, at the end of it, where the weak point of his safety lay.

He slept little that night, though he was weary from the mad ride and shaken by the strain under which he had lately lived. Again and again he dreamed that he was doing the deed, and awoke each time with a start in the dark. And the familiar perfume of Francesco's dressing things disturbed him, even through the stale smoke of the cigarette he had smoked. Yet one of his chief characteristics was that he was always ready and not easily surprised. Waking, he realized each time where he was, who he was, what he had done, and the fact that he must be up early in the morning, and each time he laid his head upon the pillow again with the determination to sleep and get the rest he needed.

Apart from the elements of fear and honour, and in so far as the mere act of killing is concerned, there is but a difference of degree between the homicide who has stabbed a man in anger, and the soldier who has killed one enemy, or ten, in battle. In most cases the homicide is pursued by a fear of consequences to which the soldier is not subject. Tebaldo felt himself safe.

He had lost no time in so fully indemnifying Taddeo, the grocer, for the death of his horse, that the excellent 'maffeuso' had no difficulty in providing him with another in the morning. He rode up to the carabineers' quarters and gave notice of his movements before going down to Randazzo, for he did not wish to appear to leave Santa Vittoria without informing the authorities. He was told that Ippolito had been taken to Messina before dawn, and that Orsino had accompanied him. He had decided that his brother should be buried on the following day, and meanwhile the coffin lay in the little church surrounded by many burning candles, and preparations were being made for a solemn requiem. Many of the people went in, on their way to their work, and knelt a moment to say a prayer for the soul of Francesco Pagliuca, and a short but heartfelt one for the destruction of all the Saracinesca in this world and the next. This seemed to them but simple justice, though the more devout of them were aware that it was sinful to wish death to anyone.

Tebaldo dismounted at the door of the church, and bade a loiterer hold his horse while he went in. He knew that the whole population would think it strange and unnatural if he should pass by, on his business, without stopping, after giving such elaborate orders for the funeral.

For his own part, he would gladly have escaped the ugly necessity, not because the hypocrisy of it was in the least repugnant to him, but because he had the natural animal dislike of revisiting a place where something terrible had happened. It was so strong that he grew pale as he went in under the door and walked up the aisle to the catafalque.

But the whole place seemed changed. He had no realization of the fact that his brother's body lay in the angular thing under the black pall. There was a strong smell of incense and many lights were burning. He felt that he was observed, and his nerves were singularly good. He knelt some time with bent head at the foot of the coffin, then crossed himself, rose, and went out. The people about the door made way for him respectfully. There were two or three of the very poor among them. No one begs in that part of Sicily, but Tebaldo gave them the copper coins he had loose in his pocket, and passed on.

"God will render it to you," said the poor

people, kissing the backs of their own fingers toward him as a way of kissing his hand by proxy. "God bless you! The Madonna accompany you!"

As he mounted, one old woman touched his knee and then kissed the hand with which she had touched it. He nodded gravely and rode away, glad to turn his back on the church at last and get out upon the high road.

The news of Francesco's death had already reached Randazzo by a wine-carrier who had come down with a load in the night. Tebaldo expected that this would be the case, and he considered that his interview with Aliandra would be facilitated thereby. He went to the inn and put up his horse. The people treated him with a grave and sympathizing respect. He had arrived there on the previous day with a few belongings, but in the suddenness of events the landlord did not consider it strange that he should not have returned during the night. Tebaldo did not volunteer any explanations, but went to his room, refreshed himself, changed his clothes, and then told the landlord that he was going to see Basili, the notary. This, also, seemed quite natural, in such a case, as Basili had always been the Corleone's man of business.

Gesualda opened the door, and he at once saw, by the gravity in her ugly face as she greeted him, that she knew what had happened. She ushered him into the front room downstairs and went up to call Aliandra, for Tebaldo said that he wished to see her before visiting her father. He stood waiting for the young girl, and going to the window he saw that the fastenings of the blinds were broken, and he remembered that he must have broken them when he forced them to look out after Francesco. The fact brought the whole scene vividly to his memory again, with all its details, and he remembered, by the connexion of little events, much that he had forgotten. Notably he recalled distinctly the very few words he had spoken to Aliandra during a meeting which had scarcely lasted two minutes, but which, by the operation of his anger, had hitherto seemed almost a blank in his recollection.

Aliandra entered the room and spoke to him first. To his own surprise, he started nervously at the sound of her voice, as though she were in some way connected with Francesco, and should have been dead with him, or he alive with her. For since his brother's sudden departure from Rome, the two had been constantly linked in his mind by his desperate jealousy.

Aliandra wore a loose black silk morning gown, and she was pale. She did not come up to Tebaldo, after she had closed the door, but seemed to hesitate and laid her hand upon the back of a chair, looking at him earnestly. His face was grave, for he knew his risk.

"I have just heard," she said in a low voice.

"Yes," he said after a short pause. "I thought that you must know. I wished to see you at once, so I came, though he is not buried yet."

"I am glad," she answered, "for I do not understand. It all seems so strange and terrible."

"It is. Sit down beside me, and I will try to tell you. It will not be so hard as it was to tell the authorities up in Santa Vittoria yesterday. I love you, Aliandra. That is why I came to you."

It was true that he loved her, but that was not the reason of his coming. Yet he spoke simply and sincerely, and she said nothing, but sat down at a little distance from him and folded her hands, waiting for him to tell his story.

"I love you," he repeated slowly and thoughtfully. "When he left Rome, I knew that he must have come to you, and as soon as I could get away, I followed him, sure that I should find him here, for I was jealous of him, jealous to madness. People laugh at jealousy. They do not know what it is." He paused.

"No," she answered gravely, for she remembered how he had looked when he had entered the house on the previous afternoon. "No. People do not understand what it is. Go on, please."

"It is a hell in soul and body. When I came here yesterday, I meant to come in at once. As I passed under the window I heard your voices distinctly. There was no one in the street, and I leaned against the wall and heard what you said. I touched the blinds once or twice, moving them a little, so as to hear better. Then I heard him tell you that falsehood about my engagement to Miss Slayback, and I put my hand on the sill, to draw myself up and deny it. But I struck my head under the blinds that were pushed out. Then I heard him come to the window, and I asked him to come outside. You know how he fled, while I was here, and I took your father's mare, without saddle or bridle and chased him."

"Yes, you frightened me," said Aliandra, as he paused again. "I had to tell my father that you had borrowed the mare. She came back of her own accord and was standing outside the stable gate this morning, waiting to be let in, all covered with mud. Please go on quickly."

"It rained. There was a terrible thunderstorm. I overtook him two or three miles on, where the road winds, for he saw that it was senseless to run away, as though I wished to injure him."

"You looked as though you did," said Aliandra, thoughtfully. "I do not wonder that he fled."

"I do not say that if I had found him here, I might not have handled him roughly," said Tebaldo, wisely. "But the gallop cooled us both, I suppose. And you know that when he chose he had a gentle, good-natured way of speaking that disarmed one. Yes — we quarrelled about you at first for a while, and then, being cooler, as I said, we rode quietly along together, though we did not say much. On the more level part of the road higher up, he began to talk of the horse he was riding, which belonged to Taddeo, the grocer, and was a good beast, but I said that your father's mare was the fleeter, and he denied it. At last he proposed that we should settle the question by racing up to the town. The one who got into the little church of Santa Vittoria outside the gate was to win. I gave him four minutes' start by my watch, because I was lighter and was riding bareback. Do you understand?"

He looked at her keenly and expectantly, for the story sounded very plausible to him. She nodded slowly, in answer, with a little contraction of the eyelids, as though she were weighing the possibilities.

"I had him in sight, and then I fell with the mare at a jump, for I had no bridle and could not lift her properly. But we were not hurt, and I got on again. I saw him again before me on the long, straight stretch up to the cemetery. Taddeo's horse must have had an aneurism, I should think, for just beyond the gate it rolled over stone dead. I saw Francesco jump off as the beast staggered, for he knew what was the matter. But he meant to win the bet and be in the church first. He ran up the last bit like a deer, and disappeared over the shoulder of the hill. It all happened in a moment, and I had still a quarter of a mile to make. Seeing that he must win, I did not hurry the mare, but she took fright at the dead horse and bolted up the last bit. At the church I got off and hitched the halter to a stake that had been driven into the ground for a banner at the last festa. I did it carelessly, I suppose, for the mare got loose. I do not know. When I entered the church I saw my brother wrestling with Ippolito Saracinesca on the steps of the altar, and the priest had a big knife in his hand and struck him before I was half way up the church."

Tebaldo was now excessively pale, and there was a nervous tremor in his voice. Aliandra was almost as pale as he, but still her lids were a little drawn in, and she kept her eyes on him.

"You have heard the rest," said Tebaldo, and his mouth was so dry that he could hardly speak. "I locked the priest into the church, which has no other door, and I went for the carabineers. They took him down to Messina early this morning, before the people were about in the streets, and he will be committed for trial without doubt. His hands were covered with blood, and he had the knife in his pocket. He had cleaned the blade carefully on his pocket handkerchief, like a fool, instead of throwing it away into a corner. As for the reason of the murder, Francesco and he had come to blows on the day before yesterday in the road. The priest admitted the fact. Heaven only knows what they were quarrelling about, but it must have begun again in the church. At all events, that is what happened, and my poor brother is dead. God rest his soul."

"Amen," said Aliandra, mechanically.

Tebaldo wiped the moisture from his pale forehead, glad that he had told his story and told it so well. It was, indeed, a marvellously lucid narrative, in which he had taken full advantage of every available fragment of truth to strengthen and colour the general falsehood.

Aliandra, like any reasonable person, would have found it hard to believe that a man supposed to have the manners and civilization of a modern gentleman could do what Tebaldo had really done. But, on the other hand, it was even harder to see how the deed could have been done by one who was not only just as civilized, but a churchman besides.

She had been terribly shocked by the news of Francesco's death, which had reached her only a few minutes before Tebaldo had appeared. She remembered the latter's face, and the terror of the former on the previous afternoon, she remembered that the other brother had been a brigand, or little better, and she knew many stories of the Pagliuca's wild doings before they had gone to Rome. It would have surprised her far less if Gesualda, who had heard the story from the carter himself, had told her that one brother had killed the other, than it did to be told that the guilty man was a Roman, a priest, and a Saracinesca.

But Tebaldo's story was plausible, and she had to admit that it was as she thought it over. He had evidently been under a strong emotion while telling it, too, and the fact was in his favour, in her eyes, for she had been fond of Francesco.

"Have you told me the whole truth?" she asked suddenly, after a long silence.

"Of course I have told you the truth," he answered, with a half-startled, nervous intonation.

"You have not always done so," said she, leaning back in her chair. "But I do not see why you should conceal anything from me now."

"You will see it all in the account of the trial."

"It is terrible!" she exclaimed, realizing once more what it all meant. "Terrible, terrible," she repeated, passing her hand over her eyes. "Only yesterday he was here, sitting beside me, telling me—"

She stopped short.

"Yes, I heard what he told you," said Tebaldo, in an altered voice. "It is of no use to go over it."

"I was fond of him," she answered. "I was

very fond of him. I have often told you so. It is dreadful to think that we shall never see him again — never hear his voice — "

Her eyes filled with tears, for beyond the first horror of his death there was the sadness. He had been so young, so full of life and vitality. She could hardly understand that he was gone. The tears welled over slowly and rolled down her smooth cheeks, unheeded for a few moments.

"I wish I knew the truth," she said, rousing herself, and drying her eyes.

"But I have told you the truth," answered Tebaldo, with a return of nervous impatience.

"Yes, I know. But there must be more. What was there between him and the priest? Why did they fight in the road? It all seems so improbable, so mysterious. I wish I knew."

"You know all that I know, all that the law knows. I cannot invent an explanation."

"It is a mystery to you, too, then? You do not understand?"

"I do not understand. No one knows all the truth but Ippolito Saracinesca. He will probably tell it in self-defence. If he could prove that my brother attacked him first, it would make a great difference. He will try to make out that he killed him in self-defence."

"It is very mysterious," repeated Aliandra.

They talked in the same way for some time.

Gradually her distrust of him disappeared, because he did not try to prove too much, and his own story, as he went over the points, seemed to her more and more lucid. He took advantage of little questions she put to him, from time to time, in order to show her how very complete the account was, and how utterly beyond his own comprehension he thought the fight at the cemetery on the day before the murder. He was amazingly quick at using whatever presented itself. Her doubts did not really leave her, and they would return again after he was gone, but they sank out of her reach as she listened to him.

Then she made him go upstairs with her and tell the whole story to her father. Tebaldo submitted, but the strain on him was becoming very great, and the perspiration stood in great drops on his brows, as he went over it all for Basili. He knew that the notary was a man not easily deceived, and was well aware that his opinion would be received with respect by the principal people in Randazzo. He was, therefore, more careful than ever to state each point clearly and accurately. He saw, moreover, that Aliandra was listening as attentively as before. Possibly, now that he was no longer speaking directly to her, her doubts were coming to the surface again. But Tebaldo's nerves were good, and he went to the end without a fault. The notary only asked three or four simple and natural questions, and he did not seem surprised that Tebaldo should not know the cause of the disagreement between his brother and Ippolito.

Aliandra went downstairs with Tebaldo. She seemed to expect that he should go away, for she stood still in the hall at the foot of the stone staircase.

"When are you going back to Rome?" he asked, for he wished to see her again.

"As soon as my father can spare me," she answered.

"I shall have to go down to Messina to give my evidence," he said. "When the funeral is over, to-morrow morning, I shall come here, and go on to Messina the next day. May I see you to-morrow afternoon?"

To his surprise, she hesitated. She herself scarcely knew why she did not at once assent naturally.

"Yes," she said, after a pause. "I suppose so, if you wish to."

"I do wish to see you," he answered. "You have no reason to doubt that, at all events."

"You speak as though I had reason to doubt other things you have said." She watched him keenly, for the one incautious little speech had weakened the effect he had produced with such skill.

"You pretended to doubt," he answered boldly. "You asked me if I was telling you the truth about my brother. That was doubting, was it not? You always do. I think you do not even believe that I love you."

"I only half believe it. Are you going over the discussion we had in Rome, again?"

"No. It would be useless."

"I think so too," she said, and her eyes grew suddenly cold.

He sighed and turned from her, towards the door. It was the first perfectly natural expression of feeling that had escaped him, and it was little enough. But it touched her unexpectedly, and she felt a sort of pity for him which was hard to bear. That one audibly drawn breath of pain did more to persuade her that he really loved her than all the words he had ever spoken. She called him back when his hand was already on the door.

"Tebaldo — wait a moment!" Her voice was suddenly kind.

He turned in surprise, and a softer look came over his drawn and tired features.

"I shall be very glad to see you when you come," she said gently. "I do not know why I hesitated — I did not mean to. Come whenever you like."

She held out her hand, and he took it.

"You may think the worst you will of me,

Aliandra," he said. "But do not think that I do not love you."

"I believe you do," she answered in the same gentle tone, and she pressed his hand a little.

Just as he was about to open the door, her eyes fell upon the rifle Francesco had left standing in the corner.

"Take your brother's gun," she said. "I do not like to see it here. I am sad enough already."

He slipped the sling over his shoulder without speaking, for the odd sensation that Francesco was not dead, after all, came over him as on the previous evening, and with it the insane longing to see his brother alive. He felt that his face might betray him, and he went out hastily into the noonday glare. The heat restored the balance of his nerves, as it generally did, and when he reached the inn he was calm and collected.

Aliandra went upstairs to her father's room, and sat down beside his couch, in silence. The sunlight filtered through the green blinds, and brought the warm scent of the carnations from without. The notary lay back, with half-closed eyes, apparently studying the queer outline of his splinted leg as it appeared through the thin, flowered chintz coverlet.

"For my part," he said, without moving, and as though concluding a train of thought which he had been following for a long time, "I do not believe one word of the story, from beginning to end."

"You do not believe Don Tebaldo's story?" asked Aliandra, more startled than surprised.

"Not one word, not one half word, not one syllable," replied the notary, emphatically. "We can say it between ourselves, my daughter. If my sister were here, I should not say it, for she is not discreet. It is a beautiful story, well composed, logical, studied, everything you like that is perfect. It must have taken much thought to put it together so nicely, and it is not intelligence that Tebaldo Pagliuca lacks. But no one will make me believe that a quiet little Roman priest could have killed one of those Corleone in that way. It is too improbable. It is a thing to laugh at. But it is not a thing to believe."

"I do not know what to say," answered Aliandra, all her doubts springing up again.

"We are not called upon to say anything. The law will take its course, and if it condemns an innocent Italian — well, it has condemned many innocent Sicilians. The one will pay for the other, I suppose. But as for the facts, that is a different matter. I daresay the priest had a knife of his own in his pocket, but it was not the knife that killed Pagliuca. Now, I do not wish to imply that Don Tebaldo killed him — "

"That is impossible!" exclaimed Aliandra.

"He could not come here and talk about it so calmly. The mere idea makes me shiver. What I think is that someone else killed him, — a brigand, perhaps, for some old quarrel, and that Tebaldo has thrown the blame on the priest, just because he is a Saracinesca."

"Perhaps. Anything is possible, except that the priest killed him. But as we know nothing, it is better to say nothing. It might be thought that we favoured the Romans."

"It is strange," said Aliandra. "When he is speaking, I believe all he says, but now that he is gone, I feel as you do about it. He said he should come back to-morrow."

"It is of no use for you to see him again. Why does he come here? I do not wish to be involved in this affair. Make an excuse, if he comes, and do not see him."

"Yes," answered Aliandra. "I will manage not to see him. It is of no use, as you say."

Tebaldo rode back to Santa Vittoria to bury his brother. Almost the whole population followed the funeral from the church to the cemetery, and it was easy to see how the people looked at the matter. Tebaldo received a summons to appear and give his evidence in two days, and he left the village early in order to have time to spend in Randazzo with Aliandra before taking the afternoon train from Piedimonte to Messina.

One thing only he had left undone which he had intended to do, for it had been impossible to accomplish it without attracting attention. He had meant to get into the little church alone and recover the knife he had dropped through the grating that stood before the glass casket in which the bones of the saint were preserved. As the details of those short and terrible moments came back to him, he remembered that the thing had not dropped far. He had heard it strike the stone inside immediately, and though it was improbable that the grating should be opened for a long time, yet the weapon was there, waiting for someone to find it, and possibly for some to recognize it, for he had possessed it several years.

The first requiem mass for Francesco had been sung in the parish church, for the curate had said that Santa Vittoria must be reconsecrated by the bishop before mass could be celebrated there again, the crime committed being a desecration. Tebaldo thought it just possible that at the bishop's visit the grating might be opened in order to show him the casket. But this was by no means certain. On the whole, he believed himself safe, for there was no name on the sheath of the knife, and he did not remember that he had ever shown it to anyone who could identify it as belonging to him.

He had sent for a carriage and drove down to Randazzo, stopping at the inn, as usual. He knocked at the door of the notary's house a few minutes later, expecting to be admitted by Gesualda. To his surprise, no one came to let him in. He knocked twice again with the same result, and was about to go away, when Basili's man, the same who had accompanied San Giacinto and Orsino to Camaldoli, opened the stable gate and came up to him.

"There is the notary," he said. "No one else is at home. The Signorina Aliandra has taken Gesualda and is gone out to visit friends in the country. They will not come back before tomorrow. The notary sleeps."

Tebaldo was very much surprised and disconcerted. He remembered how kindly and gently Aliandra had spoken when he had parted from her, and he could not understand. She had left no message, and it was clear enough that she had gone away in order to avoid him. He went back to the inn, a good deal disturbed, for if she wished to avoid him, it must be because she had some suspicion. That was the only conclusion which he could reach as he thought the matter over. It was by no means absolutely logical, being suggested by the state of his conscience rather than by the operation of his reason.

He was disturbed and nervous, and he realized with a vague trepidation that instead of forgetting what he had done, and becoming hardened to the consciousness of it, he was suffering from it more and more as the hours and days went by. Little things came back to their lost places in his memory, which might have been noticed by other people, and might betray him. To himself, knowing the truth, the story he had invented looked far less probable than it appeared to those who had heard it from him.

He thought of writing to Aliandra, for he was bitterly disappointed at not seeing her; but when he considered what he could say in a letter, he saw that he could only tell her of his disappointment. What he unconsciously longed for, was the liberty to speak out plainly to someone, and tell the whole truth, with perfect safety to himself. But that desire was still vague and unformulated.

There was no possibility of waiting till the next day to see Aliandra when she returned. He was expected to appear on the following morning in Messina, to give his evidence, and he had no choice but to go at once. He left Randazzo with a heavy heart, and a feverish sensation in his head.

CHAPTER XXXI

IPPOLITO was committed for trial on the charge of having killed Francesco Pagliuca in the church of Santa Vittoria, and Tebaldo Pagliuca was the principal witness against him. That was the result of the preliminary examination in Messina.

No one believed that Ippolito had committed the crime, neither the judge nor the prefect of the province, nor the carabineers who had arrested him and brought him down. Yet the evidence was such that it was impossible to acquit him, and his obstinate silence, after a simple denial of the charge, puzzled the authorities. It was the expressed opinion of the judge that, in any case, and supposing that the priest were guilty, it was not a murder, but a homicide committed in a struggle, which had been the result of a quarrel entirely unaccounted for. Taking Tebaldo's own story as true, it was clear that Francesco's appearance in the church had been too sudden and unexpected to allow of the smallest premeditation on Ippolito's part. Tebaldo said that he had come in and seen the two fighting. The judge observed that, if a struggle had taken place, it was more than probable that Francesco, coming suddenly upon Ippolito, had sprung upon him to avenge himself for having been maltreated by the priest on the previous day. Here Orsino rose and told the story of that first quarrel, as he had heard it from his brother immediately after it had occurred. On being questioned, Ippolito admitted the perfect truth of the story, and the judge ordered that Concetta's evidence should be taken at Santa Vittoria by a deputy of the court.

Tebaldo had been in complete ignorance of the truth about Concetta, but he saw that it would be best to take the judge's view. For all he knew, he said, his brother might have attacked Ippolito on entering the church. Ippolito was at liberty to say so, if he chose, observed Tebaldo. The fact did not militate against his own story, in the least. On the contrary, it accounted for the struggle. Francesco was unarmed, however. Tebaldo was prepared to swear to that, and did. Ippolito did not know it, and, being attacked suddenly, might have drawn his knife and defended himself.

The worst of all this was that it lent a faint air of probability to the accusation, of which Tebaldo, with his usual quickness, took advantage at once. But the judge, in his heart, was no more inclined to believe Ippolito guilty than before, though he saw no way of acquitting him. The young priest stood calm and self-possessed between the carabineers throughout the whole examination, and his quiet eyes made Tebaldo uncomfortable.

San Giacinto arrived from Rome before the hearing was finished, and entered the courtroom when Tebaldo was speaking. There was something so gloomily ominous about the grey old giant's eyes that even Tebaldo's voice changed a little as he spoke. San Giacinto had twice, in serious affairs, been the means of clearing matters up suddenly and completely, and as Orsino grasped his huge hand, he felt that all would be well.

The judge admitted Ippolito to bail, and San Giacinto offered himself and was accepted as surety, being a large landowner in Sicily and a person well known throughout the country. The trial would probably not take place before the autumn, but there is a great latitude allowed in Italy, in the matter of bail, except when the prisoner is charged with premeditated murder.

"I think," said San Giacinto to the judge, when the proceedings were officially closed, "that it would be worth your while to visit Santa Vittoria in person."

Tebaldo heard and listened, and he thought of the knife under the altar. If the judge should go to the church and insist upon examining everything thoroughly, it might be found.

"The second hearing will not come before me," observed the judge. "Nevertheless —" He hesitated a moment and then spoke in a lower tone. "The case interests me very much," he said. "I should like to see the place where it happened. I might take that country girl's evidence myself, and visit the church at the same time. Yes, I think I shall accept the suggestion."

Though he had lowered his voice, Tebaldo had heard most of what he had said, and more than enough to increase the fear of discovery, which was rapidly growing up in the place of the cynical certainty of safety which he had at first felt. Nor had the examination gone so absolutely against Ippolito as he had hoped. The judge and the officials were evidently in sympathy with the accused man, and Tebaldo had been heard with a sort of cold reserve which suggested a doubt in his hearers. Like Aliandra and her father, they all felt the utter improbability of the story, as they compared the accused with the accuser, though they had been obliged to admit just so much as they had no means of denying.

The view taken by the law on the strength of the whole evidence can be summed up in a few words. Francesco Pagliuca had assaulted a young country girl on the high road. She had screamed for help. Ippolito Saracinesca had been near and had saved her and soundly beaten her assailant. On the very next occasion of meeting him by accident, Francesco had rushed at the priest to repay his score of blows, and the priest, taken unawares, had defended himself with a knife he had about him, and which his brother had insisted that he should carry, for the very reason that he might, at any moment, be assaulted by Francesco. It was not justifiable homicide, assuredly, but there were a great many extenuating circumstances. That was as much as the men of the law could say for Ippolito, on the evidence; but not one of them believed that he had killed Francesco.

The three Saracinesca men left the court together and drove away in a closed carriage. They decided that Orsino and Ippolito should return to Rome at once and quiet the family by their appearance, while San Giacinto went up to Camaldoli, to keep matters in order as far as he could. Orsino offered to go back alone, if San Giacinto would accompany his brother, but the big man preferred to take matters into his own hands, as he usually did when there was a crisis of any sort.

When the two brothers were alone in their compartment in the train that left Reggio that evening, Orsino drew a long breath. The sunset glow was over the hills, and the rushing breeze that blew in through the open window was sweet and clean to the taste after the foul air of filthy Messina and the almost more poisonous atmosphere of the courtroom. Orsino looked out in silence for a few moments, too glad to speak to

Ippolito. When he looked round at last, he saw that his brother was leaning back in the opposite corner, with closed eyes, one hand thrust into the bosom of his cassock, the other lying upon the seat behind him. Orsino watched him, expecting that presently he would open his eyes and begin to talk. But Ippolito had fallen asleep almost instantly in his corner, exhausted by the long strain of days and nights spent in terrible anxiety.

No one ever knew what he had suffered during that time. Though of a fibre different from his father and his brothers, he was strong and healthy, but in those few days he had become thin and white, so that he looked positively delicate now, as he leaned back in his corner.

His anxiety had not been all for himself. It was a fearful thing, indeed, to be accused of murder, and be led like a murderer through a yelling rabble, to be lodged in a prison, to be thrust forward to the bar of a crowded courtroom to answer for a great crime. But it was worse to be accused by the real murderer and to be bound by one of the most solemn of all vows to keep that murderer's secret and bear his accusation without giving one hint of the truth.

It was no wonder that at the first relief from such a tension, he should fall asleep at last, and Orsino was glad when he saw and partly understood. He had slept little himself since the night of Francesco's death, but he could not have rested now, for he still had much anxiety and many things to disturb his peace. He was in profound ignorance of what had happened to Vittoria and her mother, though he had been almost hourly in communication with his own family.

Corona's first impulse had been to leave Rome instantly and join her sons, and it had been with the greatest difficulty that Giovanni had persuaded her to await the result of the preliminary hearing. He himself was afraid to leave her, and he had perfect confidence in San Giacinto. He was in reality most preoccupied about his wife; for he, like everyone else, was struck from the first by the outrageous improbability of the accusation. He hardly ate nor slept, himself, it was true, but he was all along perfectly certain that Ippolito must be at liberty in a few days, and that the whole truth must be known before long.

Corona said little after she had consented to remain at home, but she suffered intensely. The beautiful high features were like a white marble mask, and when she spoke at all, her words were brief, nervous, almost hard. Her eyes were like black steel, and her figure grew slighter, and seemed to grow taller, too. Giovanni thought that the little, soft, grey streaks in her intensely black hair were suddenly growing broad and silvery. He was almost more anxious for her than for Ippolito.

But she never broke down in any way. She showed herself to the world, in her carriage, as if nothing had happened, though she received no one during those days. She knew how to bear suffering, for she had borne much in early life, and Giovanni needed not to fear for her. He hardly left her. They so belonged to each other that it was easier to bear trouble together. Possibly, though he did not know it, he looked to her in his anxiety quite as much as she looked to him. It would have been hard to say; for where there is such sympathy, such trust, and such love, there is also a sort of community of courage and of strength and of endurance for a joint suffering.

When the news of the decision in Messina came, however, Giovanni considered the trouble to be at an end. Corona only smiled faintly as they read the telegram together.

"At liberty on bail," she said slowly. "That is not an acquittal. He is still accused of the murder."

"Long before the trial we shall have discovered the truth," answered Giovanni, confidently.

"Until we do, he is still accused of the murder," repeated Corona, with slow insistence.

She had not believed it possible that he could be held for trial. But the gladness of a near meeting with him stole upon her anxiety.

As soon as the first greetings were over, he went

with her to her own sitting-room, and they remained alone together. For a long time she held his hands and looked into his eyes, while he spoke to her.

"Do not ask me any questions, mother dear," he said, smiling at her. "You know that I did not kill the poor man, and no one believes that I did. Do not let them torment me with all sorts of questions. If I could answer them, I should have answered them at once. I cannot."

Still she did not speak, for Orsino had written and telegraphed every detail, and had again and again spoken of Ippolito's inexplicable silence.

"Mother, trust me, and do not ask me questions," said the young priest, earnestly.

"Yes," she said at last. "I trust you, and I always have. I was not hesitating, my dear, and I shall never ask you anything about it, nor allow anyone else to do so, if I can prevent it. But it has dawned on me — the truth I wanted. I believe I understand."

A startled look came into Ippolito's eyes, and his hands closed suddenly upon hers. He opened his lips to speak, but could not find wise words, for he believed that she had guessed the truth, by some extraordinary and supernormal process of intuition.

"No," she said reassuringly, "do not be afraid. I shall not even tell you what I think, and I shall certainly not tell anyone else. But—" She stopped suddenly.

"But what?" he asked, in the utmost anxiety, searching her eyes.

"Nothing that I need say, my dear boy," she answered quietly. "It is better to say nothing about such things when one is not sure. Sit down beside me, and let us be together as we used to be before all this happened."

He sat down, and they remained long together.

There was but one opinion in Rome. Everyone said that Tebaldo Pagliuca knew more about his brother's death than he chose to tell, and had managed to cast the burden of evidence against Ippolito. Hundreds of people called at the Palazzo Saracinesca, and Ippolito had scores of notes from friends, congratulating him on having regained his liberty.

Old Donna Francesca Campodonico came to see Corona, a saintly, shadowy woman, who lived alone in a beautiful old palace near the Tiber.

"A Corleone, my dear!" she said. "What do you expect? We are told to love our enemies, it is true, but we are at liberty to love them as enemies, and not as friends. In order to do that it is necessary to distinguish them, and the more clearly we draw the line, the better."

"It is refreshing to hear you speak of anyone as an enemy," answered Corona, with a smile.

"My dear," said Donna Francesca, "I am very human, I assure you. Never have anything to do with a Corleone or a Braccio. There is very little to choose between us. We are hereditary sinners!"

She was a Braccio herself, and Corona laughed, though she knew there was truth in the saying. The Braccio people had many friends, but so far as the Corleone were concerned, all Rome agreed with Donna Francesca, and congratulated the Saracinesca, quite regardless of the fact that Ippolito was not really acquitted.

But Corona was not as she had been before, and her eyes followed Ippolito about, when he was within sight, with a sort of wondering, anxious expression that showed how perpetually her thoughts were occupied with him.

CHAPTER XXXII

ORSINO made an attempt to see Vittoria on the day after his return. The liveried porter put his ear to the speaking-tube as of old, and then, shaking his head, told Orsino that the ladies could see no one. He volunteered the information that Donna Maria Carolina was very ill, and that her servants believed her to be out of her mind, since the death of her second son. The young lady did not go out every day, he said. When she did, he always heard her tell the coachman to drive to the Hotel Bristol. There were two sisters of the French order of the Bon Secours who took turns as nurses, with her mother. The doctor came twice daily, and sometimes three times. The porter had asked the doctor about Donna Maria Carolina, and he had answered that she was in no danger of her life. That was all.

The porter, as has been said, volunteered the information; but if he did so, it was because he knew Orsino and had read in the newspaper a full account of Francesco's death, and of the hearing at Messina. Being a good Roman, he felt personally outraged at the idea that any member of a great old Roman house should be accused of killing a Sicilian gentleman. He might kill him, if he chose, the porter thought, but it was an abominable insult to accuse him of it. The man had never liked Francesco, who had been stingy and self-indulgent, spending money on himself, but never giving a present to a servant if he could help it, and generally ready to find fault with everything. Tebaldo was not mean. Orsino, when he gave at all, gave lavishly, and he gave whenever he happened to think of it, as he did to-day. The porter bowed low, as much to the bank-note as to the heir of all the Saracinesca, and Orsino went away.

He wondered why Vittoria went to the Hotel Bristol whenever she went out. He remembered having once or twice left cards there on foreigners, but he could not remember their names. He might recognize them, however, if he saw them, and he drove to the hotel at once. Looking down the list of the guests, he immediately came upon the names of Mrs. and Miss Slayback, and he remembered how it had been said of late that the young American girl was to marry Tebaldo Pagliuca. It was tolerably clear that these were the people whom Vittoria visited when she went out at all. Orsino remembered that he had been introduced to them at some party. Without the smallest hesitation he sent up his card to Mrs.

Slayback, and in a very short time was requested to go upstairs.

Mrs. Slayback received him with cool interest, and showed no surprise at his visit.

"I have been in Sicily most of the time since I had the pleasure of being introduced, or I should have done myself the honour of calling sooner," said Orsino, rather formally.

"Of course," answered Mrs. Slayback. "I quite understood."

She was silent, as though expecting him to open the conversation. That, at least, was what he thought.

"You are staying in Rome very late," he began. "Of course it is cool here compared with Sicily, and June is really one of our best months, but, as a rule, foreigners are afraid of the heat."

But she had not wanted that sort of conversation, and had only been making up her mind how she should speak, being taken at short notice by his visit. He was a good deal surprised at what she said.

"Please do not talk about the weather, Don Orsino," she began. "I am very glad that you have come to see me, for I am in great perplexity. I know that you will tell me the truth, and you may help me. Will you?"

"Certainly," answered Orsino, becoming grave at once. "Anything that I could do — " He waited.

"My niece is engaged to be married to Don Tebaldo Pagliuca. She is an orphan, a niece of my husband's, and is — well — rich, to say the least of it. She has fallen in love with this young Sicilian and insists upon marrying him. The Romans say that it is a family of brigands. You shot one of them in self-defence not long ago, and now the papers say that your brother has killed Don Francesco, whom we knew. It is rather an awful double tragedy for civilized modern life, you know. Such things happen with us in the West, though not so often as formerly, but they do not happen to people who live in New York, for instance."

"I hope not," said Orsino, gravely. "Sicily is a good deal less civilized than your West, I fancy. But I assure you that my brother did not kill Francesco Pagliuca, though I believe he knows who did kill him. He only tells me that he did not, and I am willing to give my word for him, on the strength of his."

"But Don Tebaldo gave evidence on oath that he saw your brother do it," objected Mrs. Slayback.

"And Don Tebaldo is engaged to marry your niece," answered Orsino. "You will allow me to say that the fact silences me."

"I hope not," said Mrs. Slayback, "for I do not wish my niece to marry him. I come to you for an argument against the marriage. I do not wish to silence you, as you call it."

"You know Don Tebaldo very well," replied Orsino. "You have probably formed an opinion about his character. I am in a very difficult position with regard to him, myself."

He wondered whether Vittoria, growing intimate with the American girl, had spoken of him.

"Your position cannot be half so hard as mine."

Mrs. Slayback spoke with a conviction which reassured him, and he merely bent his head a little, as though assenting to what she said.

"It is clear," she continued, "that since you know that Don Tebaldo has sworn to this evidence, while you yourself, on your brother's word, are willing to swear to the contrary, you believe that Don Tebaldo is deliberately perjuring himself. That is perfectly clear, is it not?"

Orsino said nothing, but he could hardly keep from smiling a little at her directness.

"Very well," she went on; "should you allow your niece, or your sister, or anyone belonging to you, to marry a man who has deliberately perjured himself?"

"You are perfectly logical," said Orsino.

"Oh, perfectly! I always was thought so, in my family. And now that you have helped me so far, for which I am really very grateful, can you tell me whether Don Tebaldo is coming back to Rome at once?"

"I am sorry, but I know nothing of his movements. I believe you know his sister, Donna Vittoria, very well, do you not? I should think she might be able to tell you. His mother is very ill, poor lady."

He had taken the first possible opportunity of introducing Vittoria's name.

"Vittoria comes to see Lizzie whenever she can get out for an hour," answered Mrs. Slayback. "But yesterday, when she was here, she did not know anything about her brother. I think she does not like to talk of him, for some reason or other. Have you seen her lately?"

She asked the question very naturally and easily.

"No," said Orsino. "Her mother is ill, and she has no one else with her. She could not receive me, of course."

"I suppose not. She could in America. She is sure to come to-morrow afternoon about five o'clock, I should think, unless her mother is much worse. We shall be very glad to see you if you like to come in for a cup of tea."

"You are very kind — very kind, indeed, and I will come with pleasure," Orsino answered, surprised and delighted by the unexpected invitation.

"That is," said Mrs. Slayback, as though correcting herself, and not heeding his answer, "that is, you know, if you have no objection to meeting Donna Vittoria after all this dreadful business. If you have, come in the next day, and we shall be alone, I daresay."

Again Orsino found it hard not to smile, though he was very far indeed from anything like mirth.

"It would be more likely that Donna Vittoria might object to seeing me," he said.

"Oh, no!" replied Mrs. Slayback, with alacrity. "I think she likes you, by the way she sometimes speaks of you, and she does not believe her brother any more than you or I do, I can see, though she does not quite say so. Indeed, I hardly understand her. She wears black, of course, and they see no one since that poor man's death, but she comes here just the same. As for being sad, she was always sad, ever since I knew her."

"She has had enough to sadden her," said Orsino, gravely. "None of us who have been concerned in this dreadful affair can be anything but sad just now."

When he went away he could not make up his mind as to whether Mrs. Slayback knew anything of his love for Vittoria or not. Foreigners, and especially Americans, were unlike other people, he thought. It never would have occurred to any Roman lady, a mere acquaintance, to ask him to come for a cup of tea and meet two young girls.

An intimate friend might have done it, in order to do him a service, but not a mere acquaintance. But foreigners were different, as he knew.

He pondered the question all night, and the next day seemed very long until it was time to go up to the Hotel Bristol at five o'clock. He thought the correct Swiss porter's face relaxed a little when he saw the card Orsino gave, as if he had been told to expect him. This was the more apparent when Orsino was ushered upstairs at once.

He heard an exclamation in Vittoria's voice as he entered the drawing-room, and then for a moment he seemed to himself to lose consciousness, as he advanced. He had not known what it would be to be brought face to face with her after all that had happened.

Neither she nor Miss Slayback saw anything unusual in his face as he came forward, and the latter certainly had no idea how disturbed he was, as she smilingly held out her hand to him. Vittoria had uttered the one little cry of surprise, and then she felt very cold and frightened for a moment, after which she apparently regained her composure.

"My aunt is lying down in the next room, so it is perfectly proper," said Miss Slayback, in the very words she had used to Tebaldo.

Her voice brought Orsino back to lively consciousness at once, and as he sat down nearly opposite to the two young girls, he glanced from the one to the other quickly, before looking long at Vittoria. Miss Lizzie seemed worn and harassed, he thought, and much less pretty than when he had last seen her. There was a nervous restlessness about her, and she was unable to sit still for a moment without moving her hands, or her head, or her shoulders, to look round, when there was nothing to look at.

Vittoria's gentle young face was undeniably sad. She did not look weary like her friend, for she was not naturally nervous; but there was something shadowy and half ethereal about her eyes and features that moved Orsino strangely. He made a civil remark to Miss Slayback, in order not to be silent, and she answered him in short, broken little sentences. Somehow the whole position seemed odd to him. All at once Miss Lizzie rose to her feet.

"I knew I had forgotten something!" she said. "It is the day for letters to catch the French steamer, and I have not written to Uncle Ben. I always write him a line once a week. Do you mind amusing Don Orsino, Vittoria? Just a moment, you know — I can write a letter in ten minutes."

And before Vittoria could answer, she was gone, talking as she went, and not looking back. As the door closed after her, Orsino was beside Vittoria, with both her hands hidden in his and looking into her face. She met his eyes for a moment, and her head sank on his breast, as though she were very tired.

"It is not meant to be, love," she said, and he could but just hear the words.

"It shall be, whether it is meant or not," he answered, bending down to her little ear.

"It is, all too terrible!" She shook her head against his coat, hiding her face. "Nothing but death, death, everywhere — my poor brothers — one after the other." She roused herself and laid her hands upon his shoulders, looking up suddenly into his face with wide, searching eyes. "Tell me that Ippolito did not kill him!" she begged. "Tell me that it is not true! I shall believe you. I cannot believe myself, when I say it."

"It is not true," answered Orsino, earnestly. "I will pledge you what you will for my brother, my word of honour — everything. It is not true." He repeated the words slowly and emphatically.

"I know it is not, when you say it." Her head sank upon his shoulder. "But it is all so terrible, so horrible! Tebaldo killed him. I know it. I knew he would, when I saw his face that night, after they had quarrelled. Tebaldo has put it upon your brother — I know it, though I do not know how it was."

He kissed her hair, for he could not see her face.

"It is a worse crime than if Ippolito had killed him to defend himself," she said. "I feel — I do not know — but I love you so — and yet — oh, Orsino, Orsino! How will it all end?"

She rocked herself a little, to and fro, her forehead against his coat, and her hand twisted painfully upon his, but there were no tears in her voice, for she had shed all she had in the lonely nights since she had seen him last.

"It shall end in our way," said Orsino, in the low tone that means most with a man.

"You and I? Married?" Again she shook her head. "Oh, no! It will be different — the end! I am not cowardly, but this is killing me. My mother — " She lowered her voice still more, and hesitated. "My mother is going mad, they say."

Orsino wondered how fate could do more than it had done upon the Corleone.

"Nothing shall take you from me," he said, his arms going round her and folding her to him. "Nothing, neither death, nor madness, nor sorrow."

She was silent for a moment, and the mirage of happiness rose in the mist of tears.

"But it is not possible," she said, as the brief vision faded. "You know it is not possible. Ippolito did not do it — I know. There is not that to separate us. But you could not take the sister of such brothers as mine have been to be your wife. How could you? And your father, your mother — all that great family of yours — they would not have me, they would not — oh, it is impossible! Do not talk to me of it, love. It will make it harder to die."

"To die? You?" His voice rang with life.

Suddenly, and for the first time since he had loved her, he pressed her head gently backwards, and his lips met hers.

She started, and a little shiver ran to her small hands, and her eyelids dropped till they closed, and still he kissed her, long and passionately. And the colour rose slowly in her cheeks when her pulse beat again, for it had stopped a moment, and then she hid the scarlet blush against his coat, and heard the heavy, mysterious beating of his heart through flesh and bone and cloth, — the strong, deep sound which no woman forgets who has heard it, and has known that it was for her.

"You can make me live," she said softly. "But not without you," she added, drawing a deep breath between.

"Together," he answered. "Always together, to the very end."

Then, by degrees, as the great wave of passion subsided, they talked more quietly, he with perfect confidence in the future, and she more hopefully, and they forgot Miss Lizzie and her letter, till they heard her move the handle of the door. They both started.

"Does she know?" asked Orsino, quickly.

"I never told her," Vittoria had time to answer, before Miss Slayback could hear.

"I have written such a nice long letter to Uncle Ben," said the young girl, airily. "I hope you have not bored yourselves! Not that I am very amusing myself," she added, pausing before a mirror, on her way along the side of the room. "And I am a perfect fright! Just look at my eyes. Oh, well, it does not matter! Don Orsino does not mind, and I am sure you do not, Vittoria, do you?"

It was the girl's way of trying to jest at what was a real pain, if it was not a very great sorrow. It was not very successful, and her worn little face betrayed her, as well as the dark lines under her eyes. She had believed herself very much in love with Tebaldo, and, to tell the truth, she was in love with him still, so far as she had yet any idea of what it meant to be in love. But she had just made up her mind that she could never marry him. It was not possible to marry into such a family, where everybody was always killing everybody else, as Mrs. Slayback expressed it. The friends of the Saracinesca had found a great deal to say about the previous history of the whole tribe of Pagliuca d'Oriani, including the Corleone of old, during the last four days, and much of it had got into the Roman papers, which all took part against the Sicilians. Romance was very well, up to a certain point, Miss Lizzie thought, but it was necessary to draw the line somewhere, and she had drawn it now. Yet her heart ached for the fierce-eyed Sicilian, all the same, and her small face was weary and careworn.

CHAPTER XXXIII

TEBALDO's nerves were beginning to give way. It was of no use for him to argue with himself, and tell himself that the knife would not be found. He knew that the possibility existed. No one in Santa Vittoria would look for it, but there was the bishop, who would shortly reconsecrate the church, and there was the judge, who had told San Giacinto that he might go up to visit the scene of the murder. The bishop might order the grating to be opened in order to see the bones of the saint; and the judge, accustomed to the ways of criminals, might insist upon a search, seeing that the murder had taken place within arm's length of the altar.

In his broken dreams, the judge and the bishop appeared separately and together and turned into each other, and invariably found the knife, and then Tebaldo was suddenly in the courtroom, at the bar, where Ippolito had stood, instead of on the witness stand, and he heard all the people yell and curse his name, as the villagers of Santa Vittoria had cursed the young priest. As in the old days of torture a man was drawn up by his hands to the high vault of the prison, and then dropped all at once with a hideous wrenching and tearing of the joints till his feet were but a foot from the floor, so Tebaldo's sudden waking was but a sudden change of agony renewed each time and each time more unendurable, till the fear of dreaming was outdone by the dread of returning to consciousness.

When he was awake he imagined impossible schemes for getting possession of the knife unobserved. It might have seemed simple enough to go up to Santa Vittoria, call the sacristan, and have the church opened for him. Then he could have invented an excuse for sending the fat man away while he quietly reached down through the grating and felt for the knife. In his ordinary state of mind and health he would have done that, and there were ninety-nine chances in a hundred that he would have succeeded.

But it looked differently to him now. In the first place, a sheer physical horror of going back to the village at all had taken the place of the cynical indifference which had at first left his cunning and his coolness free to act. Everyone who has dealt with humanity under the influence of pain or fear knows that the effect of either is cumulative, and that in each individual there seems to be a limit beyond which the nerves will resist no more, and the will power altogether ceases. A man may bear a certain grievous pain on the first day without a sign; on the second day he will grind his teeth; on the third he will wince; later he will groan, writhe, and at last break down, like a mere child, under one-tenth of the suffering he bore manfully and silently at first. And it is the same with any given fear. In a smaller degree it is so also in the matter of losing one's temper under constantly renewed irritation of the same kind. Even in another direction, but in one which equally concerns the nerves, this thing is true. Often, in a farce on the stage, an indifferent action passes unnoticed; it recurs and excites attention; again it comes, and the audience smile; once more and they laugh, and cannot control their laughter each time the action is repeated, until a certain capacity for being moved to mirth again and again in one direction, which varies in each individual, is momentarily paralyzed. People afterwards realize with surprise, and sometimes with a little shame, the emptiness of the absurdities at which they have laughed so heartily; as many a man has despised himself for having been angry at a trifle, and wondered at his own weakness in having winced under an insignificant pain. But the trifle is only the drop that overfills the cup at last.

So Tebaldo had almost reached the limit of endurance, and the mere idea of going back to the village and the church was intolerable to him. It seemed to him that even if he could make up his mind to the attempt, he should be sure to fail. The sacristan would come back unexpectedly and find him with his hand through the grating, groping after the knife; or the lame boy, who always hung about the gate, would look in and see him. Yet he could not have locked himself into the church, for that also would have excited suspicion.

The idea that he might get someone else to recover the weapon for him took hold of him by degrees. At first it appeared to be madness to trust anyone with his secret, and his keen sense rejected the plan with scorn. But it suggested itself again and again with increasing persistence, because the mere thought that he might get the thing back without going to Santa Vittoria in person was an inexpressible relief, and he began to try and think of some person whom he could trust to be prompt and secret.

At first he thought of asking someone in Santa Vittoria. The fat sacristan, whom he had known for years, could do it easily. But Tebaldo recognized at once that he had no hold upon the man, who might betray him at any moment. Money would tempt the fellow, but no sum could silence him afterwards, if he should demand more, as was very probable. Besides, it would be necessary to write to him, and the man might lose the letter; even if he were able to read it well enough to understand, which was doubtful. There was Don

Atanasio, the apothecary. He would do much out of hatred for the Saracinesca, as his daughter had done already. But he was a cautious old man, dependent, in a large measure, upon the government, and would not be inclined to endanger his position to oblige Tebaldo. It would not do to risk a refusal.

Then it occurred to the wretched man that women had more than once saved men who loved them from desperate danger, and that, after all, he might do worse than to tell Aliandra the truth. If she were willing, she could go up to Santa Vittoria on a pretext and visit the little church, and get rid of the sacristan. Then, if she wore a wide cloak, she could kneel down on pretence of looking through the grating, and her slim woman's arm could run through it in a moment, and her hand could not fail to find the knife. He could remember, now, exactly at how many inches from the left he had dropped it through. The details came back to him with vivid clearness, though at first he had almost quite forgotten them.

He almost made up his mind to go to Aliandra for assistance, and the half decision was a sudden and immense relief. He could eat and drink and he felt that he should sleep. Immediately his mind outran this first plan, and he saw himself in Rome again, in three or four days at the most, engaged to marry the great heiress, resuming his regular life of wise courtship, and discussing with his future wife the details of a brilliant existence. He drove away the subconsciousness that the thing was not yet done and revelled in visions in which there was no fear.

But that did not last long, for he could not sleep, after all; and the knowledge that he must act quickly grew constantly more disturbing, till he rose in the night and sat by the open window, working out his plan. He must go to Randazzo again and see Aliandra; then he must wait at the inn, while she went up to Santa Vittoria. The hours of waiting would be hard to bear, but at the end of them there would be freedom. She would come back, and he should see her pass. He should go to her father's house. She would meet him at the door and draw him into the familiar sitting-room, and a moment later the weapon would be in his hand. After all, if he once had it, she could have no proof against him, beyond her mere assertion, if she should ever turn against him. For the sake of his love for her, she would never do that, he thought.

He telegraphed to Tatò at dawn to meet him at the Piedimonte station. It was a Thursday, and he felt sure that the judge would not be at leisure to go up to Santa Vittoria before Sunday. It was most probable, too, that the bishop would choose the Sunday to reconsecrate the church, and it occurred to Tebaldo that it would be strange if the two should meet as they were always meeting in his dreams. But there was plenty of time before that, and all would come right. Aliandra would not refuse to do him this service.

Tatò met him at Piedimonte in person, instead of sending down his man, and in obedience to Tebaldo's telegram he had brought a light conveyance in which the two sat side by side, with Tebaldo's little valise at their feet, and his rifle between them. They were old acquaintances, for Tatò had driven the Corleone family for years himself, and by deputy, as it were, while he had been serving his time in Ponza. He had a profound respect for Tebaldo, for he knew how the latter with his brothers had long ago led the soldiers astray when pursuing the brigands in the neighbourhood of Camaldoli. There was probably no man in that part of the country who knew as much about people of all sorts and conditions, and about their movements, as the smart-looking owner of the stable at Piedimonte, nor anyone who could keep his own council better. He was a thorough type of the 'maffeuso,' at all points, as San Giacinto had at first observed to Orsino. San Giacinto had always believed that the man had known of Ferdinando's intended attack, and of the pitfall in the avenue.

Tatò told Tebaldo that he had driven San Giacinto alone up to Camaldoli on the previous evening, returning during the night.

"What courage!" he exclaimed, with some genuine admiration, as he spoke of the big man. "After all that has happened! He is a man of iron, full of courage and blood."

"There was no particular danger in driving up to Camaldoli," observed Tebaldo, indifferently.

Tatò looked at him curiously for a moment, to see whether he were in earnest.

"Then you do not know?" he enquired. "They are in the woods above Maniace."

'They' means the outlaws, or the carabineers, as the sense requires.

Tebaldo looked quickly at Tatò in his turn.

"How many?" he asked.

"A dozen or fifteen," said Tatò. "There is Mauro, and Leoncino, and the one they call Schiantaceci — he was a gentleman of Palermo, but no one knows his real name, and the Moscio — eh, there are many! Who knows all their names? But Mauro is with them."

"Leoncino is a good man," observed Tebaldo, quite naturally.

"Souls of his dead! You have spoken the truth. It was he that wore the carabineer's uniform when they took the Duca di Fornasco's bailiff. He has a face like a stone. Yet Mauro himself is the best of them, though he is often ill with his liver. You know the life they lead. The food is sometimes good, but sometimes it is badly cooked, and they eat in a hurry, and then that poor Mauro's liver troubles him."

"Why have they come over from Noto? Do you know?"

"For a change of air, I suppose," answered Tatò, imperturbably. "But they say that the Fornasco is coming from Naples. Perhaps they would like to try for the Saracinesca. Who knows what they want?"

"Do the carabineers know that they are near Maniace?"

"How should they know? Mauro and the Leoncino rode into Santa Vittoria yesterday afternoon to see — good health to you — to see where Don Francesco died. They asked the little lieutenant of infantry to tell them the way to the church, as though they were strangers. Do you think he has their photographs in his pocket? He took them for two farmers going from Catania to Randazzo."

"They might have caught San Giacinto last night when you drove him up," said Tebaldo.

"If everyone knew where to look for money, there would be no poor men," returned Tatò. "They did not know about the Saracinesca, and the carabineers do not know about them. Thus the world goes. Each man turns his back on his fortune and chases flies. Should you not like to see the Moscio, Don Tebaldo? You know that it was he who helped that angel of paradise, Don Ferdinando. He goes everywhere, for he is not known."

"Yes. I should like to see him. But I do not care to go up to the Maniace woods, for I am known, though he is not. How can I see him? I should like to ask him about my brother."

"Where shall you stay to-night?" enquired Tatò.

"At the inn at Randazzo. I am not going to Santa Vittoria. I have business with Basili."

"I will arrange it," answered Tatò. "Leave it to me."

Tebaldo assented and remained silent for some time. As they drove on, nearer and nearer to Randazzo, the folly of his present plan became clear to him, and in the place of Aliandra, as an agent for getting back the knife, the possibility of employing the young outlaw known as the Moscio presented itself, and the possibility of confiding freely in a man whose position was ten times more desperate than his own, and whose evidence could never be of any value in the eyes of the law. Mauro himself was under obligations to Tebaldo, who could have betrayed him to the authorities on more than one occasion, less than a year earlier.

Again and again both Mauro and the Moscio, as well as three or four others of the band, had been at Camaldoli, and the Corleone had given them food and drink and ammunition at a time when a great effort had been made to catch them.

"Are you quite sure of being able to send a message to the Moscio?" asked Tebaldo.

"Leave it to me," said Tatò, again. "I have a little bundle for him in the back of the waggon. How do I know what is in it? It feels like new clothes from the tailor in Messina. The Moscio is fond of good clothes. He writes to his tailor, who sends the things when he can, by a sure hand. You know how they live, as well as I do. They always wear new clothes, and give their old things to the peasants, because they can only carry little with them. And then, they are well brought up and are accustomed to be clean. But I speak as though you were a Roman. You know how they live. The Moscio will have his bundle this afternoon, and this evening he will come down and have supper with you at Randazzo, at the inn. I know this, therefore I asked if you wished to see him, and not another."

Before Randazzo was in sight, Tebaldo had quite made up his mind to confide in the outlaw, and he could hardly have believed that he had left Messina that morning with the firm intention of imploring Aliandra to help him. But he looked forward to seeing her and to spending most of the afternoon with her.

He was disappointed. Everything happened exactly as at his last visit. Basili's man appeared at the door of the house, instead of from the stable, and gave precisely the same message. Aliandra had taken Gesualda to the country to visit some friends, and had not come back. No one knew when she meant to come.

"Tell me something else," said Tebaldo, offering the man money, for he knew that the story could not be true.

The man threw back his head in refusal.

"You might give me also Peru," he answered. "This is the truth, and this I have told you."

"I should like to see Signor Basili," said Tebaldo, thinking that he might get into the house.

"The notary sleeps," answered the man, stolidly, and he began to shut the door.

To force an entrance seemed out of the question, and Tebaldo went away angry and disappointed. He could see that it would be of no use to try again, for the same answer would be given to his enquiries. It was enraging to know that the woman he loved was within a few yards of him, and able to keep him away from her. But his anger was a relief from the perpetual anxiety about the knife, which was wearing out his nerves, day and night.

In the afternoon he shut himself up in the room he had taken and tried to write to Aliandra, but he was in no condition for composing love-letters. He could find nothing but reproaches for her unkindness in refusing to admit him; and as soon as he had expressed them, he felt that his own words exhibited him in an absurdly undignified position. Besides, he was really waiting in the unconscious hope of explaining her conduct to himself, when he knew that it was as yet inexplicable. Meanwhile he tore up the pages he had covered, and threw the whole blame upon Basili, unwilling to admit that the woman he loved could turn against him.

In the hot hours of the afternoon he shut the windows and dozed restlessly on a hard sofa, and his evil dreams came upon him once more and tormented him, waking him again and again just when the sweetness of rest was within reach. At last, his body being very weary, the dreams could no longer wake him, and tortured him at their will while he lay in a heavy sleep.

It was already dark when he awoke with a start. The door had opened, and a youth was standing beside him holding a candle in a brass candlestick, shading the flame a little with the other hand and looking down into his face.

"I regret that I disturb you," said the young man, in a gentle, girlish voice. "I hope you have slept well?"

Tebaldo was already sitting up on the sofa, and had recognized the Moscio. The outlaw could not have been more than twenty-two years old, and looked a mere boy. He was of medium height, delicately made, very carefully shaved, and dressed with a sort of careless good taste, wearing a black velvet jacket, immaculate linen, riding-trousers with gaiters, patent leather shoes, and silver-plated spurs. He was hatless, and his short, soft brown hair curled all over his head, close and fine, like curly Astrachan fur. There was a tender, youthful freshness in his skin, and he had beautiful teeth. He had studied for the bar and had been driven to outlawry because, failing to pass his final examination, he had shot his teacher through the head at the first opportunity. But he had killed a number of men since then and had almost forgotten the incident.

Tebaldo rose to his feet and greeted him.

"A friend told me you were here and wished to see me," said the Moscio. "I am at your service, though to tell the truth I am somewhat ashamed to meet you, after that unfortunate affair at Camaldoli."

"Why?" asked Tebaldo. "I do not see—"

"It was I that fired over the carriage to draw away the escort," replied the other. "Your poor brother was too enthusiastic. I was afraid that something would happen to him, for the plan did not seem to be very well thought out. In a manner I feel responsible for his misfortune, for I should not have consented to what he proposed. I hope, however, that there need be no bad blood between you and me on that account."

"Ferdinando was always foolish," answered Tebaldo. "It was certainly not your fault."

"And now you have had another misfortune in the family," said the youth, sadly. "I take the first opportunity of offering you my most sincere condolence."

Tebaldo knew that with such a man it was better to be frank, or to say nothing. He bowed gravely, and proposed that they should have supper. The Moscio answered with equal gravity, and made a little bow on his side, by way of acknowledgment.

"I was about to ask you to be my guest," he said. "I supped with you at Camaldoli the last time we met. We might have supper here in your room," he suggested. "But I fear to inconvenience you—"

"Not at all," replied Tebaldo. "I prefer it also. We shall be more at liberty to talk."

"For that matter," said the brigand, "the conversation in the public room is often amusing and sometimes instructive. The lieutenant of carabineers sat at the table next to me the last time I spent the evening here. He was very friendly and asked my opinion about catching the Moscio."

"If you prefer to have supper downstairs, let us go down," said Tebaldo, laughing a little. "But the fact is that I wished to consult you on a little matter of my own."

"In that case, it is different. But it was I that proposed your room."

While the waiter came and went, preparing the table, the two men talked a little, continuing to exchange small civilities. The waiter knew them both perfectly well, and they knew him. In twenty minutes they sat down opposite each other, as proper and quiet a pair to see as one could have found in that part of the country. The Moscio had good manners, of a slightly provincial sort, and a little too elaborate. He watched Tebaldo quietly, with a view to profiting by the example of a gentleman who had lately been much in the capital. He ate sparingly, moreover, and mixed his black wine with a large proportion of water.

Tebaldo watched the girlish face, the bright, quiet eyes, and the child-like complexion of the man who had done half a dozen murders, and envied him his evident peace of mind. He knew, however, that his guest would not stay long, and that it was necessary to tell him the story. The Moscio gave him an opportunity of doing so, almost as soon as the waiter had gone away.

"It was with the deepest regret that I heard of Don Francesco's accident," he said, looking up at Tebaldo.

"For that matter," answered Tebaldo, boldly, "I killed him myself."

"I always supposed so," replied the outlaw, quite unmoved. "Are you going to join us, if you are found out? It would be a pleasure to have you among us, I need not assure you. But, of course, so long as there is no suspicion, you will remain in the world. I should, in your place. Poor Ferdinando, whom we all loved as a brother, liked the life for its own sake. Poor man! If he had ever made an enemy, he would have killed him, but having none, his hands were clean as a child's. And in his very first affair, he was shot like a quail by a Roman. Heaven is very unjust, sometimes. Yes, we all thought that you must have sent Francesco to paradise yourself and put the blame on the priest. It was well done. The priest will go to the galleys for it, I daresay."

The youth's manner was as quiet as though he were speaking of the most ordinary occurrences. The knowledge of what he really was, and of what desperate deeds of daring he had done, somehow acted soothingly upon Tebaldo's nerves, for he needed just such an ally.

"Yes," he said. "It was done well enough. But I made a little mistake which I hope you will

help me to rectify for the sake of any service I
may have done you all before I sold Camaldoli."

"Willingly," answered the Moscio, with courteous alacrity. "But if it is for to-night, I hope
you can lend me half a dozen Winchester cartridges, for I am a little short."

Tebaldo explained briefly what he wanted. The
Moscio smiled quietly.

"Nothing could be easier," he said, when
Tebaldo had finished. "I will ride into the village to-morrow morning and get your knife. But,
for another time, I should advise you to keep your
weapon about you when you have used it. If you
are caught, it is because you are suspected already
on some good ground, and the weapon makes little
difference. But if you get away quietly, you
leave no evidence behind you."

"That is true," answered Tebaldo, thoughtfully.
"But there is no name on the knife."

"Nevertheless, someone might recognize it as
yours, if anyone had ever seen it."

"No one ever saw it, excepting my brothers
and, perhaps, my sister, when it lay on my
table. But your advice is good. I might have
saved myself much disquiet if I had brought it
away."

The Moscio made Tebaldo explain very exactly
to him where the knife lay. He knew the village
and the position of the little church well enough.

They talked over the details of the matter for a while, speaking in low tones.

"I suppose you do not want the thing when I have recovered it," observed the outlaw, with a smile.

"I should like to see it," answered Tebaldo.

"Then I should throw it away, I suppose."

"Again?" The Moscio smiled in a rather pitying way. "Then you might wish to get it back a second time. It has no name on it, you say. If it is a good knife, I shall put it into my own pocket, with your permission, as a remembrance of this very pleasant meeting."

"I should like to see it once," repeated Tebaldo.

"You do not trust me? After trusting me with the story? That is not right."

"I have proved that I trust you," replied Tebaldo. "But the thing makes me dream; I shall not get a good night's rest till I have seen it. Then keep it, by all means."

"I see!" The brigand laughed a little in genuine amusement. "I understand! Forgive me for thinking that I was not trusted. You have nerves — you do not sleep. We have a friend with us who is troubled in the same way. Do you remember the man we call Schiantaceci? He killed his sweetheart for jealousy, and began in that way. That was five years ago, in Palermo. If you will believe it, he dreams of her still, and often cannot sleep for thinking of her. Some men are so strangely organized! Now there is our captain Mauro himself. Whenever he has killed anybody, he gets a gold twenty-franc piece and puts it into a little leathern purse he carries for that purpose."

"Why?" asked Tebaldo, with some curiosity.

"For two reasons. In the first place, he knows at any time how many he has killed. And secondly, he says they are intended to pay for masses for his soul when he is killed himself. One tells him that someone will get the gold, if he is killed. He answers that Heaven will respect his intention of having the masses said, even if it is not carried out when he is dead. That man has a genius for theology. But I must be going, Don Tebaldo, for I do not wish to tire my horse too much, and I have far to ride."

"I will not keep you. But how shall I see the knife? You cannot come down again to-morrow."

"We should be glad to see you in the forest, if you can find us. Mauro would be delighted. I have no doubt you will be able to find your way, for you know the woods as well as we do. I cannot tell you where we are, for we have a rule against that, but I daresay you can guess."

"I will come," answered Tebaldo.

"If you come alone, you will be safe," said the Moscio. "Safer than you are here, perhaps, while your knife is lying under the altar of Santa Vittoria. But it will not be there any longer, to-morrow night."

The Moscio protested courteously, when Tebaldo thanked him, and he took leave of his entertainer. His coolness was perfectly unaffected, and was the more remarkable as he was certainly a rather striking young man on account of his good looks, his extremely youthful appearance, his perfectly new clothes, and a certain gentleman-like ease in all he did. He was known by sight to hundreds of people in various parts of the island, but he did not believe that any of them would betray him, and he passed the open door of the guest-room, where the lieutenant of carabineers was playing dominos with the deputy prefect, with perfect indifference, though there was a large reward on his head, and he was well known to the landlord and the waiter. To tell the truth, he was utterly fearless, and would never have allowed himself to be taken alive. But, on their side, if they were ever tempted by the reward, they knew how short and how terrible their own lives would be if they betrayed him to his death. The man who betrayed Leone still lives, indeed. He is a blind beggar now, without feet or hands, in the streets of Naples. He left Sicily with his life, such as the outlaws left it to him, to be an example and a terror to the enemies of the mafia.

Nor did the waiter show by any sign or word that he knew anything about the guest who had gone, when he came to clear the little table in Tebaldo's room. He did his work silently and neatly and went away. Tebaldo sat a long time by the open window, thinking over what he had done, and he congratulated himself on having acted wisely in an extremity from which there had been no other escape.

It all looked easy and simple now. To-morrow night, he thought, he should be sure of his safety. Then he would return to Rome again. His thoughts reverted more easily now to the dreams which Rome suggested, and he fell asleep with a sense of present relief mingled with large hopes for the immediate future.

The Moscio, on his part, would not perhaps have responded so promptly to Tebaldo's message, nor have undertaken so readily to carry out Tebaldo's wishes, if there had been nothing for the outlaws to gain thereby. But the alliance of such a man was not to be neglected at any time. He had served them in the past, and he could be of considerable service to them now.

Mauro had made up his mind to take one of the Saracinesca, if the capture were possible, and to extort an enormous ransom, sufficient to allow him to leave the country with what he should consider a fortune. He was well informed, and he recognized that a family which had such power as the Saracinesca had shown in getting Ippolito's case heard and disposed of in a few days, and, previously, in persuading the authorities to move a body of troops to Santa Vittoria, must be able to dispose of a very large sum of money. Moreover, as the Moscio had frankly admitted, the outlaws had all believed that Tebaldo had killed his brother, and, consequently, that he could be completely dominated by anyone who had proof of the fact. The Moscio had taken advantage of this instantly, as has been seen. Tebaldo, though now on bad terms with the Saracinesca, was well acquainted with their habits and characters, and knew, also, the by-paths about Camaldoli, as none of the brigands themselves did. He could be of the greatest use in an undertaking which must require all the skill and courage of the band. For it was no light thing to carry off such a man as San Giacinto or Orsino, protected as they were by a force of carabineers in their own dwelling, and by the fifty soldiers of the line who were quartered in Santa Vittoria.

When Tatò's message had arrived, Mauro had not only advised the Moscio to go down at once, but had instructed him to use every means in his power, even to threatening Tebaldo with a revelation of his former services, in order to get from him the truth about Francesco's death, as a means of controlling him in the future. It had been an easy task, as has been seen, and when the Moscio returned to the band that night, his account of the meeting was heard with profound attention and interest.

Mauro, who had a curious taste for churches, would have gone himself to Santa Vittoria, had he not been there on the previous day. A second visit might have roused suspicion, whereas, since the murder, no one was surprised if a stranger asked to see the place where it had happened. The Moscio was, therefore, directed to go himself, as he had intended.

The outlaws were encamped at that time in certain abandoned huts which the Duca di Fornasco had built as a safe retreat for some of his people during the cholera season of 1884. They were so completely hidden by underbrush and sweet hawthorn that it required a perfect knowledge of their locality to find them at all; but having been built on an eminence in the hills, in order to obtain the purest air, it was easy to keep a lookout from them, by climbing into the big trees which surrounded them on all sides. A spring, situated on the eastern slope, at a distance of three hundred yards, supplied the outlaws with water for themselves and their horses. Tebaldo, in former days, had led the carabineers to this spring, in their search for the band, but though the soldiers fancied that they had then quartered the hillside in all directions, Tebaldo had skilfully prevented them from coming upon the disused huts in the brush, wisely judging that it could be of no use to betray such a hiding-place, which might be useful to his friends in the future. The Moscio knew that Tebaldo would probably make first for the spot when he came to keep his engagement on the following day.

CHAPTER XXXIV

THE Moscio slung saddle-bags over his saddle, as though he were travelling some distance, and led his horse down from the huts by by-paths in the woods till he came to a place where the trees descended almost to the road, so that he could reach the latter without crossing any open country. Before emerging from cover he looked long and carefully up and down the valley to be sure that no carabineers were in sight, who might be surprised at seeing a well-dressed man come out of the forest. A few peasants were visible, straggling along the road, and far away a light waggon was ascending the hill. The Moscio led his horse carefully across the ditch, and then mounted in leisurely fashion and rode slowly away towards Santa Vittoria. The outlaw, who may at any moment need his horse's greatest powers, spares him whenever he can, and when not obliged to escape some danger will hardly ever put him to a canter.

It was a full hour before the village was in sight. Once on the highway, the Moscio felt perfectly at his ease, and barely took the trouble to glance behind him at a turn of the road. He had excellent papers of various descriptions about him, including a United States passport of recent date, in which he appeared as an American citizen, and a proper discharge as corporal from the military service, together with a highly commendatory letter from the captain of the troop in which the unlucky individual to whom the paper had belonged had served his time in Milan. He also possessed a gun license in the same man's name, and the description of him which accompanied it suited him very well. Some of the papers he had bought at a good price, and some he had taken without much ceremony, because they suited him. To-day he did not even carry a gun and was, in reality, altogether unarmed, though he would naturally have been supposed to have a pistol or a knife about him, like other people in Sicily. If anyone had asked his name, he would have said that he was Angelo Laria of Caltanissetta, a small farmer. The name corresponded with the papers of the soldier, and as he was unarmed it would have been hard to find any excuse for arresting him on a mere suspicion.

If a man carries so-called forbidden weapons, on the other hand, the carabineers can arrest him for that offence alone, if they find it out, and can hold him till he can prove his identity. A knife, such as one can stab with, is forbidden, and the special license, which is required to carry a pistol, is not often granted except to very well known persons, though a vast number of people really carry revolvers without any license at all.

The Moscio dismounted at the gate, walked up the street with his horse, enquired for the sacristan, and brought him back to the little church with the keys.

"Have the goodness to hold my horse," he said to the fat man. "I only wish to look at the church for curiosity, and I will go in alone."

The sacristan did not know him by sight, but with a true Sicilian's instinct recognized the 'maffeuso' in his manner. He proposed, however, to tether the horse to an old stake that was driven into the ground near the door, in order to go in with the stranger and explain how the priest had murdered Francesco. He had got the account off very glibly by this time.

"My friend," said the Moscio, "in those saddlebags I have important papers and a quantity of valuable things, the property of an aunt of mine who is dead, and may the Lord preserve her in glory! I am taking these things myself, for greater safety, to my cousin, her son, who lives in Taormina. Now the reason why I begged you to hold my horse is not that I fear for him, though he is a good animal, but because some evilly disposed person might steal the property of my poor aunt.

You understand, and you will have the goodness to hold the horse while I go in."

The sacristan looked at him and smiled. The Moscio smiled very sweetly in answer, pushed the door open and went in, closing it behind him and leaving the keys on the outside. But when he was in the church, he took from his pocket a small wedge of soft pine wood, gently slipped in under the door and jammed it noiselessly. It would have been rather difficult to open the door from the outside after that. Then he walked leisurely up the church, his spurs ringing loudly so that the sacristan might hear through the door that he was in no hurry.

He went up the altar steps, and smiled as he noticed a few round, dark spots on the marble, and one irregular stain. That was the very place where it had happened. He knelt down and tried to put his arm through the grating, but the space was too narrow. With the same leisurely certainty he slipped off his velvet jacket and laid it on the altar, rolled up his sleeves, and tried again, with his bare arm. No one, seeing him in his coat, and glancing at his small hands, would have suspected the solid muscles above. Even now the grating was too close. It was of light iron, however, and twisted in a decorative design. He easily forced a scroll in one direction, a winding stem in another, and got his hand down to the bottom of the depression in which the glass casket was placed.

He withdrew the knife, and slipped it into the pocket of his riding-breeches; then he readjusted the iron ornaments, buttoned his shirt sleeve, and put on his jacket. As he walked down the church again he took the weapon out. The broad blade was stuck in its black leathern sheath, and it required all his strength to loosen it. When he got it out, he saw that the steel was covered with dark rust.

It was a pity, he thought, as he dropped it into his pocket again, for it had evidently been a good knife. He would clean it with sand and a brick, and sharpen it on a stone, during the evenings, not because he could not have got a better one easily enough, but because it was an agreeable and interesting remembrance. He drew the wedge from under the door without making any noise and went out into the open air. The fat sacristan had lit a clay pipe with a wild cherrywood stem, and was slowly walking the horse up and down in the shade. The Moscio took a small note from a neat pocketbook. Even when notes are scarce, in the wild finances of modern Italy, the outlaws manage to have them because they are easily carried.

"Do you wish me to change it for you?" enquired the sacristan, holding the flimsy bit of paper between his thumb and finger.

"Keep it for yourself, my friend, with a thousand thanks," replied the Moscio.

But the sacristan refused, and held the note out to him, returning it.

"We are not of that kind," he said, with dignity. "We do not wish to be paid for courtesy."

"There are doubtless many poor persons in the village," answered the Moscio, smiling, and beginning to mount. "You will do me a favour by giving the money to those who need it, requesting them to pray for the soul of my poor aunt."

"In that case it is different," replied the fat man, gravely. "I thank you in the name of our poor people. As for me, I am always here to serve you and your friends."

The Moscio glanced at the man's face as the last words were spoken. Tebaldo had told him who the sacristan was, and had described him accurately.

"A greeting to your brother, Don Taddeo the grocer," said the outlaw, settling himself in the saddle.

The sacristan looked up sharply. Being cross-eyed, it was almost impossible to know with which eye he was looking at one. But the expression did not change as he answered.

"Thank you. You shall be obeyed. Our service to your friends."

They understood each other perfectly well, and

the Moscio rode slowly away into the brilliant light, leaving the fat man to lock up the church and go home. The outlaw had made a friend of him, but had not thought fit to ask him any questions about the state of the village or the movements of the Saracinesca. It was of no use to go any further than necessary at a first meeting, and the band had plenty of good sources of information.

Tebaldo spent the morning in a sort of feverish anxiety against which he struggled in vain. He went out for a stroll and passed twice before Basili's house. The weather was beginning to be hot, and the blinds were as tightly closed as though the house were not inhabited. As he passed for the second time he fancied he heard Aliandra's voice singing softly in the distance. He could hardly have been mistaken, for it had the quality and carrying power, even when least loud, which distinguishes the great voices of the world, the half a dozen in a century that leave undying echoes behind them when they are still. His blood rushed up in his throat at the sound and almost choked him, so that he pulled at his collar with his finger, as if it were too tight.

He had not intended to try to see her again, but the fascination of the light and distant song was more than he could resist. He knocked and waited on the little steps outside the door. He was sure that he heard someone moving upstairs and approaching a window, and he guessed that he could be seen through the slats of the blinds. A long time passed and he heard no sound. Then, as usual, the stable-man came to the door, with his faithful, stolid face. He began to give the customary answer.

"The Signorina Aliandra has gone to the country with —"

"Let me come in," said Tebaldo, interrupting the man roughly.

He was active, strong, and in a bad temper, and before the man could hinder him, Tebaldo had pushed himself into the house and was shutting the door behind him.

"And the notary is asleep," said the man, concluding the formula, in a tone of surprise and protest, but attempting no further resistance.

"Wake him, then!" cried Tebaldo, his naturally smooth voice rising to a high and almost brassy tone. "And the devil take you, your mother, and both your souls!" he added, relapsing into dialect in his anger.

He must have been heard to the top of the house, and by Gesualda in her kitchen. Immediately there came a sound of footsteps from above. But Tebaldo was already mounting the stairs. Aliandra was coming down to meet him, her face flushed with annoyance and her eyes sparkling.

"What is this, Don Tebaldo?" she asked, as

soon as she caught sight of him. "By what right do you—"

He interrupted her.

"Because I mean to see you," he answered. "When you are in the country with Gesualda visiting your friends, one ought not to hear you singing in Randazzo as one passes your house."

Aliandra was not really very angry that he should have got in, for she was beginning to find her father's company a little dull. But she made a movement of annoyance as though displeased at having betrayed herself by her singing.

"Well—go down to the sitting-room," she said. "I cannot turn you out, since you have got in."

They descended, and she sent away the stableman, and made Tebaldo go into the front room, leaving the door open, however, as she followed him. His anger disappeared when her manner changed. He took her hand and tried to make her sit down, but she smiled and shook her head.

"I cannot stay," she said. "But as for your having been kept out, that is really my father's doing. I suppose he is right, but I am glad to see you for a moment. I was afraid you had gone back to Rome."

"Not without seeing you. But what absurd idea possesses your father—"

"Hush! Not so loud! The doors are open upstairs, too, and one hears everything."

"Then I will shut the door —"

"No, no! Please do not! He would scold, for he would certainly know. Besides, you must go."

"I do not understand you at all," said Tebaldo, lowering his voice. "The last time I saw you, you were just like yourself again, and now — I do not understand. You are quite changed."

"No. I am always the same, Tebaldo." Her voice was suddenly kind. "I told you the whole truth in Rome, once for all. Why must I say it over again? Is it of any use?"

"It never was of any use to say it all," answered Tebaldo. "You do not believe that I love you —"

"You are wrong. I do believe it — as much as you do yourself!" She laughed rather irrelevantly.

"Why do you laugh?" he asked.

"Such love is a laughing matter, my dear Tebaldo. I am not a child. It is better that love should end in laughter than in tears."

"Why should it end at all?"

"Because you are engaged to marry another woman, dear friend. A very good reason — for me." She laughed again.

"You have only a dead man's word for it," said Tebaldo, grimly. "Unfortunately he is where he cannot take it back. But I can for him. It is not true."

He set his eyes, as it were, while he looked at

her, in order to make her believe that he was telling the truth. But she knew him well, for she had known him long, and she doubted him still. She shook her head.

"It may not be literally true," she said. "But practically it is the fact. You mean to marry the American. That is why neither my father nor I wish you to come to the house. You injure my reputation here, in my own town, as you do in Rome. If you loved me, you would not wish to do that. I have held my head high at the beginning, and that is the hardest. I did not mean to say it over again, but you force me to. Do you want me? Marry me. If you were a rich man, I suppose I should be ashamed to speak as I do. But we are both poor, you for a nobleman and I for an artist. So there is no question of interest, is there? I have not seen your American heiress. She may be handsomer than I, for I am not the most beautiful woman in the world. She is rich. That is her advantage. She may be a good girl, but she is no better than I, the singer, the notary's daughter, who have nothing in my whole life to blush for. Look at me, now, as I am. You know me. Choose between us, and let this end. I am willing to marry you if you want me, but I am not willing to sacrifice my good name to you, nor to any man in Europe, king, prince, or gentleman. Here I stand, and you may look at me for the last time, compare me with your foreign young lady, and make up your mind definitely. If it is to be marriage, I will marry you at once. If not, I will not see you again, if I can possibly help it, either here or in Rome."

As she finished her long speech she crossed her arms behind her and faced him rather proudly, drawing herself up to her full height, smiling a little, but with an earnest look in her eyes. She had never looked so handsome. The few days of country life had completely rested her young face.

"You are frank, at all events," said Tebaldo, half mechanically, for he was thinking more of her than of her words.

"And it is time that you should be frank, too," she answered. "You must make your choice, and abide by it. Aliandra Basili or the American girl."

He was silent, for he was in a dilemma and was, besides, too nervous from all he had been through to like being driven to a sudden decision. On the other hand, her beauty stirred him now, as it had not done before, and the idea of giving her up was unbearable. She looked at him steadily for several seconds. More than once his lips parted, as though he were going to speak, but no words came. Gradually her mouth grew scornful and her eyes hard.

All at once she laughed a little harshly and turned towards the door.

"You have chosen," she said. "Goodbye."

But the passionate longing that had assailed him outside, in the street, at the sound of her voice, had doubled and trebled now. As she turned, the folds of her gown followed her figure in a way that drove him mad.

"Aliandra!" he cried, overtaking her in an instant, and catching her in his arms.

She struggled a little as he forced her head backwards upon his shoulder.

"You!" He kissed the word upon her lips again and again. "You! You!" he repeated. "I cannot live without you, and you know it! Yes — I will marry you — before God, I will—"

And many passionate, broken words and solemn vows mingled with his kisses as he stood there pressing her to him. It was not a noble love, but it was genuine and fierce, as all the man's passions were, whether for love, or hatred, or revenge. It was when he had let them drive him to reckless deeds that his other nature asserted itself, calm and treacherous and self-contained.

As for Aliandra herself, she had saved her self-respect, though few people might respect her for what she had done. She was not a very romantic or sentimental young woman, but according to her lights she was a good girl. She had been taught to consider that all men were originally and derivatively bad, and that every woman had a genuine right to make the most advantageous marriage she could. She did not in the least expect that Tebaldo would be faithful to her, but she firmly intended to be an honest wife, on general principles. What she most wanted was his name, for which she meant to earn a fortune by her art. She had never been in love and, therefore, did not believe that love had any real existence, a view not uncommon with very young people who have no particular sentimentality in their composition. And so rigid were her ideas in one direction that she resented the demonstrative way in which Tebaldo expressed his decision.

He was almost beside himself, for his nerves had been already unstrung, and her beauty completely dominated him for the time being, so that he forgot even Miss Slayback's millions, his own evil deeds, and his meeting with the outlaw. There was nothing which he was not ready to do. Basili should draw up the marriage contract at once, and on the following morning they would be formally betrothed. Only the fact that he could not with propriety be married within less than three months of his brother's death recalled him to himself.

The afternoon was already advancing when he left the house and went back to the inn, half dazed and almost forgetful alike of past and future, as he walked up the street. Before he had gone a hundred yards, however, he had regained enough composure to think of what he had to do, and when he reached the inn, no one would have supposed that anything unusual had happened to him.

As he rode out of the town, half an hour later, he vaguely wondered at himself for what he had done, and wondered, also, how he could get out of his present difficult position.

He looked at his watch, and saw that it was growing late. He had far to ride, and had intended to start much earlier in the afternoon. He had the innkeeper's best horse, but it was rather a slow animal, not to be compared with Basili's brown mare. He quickened his pace as well as he could, however, and cantered along the more level stretches of the high road. At the first opportunity he struck off into a bridle path to the right which led westward towards the heights above Maniace.

He had ridden several miles, in and out among the little undulations of the upper valley, when he came out upon a broad bit of meadow, such as one occasionally finds in that region, just beyond the black lands. He put his horse at a gallop, taking advantage of the chance to gain a little time, and riding diagonally for a point at the opposite side from which the bridle path led up to the hills, as he well knew.

He was less than half way across the grass when he heard the heavy tread of horses galloping after him, with the clanking of arms and a sound of deep voices calling out to him. He looked round, but he knew already that he was followed by mounted carabineers, and that they could overtake him easily enough. After a moment's hesitation he drew rein and waited quietly for the troopers to come up. He wished that he had carried his rifle across his saddle-bow instead of at his back, for he at first believed that there was some information against him from Santa Vittoria, and that they meant to arrest him. On the other hand, to have unslung his rifle, after seeing that they were carabineers, would have been to acknowledge that he feared them. His mind worked quickly as he sat still in his saddle, waiting for them.

But when they were fifty yards away one of them spoke, and reined in his charger.

"It is Don Tebaldo Pagliuca!" he exclaimed in a tone of surprise, and in the desolate stillness of the lonely field, Tebaldo heard the words and understood that he had been mistaken for someone else.

The other trooper laughed a little, and they both trotted up to Tebaldo, saluting when they were near him.

"I beg your pardon," said the older soldier. "We took you for a stranger. It is a lonely place, and we have news that the brigands are somewhere in the neighbourhood. I trust we have not annoyed you, signore. Accept our excuses."

Tebaldo smiled easily.

"You took me for an outlaw," he said. "It is natural enough, I am sure. Do you know your way? Can I be of service to you?"

The elder trooper asked one or two questions about the directions in which the bridle paths led. He evidently knew the country tolerably well, and Tebaldo was wise enough not to deceive him. After a few moments' conversation, he offered the men a couple of cigars, which they gratefully accepted and hid in the inner pockets of their tunics, after which they saluted again and rode away in the direction whence they had come. In disturbed times such patrols are to be met with occasionally on almost every practicable bridle path, and the foot-carabineers scramble up and down through the country in pairs, even where there are no paths at all.

As he rode on alone Tebaldo was aware that his heart was beating faster than usual. He had been startled by the unexpected meeting, and for one moment had expected to be arrested. He now reflected that he had no real cause to fear any such catastrophe, since, by this time, the Moscio had certainly recovered the knife, which represented the only possible evidence against him. But the physical impression remained, and it was very like fear. He had rarely been afraid of anything in his life, and the sensation was disturbing, for it warned him that the strain on his whole nature was beginning to weaken him.

He pressed on, urging his lazy horse whenever the ground permitted, and cutting across through the woods, from one bridle path to another, as often as he could, shortening the way to gain time. He was near the foot of the hill on which the outlaws were camping and was just about to cross the streamlet which ran down from the spring, when a man in tweed clothes, that had an English look, quietly stepped out from behind a bush and stood in his way, at the water's edge, holding a rifle in his hand. Tebaldo's horse stopped of his own accord.

"Your name, if you please," said the outlaw, civilly.

"Tebaldo Pagliuca. I come by appointment to visit one of your friends."

"Name him, if you please."

"The Moscio," said Tebaldo, knowing that if the names had not agreed with those given to the sentinel as a pass, the man would probably have killed him instantly as a spy.

"I will show you the way," said the brigand, slinging his rifle on his shoulder.

"I know the way perfectly," answered Tebaldo. "Pray do not trouble yourself."

"It is a pleasure," returned the other, and he cleared the little stream at a bound.

Tebaldo guessed that he was not altogether trusted, even now. As the man walked up the hill he whistled softly, and in a few moments, emerging from the brush into a little clearing, Tebaldo saw the Moscio waiting for him. It was dusky under the trees, but Tebaldo could see the pleasant smile on the girlish face. The Moscio had his rifle under his arm, and was smoking a cigarette. The man who had led Tebaldo to the spot disappeared into the brush, returning to his post by the stream. Tebaldo dismounted.

"Have you met anyone?" enquired the outlaw, shaking hands.

"No," answered Tebaldo, "not since I left the high road."

He had reflected that he had done unwisely in not turning back with the carabineers and riding with them as far as the road, in order to disarm any possible suspicions, and he knew that the Moscio would think so, too. He should, if necessary, have even waited till the next day before coming up to the camp, but his anxiety to see the knife safe in the Moscio's possession had outweighed everything else.

"So much the better," answered the outlaw, unsuspiciously. "By the bye, here is your knife. Is this it?"

He held it out to Tebaldo, who took it eagerly, his fingers closing round the sheath, as though he were afraid of dropping it. He breathed hard between his teeth once or twice, as he looked at it, in sheer satisfaction.

"It is yours, I suppose?" observed the Moscio, interrogatively, for Tebaldo had forgotten to speak. "There was no other."

"Yes. I thank you. I am very grateful to you." The words were as sincere as any the man had ever uttered, and he handed the knife back.

"Not at all," answered the outlaw. "It was interesting to see the place. I am glad to have served you. Since you have taken the trouble to come so far, will you accept our hospitality this evening? You can hardly get back to Randazzo to-night. Mauro is in a very good humour this evening, and the weather is pleasant. You will not suffer much inconvenience. The huts are quite dry. We will try and make you some return for your former hospitality."

Tebaldo accepted readily enough, and they began to ascend the hill at once. It was some distance to the top. The Moscio turned to the right at a big, old chestnut tree.

"That is not the best way," remarked Tebaldo.

"Keep on another ten yards and then turn to the left. There is an old bridle path on the other side of the hawthorn bushes."

The Moscio laughed softly.

"It is a pity that you are not with us," he said. "You know the paths better than we do."

"I was born near here," answered Tebaldo. "I have known these woods since I was a boy."

"I wish I had! I sometimes lose my way in this part of Sicily."

The path began exactly where Tebaldo had said that it did, the entrance being hidden by hawthorn and blackberry bushes. He went on a few steps, doubled behind the brambles, and led the Moscio along a much better way than the outlaws had discovered for themselves. The outlaw appreciated the advantage, and reflected that Tebaldo could help the band in a thousand ways if he chose. Without passing by the spring, they suddenly found themselves at the top of the hill. The path stopped abruptly against the back of one of the wooden huts, having formerly crossed the summit at this point.

"Let me go first," said the Moscio, and he passed Tebaldo and his horse and went round the corner of what was really little more than a shed, roughly enclosed with half-rotten planks.

Various exclamations of surprise greeted their appearance from an unexpected quarter.

"Our friend, Don Tebaldo Pagliuca," said the Moscio, addressing a number of men who were sitting and lying about on the dry ground. "He knows the woods better than we, and has shown me a new path from the big chestnut tree."

"He is welcome," said Mauro, in a dull and muffled voice, but with some cordiality.

He and most of the others rose and greeted Tebaldo warmly. Some had known him already, and almost all had known Ferdinando well.

They were a strange looking set of men. Most of them were well dressed, and so far as their clothes were concerned might have been taken for a party of southern country gentlemen and rich young farmers, camping during a day's shooting. Mauro, who was by far the oldest, might have been seven or eight and thirty years of age, but not more, and most of the others were evidently under thirty. They were all strong looking, with the toughened appearance of men accustomed to live in the open air and to take exertion as a matter of course. The Moscio alone had preserved his marvellous, child-like freshness of complexion. The 'Moscio' means the ' soft,' being similar to our English word 'mush,' and the youth's looks accounted for the name, while his remarkable strength and utter fearlessness contrasted rather comically with the epithet.

The peculiarities in the appearance of his companions were chiefly in their faces and expressions. Most of them had the oddly sinister, unchanging smile with something contemptuous in it which so often characterizes adventurers, both within the pale of society and beyond its bounds. Such men do not laugh easily. In their eyes, too, there was the look one sees in those of some Red Indians and of dangerous wild animals aware of pursuit and always inclined to turn at bay rather than escape. Tebaldo felt, rather than saw, the glances that were turned upon him as he stood in their midst, still holding his horse by the bridle.

Mauro himself was dark, clean shaven, close cropped, and already bald on the top of his head. He had often disguised himself successfully as a priest, for he had been educated in a seminary, had turned atheist, had been a journalist, and had finally got into trouble by shooting his editor in consequence of a quarrel which had apparently begun about a question of grammar, but had in reality been connected with politics, so that the deed had been regarded as an act of justice and patriotism by the mafia. There had been a reward of twenty thousand francs on Mauro's head, dead or alive, for several years, and photographs of the famous brigand were sold everywhere in Palermo, Messina, and Catania, but there was not a carabineer in the island who could boast of having seen the man himself. He was taciturn and reticent, too, though he could be fluent enough when he pleased ; and although he put a gold piece into his purse for everyone he killed, as the Moscio had said, he could never be induced to tell how many there were in the little leathern bag. He never did anything unnecessarily, but was capable of the most blood-curdling cruelty when any end was to be gained, and was merciless to informers when they fell into his hands, not exactly out of a love for inflicting pain, but in order to inspire a salutary terror. He was extremely temperate in his habits and simple in his clothes, though his weapons were always of the best and of the newest device, and he had a large account with the leading bank of Palermo. He intended to emigrate, he said, when he should be rich enough, but those who knew him did not believe that he could be satisfied to settle down as a well-to-do proprietor in the Argentine Republic. The Moscio always said that Mauro would yet repent of his ways, enter a monastery, mortify the flesh, and die in the odour of sanctity. Whereat Mauro generally nodded thoughtfully, as though he himself regarded such a termination to his career as quite within the bounds of possibility.

As for the rest of the band, none of them were in any way so remarkable as their leader. The man known as Leoncino was believed to be a son of the famous Leone, and boasted of it. He had stabbed a rival in a village love affair, after having been brought up rather mysteriously in the house of a rich farmer. Schiantaceci was undoubtedly a gentleman by birth, a sad young fellow, with a drooping brown moustache, fiery eyes, and a very sweet voice in which he often sang softly on a summer's evening when it was not dangerous to make a noise in the camp. No one knew his real name. In a fight he always behaved as though he wished to be killed, which is generally the surest way of killing others.

Among the rest there were men of all classes. There was a man who had been mayor of his village, there was a butcher, there were three or four deserters from the army, who had each killed a comrade, and one who had attacked his lieutenant but had not killed him. There was a chemist's apprentice who had poisoned his master, and an actor who had strangled his manager's wife in a love quarrel. There were also two anarchists who had escaped imprisonment under Crispi's rule. But there was not one in the number who had done less than two murders at the time when Tebaldo went up to the camp.

One of the outlaws led his horse away, and he sat down by Mauro a little apart from the rest. In the middle of the open space a fire was burning down to a bed of coals. It had been very carefully built and slowly fed so as to produce the smallest possible amount of smoke. A well-cleaned gridiron was stuck upright in the earth by the handle, and at the entrance to one of the huts the man who was a butcher was cutting a huge piece of fresh meat into steaks.

After the first greetings, the men relapsed into silence, and paid little attention to Tebaldo. Mauro talked with him in low tones. The chief seemed, indeed, unable to speak loud. He asked many questions about the Saracinesca, but he would have considered it a breach of civility to refer to the truth about Francesco's death.

"These Saracinesca are naturally antipathetic to you," he observed, "and I daresay you would not be sorry if one of them put his ears in pawn at my bank."

"They are a powerful family," answered Tebaldo, cautiously. "If one of them were taken by you, there would be reinforcements of carabineers throughout Sicily."

"These carabineers are much like flies," said Mauro, thoughtfully. "They come in swarms, they buzz, and they fly away again, leaving nobody much the worse. It means a little more caution for a month or two. That is all. But the Saracinesca would pay a good sum to keep the young heir's nose on his face, and San Giacinto would probably write a cheque at my dictation before he were half roasted."

He spoke quietly and in a reflective tone.

"For my part," replied Tebaldo, "I wish them no good, as you may imagine. But the younger Saracinesca is in Rome. San Giacinto came back last night, it is true, but he is safe at Camaldoli."

"Safe is a relative term when we are in the neighbourhood," remarked Mauro. "Especially if you will give us your assistance," he added. "On the whole, it would be more convenient to take San Giacinto. He could write the cheque, and I could cash it almost before there were any alarm, holding him until we got the money. If we took the young one, we should have to communicate with the family. That is always disagreeable."

"You might have difficulty in cashing the cheque," suggested Tebaldo.

"None whatever," replied Mauro. "You are quite mistaken. That is always easy, though of course money in cash is preferable. A cash transaction is always better, as a mere matter of business."

Tebaldo had not by any means anticipated that he was to be called in as an ally in such an affair, and did not like the prospect at all. He promised himself that he would return to Rome as soon as possible. For the present he put aside the extremely complicated position in which he was placed by having given two promises of marriage. He felt uncomfortable, too, and chilly. He shivered a little, and Mauro noticed it, and called for a cup of wine. Tebaldo swallowed it eagerly and felt better.

"It will be necessary for you to help us," said Mauro, presently, and in a tone of quiet decision. "No one knows the land about Camaldoli as well as you do, and the approaches to the house."

"I would rather not be involved in the capture," answered Tebaldo.

"I am sure you will not refuse," replied Mauro, smiling at him. "It will be a little return for the service the Moscio has done you. He was very glad to help you, of course, but you must not forget that you are one of us, now, and that we always help each other when we can. I am sure you will not refuse."

Tebaldo glanced sideways at the quiet, priest-faced man who had been the terror of Sicily for years. He realized that the outlaw had spoken the truth, and that he might at any moment have to turn outlaw himself, if the secret of the knife were known. He knew the brigands and their ways. They would keep faith with him, even at the risk of their own lives, but he must submit to their conditions. They had him in their power, and he must help them if they required him to do so. If he refused, information would be in the hands of the carabineers in twelve hours, which would drive him into outlawry, if he escaped at all. But if he helped them, they would stand by him. He had not foreseen such a situation.

"What is it that you wish me to do?" he enquired after a short pause.

"I will tell you," answered Mauro. "There are now only four carabineers quartered at Camaldoli, and as they ride on patrol duty like the rest, there are never more than two in the house at a time. There is San Giacinto himself, so that there are three men to deal with. The rest of the people are Sicilians, and will give no trouble."

"San Giacinto is equal to two or three ordinary men," observed Tebaldo.

"Is he?" Mauro spoke indifferently. "One man is very like another, at the end of a rifle barrel," he continued, "and if one pulls the trigger, they are all exactly alike. The point is this. We intend to surprise Camaldoli to-morrow night. You must lead us by the ways you know to the low rampart at the back, behind the stables and over the river. There is a way up on that side, but we do not know it. We shall find a ladder resting against the wall on that side. A friend will place it there."

"Why do you not get him to show you the way?" asked Tebaldo.

"He lives in the house," answered Mauro. "The gates are shut at Ave Maria, and there is a roll-call of the servants and men. San Giacinto, or whichever of the Saracinesca is there, locks the gate himself and keeps the keys in his own room. They all go to bed early, and the house is always quiet between midnight and two o'clock. There is no moon just now, and if we can get round to the back without rousing the dogs, or attracting attention in any way, we can get possession of the place in five minutes. The carabineers sleep in a room on the court. They have to sleep sometimes, like other people. Barefooted we shall make no noise on the stones. Leave the rest to us."

"And have they no sentinels at night?" enquired Tebaldo. "Do they keep no watch?"

"No. The house would be hard to enter without a ladder at the one weak point. One would be sure to rouse everybody before one got in. But once in the court, we can silence the two carabineers in a moment, and then we shall be fifteen to one against San Giacinto. I would not give much for his safety, then. The main thing is to reach the ladder quietly and all together. The paths are difficult, there is water in the stream still, and we must know where to ford it in the dark, for we could not safely approach from the other side. Your help is absolutely necessary to this enterprise. As I said, I am quite sure that you will give it — quite sure."

He emphasized the last words a little, and Tebaldo knew what he meant. There was no choice.

"I will do as you wish," he said reluctantly. "I will come here before sunset, and when it is time I will lead you by the shortest way."

The Moscio's eyes were watching him and met his own as he looked up.

CHAPTER XXXV

THE two carabineers who had met Tebaldo in the field had treated him with the greatest civility, but when he was out of hearing they discussed the rather singular meeting. The more they thought of it, the more strange it seemed to them that he should have been riding alone, without so much as a portmanteau, by way of luggage, towards the Maniace woods, and at such an hour. It must be remembered that before Francesco's death, and since Ferdinando's, the authorities had everywhere been warned against the Corleone family, in the expectation of some outrage against the Saracinesca or their property; and the impression was universal that Ippolito had not killed Francesco, while many who had known the brothers since they had been wild boys at Camaldoli believed that Tebaldo had done the deed, or that he had caused it to be done, and had cleverly managed to throw the guilt upon the priest. The carabineers quartered in the neighbourhood all believed this and scouted Tebaldo's story of a race. They had no more opinion of the law's wisdom than the outlaws whom they were continually hunting, for their experience had shown them how easily the law could be defeated in a country where the whole population was banded together to defy it.

The troopers discussed the question as they rode down to Randazzo. They had seen nothing else worth mentioning, on their patrol, and when they reported themselves to the sergeant at quarters, they told him exactly what had passed. The sergeant was the one who had at first accompanied the Saracinesca to Camaldoli. He dismissed the troopers to their supper, thought the matter over, and went to the inn to find the lieutenant. The latter was playing dominos, as usual, with the deputy prefect, before going home to supper.

He was a grey-haired man of forty, prematurely aged by hard service and constant anxiety, a tall, spare figure, the perfection of military neatness in his dress, with a grave manner and a rare but kindly smile. For the rest, he was brave, honourable, and energetic, and, like the men under him, he was not much inclined to believe in the law on its own recommendation. He was as firmly persuaded as they that Tebaldo was a bad character, and had quietly watched him on the several occasions on which he had lately appeared at the inn.

He went outside with the sergeant and listened to his story attentively.

"The brigands are in the Maniace woods," he

said at last. "They left Noto some days ago. But one might as well try to find pins in a ploughed field, on a dark night. It would take at least five hundred men to beat the woods through and surround the fellows."

"A thousand, sir," suggested the sergeant, by way of comment. "It took a regiment to catch Leone alone, in the old days."

The lieutenant broke off the end of a black cigar thoughtfully, but seemed to forget to light it, becoming suddenly absorbed in his own reflexions. The sergeant stood patiently at attention.

"Have we any information this evening?" asked the officer, suddenly, as though he were looking for something.

"No, sir."

"Any arrests to-day? Any suspicious characters?"

"No, sir."

The lieutenant seemed dissatisfied, and looked a long time at his unlighted, black cigar, in deep thought.

"Very well. Good night, sergeant." He nodded and turned away, but looked round before he had made two steps. "Have two men ready all night, in case I should need them," he added.

"Yes, sir." The sergeant saluted again, and went back to his quarters.

The officer returned to his game of dominos.

He made one or two moves and then called the servant.

"Don Tebaldo Pagliuca is staying in the house, is he not?" he enquired. "Present my compliments and ask if he will not come down and play a game."

"The signore is out, Signor Lieutenant," answered the servant.

"Indeed? I am sorry. I suppose he is strolling in the town. It is cooler in the streets."

"I do not know," the man replied, though he knew very well that Tebaldo had the innkeeper's horse.

The officer nodded, as though satisfied, and went on with his game. The deputy prefect looked at him enquiringly, but he vouchsafed no information. The official representative of the government was a rather foolish man, very much afraid of the Sicilians and of doing anything to attract the ill-will of the mafia.

The lieutenant sat over the game later than usual. The windows of the public room, which was at once the dining-room and the café of the clean little inn, looked upon the main street and were open, for the air was hot. It would have been impossible not to hear Tebaldo's horse if he came back. But he had not come when the officer went home. The latter's own lodging was also on the main street, towards the upper gate, and Tebaldo would have to pass it to reach the inn. The lieutenant sat up very late, but still Tebaldo did not come.

"They have either taken him," reasoned the officer, "and in that case he will not come back at all. Or else he is on good terms with them and is spending the night with them, and will return in the morning."

But at seven o'clock in the morning, being about to show himself at his window, the lieutenant heard the tread of a shod saddle horse in the street. It was Tebaldo, looking pale and weary, leaning a little forward and dangling his feet out of the stirrups, as though he had ridden far and wished to rest himself. He had the unmistakable look of a man who has worn his clothes twenty-four hours, and the soldier's sharp eyes, looking after him when he had passed the window, saw little bits of bramble and leaf clinging to his coat.

The lieutenant shaved himself carefully and thoughtfully and dressed with his usual scrupulous care. When he had buckled on his heavy cavalry sabre, he opened a drawer in an old Sicilian cabinet and took out two little Derringer pistols, examined them to see that they were properly loaded, and slipped one into each pocket of his trousers. The tight swallow-tailed tunic of his uniform made it impossible to carry a revolver concealed. He might be going to risk his life as well as his reputation on that morning.

When he left his lodging, he went first to the quarters of the carabineers and gave the sergeant an order. Then he went straight to the inn, and asked to be shown to Tebaldo Pagliuca's room. An hour had passed since the latter had come back. The servant looked up in surprise, for though the officer and Tebaldo were on terms of civility, the man knew that they were not well acquainted. He had to obey, however, and led the way up one flight of stairs, and knocked at a door on the landing.

"Come in," answered Tebaldo's voice, indifferently, for he supposed it was the servant.

The officer entered at once, taking off his cap.

"Good morning, Don Tebaldo," he said courteously, before the other could speak. "Pray forgive my intrusion, but could you lend me your revolver for a few hours? I suppose you have one? My only one is out of order, and I prefer to carry one for what I have to do. I should be extremely obliged."

"Certainly," answered Tebaldo, rather coldly, but a good deal surprised by the request.

He crossed the room and took the weapon from a table, with its leathern case.

"I should be glad if you could return it by two o'clock," he said, "as I am going away."

"Certainly," replied the officer, quietly taking the revolver out of its case. "It is loaded, I see. Thank you. Now Don Tebaldo, will you kindly sit down for a few moments? I wish to speak to you."

He held the revolver in his right hand, and his quiet grey eyes looked gravely at the man he had caught. Tebaldo started at the sudden change of tone, and faced him, in renewed surprise.

"I borrowed your revolver in order to speak with you," said the lieutenant, "for I have heard that you have a sudden and violent temper. But I wish to speak in a quiet and friendly way. Shall we sit down?" He took a chair with his left hand.

"I am at a loss to understand you," answered Tebaldo, with rising anger. "What do you want?"

"I will explain. I am aware that you have spent the night with the brigands, who are friends of yours. You will either lead me to them, or you will go to prison. I have a couple of men downstairs, waiting. Now choose."

"This is outrageous!" Tebaldo's voice rang high, as he sprang forward.

But the sight of the revolver's muzzle close to his face stopped him, though his eyes blazed with fury.

"It is of no use to be angry," said the officer, who was perfectly cool. "Choose, if you please."

"It is outrageous! You cannot prove anything against me!"

"You are mistaken," answered the other, boldly. "I can prove many things."

"What? What can you prove?"

"I do not intend to provide you with the means of defending your case by telling you what I know. But I give you your choice. I have full power to do so. Lead me and my men to a place where we can catch Mauro, and I give you my word of honour that no accusation shall be brought against you. Refuse to do so, and I give you my word that you will be handcuffed in five minutes and taken to Messina this afternoon. You know, of course, that complicity with a band of outlaws entails penal servitude."

He saw plainly enough that he had not risked his reputation for nothing. Tebaldo was brave still, though he was unstrung and broken, but his face now showed the perplexity he could only feel if he were really in the situation the officer had prepared for him.

"I deny the whole charge," he said, after a moment's thought. "This is an outrage for which you will have to answer. Be good enough to stop threatening me, and leave my room."

The lieutenant drew a nickel whistle from the bosom of his tunic with his left hand.

"If I whistle for my troopers," he said, "you

will be in handcuffs in five minutes. I will count twenty while you make your choice. One, two, three —" and he continued to count.

Tebaldo grew pale by quick degrees, as he listened, and his heart beat violently with excitement. The officer reached twenty in his counting, and raised the big whistle to his lips.

"Stop!" exclaimed Tebaldo, hardly able to speak.

"Well?" asked the officer, holding the whistle ready near his mouth.

"You give me your word of honour that no accusation whatever shall be brought against me?"

"None on the ground of complicity with the brigands," answered the lieutenant. "I give you my word as an officer."

"There is no other to bring." Tebaldo was white.

"None that concerns me," replied the other, coolly. "There is a good deal of diversity of opinion about your brother's death, as you must know."

"This is an insult —"

"Oh, no! I do not accuse you at all. I only wish to limit my own promise to the matter in hand. I have done so, and I understand that you agree, do you not?"

"By force, for I suppose I must," replied

Tebaldo, in a sullen tone. "You must further engage to protect me from the mafia, when you have caught the fellows," he added.

"You shall have an escort wherever you go and as long as you please to remain in the country."

"That will not be long," said Tebaldo, almost to himself.

"So much the better. And now, if you please, at what time shall we start this evening?"

Tebaldo inwardly cursed himself for having trusted the Moscio in the first instance, but he quickly reflected that he might still improve his position in the eyes of the officer and thereby, perhaps, have less to fear in the future.

"Look here, lieutenant," he said, changing his tone and sitting down. "I have been forced into this, from first to last. I was riding by myself yesterday afternoon, in the country I know so well, and I had not the slightest idea that the outlaws were in the neighbourhood. I met a couple of your men, who at first took me for one of the brigands myself, and then recognized me and apologized, telling me that the band was in the neighbourhood. They rode off, and I took a short cut through the woods. I came upon the encampment unexpectedly."

The officer listened attentively and gravely. Tebaldo proceeded.

"In former years, even a year ago, when we

lived at Camaldoli before selling the place, we were obliged, as a matter of personal safety, to put up with a great deal from these men, and if we had informed against them, we should have been murdered. That is how it happened that my brother Ferdinando knew some of them. You know the conditions of the country as well as I do."

"I wish I did!" exclaimed the soldier, devoutly.

"You know them well enough, at all events. Poor gentlefolk, as we were then, cannot always help themselves. Yesterday afternoon I found myself suddenly surrounded by the whole band. There are fifteen of them. One of them recognized me, and a long discussion began. They wish to get into Camaldoli to-night and carry off the Marchese di San Giacinto."

"Fifteen armed men might do it," observed the officer. "There are only two troopers there at night."

"Yes. But the brigands do not know the way to the weak point at the back. I will explain."

Tebaldo told the whole truth now, for he saw that his best chance of safety lay in that direction. Then he proceeded to exculpate himself.

"They also gave me my choice, something in your manner," he went on. "They offered, by way of alternative, to roast me alive, if I refused to show them the way to-night, and they assured me of what I knew perfectly well, namely, that if I did not keep the appointment they could murder me wherever I might be. This was because I insisted on coming here again before to-night. It was not easy, but they yielded at last. However, it was very late by the time we had come to an agreement, and I could not have got back to Randazzo, for there was no moon, and the woods are dark and full of pitfalls. I got back this morning, and intended to go down to Messina and catch the train at Reggio to-night, and take my chance of safety in Rome. They never could get up to the back of Camaldoli without me. There you have the whole story in a nutshell."

"I see," answered the officer, who only believed half of the plausible story. "You were in a most difficult position. But it is now in your power to do the country a great service. All that is necessary is that you should lead the band to the foot of the wall, as you promised. I will take care of the rest. In the woods it is impossible to catch them. But it is important that we should recognize you, in order not to kill you by mistake if there is any fighting, as there probably will be, though I hope to take most of them alive. The wisest thing would be that you should be the first to mount the ladder, by agreement, on the ground that you can lead them inside, whereas they might lose their way."

"Yes — that is best. It is a very complicated place, like a labyrinth, between the rampart and the court."

"You will pardon me for reverting to the conditions," said the lieutenant, suavely. "You realize, of course, that in case you should not wish to carry out your part of them, you are always in the power of the law, unless you turn outlaw yourself, which, in your position, you would hardly like to do."

"I understand my position perfectly," answered Tebaldo, coldly. "I shall lead the band to the foot of the ladder at about one o'clock, I fancy."

"Thank you," said the officer. "I am much obliged for the loan of your revolver, which I return to you, as you may need it this evening."

He laid it on the table, bowed civilly, and went out, leaving the betrayer to his own reflexions.

CHAPTER XXXVI

TEBALDO would have given half his life and all his soul to undo the work of the past twenty-four hours. But it was now absolutely impossible for him to draw back. His only chance of future safety lay in serving the government, though he did not like to think what his fate might be if he should fall into the hands of any friend of the outlaws after betraying them. Yet, short of joining them outright, he could not possibly escape arrest if he did not carry out the conditions of his agreement with the lieutenant; and, if once arrested, the latter would only need to tell exactly what had happened in order to convict him of complicity with brigands and send him to penal servitude. He was literally caught in a vise and could not move without ruining himself.

It was early in the afternoon when he set out to ride to the Maniace woods again. In spite of everything, he had been to Basili's house and had seen Aliandra again. Though what he was going to do was not noble, it was dangerous, and the sight of the woman he loved cheered him in his need. He looked ill, and said that he had a touch of the fever, and Aliandra believed him, and was very kind and gentle with him. He was really too naturally courageous, with all his hideous faults, not to enjoy the passing moment to the full. His marriage with Miss Slayback looked less and less possible, as Aliandra's influence gained the ascendant, and he formally bound himself to marry the Sicilian girl.

It was like a pleasant dream between two spells of torture, and as he rode up towards the woods it faded again into an improbability, and the ugly present truth rose in its place. Even to him, the idea of such a deliberate betrayal as he contemplated was revolting. He was far too much a Sicilian to think otherwise. Apart from any apprehension for his own subsequent safety, he honestly detested the thought of leading men who trusted him to certain destruction, no matter how bad they might be. Even the fact that they had forced him to be their guide, against his will, had little weight. He knew instinctively that if there were any worldly honour concerned in so dishonourable a matter, it should have bidden him either refuse to serve the law and let the law do its worst against him, or turn outlaw and warn the band that they were in danger. Ten days earlier he might have had the boldness to do either the one or the other, but he lacked it now. His character was momentarily and perhaps permanently broken, and though he still had the physical courage to face violent danger, he grasped at any means of returning to a peaceful existence, like the veriest coward.

All through the long ride in the desolate lands and the lonely forest, and throughout the evening that followed, his mind laboured painfully against the secret and overwhelming shame of what he meant to do, and as he sat resting among the outlaws he hardly spoke, except in answer to a question from Mauro or the Moscio, and made a bare pretence of eating a little for the sake of appearances. Again and again he felt impelled to open his lips and warn his companions of their danger, and once his resolution almost broke down. But as he glanced at Mauro's quietly superior smile, a sort of sullen resentment got hold of him against the man who had forced him into his present position, and he held his peace. Once or twice he thought of the knife which the Moscio had in his pocket, but he knew that a brigand's evidence would be worth nothing in law, and would be regarded as a mere attempt at vengeance for having been betrayed. It had been very different so long as the knife had lain under the altar, where anyone might find it. There were hundreds of knives like this one in Italy, and there could be nothing surprising in the fact that one belonging to a brigand should be rusty with blood. The bare assertion of the Moscio would not be worth much.

It was Mauro's intention to kill the carabineers in their sleep, if possible, to bind and gag San Giacinto and get him out through the postern gate, and to bind in the same way all the Sicilian servants in the house, so that they could neither free themselves nor make a noise. They would themselves prefer this, and would submit patiently, as they generally did in such affairs, because if they were not made fast they would afterwards be blamed for not immediately giving an alarm, whereas if they roused the village they would expose themselves to Mauro's vengeance as informers. It must be admitted that the position of the servants was not precisely enviable.

The postern of Camaldoli would then be locked again by means of the keys found in San Giacinto's room, and the keys would be thrown into the river. San Giacinto, bound on a horse, would be conveyed to a safe hiding-place before morning, and all would be over. The brigands would be many miles away by that time, scattering over the country as they usually did, while three or four of the strongest and most desperate remained with Mauro to guard San Giacinto until he should see fit to ransom himself by writing a cheque. It was all very well planned. Tebaldo was instructed to disappear from the scene as soon as he had led the band to the foot of the wall.

"I had better go up the ladder first," he suggested. "You will lose your way in the narrow passages between the rampart and the stables. The place is like a labyrinth on that side."

"Of course," said Mauro, "if you will help us further, we shall be greatly obliged, but that was not in the agreement, so I did not venture to hope—" He stopped, smiling politely.

"It will be better that I lead you into the court," answered Tebaldo. "If the carabineers are lodged there, as you say, they can only be in one room, for there is only one that would be at all suitable. It has a very small window, and in this weather they will leave the door open for coolness."

The night was clear, but there was no moon. Under the trees it was very dark, but the starlight made each opening and clearing faintly visible ahead, between the stems, as Tebaldo led the way down the hill, with the unerring certainty of a true path-finder. Again and again Mauro, who followed him closely, thought that he was taking a wrong turning, but Tebaldo never made a mistake as he swiftly and surely walked along, giving warning of any slight obstacle in a low monotonous voice, and now and then turning his head a little to listen for those behind.

They led six horses among them, Tebaldo's and five others, of which one was for San Giacinto, one for Mauro himself, and three others for the Moscio, Leoncino, and Schiantaceci. The remaining outlaws were to return at once to the huts in the woods and get their horses there.

It was characteristic of Mauro and his companions that they trusted Tebaldo's knowledge of the country, and followed him blindly after he had left the paths familiar to them. In and out he led them, always as far as possible under cover of trees and bushes, now and then over a stretch of dewy grass, then down into a little ravine, across a fork of a rough road, through more than one rivulet, ankle deep, and always by a way which the horses could safely follow, since that was essential.

At last he halted and looked at his watch by the starlight, for he had good eyes.

"It is a little early," he said to Mauro, in a whisper. "We are near. You can hear the water at the rapids where we must ford the river. It is not midnight yet, and we can reach the rampart in a quarter of an hour. Are you going to leave anyone with the horses? This would be the best place, for there are few trees between this and the water."

He felt cold. His feet were wet, and a cool night breeze blew down the valley. He turned up the collar of his coat and shivered audibly.

Mauro offered him a silver flask, and he swallowed a few drops of liquor.

"We will do as you think best," said the chief. "If you think this is a good place, we will tether the horses here, and give them their nosebags to keep them quiet."

In a few minutes the horses were tied up to separate trees by their halters, each out of reach of the other, and each had his nose in a small bag of corn. One had been brought especially for Tebaldo's, as the precaution was an important one to hinder any of the animals from neighing.

"We may as well go on," said Mauro. "They have been in bed an hour by this time, and a man in his first sleep is not so easily waked."

Tebaldo's heart was beating hard as he once more led the way. It had troubled him often of late. He felt ill, too, and his bones ached. But he did not stumble nor hesitate, as he led the fifteen men down to the ford. He shivered again as he glanced at the grey, rushing water that sparkled here and there in the starlight, at the eddies.

Mauro was already taking off his boots, and all the rest silently followed his example. On the other side of the rapids the brambles grew low down to the water's edge, and the tall eucalyptus trees made black shadows. Higher up, wild olive trees and wild figs grew out of the tangled mass of vegetation that covered the fifty or sixty feet of the precipitous ascent, all indistinguishable in the dim light. High above all, to the right, the outline of the gloomy Druse's tower was sharp and dark against the sky, and the straight line of the rampart was drawn like a black band over the more uncertain shadows below.

Tebaldo whispered to Mauro to follow him carefully through the water, and the whispered word went back from mouth to mouth along the line till it reached the Moscio, who brought up the rear.

From step to step, knee deep in the cold stream, Tebaldo felt for his footing in the familiar ford. He had known every inch of it since he had been a child, but the freshets often changed the bed, bringing great stones down in the winter rains, which sometimes lodged on the solid rock that came to the surface at that point and produced the ford. And Tebaldo felt his way cautiously with his bare feet.

Reaching the other side, he followed the edge of the water down stream for a little way, till all the men had got out of the water and were following him, barefooted, over the stones.

Then he touched Mauro to warn him that the ascent was about to begin, and each man touched the other in warning, from first to last. With their rifles on their backs and their revolvers slung in front to be ready, the fifteen men followed their guide slowly and silently upwards. Here and there the rock jutted out among the bushes, affording a firm foothold to naked feet and hands. Again, they had to climb up by the gnarled roots of a twisted fig tree, each man trying the wood with his hands before trusting to it. Even if a bough or dry stick had cracked, the sound could not have been heard above the steadily monotonous roar of the stream below. They moved like mountaineers, without haste, but without a pause.

The rampart was not more than twenty feet high above the final ledge, a rough wall of hewn stones, pierced all along the top by little slits for defence from the gallery inside. Tebaldo glanced to the right and left, and saw the ladder in its place. It was one of those very long ones used by the peasants for gathering olives, made of two light and half-trimmed poles, sharpened at the lower ends to stick into the moist ground and thus obtain a hold from below without throwing too much weight on the branches above, and with rungs nearly two feet apart.

Tebaldo went to the foot of the ladder and listened, though the river would have prevented him from hearing any but a very loud sound from within. His heart beat in his ears like a strong muffled drum. Mauro was close behind him, and touched him on the shoulder and pointed upwards to hasten his movements. But he felt as though he were paralyzed.

Mauro was impatient to get to work, and pushed him quietly aside. It was so dark that those behind could not see what happened. Mauro stepped upon the ladder first, the next man pressed after him, and the rest followed his companions, while Tebaldo stood in the shadow, dazed and shaking with excitement. But as the last man silently ascended, his wits returned, and he thought of his own safety. Peering up at the sky, he saw the man's dark figure disappear over the top of the wall.

With one strong effort he loosened the ladder, and in an instant sent it flying down, end foremost, through the bushes. Three steps he took under the shadow of the wall, and he plunged desperately down through the tangle, escaping for his life. He was swinging himself from a crooked root to a rock when an unearthly scream pierced the darkness, so loud and terrible that it might have been uttered close to his ear. He dropped ten feet in the dark, and before he touched the ground, even while he was still in mid-air, the quick fire of repeating rifles half deafened him. He rolled down, scrambled to his feet, jumped again, caught the bough of a tree, and swung himself out over the water, and still the rifle-shots cracked through the roar of the river. He plunged on, for he was below the ford, almost sank, found bottom, saved himself, and fled like a grey wolf in the starlight, right across the open, barefooted as he was. The firing had not ceased when he was in the saddle, on Mauro's horse, galloping madly along the broken ground up the valley, towards the high road to Santa Vittoria. Still he heard shots, and glancing back he saw the dim flash of the next, above the wall. Then he rode for his life, standing with his bare feet in the stirrups, his heart beating with the furious gallop, and terror behind him, — the terror he had never felt before, and which even now was not common bodily fear.

He had given way at the last to a horror of shame at the thought of leading those men to destruction, to pass unhurt himself through the waiting soldiers, to be face to face with the officer who had cowed him into such a betrayal, to meet San Giacinto's gloomy scorn, to be thanked by him with the contempt he deserved, for having served the law he had so often defied. He rode for his life from the thing he had done, rather than from the fear of any pursuit.

The fight had been short and deadly. Mauro had reached the top and had dropped to the pavement of the gallery within the rampart. It was deserted, and all was quite still. He counted his men, till he saw the head of the last appearing at the top of the ladder. Then with his rifle slung ready, with his knife in his right hand and his revolver in his left, he crept noiselessly along the stones to the entrance of a passage leading inwards. It was quite light in the starlight by comparison with the darkness in the tangle under the trees. He went on a few paces ahead of his men and turned again. Suddenly there was a tall man in front of him, who whispered as he came up.

"Are they come? Pass me, and you are safe!"

That was all, for he had been taken for Tebaldo in the gloom. In a flash he understood, and with a single movement drove his knife straight to the man's heart. The trooper groaned as he died. Then, in a moment, the passage was full of soldiers, before, behind, everywhere. Mauro yelled to his men to escape, his muffled voice breaking into the wild scream Tebaldo had heard. At the same moment he fired.

The men saw each other in the flashes of their rifles, till the flashes only lighted up thick clouds of smoke and they groped their way to kill each other. For the outlaws died hard, and their aim was cool and true when they could see, and when they could not, they felt for flesh with the muzzles of their Winchesters and fired when they struck anything soft, alive or dead. But they knew each other by their chief's name.

"Mauro, Mauro!" they repeated, as they jostled each other in the smoke.

But Mauro was dead in the dark already with a dozen bullets in him, and though five soldiers of the line lay in a heap around him and under him, the gold pieces that should have counted them were never to be slipped into the little soft leathern bag.

Still a few shots were fired, here and there, for some of the men had managed to get upon the roof of the low buildings between the stables and the rampart, and the more active of the soldiers pursued them. When all was quiet save the sound of many distant voices, and only now and then an awful groan came up out of the thick smoke, one man, who had thrown away his empty rifle and pistol, felt his way among the dead, with a knife in his hand, groping before him with the other for any living thing that might come in his way. But by some miracle he crept on and found no one, and was suddenly at the rampart and alone. He glanced quickly to right and left for the ladder, and saw that it was gone.

"Judas Iscariot!" he said in a low voice, as he thought of Tebaldo.

Then, leaving his tale of dead behind him, he unhesitatingly got over the wall, turned his face to it, and let himself down, feeling for crevices in the stones with his naked feet. And his small, strong fingers found impossibly small holding, but it sufficed for a while, and when he could hold no more, he pushed himself backwards with a little spring and dropped ten feet to the ledge.

No one had fought more desperately for himself and his comrades than the Moscio, but fate had saved him once more, and he made his way quickly down to the stream, forded it almost without wetting himself, coolly found his boots among the many that waited for those who should never need them again, shod himself, picked out his own horse, and rode away towards the Maniace woods. He had found time to notice that Mauro's horse was gone, and he knew that Tebaldo had taken it because it was the best.

"Judas Iscariot!" he repeated quietly, as he rode away, without a scratch, from that hideous carnage, man enough to wish, perhaps, that he had found his death where so many had fallen.

For it had been a terrible fight, at close quarters. Since the famous Leone had been killed, there had been no such bloody encounter between outlaws and troops. The trap had been well laid, but even the brave old officer of carabineers had not counted on having to deal with such desperate men.

Of the outlaws, five only were alive and all more or less badly wounded. The Moscio had got away unhurt, and nine were stone dead. There had been no chance of even offering quarter, for they had fired instantly as soon as they had seen themselves surrounded, and their Winchesters had done fearful work in a few moments. Four carabineers and seventeen of the line were carried out into the court, one by one, and were laid side by side on the stones, under the stars. A dozen or fifteen more were wounded, among whom were both the officer of the carabineers and the young red-haired lieutenant of foot. As for San Giacinto, a bullet had taken off the top of his ear and had just scored the grey hair above it. A thin line of blood ran down the side of his dark face as he bent to examine Mauro's body, with a lantern in his hand.

Something told him that the priest-faced man had been the famous chief, and one of the surviving outlaws confirmed the fact, being brought up handcuffed to recognize the dead men one by one.

San Giacinto coldly wished that he might find Tebaldo Pagliuca among the slain, and said so.

"Never fear," said the wounded outlaw, with an ugly smile. "Traitors die slowly in Sicily,—but they always die."

He refused to answer any questions, of course, like the others who were taken, beyond identifying the dead, and they all swore that no one had escaped, and that Tebaldo had been mistaken in saying that there had been fifteen instead of fourteen.

"But the famous Moscio?" asked San Giacinto, who had heard of the youth. "Where is he?"

"The Moscio?" The outlaw repeated the name with a blank look. "I never heard the name," he added gravely.

CHAPTER XXXVII

TEBALDO slackened his speed at last and attempted to concentrate his thoughts. Exhausted as he was by exertion and by the ever-increasing strain on his faculties, it was not easy to think at all. But his bare feet, chilled in the cold stirrups, drew his attention to the present necessity of being shod as soon as possible. He could reach Randazzo long before dawn and get into the inn by knocking and rousing the man who slept on the ground floor. He could invent some story to explain why he had ridden home on another horse. In the dark, with only a taper or a lantern, the man would not notice his bare feet, and he could get to his room in safety. After that, he did not know what he should do. He felt that if he could not get rest soon, he must fall ill. As a matter of fact, he was ill already, with the dangerous fever of the south, as the sudden chills he had lately felt would have told him at any other time.

He made up his mind that he must reach the inn; he put his horse to a canter again and got to Randazzo just as the first pallor of the dawn threw the dark outline of Etna into stronger relief against the sky. Everything happened as he had hoped. The sleepy manservant gave him the key of the stable, and he hitched his horse in a stall, came back, entered the house, and reached his room in safety, the man not having noticed that he was barefoot.

He locked the door and almost staggered to his bed, falling upon it as he was, in his wet clothes. A moment later he was asleep.

It seemed but a moment more and he was waked by a loud knocking. He started up in one of those hideous dreams of fear, of which the whole length takes but an instant of time. The knocking was the sound of rifle-shots, and he was once more plunging down through the tangle below Camaldoli. Then he saw that it was broad daylight outside, and he heard the voice of the officer of carabineers speaking to him from without in a friendly tone. Forgetting or not caring how he looked, he opened the door.

The grey-haired lieutenant entered. He was already shaved and dressed with his usual scrupulous neatness, but he was extremely pale, and his arm was in a black sling.

"I am sorry to disturb you," he said, "though, as it is nearly twelve o'clock, I had expected to find you up. The fact is, I should be very much obliged to you if you could make it convenient to go to Rome — or Paris, if you please. One of the brigands escaped us last night."

"Only one?" asked Tebaldo, mechanically.

"Only one. We suppose that it must have been the famous Moscio."

"The Moscio?"

"We suppose so. Whoever it was, he has lost no time in telling what has happened and your share in the business. You are not safe even in the town of Randazzo, unless you will consent to go about between a couple of carabineers like a prisoner. I am sorry to say that you had better go at once. The population is roused against you. You know what they are."

"Yes. I know." Tebaldo leaned against the table.

"I can protect you with soldiers," continued the officer, his own voice weak from loss of blood. "But your position will be a very unpleasant one. I have sent for a carriage for you and will give you a strong escort, but for your own safety, as well as for the quiet of the country, I must beg you to start as soon as you can dress and get your things together. To-day you may get away quietly. To-morrow your appearance might cause something like a riot."

"I knew how it would end," said Tebaldo, faintly. "Very well. I will get ready."

The lieutenant was in reality exaggerating the

danger of the man's position, though quite unintentionally. He would certainly not have been safe in such a place as Santa Vittoria, but it was extremely unlikely that he should be attacked in Randazzo, though he might very probably have been insulted in the streets.

The Moscio had in reality seen but one man with whom he had spoken before dawn, but he was the woodcutter who had chiefly supplied the outlaws with provisions during their stay in the forest of Maniace, and he had come up as usual to know if they wanted anything on that day, being as yet ignorant of the fight at Camaldoli. But as he came down, the man had met an acquaintance and had repeated the story without telling how he had learned it. Before noon the facts were known far and wide from Santa Vittoria to Randazzo, substantially as the Moscio knew that they had happened.

The feeling against Tebaldo was at once infinitely stronger than that against the carabineers and soldiers. To a certain extent the brigands always terrorized the country, and many of the better sort of people were heartily glad to know that the band of Mauro had been finally destroyed, though they did not say so, lest some survivor should wreak vengeance on them. But there was no difference of opinion in regard to Tebaldo. It was not exactly treachery to carry people off by force and extort a ransom from them, as the outlaws did. But to lead men who trusted him into a trap prepared for them by the troops was a betrayal which no Sicilian could forgive Tebaldo, even though it might have had some good results, and the name of Judas, which the Moscio had spoken alone in the solitude, was on every tongue.

It is of no use to waste words in trying to explain this feeling, which most people will understand. The fact was that the whole population shared it, as Tebaldo knew that they must, since the story had become known. He recognized at once that he ought to accept the officer's advice and get away as soon as he could. He would write to Aliandra from Messina, but he was sure that she must despise him now, like everyone else. To all intents and purposes he was a fugitive, as he drove out of the town, half an hour later, in a closed carriage with the ragged shades drawn down. Possibly he remembered, as he shivered in his corner beside the carabineer, how the light had fallen on Ippolito Saracinesca's face in the street of Santa Vittoria scarcely ten days earlier, how the people had cursed the innocent man, and had thrown things at him, trying to bruise him from a distance.

Another carabineer sat opposite in the carriage, and one was on the box beside the driver. Tebaldo vaguely understood that even the soldiers despised

him, but he was almost past caring what they
thought. The fever was slowly gaining on him,
and his nerves were utterly broken. His face was
like a yellow mask, and he hung his head so that
his chin rested on his breast. He reached Messina
in a dream and went to the wretched hotel there.
He was not able to go on to Rome that night, and
a doctor who was sent for said that he had the
'perniciosa' fever.

On the following morning, in Randazzo, Aliandra was sitting alone in her room. She had heard
of all that had happened. Twenty people had
been to see the notary on the previous day, and the
story had been repeated again and again, till she
knew every word of it by heart.

She was ashamed of ever having wished to marry
such a man. That was her first sensation, and it
had not left her yet. Though she was strong and
sensible, she had shut herself up in her own room
and had cried for hours, not for Tebaldo, but with
shame and anger at herself. She hated him now,
far more than she had ever cared for anyone in
her short life, and she was glad when she heard
that he was gone, for she never wished to see him
again. It was a perfectly simple state of mind.
The man was a despicable traitor, in her view, and
she hated herself for having ever believed in him.

Her shame at the whole thing was not her own
secret. That made it worse. Her father's friends

knew very well that Tebaldo often came to the house and was in love with her, and had not been rebuffed. The lieutenant of carabineers himself generally came once a week to pay a visit, for he liked Basili. All the townsfolk knew it. It was a reproach, and a public one, it was a blot on her good name, and she felt it all the more painfully because she had never done anything to be ashamed of.

Again and again, through the night and in the morning, the burning tears of anger at herself ran over and scalded her cheeks, and then dried as her anger rose against Tebaldo.

This morning she had just been through one of these storms of tears in the solitude of her room, when Gesualda knocked at the door. Poor, ugly Gesualda, whose innocent little sin of eating an orange on the stairs one day had started the avalanche of fate that ended in the destruction of Mauro's band, the death of Francesco Pagliuca, and the ruin of Tebaldo, would have died of horror had she known that all these things were the direct consequences of Basili's broken leg, which had brought Aliandra to Randazzo, followed by the two brothers.

She entered quietly and stupidly enough.

"Signorina," she said, "dry your eyes, for there is one who would speak with you downstairs."

"Who is it?" asked Aliandra, impatiently. "Will they ever let me alone? What does he want?"

"Do not be angry, signorina," answered the woman. "It is a young gentleman from Messina, who has a parcel for you in his hands and begs that you will kindly receive it yourself."

"A parcel from Messina? Well—" Aliandra hesitated, but her curiosity was roused. "Tell him that I will come down immediately," she concluded.

A few minutes later she descended the stairs, having plunged her face into cold water and done her best to remove the traces of her tears. She entered the front room and met a girlish looking youth with close and curling brown hair, and extremely well dressed in light grey. A rather delicate hand held out a parcel to her, as he bowed respectfully.

"I was commissioned to hand you this parcel, signorina," said the Moscio. "It is from one of your greatest admirers."

"From whom is it?" she asked quickly, as she took the heavy little package.

"That is your friend's secret. He only begs that you will open it when you are alone. It contains a little surprise for you. I thank you for your kindness in receiving me, signorina. Good morning."

He bowed and moved quickly towards the door.

"But you, signore — what is your name? I am infinitely obliged —"

"My name is Angelo Laria, signorina. Good morning."

Before she could stop him, he had left the room, and she heard the front door shut immediately afterwards. She looked out through the closed blinds, and there was no one within sight. It was as though she had dreamed of the visitor. Then she felt the package, shook it, weighed it, began to undo it, changed her mind, and went swiftly up the stairs to her own room. It might be an ornament or a jewel, she thought, sent to the celebrated singer by an unknown admirer — possibly the well-dressed young gentleman who had brought it was himself the giver, in spite of what he said. At all events she would look at it in private. She bolted the door of her room, sat down near the window in order to have plenty of light, and opened the parcel carefully.

It contained a letter sealed, addressed to her, and folded round the black leathern sheath of Tebaldo's knife. She took the letter in one hand and the knife in the other, turning over the latter curiously. But she was too much a Sicilian not to have heard of such messages, and she guessed that the letter contained either a threat or a warning. She tore open the envelope and read the contents eagerly. There were two large sheets, tolerably closely written in excellent handwriting, and beginning as follows:

"SIGNORINA,— We, who are beyond laws, do not betray even our enemies to the law, much less our friends. We have little, but we have honour. The man to whom this knife belonged has neither, and against him, and such as he, we warn women like yourself, who are young, beautiful, and honest. These words are not written to the incomparable artist, the matchless singer, the wonder of Sicily, and the pride of the nation. They are addressed to you — simply as Aliandra Basili, an honourable Sicilian maiden, the daughter of an honest Sicilian notary. It is known to us all that you have put your faith and trust in Tebaldo Pagliuca. Consider what is here written, your own honour, and your father's name, and do not marry one who has betrayed his friends to death and captivity, and who, moreover, murdered his own brother with the weapon I now place in your hands. Judas was an honourable man compared with your betrothed husband, Tebaldo Pagliuca."

Aliandra stopped at this point, read the last sentences again, and glanced at the knife she still held in one hand. With a movement of horror and disgust she threw it from her. Then she hesitated, rose, picked it up, and hid it in a drawer before she continued reading.

The letter went on to tell the story of the last four days in detail, from the time when Tebaldo had sent for the Moscio to sup with him at the inn, till Tebaldo's departure from Randazzo. Aliandra did not pause till she reached the last sentences, but there was the bright red flush of anger and shame in her cheeks. There is perhaps no such cruel shame in human nature as that a woman feels at the disgrace of the man she has accepted as husband or lover. She paused, bit her lips, and then read to the end.

"This is not an anonymous letter, signorina. I who write to you am known as the Moscio, but many people call me Angelo Laria. I am he who by a miracle escaped from the massacre the night before last, when all my friends were dead or taken and I had not a shot left to fire. When I leave you I am going to the inn where Tebaldo Pagliuca stayed, for I will not send such a letter as this and then slink away like a thief. It is in your power, if you have read this at once, to inform the authorities and have me taken. I am not even armed. We, who have no laws, do not betray our friends, but we warn our women against such men as Tebaldo Pagliuca, and we know that they will not betray us treacherously as he did."

There was no signature, for none was necessary. There were few in Sicily who had not heard the name of the Moscio, and many strangely romantic stories were told of him. Some may think that considering what the man was, Aliandra should have delivered him up forthwith to justice. She would as soon have stabbed her father in the back.

But gradually, as she leaned back in her chair, staring at the wall, the angry flush subsided from her cheeks and a dreamy look came into her face.

"This outlaw is at least a man and a brave one," she said to herself, as she thought of him.

The Moscio was quite safe, so far as she was concerned. She folded the letter carefully, returning it to its envelope, and then, taking the stout paper in which it had been wrapped, she opened the drawer, took the knife and rolled it up with the letter again, tying it, as she had received it. After that she took sealing-wax and sealed it with the little emblem of Sicily which she carried on a thin chain with other trinkets — the three legs growing out of a human head, for the three capes of the triangular island.

Tebaldo had disappeared without a word, and she naturally believed that he had gone to Rome to escape the vengeance of the Moscio and of any friends the latter might have. Aliandra was sure he must know that she would never see him again, for though many of the details written by the outlaw were new to her, besides the main fact of Francesco's murder, the fact of the betrayal of the band by Tebaldo was public property. He had gone to Rome without so much as attempting to defend himself.

And now she had in her hands the proofs that Tebaldo had killed his brother, or what she believed to be proofs, though the law might have thought differently. She had, at least, the certainty, for it did not enter her head that the Moscio could be trying to deceive her.

Yet she would not take these proofs to the deputy prefect, nor show them to her father. She was not a detective. The idea of giving the murderer up was repugnant to her, though in a less degree than the thought of informing against the Moscio himself. She wondered what Tebaldo would do next.

Thinking it over, she came to the rather unexpected conclusion that he had gone to Rome in order to marry the American heiress at once. At first this seemed wild, but she grew accustomed to the thought in a few moments, and it impressed her. There would be much in favour of the plan, if he could carry it out. Once married to Miss Slayback and her millions, Tebaldo could leave Italy for ever and spend the rest of his life as he pleased. The mafia could not pursue him to a foreign country. Even in Rome he would be comparatively safe, for Rome, she thought, was a very civilized capital, and one man could not easily wait for another in the Villa Borghese as he could at the turning of a lonely Sicilian road.

The more she thought of it, the more certain she felt that he meant to marry Miss Slayback. All the details of her last interview with Francesco came back vividly. Knowing, now, that Tebaldo had killed him, she was more willing than before to believe everything Francesco had said. Tebaldo had loved her, in a fierce and brutal way, but he had never meant to marry her at all. He had meant something else. Her cheeks burned once more, and her eyes flashed dangerously. He should not marry Miss Slayback, either, she thought.

Then she reflected a little more calmly on her own position, and she decided to leave Randazzo at once. After what had happened, she could not stay in her native town, ashamed to show her face in the streets. Even the outlaw had known that she was engaged to marry Tebaldo Pagliuca. The very children would point at her.

Her father was much better, and she communicated her decision to him. He was very grim and silent about it all, but he thought she was wise. He should soon be on his legs again; at all events, she had helped him to get over the most tiresome part of his recovery from the accident, and he now attended to his business regularly with his clerk and received his clients in his room. Aliandra made her preparations and left on the following day, in the very carriage which had taken Tebaldo to the station of Piedimonte. And she, too, had the old carriage closed and drew down the ragged blinds. The boys in the street did not know who was inside, but they had heard how Tebaldo had driven away, and seeing the blinds down, they ran along by the door, yelling in derision.

"Another betrayer! Another Judas! Curses on the souls of his dead!" they cried.

The coachman lashed at them with his whip, and they fell behind, but Aliandra had understood, and her eyes flashed and the burning blush came back.

She had telegraphed to her aunt, and the Signora Barbuzzi met her at the station in Messina. They reached Rome on the second day, a little less than a fortnight after they had left, and early in the afternoon.

CHAPTER XXXVIII

MARIA CAROLINA was not exactly insane, but she was entirely unbalanced, and seemed to have no sane judgment in ordinary matters. Her first outbursts of grief had subsided into a profound religious melancholy, and she insisted upon being taken to a convent in which she might end her days in peace. She seemed utterly regardless of the fact that her daughter would be left alone until her surviving brother came back, if he ever returned at all, and that such a man, even as she knew him, was no fit guardian for a young girl. The doctors said that in all probability, if she were not allowed to do what she wished, she would really go mad, in her present state. They suggested that she should retire to one of the convents where ladies were received who wished to go into a religious retreat, and that one of the Sisters of the Bon Secours should obtain permission to live with Vittoria for a few days until her brother arrived.

Vittoria, worn out with anxiety and sorrow, did not know how to face this new difficulty. Miss Lizzie Slayback insisted that she should come and stay with her and her aunt at the hotel. After a little hesitation, she accepted, for it seemed the only solution of the difficulty. The American girl had become sincerely attached to her Italian friend, and felt herself drawn to Vittoria for the sake of having been on the point of marrying Tebaldo, a state of mind which is natural to some characters and utterly unnatural to others. It was a generous impulse, at all events.

Vittoria went with her mother to the convent and helped her to install herself, and on the same afternoon she moved with her maid to the Hotel Bristol. She was like a lovely shadow.

"I am so tired," she said, when she sat down at last beside Miss Lizzie.

"Rest, dear, rest," answered the American girl, drawing the weary head down to her shoulder.

As the hours went by, and she felt the freedom of not being obliged to go back to the sadness of her mother's society, Vittoria revived a little. But her life was almost more than she could bear. The papers had been full of the capture of Mauro's band, and of her brother's share in it, for the story had spread like wildfire over Sicily. Even the Roman papers made scathing allusions to Tebaldo's possible relations with the brigands, and while congratulating the government on its victory, made sarcastic enquiries into the state of the betrayer's conscience. It was indeed hard for

Vittoria to bear. She had no news of Tebaldo himself, who seemed to have disappeared mysteriously. Her mother had practically abandoned her in her selfish and half-insane sorrow. She felt herself utterly alone in the world.

Orsino gravely read the articles in the papers, and wished that he could silence them for Vittoria's sake. Had there ever been so much as a mention of her name, or even of her mother's, he would have taken active measures to do so. But the editors were careful never to allude to Tebaldo's family, and it was out of the question to hinder them from speaking of him as they chose. So far as Orsino knew, the man was quite able to defend himself.

Sant' Ilario read the accounts aloud to his father and to Corona. Sometimes Ippolito listened, but Orsino always made an excuse for leaving the room, preferring to read the news for himself.

There was a perpetual subdued anxiety in the great household, on Ippolito's account, with an eager expectation that in the course of the present events the mystery of Francesco's death should be cleared up. Their friends looked upon the affair very much as though it had taken place in Africa or the South Seas, for Sicily seems very remote to Roman society. They laughed at the idea that Ippolito could really ever be brought to trial. Even the Minister of Justice, who was a friend of

Sant' Ilario's, smiled and said that the law had means of putting off the trial for a long time in order that satisfactory evidence might be obtained. But no such evidence was forthcoming. The judge who had heard the case in Messina had been to Santa Vittoria, but had met with the most complete substantiation of Tebaldo's own story. He had not even thought of causing the grating under the altar to be opened. Nothing new transpired, and Ippolito resolutely held his tongue. In order to avoid being questioned by his many acquaintances, he saw as few people as he could, and spent much time over his music in Orsino's room. The two brothers were as fond of each other as ever, but when they were together they were much more silent than formerly. The secret preoccupation of each conflicted with that of the other, and the peace between them depended upon silence for its security.

Nor did anyone in the household know that Orsino had seen Vittoria several times at Mrs. Slayback's, still less that the American lady and her niece always managed to leave the two alone together for a while on such occasions. Orsino was determined that nothing should come between him and Vittoria, but at the present juncture it was impossible for him to insist upon his family's consent to his marriage.

Vittoria, on her side, had given up all hope,

though her love gained upon her sorrows in the struggle for her soul. She was too lonely not to love her love for its companionship, too weary not to love Orsino for his strength, and yet too desolate to believe that happiness could wait for her while the cruel hours and days crawled slowly on.

It had seemed easy long ago — a month or a little more, at most — when Orsino had first gone to Sicily. It had seemed possible when he had come back that first time, even though he had killed her own brother in self-defence. But there was no more possibility now. She felt that this was the end of her race. Some fearful thing must happen to Tebaldo, and she should be left alone, the last of the long and evil line of the Corleone. It would be better for her, too, to go back to the convent, to the dear old nuns who knew her and had loved her and would take her back as a sister, now, to end her days in peace and innocence and devotion. Her name should be forgotten, and while she lived she could pray that the evil of it might be forgiven and the remembrance of it blotted out among men.

Once or twice she had spoken in this way to Orsino, but he had stopped her suddenly and almost roughly. Come what might, he meant to marry her, and he would. That was all he said, but he meant it, and she had moments of belief when she heard the words and saw his face.

He admitted, when she pressed him, that neither his father nor his mother would at present give their consent, and that there was little to choose between them, and that they were people whose minds being once made up, would not easily change. And Vittoria sadly answered that they were right, and that she should feel and act as Corona did, were she in Corona's place. Yet still Orsino smiled gravely and said that they should not hinder him at the last, for that he, too, had made up his mind, and that he was their son and like them, and could be as stubborn as they. Vittoria could not say that Orsino had once wavered in his determination since that night when he had kissed her on the bridge outside the ballroom. He was always the same, and it was small wonder that her weariness should find rest in his strength. But when he was gone, her courage sank again.

She was seated alone one afternoon in Mrs. Slayback's drawing-room. The two ladies were out, but Vittoria would not drive with them in their big open carriage, to meet her old acquaintances and to feel that she was pointed out as the sister of Tebaldo Pagliuca, who had betrayed Mauro and his band. She went for little walks in the morning with Miss Lizzie, before it was hot, and sometimes in the afternoon she took a closed cab and drove to the convent to see her mother. To-day she was at home, and she had come into the drawing-room and established herself in the corner of a sofa, with a book, trying to read. But she could not care for what the book said, and the volume dropped upon her lap, while her head fell back and the low sunlight filtered through the blinds and gilded her brown hair, leaving her sad young face all in the shadow.

Suddenly the door opened wide, and one of the servants of the hotel announced a visitor, in a pompous tone.

"The Signorina Basili!" he said, waited for Aliandra to enter, and he closed the door.

Aliandra came in swiftly and stood before Vittoria, who half rose from her seat, startled by the singer's sudden appearance. Aliandra held something in her hand. She had never seen Vittoria, and the sunlight made the girl's hair look fair. She had ordered the servant to show her to Miss Slayback's drawing-room without announcing her, and she naturally took Vittoria for Miss Lizzie. Her handsome face was faintly flushed with anger and excitement, and her dark eyes gleamed.

"I have brought you this," she said, holding out the Moscio's parcel, "from the man who has deceived us both, who wished to marry you and ruin me, who has come back to marry you now — "

"Who? What?" asked Vittoria, half frightened, but mechanically taking the parcel.

"Tebaldo Pagliuca," answered Aliandra, too

much excited to notice that Vittoria spoke in Italian with an Italian's accent. "Tebaldo Pagliuca, who betrayed his friends the outlaws to death, Tebaldo Pagliuca, who is trying to marry you for your fortune, Tebaldo Pagliuca, who killed his own brother Francesco on the steps of the altar with the knife that is in that package — "

"Merciful God!" The young girl's voice rang breaking through the room, as she sank back.

"Tebaldo Pagliuca, who confessed the crime to the priest," continued Aliandra, working herself into a fury, "who accused the priest of the murder, knowing that he would die with the secret rather than betray a confession — Tebaldo Pagliuca, the traitor, the betrayer, the false accuser, the murderer! The story is there, with the knife, in the paper — read it, and give him his answer when he comes to-day to kiss your hands — "

"Mercy of Heaven! Mercy of God!" moaned Vittoria, still too strong to faint or not to hear and understand every word.

Aliandra believed that she had done what she had come to do. She had foiled Tebaldo effectually and for ever in any attempt he might make to marry the American heiress. With a glance at the girl's bent head, and at the soft, brown hair that looked so fair in the flecks of sunshine, she turned and left the room as quickly as she had entered it.

Vittoria started as she heard the door close, looked up, and then glanced at the package in her hand. She did not quite remember what she did after that, till she found herself locked into her own room, breaking the violet seals from the brown paper, cutting the string with her nail scissors, tearing the stout paper to pieces with her little hands, her heart beating with horror and her eyes already frightened by the expectation of the knife they were to see. She saw it, a moment later, and then her heart stood still, for she had seen it many times in Tebaldo's room, during that winter, and once she had borrowed it of him to cut a strong cord from a parcel.

Then came the letter, and the long and painful reading of the hideous tale. She spent a terrible half hour, and then she sat still for a long time, and her face was almost restful. At last she rose, quite calm and decided, and began to dress herself to go out. In a quarter of an hour she was ready, and she went downstairs alone and told the porter to get her a cab.

"Palazzo Saracinesca," she said to the cabman, "and drive under the gate!"

She went up the great staircase and asked for Corona. The footman hesitated to say whether the Princess would receive or not. Vittoria fixed her eyes on him and spoke quietly in a tone he understood.

"Be good enough to take me to the Princess's room," she said. "The matter is urgent."

She followed the man through the long succession of state drawing-rooms till he knocked at a side door, and immediately opened it inwards.

Corona was at her table, writing a note. She looked up quickly, bending her brows, and rose rather formally. She had always liked Vittoria for herself, but she had good cause to hate her name, and she had avoided the possibility of meeting the lonely girl of late. Vittoria went forward and spoke first.

"I should not have come to you for a small matter," she said. "But I have come to make a reparation."

"There is none to make," answered Corona. "You have done nothing—" She paused, not understanding.

"You shall see. Will you sit down? It may take some time to explain—or, rather, to read. There is only one question which I must ask you first. Has Don Ippolito been acquitted or not?"

Corona's face darkened.

"He has not," she answered. "He is at liberty on San Giacinto's security."

"Here are the proofs of his innocence," said Vittoria, simply, as she produced her package, and laid it on Corona's lap.

Corona opened her eyes in surprise, and her expression changed.

"My brother Tebaldo did it," continued Vittoria. "He forced your son, as a priest, to hear his confession, because Don Ippolito surprised him in the church. Then he accused him of the murder, knowing that he would keep the secret."

Corona stared, realized what the girl meant, and suddenly grasped her wrist, looking into her face. She saw the truth there, but Vittoria understood the doubt.

"When you have read, you will understand better," said the young girl, pointing to the package.

Corona said nothing, but her fingers were quick to find the letter. Vittoria rose softly and went to the window and looked out. Her hands rested on the cold stone sill and twitched nervously from time to time, but she would not turn round. She knew that what was shame and horror to her, was the joy of heaven to the mother of the accused man. Corona read in silence, intently, quickly, almost desperately.

She was a generous woman. When she had finished, and the weight had fallen from her heart at last, she rose and went to Vittoria. The girl heard her step and turned. Corona was holding out both hands.

"What shall I do to make you know how grateful I am?" she asked.

"What should you do?" asked Vittoria, sadly.
"It was justice, so I came at once. The great singer — the Basili — came into the room an hour ago. I was alone. She took me for Miss Slayback, with whom I am staying, and before I could speak she had told the truth and given me the package and was gone. So I brought it to you. I trust you to spare my poor brother if you can. Keep the secret, if you can, now that you know the truth. Perhaps something else may prove Don Ippolito innocent, long before the trial. But if nothing else will do — why then, you have his innocence in your hands."

"Where is he?" asked Corona. "Where is your brother?"

"I do not know. It is several days since he has telegraphed. He never writes. The Basili spoke as though he were in Rome, but I do not think he is. I will go home, please. I am a little tired. You will keep the secret if you can, will you not?"

"Yes. No one shall know it unless it is necessary. But you, child —"

She put her arm round Vittoria, for the girl looked shadowy and faint, as she leaned against the table by the window. Vittoria straightened herself, and opened and shut her eyes once or twice as though waking.

"There is nothing the matter," she said rather

proudly. "I am very well. I am glad that you are happy."

"You have given me back my life," answered Corona. "Some day — but there are no thanks for such things."

Vittoria began to go towards the door. She wanted no thanks, yet somehow she had hoped that Corona would speak differently, remembering how she had once been left by her with Orsino in that very room. The Princess walked with her to the hall.

"I shall not forget this, my dear," she said, almost solemnly, as she pressed the passive little hand. "I shall come and see you soon."

As Vittoria drove back to the Piazza Barberini, she felt as though the very desolation of loneliness were beside her in the shabby little cab. But Corona had never been a woman of many words, and she meant more than she said when she told Vittoria that she should not forget.

CHAPTER XXXIX

CORONA regretted the promise of secrecy which Vittoria had obtained from her, as soon as she found herself alone and able to think over the situation calmly. She had no secrets from her husband, and few of any kind, and it was hard to keep silence when Giovanni discussed Ippolito's position and the possibilities of obtaining the evidence necessary to clear Ippolito. She had, indeed, the sort of satisfaction which a woman feels all the more keenly when she feels it alone, with the certainty that everyone else will soon know what she knows, for she saw that Ippolito had behaved with almost heroic constancy. But she would soon begin to long for the moment when others should see that he was a hero.

Being naturally a calm woman, and somewhat reserved, even with her own family, her face did not betray her at first. Yet she hardly dared to look at Ippolito that evening, lest her happiness should break like light from her eyes.

Her difficulty was a considerable one, however, and puzzled her at first. In her own room she read and re-read the Moscio's letter, and her maturer judgment told her what neither Aliandra nor Vittoria had understood in their impetuosity. The law would look upon this so-called evidence as a piece of vengeance on the part of a brigand, and would attach little value to it. Why, the law would ask, since the brigand professed to hold proofs that could ruin his enemy, had he not sent them to the carabineers? The answer must take the very unsatisfactory form of a dissertation on Sicilian character in general, and on that of the Moscio in particular; whereas, while he was still at large, his character could be but an unknown quantity. It might be proved, of course, that the knife had belonged to Tebaldo. But it would be hard to show how the Moscio had come by it. To demonstrate Ippolito's innocence, something more was necessary.

Corona made up her mind that she would see Tebaldo himself and force him to a confession of his crime. It did not occur to her to fear such a meeting nor even to hesitate, after she had once made up her mind. The difficulty lay in finding the man immediately. She did not believe that Vittoria had deceived her in saying that she did not know where her brother might be, but she supposed that he would soon come to Rome, and decided to wait for him. She sent frequently to enquire at the house where the Corleone had lived.

The servants knew nothing. She wrote a note to Vittoria at Mrs. Slayback's, but Vittoria had no news.

Corona wrote to the Minister of Justice. She knew him very well, and told him that in the matter of the accusation against her son she wished to communicate with Don Tebaldo Pagliuca, but could not find out where he was. To her surprise the Minister's answer gave her the information she wished. Tebaldo, said the note, was dangerously ill in Messina at a certain hotel. Owing to the strong feeling which existed against him in Sicily, it had been thought necessary to protect him, and the government was, therefore, kept constantly apprised of his condition through the office of the prefect of Messina. He was very ill indeed, and was not expected to recover.

The information was clear, but the thought that Tebaldo might die without having cleared Ippolito was anything but reassuring. Corona's instinct was to start at once, but she remembered her promise to Vittoria, and did not see how she could make such a journey without informing her husband and giving some explanation of her conduct. She went to his room as soon as she knew what she must do.

"Giovanni," she said, "I wish you to go to Sicily with me at once. I must go to Messina."

Giovanni looked at her sharply in surprise.

"Are you ill, my dear?" he enquired. "Is it for a change? Is anything the matter?"

Corona laughed, for she had never been ill in her life. The mere idea seemed ludicrous to her.

"Can you imagine me ill?" she asked. "No. I will tell you what I can. Someone has told me something, making me promise not to tell anyone else—"

"Your informant is a woman, dear," observed Giovanni, smiling.

"Never mind who it was. But from what was told me I know that if I can go to Messina I can get evidence which will clear Ippolito completely. So I came to you."

"Are you positively sure?" asked Sant' Ilario. "It is a long journey."

"We shall travel together," answered Corona, as though that answered every objection.

"I should like it very much. Do you wish to start to-day?"

"Yes. The man is said to be dying at a hotel in Messina."

It amused them both to make a mystery of going away together, though it was not the first time that they had done such a thing, and Sant' Ilario's presence lightened the anxiety which Corona still felt as to the result of the journey.

They reached Messina at evening and drove to the wretched hotel where Tebaldo lay dying, for there was no other in the city, in which they could have lodged at all.

Half an hour later Corona entered the sick man's room. The sister who was nursing him rose in surprise as the Princess entered, and laid her finger on her lips. Tebaldo appeared to be asleep.

"Is he better?" whispered Corona.

But the sister shook her head and pointed to his face. It was like a yellow shadow on the white pillow, in the soft light of the single candle, before which the nurse had set a book upright on the table, as a shade.

Corona stood still by the side of the bed and looked down at what remained of the man who had done such terrible deeds during the last month. The colourless lips were parted and displayed the sharp, white teeth, and the half-grown beard gave something wolfish to the face. The lids were not quite closed and showed the whites of the eyes. Corona felt suddenly that he was going to die in his unconsciousness without speaking. Even if he revived for a moment, he might not understand her. The candle flickered, and she thought the lids quivered.

"He is dying," she said in a low voice. "But he must speak to me before he dies."

"Are you his mother, madam?" asked the sister, in a whisper.

"No!" Corona's great eyes blazed upon the nun's face. Then she spoke gently again. "I am the mother of the priest he falsely accused. Before he dies he must tell the truth."

A faint smile moved the wasted lips, and the lids slowly opened. Then he spoke, almost naturally.

"You have come to see me die. I understand."

"No," said Corona, speaking clearly and distinctly. "I have come to hear the truth about my son, from your own lips, as I know it from others —"

The yellow face shivered and the eyes stared. There was a convulsive effort of the head to rise from the pillow.

"Who told you?" The question gurgled in the throat.

"Your sister told me —"

"I have no sister." The head fell back again, and the twisting smile took possession of the lips.

"Vittoria is your sister. You are Tebaldo Pagliuca." Corona bent down towards him anxiously, for she feared that he was wandering, and that the truth must escape her at last.

"Oh no! Vittoria is not my sister. I remember when she was brought to Camaldoli by the outlaws when I was a boy."

Corona bent lower still and stared into the open

eyes. Their expression was quite natural and quiet, though the voice was faint now.

"It is better that someone should know," it said. "I know, because I saw her brought. The brigands stole her from her nurse's arms. Vittoria is the daughter of Fornasco. They frightened my father and mother — they brought the child at night — in trying to get a ransom they were all taken, but none of them would tell — there is a paper of my father's, sealed — in Rome, among my things. He always said that we might be accused, though they managed to make people believe it was my mother's child, for fear of the brigands — I cannot tell you all that. You will find it in the papers."

The eyelids closed again, but the lips still moved. Corona bent down.

"Water," said the parched whisper.

They gave him drink quickly, but he could hardly swallow it. He was going fast.

"Call the doctor," said Corona to the nurse. "He is dying. Has he seen a priest? Call my husband!"

"I had sent for a priest," answered the nurse, leaving the room hastily.

For many minutes Tebaldo gasped painfully for breath. In his suffering Corona raised the pillow with his head upon it, tenderly and carefully.

"You are dying," she said softly. "Commend your soul — pray for forgiveness!"

It was horrible to her belief to see him dying unconfessed in his many sins.

"Quickly — lose no time!" she urged. "Think of God — think of one prayer! It may be too late in a moment — "

"Too late?" he cried suddenly, with a revival of strength. "Too late? But I shall catch him on the hill! Gallop, mare, gallop — there, there! So! We shall do it yet. I am lighter than old Basili! One more stretch! There he is! Gallop, mare, gallop, for I shall catch him on the hill!"

One hand grasped the sheet like a bridle, the other patted it encouragingly. Corona stared and listened breathlessly, half in horror, half in expectation. She did not hear the door open, as some one came in. The dying man raved on.

"What? Down? He has killed his horse? It shied at the woman in black! He will try the church door — on, mare, gallop! We shall catch him there!"

A hideous glare of rage and hatred was in the burning eyes. The twisted and discoloured lips set themselves like blue steel. The right hand struck out wildly. Then the eyes fixed themselves upon the young priest who stood beside Corona, and whom she had not seen till then.

Tebaldo sat up as though raised by a spring,

suddenly. He grasped the priest's ready hands and looked up into his face, seeing only him, though the doctor and the nurse were close by.

"I confess to Almighty God," he began—

And word for word, as he had confessed to Ippolito alone in the little church, he went through the whole confession, quickly, clearly, in a loud voice, holding the priest's hands.

Who should say that it was not a true confession now? That at the last, the dream of terror did not change to the reality of remorse? The priest's voice spoke the words of forgiveness, and he bent down above Corona's kneeling figure, that the dying man might hear.

But before the last merciful word was spoken, the last of the Corleone lay stone dead on his pillow. He was buried beside his two brothers in the little cemetery of Santa Vittoria, for the sister had promised him that, when he knew that he was dying.

And outside the gate, when it was all over, a figure in black came and knelt down upon the rough, broken stones, and two white hands grasped the painted iron rails, and a low voice came from beneath the little black shawl.

"Mother of God, three black crosses! Mother of God, three black crosses!"

And there were three black crosses, side by side.

CHAPTER XL

IT might have been a long and difficult matter to establish Vittoria's identity, if Maria Carolina had been really insane, as it had been feared that she might be. She was beyond further suffering, perhaps, when the third of her sons was dead, but her mind was clear enough under the intense religious melancholy that had settled upon her in her grief. The fact of her having been willing and anxious to leave Vittoria at such a time now explained itself. The girl was not her daughter, and in the intensity of her sorrow the bereaved mother felt that she was a stranger, if not a burden. Yet she kept the secret, out of a sort of fear that even after eighteen years the revelation of it might bring about some unimaginably dreadful consequence to herself, and as though the Duca di Fornasco could still accuse her of having helped to steal his child, by receiving her from the brigands.

The fact was that the outlaws had terrified the Corleone at the time, threatening them with total destruction if they refused to conceal the infant.

They were poor and lived in an isolated neighbourhood, more or less in fear of their lives, at a time when brigandage was the rule, and when the many bands that existed in the island were under the general direction of the terrible Leone. They had yielded and had kept the secret with Sicilian reticence. Tebaldo alone had been old enough to partly understand the truth, but his father had told him the whole story before dying, and had left him a clearly written account of it, in case of any future difficulty. But Maria Carolina was alive still, and sane, and she told the truth clearly and connectedly to a lawyer, for she was glad to sever her last tie with the world, and glad, perhaps, that the stolen child should go back to her own people after all. Among her possessions were the clothes and tiny ornaments the infant had worn.

Vittoria's first sensation when she knew the truth was that of a captive led into the open air after years of confinement in a poisonous air.

She had been the daughter of a race of ill fame, fatherless, and all but motherless. Her three brothers had come to evil ends, one by one. She had been left alone in the world, the last representative of what so many called 'the worst blood in Italy.' She had been divided from the man she loved by a twofold bloodshed and by all the horror of her last surviving brother's crimes. Many and many a time she had stared into her mirror for an hour at night, not pleased by her own delicate loveliness, but asking herself, with heartbroken wonder, how it was possible that she could be the daughter of such a mother, the sister of such brothers, the grandchild of traitors and betrayers to generations of wickedness, back into the dim past. She had never been like them, nor felt like them, not acted as they did, yet it had seemed mad, if not wicked, to doubt that she was one of them. And each morning, meeting them all again and living with them, there had come the shock of opposition between her inheritance of honour and their inborn disposition to treachery and crime.

And now, it was not true. There was not one drop of their blood in her veins. There was not in her one taint of all that line of wickedness. It had all been a mistake and a dream and an illusion of fate, and she awoke in the morning and was free — free to face the world, to face Corona Saracinesca, to marry Orsino, without so much as a day of mourning for those who had been called her brothers.

The fresh young blood came blushing back to the delicate cheeks, and the radiance of life's spring played on the fair young head.

"How beautiful you are!" exclaimed Miss Lizzie, throwing her arms round her.

And Vittoria blushed again, and her eyes glistened with sheer, unbounded happiness.

"But I shall never know what to call you," laughed Miss Lizzie.

"I am Vittoria still," answered the other. "But I am Vittoria Spinelli — and I come of very respectable people!" She laughed happily. "I am related to all kinds of respectable people! There is my father, first. He is on his way to see me — and I have a brother — a real brother, to be proud of. And I am the cousin of Taquisara of Guardia — but I am Vittoria still!"

Rome went half mad over the story, for the Romans had all been inclined to like Vittoria for her own sake while distrusting those who had composed her family. The instinct of an old and conservative society is very rarely wrong in such matters. The happy ending of the tragedy of the Corleone was a sincere relief to everyone; and many who had known the Duca di Fornasco in the days when his infant daughter had been carried off and had seen how his whole life had been saddened during eighteen years by the cruel loss, rejoiced in the vast joy of his later years. For he had many friends, and was a man honoured and loved by those who knew him.

"I have always believed that I should find you, my dear child," he said, when his eyes had cleared and he could see Vittoria through the dazzling happiness of the first meeting. "But I have often feared to find you, and I never dared to hope that I should find you what you are."

It seemed to her that the very tone of his voice was like her own, as his brown eyes were like hers.

And later, he took Orsino's hand and laid it in his daughter's and pressed the two together.

"You loved more wisely than you knew," he said. "But I know how bravely you loved, when you would not give her up, nor yield to anyone. Your father will not refuse to take my daughter from my hands, I think."

"He will be as proud to take her as I am," said Orsino.

"Or as I am to give her to such a man as you."

So Orsino was married at last, and this tale comes to its happy end. For he was happy, and his people took his wife to themselves as one of them, and loved her for her own sake as well as for his; and they loved her, too, for the many troubles she had so bravely borne, under the disgrace of a name not her own. But neither were her sorrows hers, any more.

"Such things can only happen in Italy," said Mrs. Slayback, after the wedding.

"I am glad that nothing worse happened," answered her niece, thoughtfully. "To think that I might have married that man! To think that I cared for him! But I always felt that Vittoria was not his sister. If I ever marry, I shall marry an American."

She laughed, though there was a little ache left in her heart. But she knew that it would not last long, for she had not been very desperately in earnest, after all.

END OF VOL. II

Lightning Source UK Ltd.
Milton Keynes UK
UKHW040707221019
352026UK00001B/16/P